The philosophy of Wang Yang-ming

Yang-ming Wang, Frederick Goodrich Henke

THE PHILOSOPHY OF
WANG YANG-MING

THE IMAGE OF WANG YANG-MING IN A SMALL TEMPLE
ON THE HILL IN YÜYAO CITY, CHEKIANG

THE PHILOSOPHY OF WANG YANG-MING

TRANSLATED FROM THE CHINESE
BY
FREDERICK GOODRICH HENKE
(PH.D., CHICAGO)

PROFESSOR OF PHILOSOPHY AND EDUCATION IN ALLEGHENY COLLEGE. FORMERLY
PROFESSOR OF PHILOSOPHY AND PSYCHOLOGY IN THE
UNIVERSITY OF NANKING

INTRODUCTION BY
JAMES H. TUFTS, PH.D., LL.D.

PROFESSOR AND HEAD
OF THE DEPARTMENT OF PHILOSOPHY IN THE UNIVERSITY OF CHICAGO

LONDON - CHICAGO
THE OPEN COURT PUBLISHING CO.
1916

THE TORCH PRESS
CEDAR RAPIDS
IOWA

TO

MY FATHER

WHO SHOWED ME HOW TO CARRY A LONG

DIFFICULT TASK TO

COMPLETION

INTRODUCTION

Scholars, like other people, may be provincial; but the spirit of scholarship recognizes and values truth and wisdom from every source. Such recognition and appreciation have always been a factor in promoting mutual understanding and good will between nations. Western scholars have for some time had access to the older Chinese classics. A general esteem for Chinese ethics has resulted, which has contributed to ensure a friendly reception to the Chinese students and travelers who have visited Europe and America. But previous intercourse between Orient and Occident is, we may well believe, only a promise of far greater acquaintance. Everything points to a rapid increase of commercial and political relations. The East is learning what the West has thought and said; it is highly important that the West should know much more of the East. Accordingly, I am glad of an opportunity to prefix a cordial word of welcome to the translation of an important Chinese author, which a friend and former student of mine is presenting to the world of scholars and to all who would understand better the civilization and ideals of China.

Dr. Henke has resided for several years in China, first as a missionary and then as a teacher of philosophy in the University of Nanking. He has had the advice and coöperation of Chinese scholars and has given a translation which, I believe, will be valuable not only in making accessible an author whose ideas suggest many interesting comparisons with those of certain thinkers, but also in adding to our understanding and appreciation of the East.

I have written "of the East," yet as Mr. Lowes Dickinson says, China is in many respects more akin to the prac-

tical mind of the West than to the contemplative mind of
the East as represented by India. Certainly the prevail-
ing emphasis of Wang Yang-ming is upon the guidance of
life, and the fact that he was a Viceroy and as administra-
tor suppressed revolts and governed his province successfully may suggest a certain kinship in thought to the Ro-
man emperor who wrote so wisely upon the conduct of life
— a kinship which will be born out by many passages.

A Western reader is likely to be somewhat repelled by
the form in which a Chinese author's thoughts are presented Instead of an essay or a logically planned system,
we have for the most part detached sayings or comments of
the sage drawn out by his disciples' questions and written
down by them or else embodied in letters Such a form of
presentation involves repetition; it requires an effort to put
together various fragments and make from them a connected whole; yet this very form is itself no doubt signi-
ficant for an understanding of the respect for the personal
source of thoughts, as distinct from their abstract or logical content, which has been a character of Chinese culture.

The central thought of the sayings and letters here translated are stated in Dr Henke's Preface. In reading the
manuscript I have been impressed with the reiteration of
the doctrine that "intuitive knowledge" is the one thing
needful It is "characteristic of all men " Though often
obscured, "it is hard to obliterate." It is not merely an
intellectual function; its "place of manifestation is to be
found in true sincerity and commiseration," or sympathetic
feeling. Filial piety, respect for the elder brother, loyalty
to the prince are different forms of its development. Nor
is intuitive knowledge abstract and mystical It is "just
the opposite of the empty, meaningless, sudden enlightenment of the Buddhists." For "my sayings regarding the
investigation of things, the development of the intuitive
faculty, the making sincere of the purpose, and the rectifying of the mind, refer to the student's use of his original

nature in his various daily tasks, in order to investigate and firmly maintain the truth." To devote yourself to learning it is not necessary to have leisure. "Since you are engaged in trying law cases, you should devote yourself to learning in connection with these law cases, for thereby you will really be engaged in the investigation of things."

Finally, the intuitive faculty which manifests itself in these various activities "is the embodiment of natural law." Nature is one. It is manifested in virtue. It is variously called heaven, Shang-ti (God), fate, disposition, mind. To study the mind is, then, to study nature.

Whatever the differences in form of presentation, these thoughts will suggest to the student of Western ethics that seekers for truth speak a common language. Since Socrates urged the importance of knowledge and the Stoic bade men follow nature and Shaftesbury pointed to inner sources of moral certainty, the West has tended to look increasingly to scientific study of nature and society for guidance in detail. But if these Western thinkers could sit down with the Chinese Teacher, they would feel that they were dealing with congenial ideas.

JAMES H. TUFTS

University of Chicago

TRANSLATOR'S PREFACE

Little has been done to provide detailed information for the European student of the history of philosophy, concerning the trend of Chinese philosophic thought since the time of Confucius and Mencius   Owing to this the impression prevails in some quarters that, apart from the Five Classics, the Four Books, and Lao-tzu's Tao-Teh-King, the Chinese have produced little that is worth while

In the year 1911, I was asked to make a special study of the philosophy of Wang Yang-ming (A.D 1472-1529) for the North China Branch of the Royal Asiatic Society, of Shanghai   As a result, I undertook a thorough investigation of his standpoint; and in the autumn of 1912 read a paper before the Society on "A Study in the Life and Philosophy of Wang Yang-ming."[1]

Having become greatly interested in his approach to the problems of philosophy and knowing that his thought is exercising a profound influence upon the Chinese and the Japanese, I decided to translate his "Biography," "Instructions for Practical Life," "Record of Discourses," and "Letters" into English. The present volume is the outcome, which I now offer to students everywhere, with the hope that it may inspire a desire for a fuller knowledge of the splendid achievements of the Chinese, and a deeper appreciation of their worth

The form and the content of the classic literature of China was fairly well fixed in the ante-Ch'in period by the work of Confucius, Mencius, and their disciples, and the classics would probably have been handed down intact to the present generation had it not been for Shih Huang-ti (B.C. 246-221) of the Ch'in dynasty   He called a great council in B C 212 to discuss the affairs of the king-

---

[1] *Journal of the North-China Branch of the Royal Asiatic Society*, XLIV (1913), pp. 46-64. *Vide* "Wang Yang-ming, a Chinese Idealist," *Monist*, XXIV (1914), pp 17-34

dom; and during this Li-ssu, the prime minister, pointed
out that scholars had always been a source of endless difficulty to the nation, because they offered their services to
the highest bidder, irrespective of state affiliations. He
suggested that all the classical literature be burned and
that all students be required to engage in the study of law
under the instruction of recognized officials of the Empire.
Shih Huang-ti, pleased with the advice, promulgated an
edict, ordering that all the classical books — except the
Canon of Changes — be delivered into the hands of the
nearest magistrate to be burned; that, under penalty of
death, no scholars should converse together regarding the
classics; and that entire families should be executed, if
any member thereof expressed himself in favor of the traditions and customs of the classics. The order was carried
out strictly, and classical learning was greatly hindered.
However, the classic literature had been committed to
memory by large numbers of scholars, and portions had
doubtless been hid away in walls, and buried in the earth.

When the Han dynasty came into power, an attempt was
made to reassemble the lost books. An imperial edict urged
the old men to bring forth from their memories portions of
the classics not forgotten — a state of affairs which en-
couraged scholars generally to write plausible substitutes
for the lost books. For these reasons, we are reasonably
certain that we do not have the classics in their original
form. On the other hand, it is probable that the substance
was preserved.

As far as the scholars of China were concerned, those
portions of the literature that were agreed upon as authen-
tic, became the philosophic, moral, and literary criterion
according to which excellence in these things was judged.
In this way the Five Classics and the Four Books took the
same place in the development of China, which the Vedic
literature held in India. To start out with, there was a
degree of latitude present in the matter of interpretation,
for the classics are written in a very schematic style.

Scholars made considerable use of this freedom, until the philosopher Chu Hui-an (A.D. 1130-1200) fixed the interpretation of the classics through his commentary.

In Chu's time, Confucianism had gained decided ascendency over its competitors, Taoism and Buddhism. Chu was a realist, believing that things exist in their own right apart from the mind: not, however, in such a way as to make knowledge of them impossible. He held that external things partake of the principles of the mind, and that for this reason knowledge may be perfected by investigating the principles of all things with which we come into contact.

Wang Yang-ming, who lived three and one half centuries after Chu, was an idealist of the monistic type. For him mind covered the entire gamut of existence: he thought that nothing exists independent of and apart from mind. His point of view was consequently at variance with Chu's. He had considerable difficulty in defending his break with the traditional interpretation of the classics, but he succeeded remarkably well.

As a rationalizing and socializing factor in the development of life, his exposition exhibits the following doctrines:

1. Every individual may understand the fundamental principles of life and of things, including moral laws, by learning to understand his own mind, and by developing his own nature. This means that it is not necessary to use the criteria of the past as present-day standards. Each individual has the solution of the problems of the universe within himself. "Man is the measure of all things."

2. On the practical side, every one is under obligation to keep knowledge and action, theory and practice together, for the former is so intimately related to the latter that its very existence is involved. There can be no real knowledge without action. The individual has within himself the spring of knowledge and should constantly carry into practice the things that his intuitive knowledge of good gives him opportunity to do.

3   Heaven, earth, man, all things are an all-pervading
unity. The universe is the macrocosm, and each human
mind is a microcosm. This naturally leads to the conceptions, equality of opportunity and liberty, and as such
serves well as the fundamental principle of social activity
and reform [2]

In the work of translation, I had a Chinese scholar of
the old school at my side, to give advice and assist in the
interpretation of difficult passages The volume herewith
presented is a faithful translation of volume one of the
four volume edition of Wang's works distributed by the
Commercial Press, of Shanghai After I had completed
the translation, three of my associates on the faculty of
the University of Nanking went over the manuscript, making valuable changes and suggestions.   Professor Liu
Ching-fu read the Biography and Book III, Professor
Alexander Y. Lee, Books I and II; Professor Liu Ching-
pan, Book IV   I hereby desire to express my indebtedness
to them for the part they have contributed in this enterprise   I am also under deep obligation to the Reverend J
E. Shoemaker, who furnished the photograph from which
the frontispiece was made, and to my wife, who read the
entire book in proof, and aided me very greatly in other
matters, especially in points of style.

The captions inserted in italics in the text were added
at the suggestion of Dr Paul Carus   Chinese names and
characters have been spelled according to the system of Sir
Thomas Wade. The numbers placed at intervals in the
text within parentheses refer to the paging of the Chinese
text   Those familiar with the Chinese will find these a
great advantage in locating the place in the original

FREDERICK GOODRICH HENKE
Meadville, Pa., February, 1916

---

[2] *Vide* The Popular Science Monthly, LXXXVII (1915), pp.
78-89

CONTENTS

THE BIOGRAPHY OF WANG YANG-MING

THE BIOGRAPHY OF WANG YANG-MING
(王 陽 明)

Ancestry and Birth

The Teacher was named Shou-jen (守 仁) and Po-an (伯 安).[1] His ancestor at the time of the Western Chin dynasty was Wang Hsi-chih, a general of the right division of the army; and the ancestral home was at Shanyin in the province of Chekiang. Twenty-three generations later, Wang Shou, an official of rank, moved the home to Yüyao, also in Chekiang. At the time when the Ming dynasty first came into power, Wang Kang, who lived six generations before Wang Yang-ming, lost his life in the service of his emperor, at the hands of the aborigines in Canton Province. His son, Wang Yen-ta, wrapped his father's remains in sheep's skin and took them back to Yüyao. A censor named Kuo Shun reported this to the emperor, who had a temple erected in honor of the father at Tseng in the province of Canton. In the fourth generation Wang Yü-chun was requested by Emperor Yung Lo to become an official, but refused, styling himself "the old man in obscurity among the rocks." In the third generation, Wang Shih-chieh was honored with the degree of Chinshih,[2] because of superior knowledge of the classics. In the second generation Wang T'ien-hsü was the first of

---

[1] The Chinese have the custom of giving each person a number of different names at various periods of life. The name Po-an was probably given to Wang at the age of twenty. The name Yang-ming (陽 明) was given to him by his students. The name Wen-ch'eng (learning completed) was a posthumous title.

[2] A graduate of the third degree.

the Hanlin.[3] He and his son Wang Hua were vice-presidents of the Board of Rites. The latter, who was styled Long-shan, was the father of Wang Yang-ming. He was the first of the Chinshih, held the office of President of the Board of Civil Office at Nanking, and was given the title of Earl of Hsinchien. Seeing that at the old home at Shanyin there was excellent mountain water, and that it was really the original family home, he moved his effects from Yuyao to Yuehch'eng at Kuanghsiangfang Wang Yang-ming built a home in Yang-ming Grotto about twenty li southeast of Yuehch'eng, and because of this was called Yang-ming by his students.

Wang Yang-ming was born in the eighth year of the reign of Emperor Ch'eng Hua, in the ninth month and the thirtieth day, having been carried by his mother for fourteen months His father's mother, named Ts'en, in a dream saw a spiritman clothed in dark red silk decorated with precious stones, playing and drumming in the clouds as he brought the child When she awoke the child was already crying His grandfather accordingly called him Yun (cloud) and the neighbors called the place Auspicious Cloud Loft.

Early Life

In the twelfth year of Ch'eng Hua, at the age of five, he was still unable to speak. A passing Buddhist priest beholding him said, "A good child, but unfortunately his name has been made known." (2) Influenced thereby, his grandfather changed his name to Shou-jen, and forthwith he was able to speak The boy often secretly repeated the contents of his grandfather's books. When his surprised grandfather asked him how this was possible, he said, "I remembered what I heard you read" In the seventeenth year of Ch'eng Hua, when he was ten, his father became a Chinshih

---

[3] The highest degree conferred upon scholars under the old system of education in China.

When the boy was eleven his father went to the capital, Peking, to be an official, and the grandfather, who accompanied him, took Yang-ming along. When they passed Chinshan, near Chinkiang, the grandfather and a friend were writing a poem. As they did not finish it, Yang-ming helped with four sentences. The friend, greatly astonished, gave the boy the subject, ''The Mountain Hides the Moon,'' and forthwith the child gave a verse, which is published in his writings.

The next year he was studying in the capital city. One day when walking on the Ch'angan Street with some companions, he met a fortune teller, who said, ''I will tell your fortune. When your beard reaches your collar, you will enter the realm of the sage; when it reaches your diaphragm, your knowledge will have begun; and when it reaches your abdomen, your knowledge will be complete.'' Wang was profoundly influenced by these words, and when he returned to school asked his teacher, ''What is the most important thing in life?'' The teacher said, ''Study to become a Chinshih.'' Yang-ming replied, ''Perhaps not. Study to become a sage: that is the first and the greatest occupation.''

When he was thirteen, his mother died. In the twenty-second year of Ch'eng Hua, when he was fifteen, a rebellion occurred in the capital, led by Shih Ying and Wang Lung, and another in the province of Shansi, led by Shih Ho-shang and Liu Ch'ien-chin. At that time Yang-ming lived at Chüyungtuan and learned to ride horseback and to use the bow and arrow. He also asked the barbarous tribes there how they protected themselves against their enemies. At this occupation he spent a month before returning. In a dream he visited the temple of General Ma Yüan and while there wrote a poem, which is published in his works. Deploring the condition of the times, he wished to present a memorial to the throne, but his father refused to allow it. (3)

Marriage

In the first year of Hung Chih,[4] the Teacher (Wang Yang-ming) was seventeen years of age In the seventh month of that year he went to Hungtu, where he married a woman named Chu, the daughter of a state counselor.[5] The day the betrothal presents were sent he happened to enter a temple called T'iehchukung, and seeing a Taoist priest sitting with crossed legs, greeted him and sat down opposite him. As he forgot to return, his wife's father sent men in search of him, but failed to find him He did not return until the next day.

In the yamen [6] there were a number of boxes of paper which he soon used up, for he wrote daily and his knowledge of writing characters rapidly increased He frequently said, "When I first wrote characters, I followed the ancient models carefully and got merely the form of the letters Afterwards I added thought to my effort and kept the shape of the characters in mind In that way after a long time I succeeded in understanding the method This continued until I had read the elder philosopher Ch'eng who said, 'When I write characters I am very reverent. It is not that I wish to write well, but because reverence itself is knowledge.' Then I said, 'Since he did not wish the writing to be excellent, why did he learn to write?' However, I see this, that the ancients at all times and in all things learned from the mind itself If the mind is discriminating and clear, skill in the writing of characters will be included." Later, when he spoke of philosophy to his students, he often referred to this

Early Efforts as a Scholar

In the second year of Hung Chih the Teacher was eigh-

_____
[4] Name of the emperor

[5] Hungtu refers to Nanchang, the capital of the province of Kiangsi

[6] The home and office of officials

teen years of age. In the twelfth month he took his wife and returned to Yüyao by boat by way of Kuanghsin (Chekiang), where he visited his friend Lou Liang and talked with him about the "investigation of things." Much pleased, the Teacher said, "One can learn to become a sage." Later when he read the works of K'ao T'ing, he realized that scholars of the past had said that things have an external and an internal, a minute (small) and a coarse (large). Every blade of grass and every tree has its principles. Seeing a bamboo, he sought to investigate it. He thought diligently, but being unable to discover the principle thereof he became ill.

Receives the Degrees of Chüjen, Chinshih, and Hanlin

In the autumn of the fifth year of Emperor Hung Chih, at twenty-one years of age, he received the degree of Chüjen [7] in his native province. At midnight while taking the examination he saw two giants, one of whom was clothed in dark red silk and the other in green. One stood toward the east and the other toward the west. (4) Both said, "Three men together can accomplish much." The Teacher, Suen Shui — later a governor — and Hu Shih-ling — later the President of a Board — received the degree of Chüjen together. When Ch'en Hao attempted to usurp the throne, Hu divulged his evil intention, Suen lost his life in the ensuing battle, and the Teacher crushed the usurper.

At twenty-two years he took the examination for Chinshih at the Nankung, but failed. A prime minister, Hsi Yai, who had profound respect for him, in jest said, "When you take another examination and become the first of the Hanlin, take the subject, 'A poem to the future first of the Hanlin.'" The Teacher forthwith took his pen and wrote a poem. Thereupon one envious of his attainment said, "If he should really become the first of the Hanlin, he would despise us." The next year he again took the

---

[7] A graduate of the second degree.

examination for Chinshih, but was hindered by those envious of him. A number of those who lived with him were ashamed because they had not received the degree, but the Teacher laughed, saying, "You are ashamed because you failed, I am ashamed because my mind is perturbed at my failure."

During the tenth year of Hung Chih, Wang lived in Peking The country at that time was harassed by enemies at the borders, and Emperor Hung Chih asked that the officials recommend a man able to lead an army, but no one was recommended Wang accordingly carefully studied military tactics Whenever he was at a feast with guests, he took the kernels from the fruit that had been eaten and arranged them in the position of troops.

At twenty-seven the Teacher read a memorial presented to Kuang Tsong (an emperor of the Sung dynasty) by K'ao T'ing, which said, "To be respectful and maintain one's purpose is the source of study. Following the regular order with utmost discrimination is the method of study " In consequence the Teacher regretted that, notwithstanding great effort, he had not attained because of being too anxious to acquire He began to study in a methodical way, but continued to consider the principles of things and his own mind as two separate things His mind was troubled for a long time, and he again, as at a previous time, fell ill. But when he heard a Taoist priest explain the principle of nourishing life, his heart rejoiced.

In the twelfth year of Hung Chih, when twenty-eight, he again took the examination for Chinshih and attained the second place, and later the seventh place in the second class of Hanlin He then was appointed a member of the Board of Works. (5) While he was still a Hsiuts'ai (A B.), at one time in a dream Wang Yueh, an Earl of Wei Ling in Kiangsi, gave him a bow and sword. In the fall of the year in which he received the Chinshih, he was ordered by the emperor to build the tomb of Wang Yueh. In superintending the workmen he had half of them work and half rest, with definite times both for rest and for meals. When he and the workmen ceased from work, he practiced the octagonal method of drilling soldiers with them. The tomb was finished, and Wang Yueh's people offered him gold and silk, but he refused to take them. They then brought forth the sword which Wang Yueh had carried, and since this was in harmony with his dream he received it. At that time the stars changed, and the emperor asked that his officials explain the reason. Yang-ming sent in a memorial stating eight things regarding the borders of the empire.

He Investigates Immortality

At twenty-nine he was given control of the Yuinnan section of the Board of Punishments, and at thirty he was Provincial Judge in Chiangpei, reversing many of the law cases that came under his jurisdiction.

When not engaged in official duties he went to Chiuhua-shan.[8] There he met a Taoist priest named Ts'ai P'eng-t'ou and asked him regarding the magic of eternal youth and immortality. The priest answered, "You are not in a position to ask about it." A second time after sending away his servants he asked, and the priest again replied, "You are not in a position to make inquiry." A third time Wang asked. Ts'ai said, "Though you have an abundance of propriety, you still do not forget the manner of an official," and laughing aloud left him.

In the Titsang Grotto there was a strange and extraordinary man who sat and slept on pine needles, and who never cooked his food. The Teacher climbed cliffs and passed dangerous places in order to see him. When he reached the cave, the man was sleeping. The Teacher sat a long time waiting for him to awaken, and when he finally awoke asked him, "What is the first virtue to be investigated?" There

---

8 A well-known sacred mountain near the Yangtze River in the province of Anhui.

was no answer given until after a long time, when the strange man said, ''Chou Lien-hsi and Ch'eng Ming-tao are two great Hsiuts'ai among scholars.'' When he had spoken he again fell asleep. The Teacher left Returning the next day, he did not see the strange man again.

In the fifteenth year of Hung Chih, in the eighth month, the Teacher was thirty-one He resigned his official position to return to his home in Chekiang in order to care for his aged parent. He built a home at Yang-ming Grotto and there engaged in Taoist practices. His friends of the company of Wang Ssu-yü came to visit him, but he sent his servants to receive them. He revealed to them their entire past life just as a prophet would have done, while they marvelled at his power, believing that he had become perfect. (6) After some time the Teacher coming to a state of realization said, ''This humbugging, these worthless dregs, are not in accordance with the true way.'' He discontinued the Yoga practices

He Influences a Buddhist Priest to Abandon His Calling

Though he wished to leave his home and go to a far-distant place, he remembered that his grandmother and his father still lived and consequently was unable to come to a decision. One day, however, he came to himself and said, ''Though these are the thoughts of a child, yet should they perish, the original disposition (nature) would therewith be destroyed '' Accordingly he moved to Hsihu, spending much of his time between Nanp'ing and Hupao A Buddhist priest had been sitting for three years in contemplation without speaking or looking at anything The Teacher in a loud voice said, ''This priest sits here the entire day moving his lips But what does he say? He sits here with his eyes open all day, and what does he see?'' The priest was startled, and the Teacher made inquiry about his home The priest said, ''My mother lives '' ''Are you ever homesick for her?'' asked the Teacher. ''It is impossible not to have such thoughts,'' said the priest The

Teacher then talked to him about the natural love of one's own. The priest wept and thanked him; then took his almsbowl and returned home.

At thirty-three the Teacher was delegated to conduct the Chüjen examinations in the province of Shantung, and himself examined all the essays. In the ninth month of this year he was placed in control of the officers of the army.

At thirty-four he became the friend of Chan Kan-ch'üan (Jo-shui). Together they proclaimed the importance of devotion to the doctrines of Confucius. As a result many now first came to him to study these doctrines.

Having Offended the Eunuch Liu Tsing, He is Exiled to Lungch'ang

In the first year of Cheng Te, Wang was thirty-five years of age. At that time a eunuch, Liu Tsing, usurped much power. Two Taotais [9] at Nanking, Tai Hsien and Po Yen-hui, sent a memorial to the emperor asking that he dismiss Liu Tsing and thereby offended the emperor, who accordingly had them cast into prison. In the second month the teacher sent in a memorial and rescued them, and thereby offended Liu Tsing. Liu Tsing then falsely in the emperor's name had him struck forty blows with the bamboo and disgraced him by sending him to Lungch'ang, Kweichow, in the governmental dispatch service. [10] (7)

In the summer of the second year of Cheng Te, at the age of thirty-six, the Teacher, disgraced, started his journey and reached Ch'ient'ang. Liu Tsing deputized a man to follow him secretly. When the Teacher saw that he could not evade him, he pretended to drown himself in the river and secretly escaped to Choushan on a merchant vessel. A typhoon arose and in one night drove the ship to the bor-

[9] A Taotai under the old government was an official in charge of several prefectures.

[10] His principal duty was that of providing fresh horses for quick dispatch.

der of Fukien. When the Teacher had landed he wandered in the mountains some tens of li [11] As night came on he knocked at the door of a Buddhist temple, but the priest refused him hospitality. Hastening, he reached a deserted temple and supporting himself against the incense-table slept. The place was the resort of a tiger, who at midnight prowled around roaring, but was afraid to enter. At the break of day the Buddhist priest, thinking that the Teacher had surely been killed by the tiger, went to get his bag, for he used the tiger to help him pillage strangers. When he saw that the Teacher was just waking up, he was alarmed and said, "This is an extraordinary man!" Upon his invitation Wang went with him to the temple, where he met the Taoist priest who had formerly sat with him in the T'iehchukung. This one laughed and taking a poem from his sleeve gave it to the Teacher to see The ode read: "Twenty years ago I saw the gentleman. Today he comes, but the news of his deeds precedes him." He asked Wang where he wished to go. "If the anger of Liu Tsing," he said, "should fall upon your father, he would falsely report that you have either gone north to the Tartars or south to Kwangtung. What can be done?" The Teacher, alarmed, took refuge in divination and as a result returned home, leaving a verse written on the temple wall. He chose the nearest route, passing by Wu-i and crossing Poyang Lake At Nanking he visited his father, and in the twelfth month started his journey for Lungch'ang anew. At that time his brother-in-law (younger sister's husband) Ts'ü Ai, with his face toward the north, gave him a gift, thereby fully determining to be his disciple.

His Residence in Lungch'ang

At thirty-seven, in the third month of the third year of Cheng Te, he reached Lungch'ang and took up his official position there. Lungch'ang was situated in the northwest-

---

[11] A "li" is usually considered about a third of a mile.

ern part of Kweichow, among the mountains. It was the resort of venomous snakes and poisonous worms, the habitat of babbling barbarians with whom it was impossible for him to converse. The only ones with whom he could speak were criminals who had made their escape to these distant parts. Liu Tsing at this time still hated Wang, but the latter counted as nothing gain or loss, glory or disgrace. Life and death alone he meditated upon. He had a sarcophagus made and awaited the decree of Liu Tsing. (8) It happened that his followers all fell ill. The Teacher himself chopped wood, carried water, and made soft-boiled rice for them. Moreover, he sang songs, especially their home tunes for them, and recited humorous stories in order to drive away their sorrow and comfort them.

The Enlightenment

The great object of his meditations at this time was: What additional method would a sage adopt who lived under these circumstances? One night it suddenly dawned upon him in the midnight watches what the sage meant by "investigating things for the purpose of extending knowledge to the utmost." Unconsciously he called out, got up and danced about the room. All his followers were alarmed; but the Teacher, now for the first time understanding the doctrine of the sage, said, "My nature is, of course, sufficient. I was wrong in looking for principles in things and affairs." He meditated upon the words of the Five Classics and found them entirely in harmony with this. Subsequently he wrote a commentary on the Five Classics, "Thoughts on the Five Classics."

The natives of the place daily became more intimate with him. Seeing that the house where he lived was damp, they built him a schoolhouse and called it Lungkang, also a guestroom, a study, a pavilion, and a den. The prefect of Ssuchou sent men to deceive him, but the natives were enraged and beat them. The prefect was incensed and reported it to a higher official, who ordered Wang to go to the prefect and apologize But Wang, unwilling to do this, sent a letter to the higher official When the prefect heard of this he was humiliated. A higher official named An sent the Teacher rice and pork from Shuihsi. He also sent servants, gold, silver, and a saddled horse, but the Teacher did not receive the gifts. At one time the emperor had determined to establish a military post at Shuihsi and build a wall (city) around it, but later abandoned the plan The station for transmitting dispatches, however, was still there. The official named An did not like it because it was in his way, and wished to dispose of it. He consulted with the Teacher, who wrote him a letter in which he showed that the power and influence of the imperial court should be extended. An was satisfied. A tribal chief named Ochia-ochia stirred up the natives to rebellion Wang wrote a letter to An, exhorting him; whereupon An, much alarmed, crushed the rebellion.

At thirty-eight, the deputy commissioner of education of Kweichow, Hsi Shu by name, asked the Teacher to take charge of Kueiyang College At that time the Teacher first taught that knowledge and action must go together What he said is found in his writings

He is Restored to Honor and Receives Official Promotion

At the age of thirty-nine, Wang was promoted to the magistracy of Lulinghsien in Shansi, and during the seven months he was there he used no violent punishments (9) By selecting three classes of old men to be elders and to admonish the people in virtue, he influenced many In the eleventh month of that year (Cheng Te, the fifth year) he went to Peking to have an audience with the emperor, and while there stayed in a temple called Hsinglungssu. At this time Huang Tsung-hsien first heard the Teacher discourse on learning Wang was pleased and had him study with Chan Kan-ch'üan. In the twelfth month he was promoted to President of the Board of Punishment for Szchuan at Nanking.

In the first month of the sixth year of Cheng Te, Wang was made head of the inspection department of the Board of Civil Offices. He then first discoursed upon the learning of Chu Hui-an and Lu Hsiang-shan. He also sent a letter to Ts'ü Ch'eng-chih. At that time Fang Hsien-fu on the same board, but of higher rank, gave Wang the gift of a student to a teacher. In the second month of that year Wang was appointed associate examiner of the Chinshih essays. In the tenth month he was delegated to be the official who reports to the Vice-President of the Board of Civil Offices regarding letters received.

In the seventh year of Cheng Te, in the second month, he was promoted to clerk of the merit department of the Board of Civil Offices. In the twelfth month he was promoted to Nanking as Vice-President of the Court of the Emperor's Studs. Inasmuch as the road was convenient, he returned to his native home. In that year Ts'ü Ai, who at the time was prefect at Ch'ichou, was promoted to membership on the Board of Works at Nanking. Together with the Teacher in the same boat he went to Yüyao. On the way they discoursed upon the purport of the Great Learning. The conversation is recorded in his works.

In the eighth year of Cheng Te, when he was forty-two years of age, the Teacher went to Ch'uchou. By day he sauntered near the Langya Spring with his disciples. In the evening when the moon was bright several hundred men gathered around the Dragon Pool and sang that the valleys resounded with the echo. Students of the old learning daily increased.

In the ninth year of Emperor Cheng Te, at forty-three, Wang was promoted to President of the Court of Ceremonies. In that year he first turned specifically to intuitive knowledge for instructing his disciples. (10)

At forty-four he selected his cousin's son, Cheng Hsien,

as heir, for neither he nor his three brothers had any sons. His father had chosen Cheng Hsien, who was eight at that time, as the heir.   In the eighth month of this year (Cheng Te tenth), Wang determined to send in a memorial in order to remonstrate with the emperor against his receiving Buddhism.   The servants of the emperor said that in the western country (India) there lived a Buddhist priest who could prognosticate three generations,[12] and who in consequence was called by the Tartars a living Buddha.   Cheng Te sent an ambassador named Liu Yuin to welcome him with all dispatch   He used a string of five-hundred pearls on a pendant scroll, and carried silver amounting to more than ten thousand taels, besides gold.   Cheng Te ordered that Liu Yuin should return within ten years, and gave him power to act .   Liu Yuin asked for seventy thousand ying of salt to cover his travelling expenses   A prime minister named Yang Ting-ho sent in a memorial advising Cheng Te against this, but he paid no attention   Wang had written a memorial with the intention of sending it in, but desisted   Instead he sent in a memorial, and later a second one, asking leave to return home and care for his grandmother, who at the time was ninety-six years of age.

In the ninth month of the eleventh year of Cheng Te, the Teacher was promoted to Military Governor of Kiangsi, having been recommended by Wang Ch'iung, President of the Board of War   Wang Ssu-yü said to Chi Pen, "Wang will surely acquire merit this time.   I am unable to attack him single handed."   In the tenth month he returned to his home at Yüyao.

The Robbers at Wanan Are Subdued by Wang

In the first month of the twelfth year of Cheng Te, he reached Kanchou.   He passed Wanan, where several hundred robbers along the road plundered the passers-by. Merchant vessels did not dare to advance, but the Teacher

---

[12] That just past, the present, and the next

united them into a fleet.   Hoisting flags and beating drums,
they went forward as if to battle.   The robbers became
frightened and surrendered.   "We are famine-stricken
people," they said.   "Kindly relieve us in our extremity."
Wang ordered men to tell them that when he reached
Kanchou he would send an official to help them.   "You
should continue your regular occupations," he said, "and
not bring punishment upon yourselves by committing mis-
demeanors."   The robbers all returned home.   When he entered Kanchou, he forthwith selected and raised soldiers from
the people to introduce the ten-family register system. (11)

Since the Kanchou official helpers and yamen runners
all knew the ways and devices of the robbers, the robbers
were forewarned whenever the officials tried to do anything.
At the camp gate there was an old underling who was especially villainous.   The Teacher, knowing his ways, had
him called into a secret chamber and given his choice
whether he would live or die.   As the old underling divulged the truth, Wang permitted him to live.   Moreover,
what he said was tested and proven true, and thereby the
Teacher learned the actual condition of the thieves.

In the second month of this year he subdued the rebellion
at Changchou, and in the fourth he returned the soldiers.
At that time it had not rained for three months.   The
Teacher and his soldiers were at Shanghang.   He prayed at
the Hsing T'ai yamen and it rained for three days.   The
magistrate of the place asked the Teacher to change the
name from Hsing T'ai to Favorable Rain Hall (Shih-
yut'ang.

He is Made Provincial Commander-in-Chief

In the fifth month he established a military tally.   He
sent up a memorial asking that the P'ingho magistracy be
established at Hotou, and that the sub-district deputy magistrate be moved from Hsiaohsi to Fangtou.   In the sixth
month he sent a memorial asking for a reorganization of

the salt gabelle. In the ninth month he was made Provincial Commander-in-chief of the army at Kanchou, Tingchou, and Changchou in Kiangsi. The emperor gave him a banner and authority to act on his own initiative He sent up a memorial explaining rewards and punishments and asked that he be given power to act in such matters. Some of the people laughed and called him foolish, but Wang Ch'iung said, "If the government does not give this kind of power to that type of men, to whom shall it be given?" The Teacher sent in a second memorial and received the authority for which he had asked

Pi Chen, a Kiangsi eunuch delegated to keep watch, plotted with his favorites that the emperor should appoint him to examine the Teacher's army. Wang Ch'iung sent up a memorial saying, "That which in military matters is most to be dreaded is command from the distance. In case Wang must use soldiers at Kanchou, he must first wait until plans are made at the capital Thus will he be defeated. But if there is a disturbance at the capital, then it may be heard that the Kanchou government came to the rescue." Thereupon Pi Chen's plotting ceased. Because the Teacher settled the rebellion at Changchou he gained merit. His salary was increased and a present of two thousand taels of silver and four rolls of silk was given to him

In the tenth month he quieted the rebellion at Huenshui and T'ungkang The chief of the robber band, Hsie Chihshan, was captured, and questioned by the Teacher, who asked, "How did you accumulate such a gang?" Chihshan said, "It was not easy. When I saw a man of excellent ability, I was unwilling to let him go and used many devices to get him. I assisted him in trouble, or gave him help in his extremity, or appealed to his love of wine and women, until he was grateful for kindness (12) Then, when I plotted with him, he invariably was willing " The Teacher, turning to his disciples, said, "When we really wish to find a friend, we too should use the same method " In the twelfth month he returned with his soldiers and sent in a memorial asking that a magistrate be sent to Huenshui, a guard be placed at the Ch'aliao Pass, and a sub-district magistracy be established at Shangpao, Ch'iench'ang, and Ch'anglung.

In the thirteenth year of Emperor Cheng Te, the Teacher was forty-seven. In the first month he attacked Sanli; in the third month he reduced to submission the thieves at Tamao and Lit'ou; and in the fourth month he returned with the troops and established primary schools in the country. Holding up the wine, he thanked his followers, saying, ''Thank you, Sirs, for your help! I use this feast to requite you in a measure.'' The disciples, surprised, asked him the reason. The Teacher said, ''When I first went up into the hall to reward and punish the soldiers, I experienced a fear of making mistakes and disgracing you. I did not dare to be careless. When I left the hall to meet you face to face, I still remembered the rewards and punishments and was unhappy, until finally when I went up into the hall and when I met you face to face my mind was at rest. Then I was at peace. This is the matter in which you have helped me.'' In the fifth month Wang sent up a memorial asking that a magistracy be established at Hopingt'ung and that the sub-district magistrate at Hoping be sent to Lit'ou. In the sixth month, because of the merit accruing to him for having reduced the rebellion at Huenshui and T'ungkang, he was promoted to first assistant to the President of the Censorate, and one son was honored with the office of Ching I Wei [13] for all time and with the income of one hundred families.

Hsieh K'an Cuts the Blocks of the ''Instructions for Practical Life''

In the seventh month he cut the original text of the

---

[13] A sort of imperial commissioner.

Great Learning in wood, and also the philosopher Chu's "Wan Nien Ting Luen" (Discussions of Later Life)   In the eighth month his disciple Hsieh K'an cut the blocks of the "Instructions for Practical Life" at Ch'ien in Kiangsi — a book which Ts'u Ai has transmitted.   When Ts'ü Ai died, Wang mourned deeply and sacrificed two funeral orations at his grave.   In the ninth month he repaired the Lienhsi College for the students from all quarters   In the tenth month he reestablished village headmen, and in the eleventh month he sent a second memorial asking for a reorganization of the salt gabelle.

In the fourteenth year of Cheng Te the Teacher was forty-eight.   In the first month because of merit as a result of having reduced the rebellion at Sanli, his son was made a Ching I Wei with the income from one-thousand families. Wang sent a memorial refusing, but the emperor would not listen.   He then sent up a memorial resigning his position because his grandmother was ill, but the emperor would not accept the resignation.

He Subdues the Rebellious Prince Ch'en Hao

In the sixth month he received command from the emperor to go to Fukien to investigate a rebellion among the soldiers. (13)   Starting from Kanchou on the ninth, he reached Fengch'eng on the fifteenth and heard that Prince Ch'en Hao had rebelled.   Quickly returning to Chian, he raised troops by public solicitation.   Ch'en Hao ordered troops to pursue him, but by scheming he escaped them   On the nineteenth Wang reached Chian and sent in a memorial regarding the rebellion.   Fearing that the rebels might utilize the down-river current to reach Nanking and unexpectedly invade the two capital cities (Peking and Nanking), he devised a scheme to deceive the messenger of Ch'en Hao, thinking that if the latter could be detained from ten days to a month all would be well.   He secretly counterfeited the urgent dispatch board of the Provincial

Commander-in-chief of Kwangtung and Kwangsi, the official dispatch asking the soldiers from the capital and the borders of the Empire to come to the rescue, a letter from Li Shih-shih and Liu Yang-cheng (two of Ch'en Hao's generals) revealing treachery in the camp, and also a petition of submission from Min Nien-ssu and Ling Shih-i. He ordered Lei Chi and Lung Kuang to devise a plan whereby Ch'en Hao might learn this When Ch'en Hao heard it, he was frightened and did not know what preparation to make. The details of this matter are recorded in the Fan Chien I Shih. On the twenty-first he sent in another memorial regarding the rebellion, fearing that, because of the violence of the uprising, the former memorial had perhaps not reached the emperor. On the same day he sent in a memorial asking permission to return to Chekiang that he might bury his grandmother.

On the fifth day of the seventh month he sent in a memorial stating that Ch'en Hao was slandering the emperor in an official dispatch, and on the thirteenth he led troops out of Chian. On the fifteenth a consultation was held at Changshu, ordering the magistrate of Fenghsin, called Liu Shou-hsü, secretly to destroy Ch'en Hao's ambush soldiers at Hsinchiufench'ang On the nineteenth, Wang left Shihch'a and on the twentieth he and his soldiers captured Nanchang. On the twenty-fourth the Teacher fought against Ch'en Hao near the Poyang Lake at Huangchiatu, and on the twenty-fifth at Patzunao. On the twenty-sixth Wang captured Ch'en Hao at Ch'iaoshi Kiangsi was at rest, and the government did not yet know of the affair

The Emperor and the Rebellion

At that time Li K'o-ssu, President of the Censorate, sent in a special memorial regarding this matter. The emperor called together the court officials for deliberation, but they did not dare to find fault with Ch'en Hao. The President of the Board of War, Wang Ch'iung, alone said, "His

character has always been bad. That he should thus suddenly rebel should not be enough to alarm you. Wang
Shou-jen (Yang-ming) will take the matter in hand from
upstream, pursue him, and capture him. Yet according to
ancient custom it is necessary to send a general." (14) Wang
Ch'iung sent in a memorial asking Cheng Te to issue an
edict disowning Ch'en Hao as relative (prince) and calling
him a rebel. He also asked that a general with troops be
sent to Nanking, and that the Earl of Nanho, named Fang
Shou-hsiang, and the official in charge of the guard at
Yangchow, a censor, Yü Chien by name, lead Anhui troops
to guard Nanking, and further that Wang Shou-jen lead
Kiangsi troops from Lingchi and that a President of the
Censorate, named Ch'in Chin, lead Hupeh troops from
Chingjui to Nanchang   He further asked that Li K'o-ssu,
who guarded Chinkiang, Hsu T'ing-kuang, who guarded
Chekiang, and Ts'ung Lan, who guarded Ichen, check the
rebels, and that dispatches be sent to all parts of Kiangsi
announcing that whoever should raise public troops and
capture the rebels would be made a marquis   At that time
there were many ignoble people who persuaded the emperor to go in person so that he prohibited any general from
being sent   He said, "I myself ought to lead six regiments and in the name of Heaven demand justice."   He
used the standard, "Stern Commander-in-Chief, Duke Who
Guards the Country," and ordered two eunuchs, Chang
Yung and Chang Chung, and an earl named Hsü T'ai and a
lieutenant-general Liu Hui, to lead the capital troops and
the border troops amounting to more than ten thousand,
and to follow him. A deputy named Chu Hsu and a censor
named Chang Lun followed the army to record merit.

On the sixteenth of the eighth month Wang sent in a
memorial advising the emperor not to come himself, and
on the same day he for a second time asked for leave of
absence to bury his grandmother. On the eleventh of the
ninth month Wang left Nanchang for Peking, to hand

over his prisoner of war. At this time Chang Chung, Hsü T'ai, and their followers planned to send someone to use the "Stern Commander-in-Chief" dispatch board, receive (from Wang) the rebellious Ch'en Hao, and liberate him on the Poyang Lake, that the emperor himself might battle against him, and that when a victory had been reported merit might be meted out. The Teacher had reached Kuanghsin, when Chang Chung and Hsü T'ai sent a messenger ordering him to return to Kiangsi. Wang did not obey, but instead by night passed the Yüshants'aop'ing dispatch station. At Hangchow he met Chang Yung and said, "The people of Kiangsi have long endured the injuries of Ch'en Hao. They have passed through the rebellion, and in addition they suffer from the dry weather. If now is added the furnishing of supplies for the troops from the capital and the borders of the Empire, the poverty will be unendurable. The outcome will be that they will flee into the mountain valleys and rebel. Those who in the past helped Ch'en Hao did so because they were forced. Under the present weight of poverty there will be great confusion if rebellion ensues. You have in the past surrendered your life to your country: can you not now think of your countrymen?" Chang Yung answered, "Certainly! I have come because a great band of ignoble fellows surrounds the emperor. My purpose is to protect and safeguard him. (15) I have not come because I wish to rob others of just merit; but the disposition of the emperor is such that the situation may be saved if I follow his ideas. Should I disobey him, I would needlessly anger his ignoble followers and there would then be no way of solving the difficulty." The Teacher believed him and delivered Ch'en Hao up to him, but himself feigned illness and dwelt at Hsihu in a temple.

Wang Returns to Nanchang as Governor

In the eleventh month, at the command of the emperor, he returned to Nanchang as governor of Kiangsi. At that time Chang Chung and Hsü T'ai in Kiangsi devised many schemes to detect him in some wrong. Chu Hsü and Chang Lun, hoping for benefit from them, adopted their views and circulated rumors on all sides. When Wang returned, the troops from the north reviled him and tried to stir up a feud. He was not aroused to anger, but was the more courteous to them. Secretly he ordered the inhabitants to move to the country and used weakened old men at the yamen gate. He intended to reward the northern troops, but Chang Chung and Hsü T'ai had previously forbidden them to receive anything. He issued the following proclamation: "The northern soldiers have left their homes and suffered privations. The people of this city should extend toward them the courtesy of a host to his guest." When he met northern soldiers who had lost one of their number through death, he would have his conveyance stopped, speak comforting words to them, and after contributing ample money for the coffin pass on sighing. After a time the northern soldiers were moved by his kindness. At the feast of the winter solstice he ordered the people to prepare wine and pork to sacrifice to those who had lost their lives in the rebellion. The sound of the weeping did not cease day or night, and when the northern troops heard this, they could not but think of home and weep. Chang Chung and Hsü T'ai arranged for a test shooting-match with bow and arrow, thinking that Wang was unable to use the bow and that in this way they could vanquish him. Thrice he shot and thrice he hit the target. The northern troops standing alongside shouted and held up their hands in admiration. Chang Chung and Hsü T'ai greatly alarmed said, "May not all our soldiers follow Wang?"—and withdrew their troops. In that year, on the sixteenth of the twelfth month, the emperor reached Nanking.

He is Persecuted by Chang Chung and Hsu T'ai

In the fifteenth year of Cheng Te, Wang was forty-nine years old. At that time the emperor was at Nanking. Chang Chung and Hsü T'ai, since they hated Yang-ming, sent false imperial decrees calling him, but he did not leave. They also secretly slandered him in the presence of the emperor, saying, "Wang Shou-jen will certainly start a rebellion" The emperor said, "What evidence have you?" They said, "Try to summon him: he will not come." (16) In the first month Cheng Te summoned Wang. Chang Yung ordered a private secretary, Ch'ien Ping-chung, to notify the Teacher. When he heard it he immediately started the journey, but was hindered at Wuhu by Chang Chung and Hsü T'ai He then went to Chiuhuashan, where he dwelt in a temple made of grass. Cheng Te secretly sent a messenger to see him, who upon returning reported, "Wang Shou-jen is learning to be a Taoist priest: how would he stir up a rebellion?" The emperor ordered Wang to return to Kiangsi. Passing a temple called K'aihsien, he engraved the following on a stone in the study loft: "In the fourteenth year of the reign of Cheng Te, in the sixth month and the fourteenth day, Prince Ning (Ch'en Hao) rebelled at Nanchang. He led troops toward Nanking, and both Nanking and Kiukiang were captured. He then attacked Nganking (Anking) The whole country was in a state of excitement. In the seventh month on the thirteenth day I, Shou-jen, led troops from another city, retook Nanchang, captured Ch'en Hao and crushed the rebellion. At that time Cheng Te, having heard of the rebellion, was angered and led six regiments to avenge himself I turned over the prisoner of war to him and he returned. Great is the majesty of the emperor. Holy in warfare, he yet does not kill. It may be compared to the thunders which shake and without striking cease. The throne belongs to him. Who would attempt to usurp it? Heaven beheld Ch'en Hao, vindicated the intelligence of the emperor, and re-

stored peace within the empire " It was a vision of Shih
Tsung (who was known as Chia Ching) mounting the
throne. Was the Teacher able to forecast this?

He Inspects the Troops at Kiukiang and Kanchou

In the second month the teacher went to Kiukiang to in-
spect drill. In the third month he sent in a memorial asking that the taxes be rescinded for that half-year. For the
third time he sent in a memorial asking for leave of absence in order to bury his grandmother, but the emperor
refused. In the fifth month there was a great flood in
Kiangsi, and he sent in a memorial impeaching his own
character. When in the sixth month he went to Kanchou
to review the troops and teach them military tactics, Chiang
sent a man to watch him secretly. The people were all
afraid of Wang, who wrote the following ode: ·

"In the East an old man protected himself from the ravages
      of a tiger.
The tiger entered his house at night and bit his head.
The small child in the western home did not know the
      tiger,
He took a bamboo pole in his hand and drove the tiger as
      he drove the cattle."

His disciples were solicitous about his welfare, but the
Teacher said: "Formerly I lived at the capital in the midst
of mighty ones, at the point of the bayonet and sword; but
my mind was at rest Why should you be so anxious
today?"

As it was said that there were many warriors at Wanan,
he ordered an official to go there and choose a company
from among them. "Choose only those of great strength,"
he said, "and do not inquire about military skill." He
chose three hundred men. (17) Lung Kuang made inquiry,
saying, "Ch'en Hao has been subdued, why do you select
these?" The Teacher laughed and said, "Chiao Chi

(Cochin China) is in a state of rebellion To advance against the rebels while they are not suspecting, affords an excellent opportunity.''

How They Disposed of Ch'en Hao

Ch'en Hao had not been beheaded at that time, because Emperor Cheng Te was still at Nanking. Moreover, it was exceedingly difficult to surmise the plans of Chiang Pin, for at Niushou Mountain there were startling things happening at night. Chiang Pin feared Wang and did not dare to move Why Wang conducted drills at Kiukiang and Kanchou and selected the Wanan warriors, could not well be told to the public. In the seventh month Wang a second time sent up a memorial reporting good news from Kiangsi. At that time the Chiang Pin clique planned to claim the merit of delivering over the prisoner of war, but Chang Yung said, ''That will not do; for we had not left the capital when Ch'en Hao was captured. Wang sent the prisoner forward to Peking, passing Yushan and crossing at Ch'ient'an The people have already seen and heard this: it cannot be disavowed.'' They therefore used the banner of the Stern Commander-in-Chief ordering the Teacher to send in a second memorial regarding the victory in Kiangsi He sent in a memorial containing the gist of the first, adding the names of the parties concerned. In the eighth month he sent in a memorial to the Board of Punishment, clearing up the wrong done to Chi Yuanheng. In the intercalary eighth month, on the eighth day, the emperor received the prisoner at Nanking, and on the twelfth the emperor left Nanking.

Hou T'ao said, ''This affair was due to his officials As the criminal had been taken, why create a disturbance by taking out the soldiers at all? Since the country was at peace, why kill the people for the sake of the report of a victory and thereby involve the dynasty in a wrong? Why endanger the dynasty by disturbing the country? Because

Chang Chung and Hsü T'ai sought the merit of another and violated the principles of righteousness This wrong overflowed the heavens. Moreover, Chu Hsu and Chang Lun cunningly followed the evil group. The wickedness of the gang lacked ingenuity and intelligence.''

For the fourth time Wang sent up a memorial asking for permission to bury his grandmother, but the emperor refused. At Kanchou he heard that his grandmother had died and his father had taken ill, and in consequence he wished to lay aside his official position and return home One of his disciples, Chou Yung, said, ''The Teacher's thought of returning home seems to be justified '' After a long pause the Teacher replied, ''How can it be otherwise than justified?'' In the ninth month he returned from Kanchou to Nanchang

Wang Ken, the Strange Man from T'aichou, Visits Wang

At that time there was a man at T'aichou named Wang Ken, who wore the cap and costume of the ancients. He held a wooden tablet in his hand, and using two odes came to visit the Teacher (18) Wang was astonished when he saw him, and coming down asked him to sit in the place of honor ''What cap are you wearing?'' Wang asked. He answered, ''The cap of the time of Emperor Shun.'' ''What costume are you wearing?'' He answered, ''The clothes of Lao Lai-tzu.'' The Teacher said, ''Are you learning to be like Lao Lai-tzu?'' The man said, ''Yes '' The Teacher said, ''Do you merely imitate the wearing of his costume or do you imitate his coming into the room and artfully falling?'' Wang Ken's conscience troubled him and he gradually sat farther away. They conversed about the purport of ''investigating things for the sake of extending knowledge.'' When the conversation was ended, Wang Ken understood On the following day he changed his costume and brought to Wang the gift of a disciple.

On the third of the twelfth month the emperor was at

T'ung-chou and had Ch'en Hao beheaded. On the eighth he returned to Peking.

In the first month of the sixteenth year of Cheng Te, the teacher, at fifty years of age, dwelt at Nanchang and selected the descendants of Lu Hsiang-shan [14] for employment. On the fourteenth of the third month Cheng Te died in a house made of leopard skins,[15] and in the fourth month Shih Tsung ascended the throne. In the fifth month the teacher gathered together his disciples at Pailu-tung [16] In the sixth month the emperor called him to come to the capital by the dispatch route. On the twentieth he left Nanchang, though the prime minister attempted to prevent his going to the capital. He was promoted to President of the Board of War, and was ordered to advise and aid in military matters.   When he reached Ch'ient'an he sent in a memorial asking that he might use the convenient road home to bury his grandmother.

He Visits His Old Home and Receives Further Honors

In the eighth month he reached Yuehch'eng and in the ninth month Yuyao, where he visited the grave of his grandmother.   He made inquiry about the Shuyünlou (Auspicious Cloud Loft) He wept a long time because his beloved mother had not lived long enough to have his care, and because he had not been able to be present at the death of his grandmother to dress her for burial   In the twelfth month he was made Earl of Hsinchien and entrusted to Heaven's protecting care that he might display sincerity and strength in guarding aright the civil offices. In addition the emperor added the title, "Master of the Banquetting Office and Pillar of the Government " He also filled the office of President of the Board of War at Nanking, and thus advised and aided in military affairs as be-

---

[14] Lu Hsiang-shan was a philosopher of the Sung dynasty.

[15] He was fond of dissipation and luxury.

[16] An ancient college near Kiukiang, in the province of Kiangsi

fore. His salary was one thousand picul of rice per year.[17] Three generations, including wives, obtained posthumous honors, and his descendants for all time obtained the official rank of baron.

On the day when the proclamation arrived Yang-ming's father celebrated his birthday. The Teacher took the wine goblet to drink to the age of his father, who wrinkling his brow said, "Formerly at the time of Prince Ning's rebellion everybody said you had died, and yet you were not dead. Everybody said that the rebellion would be difficult to settle, yet you subdued it. Many arose who slandered you. Calamity threatened at every hand. During the last two years danger has been avoided with difficulty. (19) Now the clouds have scattered and sun and moon appear to make your faithfulness and your virtue manifest. We are both unworthy to receive official merit, high official position, and a high degree of nobility. Is it not fortunate that we again meet in one room as today? And yet the time of greatest prosperity is the beginning of decline, and happiness is at the base of misfortune. Though we may rejoice, we may also fear." The Teacher washed the goblet and kneeling before his father said, "This has been the instruction of my father. I, your son, will constantly heed it."

The Death of Wang's Father

In the first year of Emperor Chia Ching, the Teacher was fifty-one years old. In the first month of that year he sent in a memorial declining the titles of nobility, but the emperor refused to consider it. In the following month his father died. The Teacher wept himself nearly to death, and vowed that his entire family should eat no meat for one hundred days. Not many days after taking this vow, he ordered his brothers and nephews to eat a little dry pork. He said, "They have eaten pork for a long time, I cannot force them. It will give the reins to them to do it secretly,

---

[17] A picul is equal to 133½ pounds avoirdupois.

and thus it is better that I be liberal with them and allow them to do as they think best." He mourned a long time and then stopped. A guest came to make inquiry after the death of his father, and one of his servants said to Wang, "You ought to weep." The Teacher said, "Weeping comes from the heart. If I utilize the coming of a guest to weep and the going of the guest to stop, that is to gloss over the feelings and act falsely, like the ordinary man, who does this at the death of his parents."

Wang is Charged with Heterodoxy

In the seventh month he again sent in a memorial declining the titles of nobility, but there was no reply. At that time there were a censor, Ch'eng Ch'i, and an undersecretary in the censorate named Mao Yü who, in compliance with the ideas of a prime minister, first impeached the Teacher as heterodox. One of Wang's disciples, the secretary of the Board of Punishments, a man named Lu Ch'eng, sent in a memorial discussing and refuting this in six ways. When the Teacher heard of it, he stopped him. In the ninth month he buried his father at Shich'üanshan.

In the second year of Chia Ching, Wang was fifty-two years old. In the second month the examination for Chinshih took place. Ethical themes were propounded in order to controvert the Teacher. One of his disciples, Ch'ü Shan, left the examination hall without answering; another, Ch'ien Te-hung, wrote but returned unsuccessful. When the Teacher saw him he was glad to welcome him and said, "From this time the learning of the sage will be well understood." (20) Te-hung said, "Since affairs are as they are, how will it be well understood?" The Teacher responded, "My exposition of learning will be published all over the country through the present examination. Even in the most impoverished village or the deepest valley all will hear of it. In case my doctrines are wrong, someone will surely arise to investigate the truth." In the ninth month he removed the body of his father to T'ienchufeng and his grandmother to Hsüshan   He did this because of a flood at Shihch'uan

He Gives Advice to a Prefect

In the eleventh month he discussed the doctrines of Buddhism and Taoism with Chang Yüan-ch'ung, who held that the application of the two religions also brought merit to the Confucian scholar. "Should we not also unite with them?" he asked   The teacher replied, "You say unite? No! If the sage exhausts his nature in arriving at fate, there is nothing that has not been made ready for him   Why should we unite with them?   Their culture and learning are also ours   If I exhaust my whole nature in arriving at the decree of Heaven and nourish my person completely, I am styled an 'immortal.' If I am not affected by worldly ties, I am styled a Buddha. Later generations of Confucian scholars have not recognized the perfection of the sage's knowledge, and thus emphasize the difference between it and Taoism and Buddhism. Compare it with a house which has three rooms. When a Confucian scholar sees a Buddhist coming, he gives him the room to the left, and when he sees a Taoist, he gives him the room to the right, while he himself lives in the middle room   All choose one and cast aside other things "

He Gives Advice to a Prefect

In the first month of the third year of Chia Ching, a prefect from Chekiang named Nan Ta-chi came to see the Teacher. He said he was fully occupied with his administration of the government, and asked Wang why he did not have a word of instruction for him. Wang said, "I have long since spoken."   Ta-chi did not understand. The Teacher said, "If I had not spoken, how would you have known?" He said, "I know this through my intuitive faculty." The Teacher said, "Have I not frequently spoken of intuitive knowledge of good?'' Ta-chi laughed, thanked him and left. After some days he came again saying, ''After making mistakes I am very repentant. Though I desire earnestly to change, still it is better that someone first tell me not to transgress.'' Wang replied, ''That some-one tell you is not really equal to repenting yourself.'' (21) After several days he came saying, ''The transgressions of the body I have overcome. How about the transgressions of the mind?'' The Teacher said, ''If the mirror has not been wiped clear, it will hide filth. Your mirror is now clean, so that if a little dust settles on it, it cannot stay. This is your opportunity to become a sage, if you exert yourself.''

A Feast with His Disciples

On the fifteenth of the eighth month the Teacher feasted with his disciples at T'iench'üanch'iao. That night the moon was as bright as day and there were over one hundred disciples present, who, having drunk until they were merry, began to sing. They pitched arrows into a vase,[18] beat the drum, and went boating. When the Teacher saw that they all enjoyed the sport, he returned and wrote the following ode:

''Though placed aside, the lute sounded in the spring
     breeze.
  Though T'ien was enthusiastic, he was according to my
     liking.'' [19]

The next day the disciples came to thank him. He said: ''Formerly Confucius at Ch'en thought of the pedants of Lu, because his disciples had not buried the desire for wealth and honor. They (his followers) were as though bound and imprisoned, and did not comprehend him. A few of the wisest ones dropped this desire and understood

---

[18] ''An ancient game consisting in pitching arrows into the three long necks of a vase designed for that purpose.''

[19] *Vide* Confucian Analects, Book XI, Ch. 25, ¶ 7.

that all worldly affinity is unnatural, and that unless it is really suppressed for the sake of entering into the very essence of things, it will gradually ruin mankind. There is also the defect of neglecting natural relationships and things Although one who does this is different from the ordinary mean man, yet he too has not brought his life into conformity with the doctrine For this reason Confucius determined to return to moderate their views Today, Sirs, you are thoroughly acquainted with this, and it is well that you should use your greatest energy and your strength to reach the right path. Do not think that knowledge of one kind is sufficient, and finally end by being merely eccentric.''

Wang's Disciples at Work

Ch'ien Te-hung, Ch'ien Te-chou, Wei Liang-cheng, and Wei Liang-ch'i studied at the south of the city. They visited many renowned places at Yuhsueh, but forgot to return. The father of the two Ch'iens made inquiry of the Wei brothers, saying, ''Will you not all neglect your studies?'' The two brothers said, ''There is work everywhere for the student '' He said, ''Do you also pay attention to the sayings of the philosopher Chu?'' The two brothers said, ''We investigate the sayings of the philosopher Chu by means of the intuitive faculty. If one strikes the snake in the vital spot, why should he be solicitous about getting it?'' The father of the two Ch'iens doubted and was not convinced. He went in and made inquiry of the Teacher, who said, ''Learning to be a sage is like a man governing his family His possessions — houses, clothes, provisions, furniture — all are of his own providing If he wishes to invite guests, he brings out all his belongings for their use. When the guests leave, his things are all left for him to use without limitation to the end of life. He who is studying to be a scholar is like one who takes it upon himself to borrow the things necessary for his use (22) If he wishes to invite guests, everything is borrowed from the guest-room furniture on down. When the guests come, he appears to be prosperous and wealthy; but as soon as the guests leave, everything must be returned, for not a single thing belongs to him. If he invites guests and they do not come, his luck has failed him and things are borrowed in vain. To the end of his life he bustles and toils as a poverty-stricken man. He asks and receives that which is useless, for he seeks it in external things." The next year Wei Liang-cheng was the first on the list of the successful graduates of the second degree. The father of the Ch'iens heard it and laughingly said, "He struck the snake in the vital spot."

At that time the great ceremony was discussed.[20] Huo Wu-yai, Hsi Yüan-shan, Huang Tsung-hsien, and Huang Tsung-ming asked the Teacher but he made no reply. In the tenth month one of his disciples, Nan Ta-chi, cut the blocks of a part of the Ch'uan Hsi Lu (Instructions for Practical Life).

In the fourth year of Chia Ching, Wang was fifty-four years of age. In the first month his wife died. In the fourth month she was buried at Hsüshan. In the sixth month he put aside mourning for his father. A president of the Board of Rites, named Hsi Shu, sent in a special memorial recommending that the Teacher be made an official. The memorial read: "Among those born before me, I saw a man whose name was Yang I-tsing; among those born after me, I know a man named Wang Shou-jen." In the ninth month Wang returned to Yüyao to visit the graves. He gathered all his disciples at Lungchuenshi in a council chamber. In the tenth month the Yang-ming College in Chekiang was founded.

_____

[20] The emperor had elevated his own father to the rank of father of the emperor, whereas according to Chinese custom it should have been conferred upon Cheng Te.

The Censor Nieh Pao Becomes One of Wang's Disciples

In the fifth year of Chia Ching, Wang was fifty-five. In that year Nieh Pao investigated Fukien as censor, crossing at Ch'ient'an and visiting the Teacher, who was pleased and said, "Tzu-ssu, Mencius, and the philosophers Chou and Ch'eng did not purpose mutually to meet a thousand years later." However, at that time Nieh Pao was received as a guest   Six years later when the Teacher had been dead for four years, Pao was an official at Soochow   He told Ch'ien Te-hung and Wang Chi that he had been greatly helped by the Teacher, and said, "I had hoped to see him again and bring an offering, but failed to reach him in time. (23) You now are my witnesses that I have arranged this incense altar to honor him in worship. I may thus be called his disciple." In the twelfth month his son Cheng-i was born by his second wife named Chang.

Wang as Viceroy and Teacher

In the sixth year of Chia Ching, Wang was fifty-six. In the fourth month Tsou Shou-i cut the blocks for Wang's essays and memorials at Kuangtechou   In the fifth month Wang was made Viceroy of Kwangtung, Kwangsi, Kiangsi, Hunan and Hupeh. He reduced Ssut'ien to submission. Leaving Yuehch'eng in the ninth month, he passed Nanchang in the tenth   Before this, when the Teacher's ship stopped at Kuanghsin, the disciple Ch'u Yueh, who at that time had just arrived from Pailutung, where he was learning to sit cross-legged with the purpose of becoming a Buddhist priest, boarded the ship. When the Master saw him and realized his idea, he had him mention any similarity he might detect between Buddhism and Confucianism. The Teacher said, "No" After a moment he changed his reply somewhat, saying, "No   Are our principles confined to a particular place? They may be compared to the light of this candle   Light is everywhere   One cannot say that the candle alone is light " Referring to the inside of the ship he said, "Here is light. Here is light." And alluding to the surface of the water outside the ship he said, "There too is light." Ch'ü Yueh acceded. The next day when they reached Nanp'uh, they were heartily welcomed by the people. Loudly rejoicing, the populace blocked the road, so that they could not advance. Old men quarreled about carrying the Teacher's chair into the captain's yamen. He ordered that those who came to visit him should enter at the east and leave at the west. Those who could not let him go, after leaving came in again. Starting at eight in the morning, they did not leave until three in the afternoon, and then first did he allude to the carrying out of the usual etiquette. The next day he went to the Confucian temple and discussed the Great Learning in the Minglunt'ang. All his disciples surrounded him as a screen, so that many could not hear him. A man named T'ang Yao-ch'en, who usually did not believe what he said, under guise of bringing tea reached the room and listened at the side. Astonished he said, "Since the Three Dynasties has there been such bearing?" In the eleventh month the Teacher reached Wuchou and thanked the emperor through a memorial in which he spoke of his own superficial judgment.

In the second month of the seventh year of Chia Ching, at the age of fifty-seven, the Teacher had reduced Ssut'ien to submission, and in the fourth month he established a college there. (24) In the seventh month he reduced to submission eight military outposts and broke through the mountain pass. He then sent in a memorial regarding his administration of Ssut'ien and his success in opening the mountain pass. In the ninth month, because of the merit accruing from reducing Ssut'ien, he was given fifty taels and four suits made of hemp-cloth.

Wang's Illness and Death

In the tenth month he was so ill that he sent in a memorial asking permission to leave office, but there was no reply. He visited the temple of Ma Fu-po of the Han dynasty at Wumant'an, which he had seen in a dream in his youth, and inscribed two odes on its walls. He also visited the ancestral temple at Canton — the temple of Wang Kang of six generations before Yang-ming. Kang was State Counselor when he lost his life in a rebellion of the wild tribes, called Miao   Though exceedingly ill, he removed the troops to Tayüling in the eleventh month   He said to Wang Ta-yung, a provincial treasurer, "Do you not know how K'ung Ming trusted Chiang Wei?" Ta-yung thereupon had troops protect him. He also had a carpenter make a coffin for him   On the twenty-fifth when he reached Nanan, a disciple called Chou Chi came to see him. The teacher sat up and slowly said, "How have you progressed in your study of late?" Chou Chi spoke of his government affairs and inquired regarding Wang's state of health   The Teacher said, "The disease is very severe That I am not dead is due to my strong constitution." On the twenty-eighth the boat reached Chinglungp'u. The next day the Teacher called Chou Chi to him. He opened his eyes, and seeing him said, "I am leaving." Chou wept and asked whether he had a last word to leave behind The Teacher in a low voice said, "My mind is very bright and clear. What more is there to say?" After a little while he closed his eyes and died. A disciple named Chang Ssu-ts'ung, a military official at Kanchou, received the body in the postal dispatch yamen at Nanyeh, where it was washed and clothed.

In the twelfth month Ssu-ts'ung, his under-officials, and the disciples offered a sacrifice and placed the body in the coffin, which was placed on the ship the next day. The scholars and people from far and near blocked the way, and the noise of the weeping shook the earth. When they reached Kanchou, the people along the way crowded about and wept. From Nanan they proceeded to Nanchang, where two disciples — an inspector censor, Ch'u Liangts'ai, and a provincial literary chancellor, Chao Yen — asked them to delay going until the next year. The people wept both morning and evening.

Wang's Remains are Taken to Yuehch'eng

In the first month of the eighth year of Chia Ching, the remains left Nanchang. At that time the wind was so unfavorable for several days that the ship could not proceed. Chao Yen prayed at the coffin saying, "Sir, can it be that you are left at Nanchang for the sake of the scholars and the people? (25) From Chekiang your relatives and disciples came here and have waited a long time for you." Suddenly a west wind arose so that they reached Iyang in six days. In the second month the remains reached Yuehch'eng.

Huang Kuan Sends in a Memorial in Defense of Wang

In the court there was a diversity of opinion about Wang, so that no hereditary ranks, posthumous honors, and other customary honors were granted; but instead an order from the emperor came prohibiting the disseminating of the false doctrine. Huang Kuan of the Imperial Supervisorate of Instruction sent in a memorial saying: "A loyal minister serving his prince with righteousness does not enter into illicit relations. When a superior man establishes himself his doctrine is not servile. At one time I was an assistant secretary; now I am a Shaopao.[21] Kuei O was at that time a second-degree man. I chose him in an emergency and was his friend, until I became Secretary of Records of the Court Censors at Nanking. Then I saw that he did not understand the great ceremony and we discussed it together. From that time on for more than

---

[21] An official a little lower than a viceroy.

twenty years we were constantly together. At another
time I recommended Wang Shou-jen, the Earl of Hsinchien, that he might help increase the virtue of the emperor. O was not friendly toward Shou-jen, and for that
reason did not agree to it The mean man improved his
opportunity, yet I did not because of this put him aside.
But in accordance with the principle of a serving prince
and the doctrine of a teacher and friend, I am compelled to
divulge this fact. I myself knew Shou-jen thoroughly because of his merit and his learning It was owing to his
great merit that others envied him His learning was that
of the ancients but was not recognized as such, and for this
reason Shou-jen was not endured on the earth.

Wang's Fourfold Merit

"His merit was fourfold. First, Ch'en Hao (Prince
Ning) was disorderly, and his machinations were not of a
day. Within the court the Wei Pin clique, favorites like
Ch'ien Ning, Chiang Pin and their associates, as well as
the Lu Wan group, were perfidious. Outside such guards
as Pi Chen and Liu Lan were treacherous, and the court
officials and the officials throughout the country nearly all
looked on. Had it not been that Shou-jen was loyal and
did not permit himself to dwell on the misfortune of ex-
terminating his own family, but took upon himself the responsibility of punishing the rebel, it would be hard to tell
whether the country would now be at peace or in danger.
Today everybody supposes that this accrues to the merit of
Wu Wen-ting This is an instance of esteeming the shooting too lightly and overestimating the dog. The second is as
follows: The camps of Tamao, Ch'aliao, Lit'ou, and T'ungkang represented the combined force of four provinces.
Soldiers had collected there for a number of years (26)
When Shou-jen reached the place as guard, he subjugated
them all. His third merit is as follows: At T'ienchou
and Ssuen confusion had reigned for years, so that quiet

could not be restored, nor could the people be pacified. In consequence, Shou-jen was sent there and caused Prince Lu's followers to bow their heads in submission. Moved to tears, they received their punishment and thus brought the trouble of this place to an end. His fourth merit is as follows: Originally the eight military outposts were the disgrace of the interior of the two Kwangs.[22] The government soldiers coöperated with the rebels, and there was no way of getting at them. Shou-jen made use of the troops that were returning to Yungshun, and Lu Wang's soldiers yielded to them. By a surprise attack he exterminated them as quickly and easily as though they had been dead wood. It accrues to the merit of Shou-jen, that he averted great calamity and was ready to work unto death. Can this merit be taken from him?

Huang Lauds Wang's Learning

"Moreover, his learning was great in three respects. In the first place, he emphasized the development of intuitive knowledge. The extension of knowledge through an investigation of things, he took from Confucius, and intuitive knowledge from Mencius. How then can he be charged with heterodoxy? In the second place, his love for the people is to be identified with loving such of the people as are not one's relatives. Whosoever loves, deems worthy, delights, and benefits the people, also shares with the people their likes and dislikes and stands for a system of proper restraint. Loving the people is to be interpreted in this way, and thus is not the creation of Shou-jen. In the third place, he insisted on the unity of learning and practice. This idea is found in the Canon of Changes, in the words: 'If one knows the best and highest essence, one should attain to it. When one knows the end, one should reach it.' Shou-jen expressed the same thought in these words: 'I would that the talk and the practice of

---

[22] Refers to the provinces Kwangtung and Kwangsi.

men agreed' Men should not merely talk ' In this he was in perfect harmony with, and supplemented the learning of Confucius and Mencius Why should he be maligned? O has used these things to injure Shou-jen, and has thereby caused the emperor to lose an able minister. He did not allow Shou-jen to make the emperor as perfect as Yao and Shun. Who, in last analysis, is to blame? Therefore I dare not say that O is right in this, for the facts of Shou-jen's learning and the extent of his merit are as I have stated. Instead of being rewarded as he should be, punishment is meted out to him. The old beneficence given to a faithful servant has been cast aside and learning has anew been put under the ban. What do you think of O's trying in this way to help our illustrious Emperor?

"Shou-jen died last year in the twelfth month, his wife and children are enfeebled; his servants have carried out his remains, and after wrapping them in straw have buried them on a hill It is enough to arouse pity among the spirits, when they learn of it! How much more among men and sages' (27) Had Shou-jen been born in a different generation, you as Emperor would have the more given him posthumous honors. Why, having yourself seen him, should you lose this opportunity? For twenty years I was the friend of Shou-jen I had been unable for a single day to arouse myself to real effort in decreasing my wrongdoing, but when I followed Shou-jen I realized that I had suddenly come to a knowledge of my need. Therefore I look upon him as my teacher. It was not that I without circumspection believed him as ordinary teachers and friends believe one another. In the presence of the Emperor I now recognize Shou-jen as teacher and friend. Inasmuch as I have it on my mind, I must finish. Formerly O was slandered by mean men, and I rose up to defend him He was exonerated and I was glad for him, though it was not my private concern.   The injustice harbored against Shou-jen at this time may be compared to the former wrong endured by O.   I would that you might make manifest similar kindness, send a special command to the department, and magnanimously using the regulations for bestowing posthumous honors, confer upon Wang posthumous honors as well as hereditary titles; also, that you might remove the prohibition against his learning, and thereby display your virtue.   If this affair is not cleared up, I shall ever be mindful of O.   I take it upon myself to speak thus straightforwardly, that I may exhaust my faithfulness in service to the Emperor and cover the wrongdoing of O.''   There was no answer to the memorial.

Wang is Buried at Hungch'i

In the eleventh month the Teacher was interred at Hungch'i.   Hungch'i lies thirty li beyond Hangchow, and in reaching it one must enter Lant'ing for five li.   The Teacher had himself selected this spot.   The waters of the stream surrounded it from right to left and wore it away at the right.   The magician did not like it.   In a dream he saw a sage in a purple garment and a gem-inlaid sash, standing on the water of the stream, saying, ''I desire to change the old bed of the stream.''   The next day during a heavy storm, as the stream became turbulent, it suddenly widened several hundred feet to the south in front of the grave.   Therefore they determined that the grave should remain there.   At that time more than a thousand of Wang's followers, who had come from all directions, mourned for him.

Posthumous Honors

In the fifth month of the first year of Lung Ch'ing, the Teacher was by imperial order made Marquis of Hsinchien, and was given the posthumous title of Wench'eng (文 成). (28) In the second year of the Emperor

Lung Ch'ing, in the sixth month, his son, Cheng-i, was given the rank of Earl of Hsinchien.   In the twelfth year of Emperor Wan Li, an imperial order was issued to sacrifice to the Teacher in the Confucian temple after sacrificing to Confucius.

THE PHILOSOPHY OF WANG YANG-MING

BOOK I

INSTRUCTIONS FOR PRACTICAL LIFE

PART I [1]

Wang's Standpoint and Personality

In all that the Teacher said regarding the "investigation of things" of the Great Learning, he always considered the use of the original edition as correct — the one which former scholars considered mistaken. When I first heard this I was startled, after that I doubted, and finally I studied it with all my energies, and compared what I considered mutual mistakes in order to ask the Teacher. Then first did I understand that his exposition was so correct that the sage a hundred generations hence would not doubt it.

The wisdom of the Teacher was from Heaven. He was interesting and unrestrained, though not imposing in external appearance. In youth he seemed to have the martial bearing of age. He wrote many long themes, but did not use unnecessarily many words. He investigated and rejected the learning of the two religions (Buddhism and Taoism). When this was heard by others, they looked upon him as a man seeking to be different from others, and not giving anything thorough consideration, but they did not know that he had dwelt three years among the barbarians, enduring physical torture and cultivating tranquility of mind. In his discrimination and undividedness he had already entered into the company of the sages and belonged completely among the orthodox.

Both morning and evening I was in his presence and saw

---

[1] These were recorded by Ts'ü Ai, arranged by Shih Ssu-ming, and later revised by Ts'ü K'un and Chu P'ei-hsing.

that his doctrines were simple, yet superior. Though to some they appeared rough and uncouth, examination showed them to be very complete. In following them they seemed near, and in attaining to them one received benefit without end. For more than ten years I was unable to see within his bamboo fence.[2] How could any man of the world, who possibly saw the Teacher but once, or did not even hear his voice, carelessly or impatiently determine the true value of his doctrines after merely hearing his brief remarks on some insignificant subject, or from hearsay reports concerning his teachings? (2) Some scholars who followed the Teacher heard his instruction but received one-third while they neglected two-thirds of what he said; like one who in examining a horse sees whether it is male or female, black or yellow, and overlooks the fact that it is a thousand li horse.[3] I have made a record of what I heard that I may secretly reveal it to those of like aspiration, and that thus we may mutually examine and correct it with a view to not losing the Teacher's instruction. I, his disciple Ts'ü Ai, have written this book.

He Discusses the Text of the Great Learning

I made inquiry regarding "to love the people",[4] which the philosopher Chu said should be translated "to renovate the people,"[5] the evidence being that a later chapter uses "to renovate the people." "You feel," I said, "that it is correct to follow the original, 'to love the people.' Is there any evidence for your point of view?"

The Teacher said: "The character hsin (新) in the later chapter naturally means that the people renovate themselves, a thought which differs from the meaning of this particular passage. Is your evidence for the new edi-

[2] Meaning that the depth of his learning was still unfathomed.
[3] A horse of exceptional ability.
[4] Great Learning, Introduction, Paragraph 1.
[5] *Ibid.*, Ch. 2, ¶ 2.

tion sufficient? The character 'to make' when used with
the character 'to love' does not have the import of renovating. The statement further down, 'govern the state
and bring mankind to a state of peace,' does not elucidate
the meaning of renovate. For instance, the expressions,
'The princes deem worthy what the people deemed worthy
and love what the people loved'; [6] 'The common people
delight in what delighted the princes and benefit by their
beneficial arrangements'; or 'Act as if you were watching
over an infant'; [7] 'Love what the people love and hate
what the people hate,' [8] imply that the superior men are as
parents to the people. This gives the meaning of love. The
term 'loving the people' (親 民) is the same as Mencius'
expression, 'loving one's parents.' Thus loving is an inward and spiritual love of mankind. The people did not
love (those above them) and Shun sent Hsieh as minister of
instruction reverently to make known the five lessons of
duty. [9] This means that he loved them. The canon of Yao
which says: 'He was able to make illustrious his lofty
virtue,' implies that he made illustrious his own lofty
virtue. [10] By loving the nine agnatic relatives up to the
point where he made no distinctions between the people
and united and harmonized the various states, he illustrated the idea of loving the people and manifested his
lofty virtue on all the earth. Again, it is like Confucius'
saying, 'To cultivate one's self so as to give peace to the
people.' [11] To cultivate one's self is to make illustrious lofty
virtue. Giving peace to the people implies loving the
people. Loving the people embraces the idea of nourishing

---

[6] Great Learning, Ch. 3, ¶ 5.

[7] *Ibid.*, Ch. 9, ¶ 2.

[8] *Ibid.*, Ch. 10, ¶ 3.

[9] These correspond to the five human relationships: (1) sovereign
and subject; (2) father and son; (3) husband and wife; (4)
brothers; (5) friends.

[10] Great Learning, Ch. 1, ¶ 3.

[11] Confucian Analects, Book XIV, Ch. 45.

and educating. In saying, 'To renew the people,' one becomes conscious of error."

The Highest Virtues are Innate

I made inquiry regarding the saying from the Great Learning, "Knowing where to rest, the object of pursuit is determined." [12] "The philosopher Chu," I said, "held that all affairs and all things have definite principles. This appears to be out of harmony with your sayings." (3)

The Teacher said: 'To seek the highest virtue in affairs and things is only the objective side of the principles of righteousness. The highest virtues are innate to the mind. They are realized when the manifesting of lofty virtue has reached perfection. Nevertheless, one does not leave the physical realm out of consideration. The original notes say that the individual must exhaust heaven-given principles to the utmost and that no one with any of the prejudices of human passions will attain to the highest virtue."

I made inquiry saying, "Though the highest virtue be sought within the mind only, that may not enable the individual to investigate thoroughly the laws of the physical realm."

The Mind is the Embodiment of Natural Law

The Teacher said: "The mind itself is the embodiment of natural law. Is there anything in the universe that exists independent of the mind? [13] Is there any law apart from the mind?"

I replied: "In filial obedience in serving one's parents, or faithfulness in serving one's prince, or sincerity in intercourse with friends, or benevolence in governing the people, there are many principles which I fear must be examined."

The Teacher, sighing, said: "This is an old evasion. Can it be fully explained in one word? Following

---

[12] Great Learning, Introduction, ¶ 2.

[13] May in modern terminology best be translated "experience."

your order of questions I will make reply. For instance, in the matter of serving one's father, one cannot seek for the principle of filial obedience in one's parent, or in serving one's prince one cannot seek for the principle of faithfulness in the prince, or in making friends or governing the people one cannot seek for the principle of sincerity and benevolence in the friend or the people. They are all in the mind, for the mind is itself the embodiment of principles. When the mind is free from the obscuration of selfish aims, it is the embodiment of the principles of Heaven. It is not necessary to add one whit from without. When service of parents emerges from the mind characterized by pure heaven-given principles, we have filial obedience; when service of prince emerges, faithfulness; when the making of friends or the governing of the people emerge, sincerity and benevolence. It is only necessary to expel human passions and devote one's energies to the eternal principles."

I said, "Hearing you speak thus, I realize that I understand you in a measure, but the old sayings trouble me, for they have not been completely disposed of. In the matter of serving one's parents, the filial son is to care for their comfort both in winter and summer, and inquire after their health every evening and every morning. These things involve many details. I do not know whether these details are to be investigated in the mind or not."

The Teacher said: "Why not investigate them? (4) Yet in this investigation there is a point of departure; namely, to pay attention to the mind in getting rid of selfish aims and to foster the eternal principles. To understand the providing of warmth for one's parents in winter, is merely a matter of exhausting the filial piety of one's mind and of fearing lest a trifle of selfishness remain to intervene. To talk about providing refreshing conditions for one's parents during the summer, is again a matter of exhausting the filial piety of the mind and of fearing lest perhaps selfish aims be intermingled with one's efforts. But this implies that one must seek to acquire this attitude of mind for one's self. If the mind has no selfish aims, is perfectly under the control of heaven-given principles (natural law), and is sincerely devoted to filial piety, it will naturally think of and provide for the comfort of parents in winter and summer. These are all things that emanate from a mind which truly honors the parents; but it is necessary to have a mind that truly honors the parents before these things can emanate from it. Compare it to a tree. The truly filial mind constitutes the roots; the many details are the branches and leaves. The roots must first be there, and then later there may be branches and leaves. One does not first seek for the branches and leaves and afterwards cultivate the roots.

"The Book of Rites says: 'The filial son who sincerely loves surely has a peaceful temper. Having a peaceful temper, he surely has a happy appearance. Having a happy appearance he surely has a pleasant, mild countenance.' It is because he has a profound love as the root that he is naturally like this."

The Highest Excellence

Cheng Chao-shuo asked whether it is not also necessary to seek for the highest virtue in objective affairs and things. The Teacher said: "The highest excellence consists in nothing else than a mind completely dominated by heaven-given principles (natural law). As for the method by which it may be sought in affairs and things, attempt to name a few and see."

Chao-shuo said: "Serving one's parents is an instance. Why should one carry out the warmth and refreshing formality, as well as the duty of honoring and caring for one's parents? One must search for an ought in such matters. The highest virtue thus carries with it the work of study, investigation, thought and discrimination."

The Teacher said: "If there is nothing further involved

than the formalities of providing comfort for parents in winter and summer, and the duties of honoring and nourishing them, then one or two days will suffice to investigate them completely. What study, investigation, thought, and discrimination are required for this? (5) At the time of providing warmth and coolness, it is necessary to have the mind completely dominated by heaven-given principles; and at the time of honoring and nourishing the same holds true. Without applying study, investigation, thought, and discrimination to the mind, it will be difficult to avoid a slight error on the subjective side, with a resultant gross mistake on the objective side. Even in the case of a sage, it is highly important to urge the necessity of being discriminating and undivided. If the highest virtue is only a matter of mood, manner or ceremony, the actor of today who disguises himself in much providing of warmth, coolness, honoring, and nourishing according to usage, may be classed as having the highest virtue." That day I again comprehended.

The Unitary Character of Knowledge and Practice

Because I did not understand the admonition of the Teacher regarding the unitary character of knowledge and practice, Tsung-hsien, Wei-hsien and I discussed it back and forth without coming to any conclusion. Therefore I made inquiry of the Teacher regarding it. He said: "Make a suggestion and see." I said: "All men know that filial piety is due parents, and that the elder brother should be treated with respect; and yet they are unable to carry this out in practice. This implies that knowledge and practice really are two separate things."

The Teacher replied: "This separation is due to selfishness and does not represent the original character of knowledge and practice. No one who really has knowledge fails to practice it. Knowledge without practice should be interpreted as lack of knowledge. Sages and virtuous men teach men to know how to act, because they wish them to return to nature. They do not tell them merely to reflect and let this suffice. The Great Learning exhibits true knowledge and practice, that men may understand this. For instance, take the case of loving what is beautiful and despising a bad odor. Seeing beauty is a result of knowledge; loving the beautiful is a result of practice. Nevertheless, it is true that when one sees beauty one already loves it. It is not a case of determining to love it after one sees it. Smelling a bad odor involves knowledge; hating the odor involves action. Nevertheless, when one perceives the bad odor one already hates it. One does not determine to hate it after one has smelt it. A man with his nostrils stuffed may see the malodorous object before him, but does not smell it. (6) Under such circumstances it is a case of not perceiving it, rather than of disliking it. No one should be described as understanding filial piety and respectfulness, unless he has actually practiced filial piety toward his parents and respect toward his elder brother. Knowing how to converse about filial piety and respectfulness is not sufficient to warrant anybody's being described as understanding them. Or it may be compared to one's understanding of pain. A person certainly must have experienced pain before he can know what it is. Likewise to understand cold one must first have endured cold; and to understand hunger one must have been hungry. How, then, can knowledge and practice be separated? This is their original nature before selfish aims have separated them. The sage instructs the individual that he must practice before he may be said to have understanding. If he fails to practice, he does not understand. How thoroughly important a task this is! Why do you so insistently say that knowledge and practice are two separate things, while the sage considers them as one? If one does not understand the purport of well-established truths but merely repeats one or two, what advantage accrues?''

I said: ''The ancients said that knowledge and practice

are two different things. Men should also understand this clearly. One section treats of knowledge, another of practice. Thus may one acquire a starting-point for one's task."

The Teacher said: "But thereby you have lost the meaning of the ancients. I have said that knowledge is the purpose to act, and that practice implies carrying out knowledge. Knowledge is the beginning of practice; doing is the completion of knowing. If when one knows how to attain the desired end, one speaks only of knowing, the doing is already naturally included; or if he speaks of acting, the knowing is already included. That the ancients after having spoken of knowledge also speak of doing, is due to the fact that there is a class of people on earth who foolishly do as they wish and fail to understand how to deliberate and investigate. They act ignorantly and recklessly. It is necessary to discuss knowledge so that they can act correctly. There is another class of people who vaguely and vainly philosophize but are unwilling to carry it out in practice. (7) This also is merely an instance of estimating shadows and echoes. The ancients of necessity discussed doing, for only then can such people truly understand. The language of the ancients is of necessity directed toward rectifying prejudices and reforming abuses. When one comprehends this idea, a word is sufficient. Men of the present, however, make knowledge and action two different things and go forth to practice, because they hold that one must first have knowledge before one is able to practice. Each one says, 'I proceed to investigate and discuss knowledge; I wait until knowledge is perfect and then go forth to practice it.' Those who to the very end of life fail to practice also fail to understand. This is not a small error, nor one that came in a day. By saying that knowledge and practice are a unit, I am herewith offering a remedy for the disease. I am not dealing in abstractions, nor imposing my own ideas, for the nature of knowledge and practice is originally as I describe it In case you comprehend the purport, no harm is done if you say they are two, for they are in reality a unit. In case you do not comprehend the purport thereof and say they are one, what does it profit? It is only idle talk."

The Philosopher Chu's Mistaken Interpretation of "Investigation of Things"

I made inquiry saying: "Yesterday I heard the Teacher's instructions about resting in the highest virtue. I realize that I am beginning to get a grasp of this task. Nevertheless, I think that your point of view cannot be reconciled with the philosopher Chu's instruction with reference to the investigation of things."

The Teacher said: "Investigation of things is what is meant by resting in the highest excellence He who has knowledge of the highest excellence also understands the investigation of things."

I said. "Using the instruction of the Teacher, I yesterday pushed forward in the investigation of things, and it seemed as though I comprehended it in general; and yet the instruction of the philosopher Chu is all substantiated in what is called 'a state of discrimination and undividedness' by the Book of History, 'extensive studying and the keeping of one's self under restraint' by the Confucian Analects, and 'the exhausting of one's mental constitution in knowing one's nature' by Mencius As a result, I am unable to understand fully."

The Teacher said: "Tzu-hsia was earnest in his belief in the sages, while Tseng-tzu sought within himself for help. To be earnest in belief surely is correct, but not as much so as genuineness in application. Since you cannot grasp this, why should you cling to the, sayings of the ancients and thereby fail to apply yourself to what you ought to learn? The philosopher Chu believed the philosopher Ch'en, and yet when he reached places in which he did not understand him, did he ever suddenly and thoughtlessly accept his point of view? (8) Discrimination, undividedness, 'extensive studying,' 'keeping one's self under restraint,' and 'exhausting one's mental constitution' are *ab initio* harmoniously blended with my sayings. But you have never thought about this. The philosophic teaching of Chu cannot but be related to and adapted from the views of others. It does not express the original meaning of the sages. Devotion to the essence implies a united task; extensive studying implies keeping one's self in restraint. I say that the virtuous man already knows that knowledge and practice are a unity. The mere saying of this is enough to show it. 'To exhaust one's mental constitution in order to understand one's nature and know heaven,' implies that the individual is born with knowledge of the duties and carries them out with ease. Preserving one's mental constitution and nourishing one's nature so as to serve heaven,[14] implies that the individual acquires knowledge of them by study and practices them from a desire for advantage. The saying, 'Neither a premature death nor a long life causes a man any double-mindedness,'[15] implies that the individual acquires knowledge of them after a painful feeling of his ignorance and practices them by strenuous effort. The philosopher Chu made a mistake in his teaching regarding the investigation of things because he inverted this idea, using 'the exhausting of one's mental constitution in knowing one's nature' as 'investigation of things for the purpose of extending knowledge to the utmost.' He wanted those who were learning for the first time to act as though they had been born with knowledge of duties and carried them out with natural ease. How can that be done?"

I made inquiry saying, "In what way can exhausting one's metal constitution in knowing one's nature be con-

---

[14] Mencius, Book VII, Pt. I, Ch. 1, ¶ 2.

[15] *Ibid.*, Book VII, Pt. I, Ch. 1, ¶ 3.

strued as acting with ease as a result of innate knowledge?"

The Teacher said: "Nature is the original character of the mind (one's mental constitution). Heaven is the source of nature. To exhaust one's mind means to exhaust one's nature. Only he who is possessed of the most complete sincerity is able to exhaust his nature and understand the nourishing power of heaven and earth   He who preserves his mental constitution has not exhausted it. Knowledge of heaven is as the knowledge of the *Chihchou* and *Chihhsien*, whose knowledge of the territory they govern is a thing in line with their duty. It implies considering one's self as one with Heaven. Serving Heaven is like the son serving his parents, and the minister serving the prince   It must be done reverently if it is to be perfect. The implication is that the individual may consider himself as separated from Heaven. At this point the sage and the virtuous man are different from others. As for the saying, 'Neither premature death nor long life cause doublemindedness,' this teaches the student to apply himself to virtue with a whole heart, and not to allow failure or success, premature death or long life, to alter his mind, but to cultivate his person while awaiting the decrees of Heaven   The failure or success, premature death or long life which he experiences, are for him the decrees of Heaven, and therefore they do not excite and disturb his mind. Though the idea of serving Heaven carries with it the idea that the individual is in a way separated from Heaven, it also means that he lives in the presence of Heaven   To await the decree of Heaven implies that one does not know it, but is waiting for it   Here we have the starting-point of learning and of fixing one's mind, and of course weariness and strenuous effort are implied   Present-day scholars are reversing the order, so that the student has no place where to begin " (9)

Wang's Interpretation of a "Thing"

I said, "Yesterday when I heard your teaching I clearly realized that the task is as you describe it: having heard your words today, I am still less in doubt. Last night I came to the conclusion that the word 'thing' of 'investigating things' is to be identified with the word 'affair.' Both have reference to the mind."

The Teacher said: "Yes. The controlling power of the body is the mind. The mind originates the idea, and the nature of the idea is knowledge. Wherever the idea is, we have a thing. For instance, when the idea rests on serving one's parents, then serving one's parents is a 'thing'; when it is on serving one's prince, then serving one's prince is a 'thing'; when it is occupied with being benevolent to the people and kind to creatures, then benevolence to the people and kindness to creatures are 'things'; when it is occupied with seeing, hearing, speaking, moving, then each of these becomes a 'thing.' I say there are no principles but those of the mind, and nothing exists apart from the mind. The Doctrine of the Mean says: 'Without sincerity there would be nothing.' [16] The Great Learning makes clear that the illustrating of illustrious virtue consists merely in making one's purpose sincere, and that this latter has reference to investigating things."

The Teacher spoke again saying: "The 'examine' of 'examining into the nature of things', just as the 'rectify' of 'the great man can rectify the mind of the prince', of Mencius, [17] has reference to the fact that the mind is not right. Its object is to reinstate the original rightness. But the idea conveyed is that one must cast out the wrong in order to complete the right, and that there should be no time or place in which one does not harbor heaven-given principles. This includes a most thorough investigation of heaven-given

[16] Doctrine of the Mean, Ch. 25, ¶ 2.
[17] Works of Mencius, Book IV, Part I, Ch. 20.

principles.[18] Heaven-given principles are illustrious virtue; they include the manifesting of illustrious virtue.''

Innate Knowledge

Again he said: "Knowledge is native to the mind; the mind naturally is able to know. When it perceives the parents it naturally knows what filial piety is; when it perceives the elder brother it naturally knows what respectfulness is; when it sees a child fall into a well it naturally knows what commiseration is. This is intuitive knowledge of good, and is not attained through external investigation. If the thing manifested emanates from the intuitive faculty, it is the more free from the obscuration of selfish purpose. This is what is meant by saying that the mind is filled with commiseration, and that love cannot be exhausted. (10) However, the ordinary man is subject to the obscuration of private aims, so that it is necessary to develop the intuitive faculty to the utmost through investigation of things in order to overcome selfishness and reinstate the rule of natural law. Then the intuitive faculty of the mind will not be subject to obscuration, but having been satiated will function normally. Thus we have a condition in which there is an extension of knowledge. Knowledge having been extended to the utmost, the purpose is sincere.''

Propriety in Its Relation to Principles

I made inquiry of the Teacher saying, "Though I ponder deeply I am unable to understand the use of 'extensive study of all learning' in the task of keeping one's self under the restraint of the rules of propriety.[19] Will you kindly explain it somewhat?''

The Teacher said: "The word 'propriety' carries with it the connotation of the word 'principles.' When prin-

---

[18] Used here and hereafter largely in the sense of natural law.

[19] Confucian Analects, Book VI, Ch. 25.

ciples become manifest in action, they can be seen and are then called propriety. When propriety is abstruse and cannot be seen, it is called principles. Nevertheless, they are one thing. In order to keep one's self under the restraint of the rules of propriety it is merely necessary to have a mind completely under the influence of natural law (heaven-given principles). If a person desires to have his mind completely dominated by natural law, he must use effort at the point where principles are manifested. For instance, if they are to be manifested in the matter of serving one's parents, one should learn to harbor these principles in the serving of one's parents. If they are to be manifested in the matter of serving one's prince, one should learn to harbor them in the service of one's prince. If they are to be manifested in the changing fortunes of life, whether of wealth and position, or of poverty and lowliness, one should learn to harbor them whether in wealth and position, or in poverty and lowliness. If they are to be manifested when one meets sorrow and difficulty, or is living among barbarous tribes, one should learn to harbor them in sorrow and difficulty, or when one is among barbarous tribes. Whether working or resting, speaking or silent, under no conditions should it be different. No matter where they are manifested, one should forthwith learn to harbor them. This is what is meant by studying them extensively in all learning, and includes the keeping of one's self under the restraint of the rules of propriety. 'Extensive study of all learning' thus implies devotion to the best (discrimination). 'To keep one's self under the restraint of the rules of propriety' implies devoting one's self to a single purpose (undividedness).''

The Mind is a Unity

I made inquiry saying: ''An upright (righteous) mind is master of the body, while a selfish mind is always subject to the decrees (of the body). Using your instruction regarding discrimination and undividedness, this saying appears to be mistaken "

The Teacher said: "The mind is one. In case it has not been corrupted by the passions of men, it is called an upright mind. If corrupted by human aims and passions, it is called a selfish mind. When a selfish mind is rectified it is an upright mind, and when an upright mind loses its rightness it becomes a selfish mind. Originally there were not two minds. (11) The philosopher Ch'eng said, 'A selfish mind is due to selfish desire; an upright mind is natural law (is true to nature).' Even though his discourse separates them, his thought comprehends the situation correctly. Now, you say that if the upright mind is master and the selfish mind is subject to decrees, there are two minds, and that heaven-given principles and selfishness can not co-exist. How can natural law be master, while selfishness follows and is subject to decrees?"

Wang Compares Wen Chung-tzu with Han T'ui-chih

I asked concerning Wen Chung-tzu and Han T'ui-chih.[20]

The Teacher said· "T'ui-chih was one of the best of literary men, while Wen Chung-tzu was a virtuous scholar. Because of T'ui-chih's literary style, later generations gave him a position of honor, whereas he was really much inferior to Wen Chung-tzu "

I asked: "How is it that Wen Chung-tzu was faulty in his estimation of the classics?"

The Teacher said· "Perhaps he was not entirely mistaken in his estimation of the classics. Tell me how the ideas of later commentators compare with his."

I answered· "There are none among the ordinary commentators who are not writing for reputation. It is true that they aspire to understand and elucidate the doctrine,

---

20 Wen lived at the time of the Three Dynasties and was a virtuous scholar. Han lived in the T'ang dynasty and was also a scholar, but did not emphasize ethics.

but their interpretation of the classics is influenced by their desire for reputation.''

The Teacher said: ''Is there not some one or something that can be used as a pattern when making comments to elucidate the doctrine?''

Confucius Revised the Six Classics

I said, ''Confucius revised the Six Classics in order to shed light on the doctrine.''

The Teacher said: ''Yes. But in interpreting the classics does one not follow Confucius?''

I said: ''The writing of comments implies that there is something to be made clear in the doctrine. Interpreting the classics refers only to judging their effect and may not add anything to the doctrine itself.''

The Teacher said: ''Sir, do you consider him who understands the doctrine as thereby returning to honesty, reverting to sincerity, and perceiving the genuine method of conduct? Or do you think that he improves his composition, but merely for the sake of being able to dispute? The great confusion in the Empire is due to the victory of false learning and the decay of genuine conduct. It is not necessary to publish the Six Classics in order to cause the doctrine to be understood. Confucius revised them because that was the only thing feasible. From the time when Fu Hsi drew the eight diagrams up to the time of Wen Wang and Chou Kung, portions of the Book of Changes, such as Lienshan and Kueits'ang, were discussed, often in a noisy, disorderly way.[21] I do not know how many scholars discussed them, but the doctrine of the Book of Changes was greatly perverted. Because the custom of admiring literary style daily increased within the Empire, Confucius, realizing that the discussions about the Book of Changes

---

[21] The eight diagrams consist of eight combinations of a line and a divided line. They are said to have been copied from the back of a tortoise by the legendary monarch Fu Hsi. They were used in philosophizing and in speculating about nature.

would be endless, chose the interpretation of Wen Wang and Chou Kung and eulogized it as being the only one that grasped the underlying idea (12) Thereupon the confused interpretations were entirely discarded and a unanimity of opinion was reached among expositors   The same situation prevailed in the case of the Book of History, the Book of Poetry, the Book of Rites and the Annals of Spring and Autumn.   In the Book of History from the Tienmo on, and in the Book of Poetry from the Erhnan on — as, for example, in the Chiuch'iu and the Paso — all expressions of lewd wantonness and licentious excess, including I know not how many hundreds or thousands of leaves, were rejected, expunged, or revised by Confucius.   Moreover, he did the same with the names of distinguished persons, things, and measures without limit.   This was the first time that such sayings were discarded.

"Where did Confucius add a single sentence to the Books of History, Poetry, or Rites?   The many present-day interpretations of the Book of Rites have all been agreed upon and adopted by later scholars, and are not the interpretation of Confucius.   Though the Annals of Spring and Autumn are attributed to Confucius, in actual fact they are an ancient record of the history of Lu Kuo.   The one said to have written it wrote about ancient things; he who corrected it expunged much, abbreviating without making any additions   When Confucius transcribed the Six Classics, he was afraid that multitudinous characters would confuse the Empire   He decided to abridge them in order that the scholars of the Empire might get rid of the mere literary learning of the classics, and, seeking for what was genuine about them, no longer teach merely by using the literary style.   After the revision of the Annals of Spring and Autumn, the more the multitude of characters increased, the more confused the Empire became

The Work of Confucius Has Been Partly Undone

"(Ch'in) Shih Huang mistakenly burned the books from private motives, though he had no justification for doing so. If his purpose at that time was to exhibit the doctrine, he should have known enough to collect and burn all the sayings that were opposed to the classics and violated moral principles. That would have been in accord with the idea of revision. From the time of the Ch'in and Han dynasties, literary productions again daily increased in number. Though anyone should desire to dispose of them entirely, it would be utterly impossible. One should adopt the plan of Confucius: record that which is approximately correct, and publish it. All superstitious and perverse sayings should, of course, gradually be dropped. I do not know what interpretation of the classics prevailed contemporaneously with Wen Chung-tzu. As I look the matter over privately, I believe that a sage had arisen but was unable to effect a change. The misrule of the Empire was due to the fact that literary productions were abundant, but sincerity had decayed. Men, following their own opinions, sought for new mysteries that they might increase their fame. Ostentatious for the sake of becoming prominent, they confused the wise of the Empire, dulled the ears and eyes of the people, and caused them to dispute extravagantly. (13) They assiduously corrected literary style in order to seek notoriety before the world, but did not understand the practice which is generously original and nobly true, and which returns to honesty and reverts to sincerity. All commentators use their literary productions to promote this."

I said: "Among commentators there are some that are indispensable. The classic called the Annals of Spring and Autumn would probably be difficult to understand if it were not for the Tso Chuan." [22]

---

[22] The famous commentary of Tso Ch'iu-ming upon the Spring and Autumn Annals.

The Teacher said. "You say that the interpretation of the Annals of Spring and Autumn depends upon the Tso Chuan and can be understood only after the latter has been read The Annals of Spring and Autumn consists of abridged sayings Why should the sage devote himself strenuously to profound, abstruse phraseology? The Tso Chuan consists mostly of the ancient history of Lu Kuo If the Annals of Spring and Autumn can really be understood only after the reading of the Tso Chuan, why did Confucius revise it?"

- I said· "The philosopher Ch'eng also said that the Tso Chuan is the case (speaking from a legal standpoint) and the Spring and Autumn Annals are the judgment For example, a certain book gives an account of the murder of a prince or the devastation of a state by war. But if the individual lacks knowledge of the particular affair it is difficult for him to pass judgment "

Why the Sages Commented on the Classics

The Teacher said: "Perhaps this saying of the philosopher Ch'eng also was influenced by the sayings of the ordinary scholar, so that he did not comprehend the idea of the original writer of the classic. As for the account of the murder of the prince, just this murdering of the prince is the crime What necessity is there of instituting inquiry into the details of the murder? A declaration of war should come from the emperor. The attacking of the state is itself the crime. Why institute inquiry into the details of the attack? The sages comment on the Six Classics because they wish to rectify the minds of men and because they wish to preserve moral principles and drive out selfish aims. In evidence notice how often they refer to the keeping of Heaven's principles and the dispelling of selfish aims. In case anyone makes inquiry, each speaks according to his capacity, but without being willing to say much. They fear that men are merely seeking an expression of their (the sages') opinion. It was for this reason that Confucius said, 'I prefer not to speak.' How could he be willing to exhibit in detail those things that tolerate passion and violate heaven-given principles? Such things increase disorder and point out the way to adultery. Mencius said, 'None of the disciples of Chung-ni (Confucius) spoke about the affairs of Hwan (sic) and Wang, and therefore they have not been transmitted to later generations.' [23] This is what is meant by the domestic discipline of the Confucianists. The ordinary literary man expounds an education of force, and for that reason strives to know how to acquire many secret plans and artful devices. All his desires center in honor and wealth. They are entirely contrary to the idea of the sages who wrote the classics. (14) How, then, can they hope to understand?'' Therefore the Teacher said, sighing, ''Because they do not understand moral excellence, it is difficult to converse with them regarding this.''

Not Everything in the Book of History Should Be Believed

Again he said: ''Confucius said, 'In my early days the historiographer left a blank in his text.' [24] Mencius said, 'To believe the books without question is worse than having no books. It would be better not to have the Book of History than to believe it entirely. In ''The Completion of the War,'' I select only two or three passages which I believe.' [25] In the books Confucius edited covering the T'ang, Yü, and Hsia dynasties, a period of four or five hundred years, he did not expunge more than a few sections, nor did he reject any affairs. Moreover, his revision went no further. The idea of the sage may be known from this, that he simply endeavored to eliminate multitudinous characters. Later literary men, on the other hand, desire to increase their number.''

---

[23] Mencius, Book I, Pt. I, Ch. 7, ¶ 2.

[24] Analects, Book XV, Ch. 25.

[25] Mencius, Book VII, Pt. II, Ch. 3, ¶ 1 and 2.

Wang Discusses the Revision of the Classics

I said: "When the sages wrote the classics their aim was to get rid of the passions of men and harbor natural law. They preferred not to give to others a minute explanation of the events which occurred after the five rulers of the sixth century. That was right. But why is it that the affairs of the period prior to Yao and Shun were still less fully discussed?"

The Teacher said: "In the time of Hsi and Huang, important events occurred rarely and those who transmitted them were few in number. From this one may conclude that at that time all was well ordered, unpretentious, and without special elegance. The methods of government of the most ancient times were of that nature. Later generations have not been able to reproduce them."

I said: "Inasmuch as the records of the first three rulers had been handed down, why did Confucius revise them?"

The Teacher said: "Granting that there were those who transmitted them, yet in a changing world they gradually proved inadequate. The attitude of the community was increasingly disclosed and literary taste increased daily until we reach the end of the Chou dynasty. At that time they desired to adopt the manners and customs of the Hsia and Shan dynasties, but it was even then impossible to do so. How much less would they have been able to adopt those of the T'ang and Yü dynasties, or those of the time of Hsi and Huang! However, the path of duty was the same, though their methods of government had changed. Confucius recorded the doctrine of Yao and Shun as if they had been his ancestors, and elegantly exhibited the regulations of Wen and Wu, which were really the principles of Yao and Shun.[26] But the methods of proper government were different, and thus it was not feasible to introduce the professions of the Hsia and Shan dynasties into the Chou dynasty. It was for this reason that the Duke of Chou

---

[26] Doctrine of the Mean, Ch. 30, ¶ 1.

desired to exhibit the virtues of the three emperors in his own person. When, however, he saw anything in them not suitable to the time, he hesitated and pondered on it from daylight to night. How much less would it be possible to restore the government of the most ancient times! This the sages surely could abridge.'' (15)

Speaking again, the Teacher said: ''To devote one's self to an affair without effecting anything and without being able, as were the three emperors, to govern according to the times; and to desire to carry out the manners and customs of the ancients, these must be considered as devices of the Buddhists and Taoists. To desire to govern according to the times, and yet not to find the source thereof in the path of duty as did the three emperors; and to rule with a mind seeking honor and wealth, this is an occupation lower than that of a tyrant. Though numerous later scholars discussed back and forth, they merely discussed violent, audacious moral conduct.''

The Restoring of Ancient Methods of Government

Speaking again, he said: ''The method of government previous to the T'ang and Yü dynasties can not be restored by later generations, but a sketch may be made of it.[27] The government after the Three Dynasties cannot be imitated by later generations.[28] It should be sloughed off. Only the method of government of the Three Dynasties may be followed. But those who discuss the Three Dynasties do not understand their fundamental principles, and vainly devote themselves to the results. It cannot be restored in that way.''

The Six Classics May Be Viewed as History

I said: ''When former scholars discussed the Six Clas-

[27] The T'ang and Yü dynasties were those of Yao and Shun, 2357-2255 B.C.

[28] The Three Dynasties were those of Hsia, Shang, Chou, 2205-255 B.C.

sics, they regarded the Annals of Spring and Autumn as history. History merely records events. Are not the Annals of Spring and Autumn perhaps somewhat different in this from the other books of the Five Classics?"

The Teacher said· "The narrating of events is called history; the discoursing on the principles of the path of duty is called a classical work. But events are really identical with the path of duty, and this path is identical with events The Annals of Spring and Autumn is a classic work, and the Five Classics are history. The Canon of Changes is the history of the emperors P'ao and Hsi, the Book of History, of the time following Yao and Shun; the Book of Poetry and the Canon of Rites, the history of the Three Dynasties. Inasmuch as the affairs and principles discussed in the Annals are the same, how can the books be said to be different?"

The Teacher spoke again, saying. "The Five Classics also are merely history — history for the purpose of explaining good and evil, and for the sake of instruction and warning The good may well be used for such instruction. Time has left its foot-print in order to exhibit precepts. The evil may well serve as a warning. If one heeds the warning and corrects in himself the corresponding evils, it may serve as a preventative of wickedness."

The Moral Purpose of the Sages

I said: "Leaving foot-prints in order to exhibit precepts also implies cherishing and defending the source of moral principles. Does not correcting the corresponding evils in order to prevent wickedness keep the passions of men from shooting forth?"

The Teacher said: "Surely the sage wrote the classics with this in mind (16) But one need not dote on literary expressions."

I again made inquiry saying "The evil may serve as a warning signal. If one heeds the warning and corrects the evils, it may serve to prevent wickedness. Since they are only in the Book of Poetry, why not expunge Chen and Wei (two odes)? Is the assertion of former scholars true, that the evils may serve to regulate the easy-going habits of men?''

The Teacher said: ''The Book of Poetry is not the original book of the Confucianists. Confucius said, 'Banish the songs of Cheng. The songs of Cheng are licentious.' [29] He also said, 'I hate the way in which the songs of Chen confound the music of Ya.' [30] That the songs of Chen and Wei are the sounds of a decaying state is according to the domestic discipline of the Confucianists. The three hundred sections which Confucius chose are all called the music of Ya.[31] All may be played in the temple of Heaven or for a village clan. All, therefore, were played pleasantly and harmoniously and greatly promoted virtuous disposition and changed evil usages. Why were the songs of Chen and Wei omitted? Because they fostered the growth of licentiousness and led to adultery. They doubtless were again adopted by ordinary scholars after the burning of the books by Emperor Ch'in, for the sake of making up full three hundred sections. They are expressions of debauchery such as are frequently gladly transmitted by ordinary vulgar people. The alleys of today are full of that sort of conversation. That wicked men may serve as a warning to the easy-going tendency of men, is a manner of approach which seeks verbal form without getting any real advantage, while at the same time it engages in apologizing discussions.''

Because of interest in the loss of the original sayings of the ancients, I at first listened to the instruction of the Teacher, but was really fearful, doubtful, and without any

[29] Analects, Book XV, Ch. 10, ¶ 6.

[30] *Ibid.*, Book XVII, Ch. 18.

[31] Refined, elegant music. Professor Alexander Y. Lee prefers to call it civil music.

point of contact. After I had heard the Teacher's instruction for a long time, I gradually realized that I must face about and rectify my steps. After that I first began to have faith that the learning of the Teacher had come direct from Confucius, and that the remaining discussions were all by-paths. Such discussions intercept the stream. He says that the investigating of things consists in making the purpose sincere; the understanding of virtue, in cultivating one's self; the investigation of heaven-given principles, in exhausting one's disposition; the maintaining of constant inquiry and study, in honoring one's virtuous nature; the extending of learning, in keeping one's self under the restraint of the rules of propriety; being discriminating, in being undivided; and other like sayings. At first these are hard to harmonize, but after one has thought about them for a long time one spontaneously gesticulates with hands and feet. (17)

INSTRUCTIONS FOR PRACTICAL LIFE

PART II [1]

Practical Ethical Instruction

The Teacher said: "Seize hold of a good resolution as if the mind were distressed. Will there be any time to engage in idle talk or to care for idle affairs, if the mind is fully occupied with its distress?"

I, Lu Ch'eng, made inquiry saying: "There is the matter of mastering one's mind. If in studying one is engaged entirely with study, or in receiving guests one is completely engaged in receiving guests, may these be considered as examples of being undivided?"

The Teacher said: "If in being fond of women one gives one's self completely to salaciousness, or in desiring wealth one devotes one's self entirely to covetousness, may these be considered as instances of mastering one's mind? This is what is called urging things and should not be considered as mastering the mind. To master one's mind implies mastering moral principles." [2]

I made inquiry regarding the fixing of one's determination. The Teacher said: "It is simply a question of keeping heaven-given principles in mind; for this in itself is what is meant by fixing one's determination. If one is able to remember this, it will obviously become gradually fixed in the mind. It may be compared to the Taoists' saying, 'a matrix which brings forth the virtues of the sage.' One who constantly harbors a regard for natural law little by

---

[1] Recorded by Lu Ch'eng.

[2] "Moral principles" here as elsewhere may also be translated "heaven-given principles" or "natural law."

little becomes a beautiful, great sage and spirit-man But it is also necessary, in obedience to this thought, to nurture and practice these principles.''

The Teacher said: ''If during the day one feels that work is becoming annoying, one should sit and rest. One should study though one feels an aversion to it. This is also giving a remedy for disease. In having intercourse with friends, mutually strive to be humble; for then you will derive benefit from your friendship. In case you strive for superiority you will be injured''

Later Scholars Wrote to Show Their Own Skill

I made inquiry saying, ''There have been many commentators in the past It is possible that some of them have brought confusion into right learning''

The Teacher replied· ''The mind of man completely embraces natural law. The books written by sages and virtuous men, just as the artist's work that gives a life-like expression, show men the general outline so that they may earnestly seek the truth in them The mental energy of the sages, as well as their bearing, their sayings, their joys, their actions, and their behavior, assuredly are things that could not be transmitted When later generations wrote commentaries they took the things the sages had outlined, and transcribed them according to the pattern (18) But they did more than this; for they also falsely separated them and interpolated them so that they might thereby show their own skill. In doing so they have strayed far from the truth.''

The Sage Lives True to Nature

I made inquiry saying, ''Does the unlimited adaptability of the sage not also first have to be acquired ?''

The Teacher said: ''How can so much be acquired? The mind of the sage is like a bright mirror. There is only brightness there, and thus the response will be true to the influence brought to bear upon it. It will reflect everything truly. Past forms do not linger there; nor does it need to prepare for those which it has not reflected. If according to the expositions of later generations it is necessary that preparation be made, it is quite contrary to the learning of the sages. Chou Kung regulated the rites of propriety and provided music in order to educate the Empire; and this all sages are able to accomplish. But why did not Yao and Shun accomplish it? Why was it delayed until the time of Chou Kung? Confucius revised the Six Classics in order to instruct all later generations. This, too, all sages are able to do. Why did not Chou Kung first accomplish it? Why was it delayed until the time of Confucius? One may know from these situations that when the sage meets with definite conditions, he does a definite work to meet the specific conditions. The only fear one need entertain is lest the mirror be clouded. One need not fear that when the thing comes before it, it will fail to reflect. Investigation of the change of events must also be carried on in accordance with the times. Naturally the student must first complete the task of brightening up the mirror. He should be grieved if his mind cannot become like a bright mirror, and should not grieve because things are continually changing.''

I said, ''Surely what you have said is of no immediate concern to me, for I have already made preparation for all sorts of imaginable circumstances. What do you think of such a reply?''

He said, ''That way of talking is originally good. But if you do not carefully consider it, it brings distress.''

The Principles of Righteousness Are Inexhaustible

The Teacher said: ''The principles of righteousness have no fixed abode and are inexhaustible. I say unto you, Do not because of having acquired some virtue say, I will cease acquiring.'' He said again, ''In ten years, twenty years, fifty years, do not cease." At another time he spoke again, saying, "Sageness is like the evil of Chieh and Chou [3] Truly after their time evil was inexhaustible. If Chieh and Chou had not died, would evil have ceased? If virtue may be exhausted, why did King Wen look toward the right path as if he could not see it?" [4] (19)

I made inquiry saying: "When I am tranquil I am conscious of good ideas, but when I meet with events (am subject to stimulation) the situation is different. How do you account for this?"

The Teacher said: "This shows that you know how to cultivate tranquility but do not understand how to control yourself. For this reason you are prostrate whenever you meet with a difficulty. When one has experience in affairs, he is able to stand firmly. Whether at rest or occupied, his purpose is fixed."

The Nature of Advanced Learning

I asked concerning the advancement of learning. The Teacher said: "When later scholars in instructing the people understood the minutiæ, they called it advanced learning. When they had not learned them, they called it lower learning. This implies that they differentiated between lower and advanced learning That which deals with things that can be seen with the eyes, heard with ears, expressed with the tongue, and thought with the mind is all lower learning On the other hand, that which cannot be seen with the eyes, heard with the ears, expressed with the tongue, or contemplated with the mind must be considered advanced learning. The planting and watering of a tree would stand for lower learning. But when the tree rests while growing both night and day, and its branch-

---

[3] The Emperor Chieh ruled about 1818 B.C He was defeated for his cruelty The Emperor Chou was the last ruler of the Shang dynasty. His crimes caused the overthrow of the dynasty at about 1154 B. C.

[4] Mencius, Book IV, Pt. II, Ch. 20, ¶ 3.

es spread luxuriantly, this stands for progressive learning. How can these two be separated? The method by means of which a man prepares himself so that whenever he is able to act he can tell those who talk with him how to proceed, is lower learning. The progressive higher learning is, however, included within the lower learning. What the sages have said, though it be given in great detail, is all lower learning. As the student applies himself in accordance with this he naturally proceeds to rise in his penetration. It is not necessary to look anywhere else for work that makes progress."

The Teacher said: "In ancient times there were only these sages." Again he said, "Man born on earth has only this one affair to which he should direct his attention."[5]

The Meaning of the Expression, "Being Discriminating and Undivided"

I made inquiry saying, "What sort of effort is involved in being discriminating and undivided?"[6]

The Teacher said: "Being undivided carries with it the purpose of being discriminating; and discrimination includes the task of being undivided. (20) It does not mean that in addition to exercising discrimination there is undividedness. The character *ch'ing* (meaning best, or essence) is derived from the character *mi* (rice) and thus should be compared with *mi* (rice). You wish to get the rice unmixed and of a clean white. This implies giving it undivided attention. Moreover, unless one adds hulling, winnowing, sifting, and selecting, discrimination is not complete. The use of discrimination includes hulling, winnowing, sifting and selecting, but in all one really does not desire more than that the rice be unmixed with tares, and pure white. Applying this, we see that extensive study, accurate in-

---

[5] To strive to become a sage is the only occupation worth while.

[6] Refers to man's nature, of which all things are the development.

quiry, careful reflection, clear discrimination, and earnest practice are included in being discriminating and undivided. The extending of learning consists in keeping one's self under the restraint of the rules of propriety; the investigation of things for the extension of knowledge consists in making one's purpose sincere; the maintaining of constant inquiry and study consists in honoring one's virtuous nature, understanding virtue consists in making the person sincere. There is no other way of explaining it.''

The Teacher said. ''Ch'i Tiao-k'ai said, 'I am not yet able to rest in the assurance of this' The master was pleased.[7] Tzu-lu got Tzu-kao appointed governor of Pi. The master said, 'You are injuring this man's son.'[8] Tseng Tien spoke of his wishes. The master permitted this[9] The purpose of the sage can be seen from this.''

Tranquility of Mind Explained

I made inquiry saying, ''May the time in which one is in a tranquil state of mind be said to be a state of equilibrium?''

The Teacher said: ''Men of today stay their minds only by controlling their passion nature, and thus when they are in a state of tranquility the passion nature alone is tranquil. This cannot be considered as the state of equilibrium in which there are no stirrings of feeling.''

I said: ''Though they are not in the state of equilibrium, are they not striving for it?''

He said: ''The individual must expel passion and cherish natural law before he really engages in the task When in a state of tranquility, one should constantly meditate how to get rid of passion and how to cherish natural law; and when at work one should also strive for the same end. It makes no difference whether one be in a state of tran-

---

[7] Analects, Book V, Ch. 5. Confucius wished him to enter official employment and this was his answer.

[8] *Ibid.*, Book XI, Ch. 24, ¶ 1 and 2.

[9] *Ibid*, Book XI, Ch 25, ¶ 7.

quility or not. If one depends upon the state of tranquility, the fault of loving tranquility and despising activity
gradually develops, and in connection therewith a great
many other faults that are hidden away in the mind and
will never be dislodged. As soon as conditions are favorable, they flourish as of old. In case action according to
principles is the motivating purpose, how can there fail to
be tranquility? But if tranquility itself is made the purpose, there will certainly be no compliance with principles.'' (21)

The Harm of Foregone Conclusions

I made inquiry saying, ''The disciples of Confucius discussed their wishes. Yu (Tzu-lu) and Ch'iu (Jan-yu)
wished to be entrusted with a government position; Kung-
hsi Chih wished to be responsible for ceremony and music.
All these are very useful. But when one reaches the words
of Tseng Hsi (Tseng Tien), only play is mentioned. Yet
the sage favored him.[10] How is this to be interpreted?''

The Teacher said: ''The three disciples had foregone
conclusions and arbitrary predeterminations. Having
these, they certainly would be turned aside from their
purpose. In case they were able to carry out their desires, they would not be able to do the other important
thing. Tseng Tien's wish, on the other hand, was without
preconceived ideas and arbitrary predeterminations, and
implied doing what is in accord with one's station and not
desiring to go beyond this. Such a viewpoint means that
when situated among barbarous tribes one does what is
proper among barbarous tribes; that in sorrow and difficulty one adapts one's self to a position of sorrow and difficulty; and that there is no situation in which one is not
self-possessed. According to the language of the three
disciples, the individual is merely a tool. Tseng Tien's
wish implied that the individual is not to be a tool. Since

---

[10] *Ibid.*, Book XI, Ch. 25. ¶ 3-7.

each of the three disciples wished to perfect his ability with majesty, they were not like the ordinary man who speaks vainly and lacks genuineness   For these reasons the master also favored their desires.''

How to Make Progress in Knowledge

I made inquiry saying, ''What shall the individual do when he finds that he is making no progress in knowledge?''

The Teacher said. ''In devoting one's self to study, one must have a point of departure   One should work from the starting-point forward, and advance by gradually completing each branch of study. The immortals have a good simile when speaking of small children· 'The child in its mother's womb consists only of pure vital force' What knowledge can it have? After birth it is first able to cry; a little later, to laugh; still later, to recognize its parents and brothers; and after that it is able to stand, walk, grasp, and carry. This is universally true   It implies that mental and physical energy increases, that strength becomes more vigorous, and intelligence more ample as the days pass. These capacities are not acquired through direct endeavor nor through a series of investigations after birth. This shows that there is a source. That the sage (Confucius) assumed regal sway over heaven and earth and nourished all things, is merely the result of progressive development from the equilibrium in which there is no stirring of pleasure, anger, sorrow, or joy. Later scholars do not understand what is meant by 'the investigation of things.' They see that the sage was omniscient and omnipotent, and thereupon desire at the very beginning to complete their quest. Is that in harmony with natural law?''

He spoke further saying: ''In fixing the determination one must work as though he were cultivating a tree. (22) When the young tree has the first rootlets it does not yet have a trunk, and when the trunk appears it does not yet have branches. After the branches come the leaves, and after the leaves, the flowers and the fruit. When you first cultivate the roots you need only care for them by watering them. You should not think of cultivating branches, leaves, flowers, and fruit. What advantage is there in being anxious? But you should not forget to care for the tree and water it, lest perchance there be no branches, leaves, flowers, or fruit."

I said: "What shall be done when one studies and is unable to understand?"

The Teacher said: "It shows that the quest is confined to the meaning of the individual characters, and that therefore one does not understand the thought of what is read. This is not equal to the method of those who devoted themselves to education in ancient times, for they read much and were able to explain it. But the unfortunate thing was that though they were able to expound very clearly, they did not really gain any advantage. It is necessary to work on the base of native endowment. Whosoever is unable to understand or unable to practice should return in his work to his original mind. Then he should be able to comprehend. The Four Books and the Five Classics discuss the original nature of the mind. The original nature of the mind is to be identified with the path of duty (truth). He who understands the original nature of his mind thereby understands the path of duty, for the two cannot be distinguished. This is the point of departure in studying."

Some one inquired about the philosopher Chu, saying, "In case a man devotes himself to study, he need pay attention only to mind and principles. How is this to be interpreted?"

The Teacher said, "Mind is nature, and nature includes law and order. The character yü (and) after 'mind' perhaps makes it inevitable that they be considered as two.

It will depend upon the way the student uses his good judgment with reference to this.''

A Tentative Explanation of Evil

Some one said, ''All men have natural endowment (mind), and the mind is the embodiment of heaven-given principles (natural law). Why then do some devote themselves to virtue and others to vice?''

The Teacher said, ''The mind of the evil man has lost its original nature.''

I made inquiry saying: ''Analyze heaven-given principles and you will find them extremely pure and not in the least confused, unite them again and you will have exhausted their greatness and there will be nothing left. How is this to be understood?'' (23)

The Teacher replied: ''Perhaps they will not be exhausted Is it really possible that natural laws will admit of being analyzed, and how can they be reassembled? When one attains what the sages call the state of being discriminating and undivided, they have then been exhausted.''

The Teacher said· ''Self-investigation should be nurtured when one is busy with the affairs of life, the nurture of self should be investigated when one is not thus occupied ''

The Great Problems of Life

I frequently made inquiry about Hsiang-shan's sayings regarding the way in which one should expend his energy with reference to human feelings and passions, as well as with reference to the vicissitudes of life [11]

The Teacher said: ''There are no crises and problems beyond those of passion and change. Are not pleasure, anger, sorrow, and joy passions of men? Seeing, hearing, talking, working, wealth and honor, poverty and lowliness, sorrow and difficulty, death and life, all are vicissitudes of

---

[11] *Vide* Biography, *footnote* 14, p. 29.

life. All are included in the passions and feelings of men. These need only to be in a state of perfect equilibrium and harmony, which, in turn, depends upon being watchful over one's self.''

I made inquiry saying, ''Is it true that we have the names benevolence, righteousness (duty to one's neighbor), propriety, and wisdom because we ourselves have manifested them?'' The Teacher said, ''Yes.''

The Connotation of the Word "Nature"

On another day I said, ''Are the feelings of commiseration, shame, dislike, modesty, complaisance, approval, and disapproval to be considered as nature manifesting virtue?''

The Teacher said: ''Benevolence, justice, propriety, and wisdom are nature manifesting virtue. There is only one nature and no other. Referring to its substance, it is called heaven; considered as ruler or lord, it is called Shang-ti (God); viewed as functioning, it is called fate; as given to men it is called disposition; as controlling the body, it is called mind. Manifested by the mind, when one meets parents, it is called filial piety; when one meets the prince, it is called loyalty. Proceeding from this on the category is inexhaustible, but it is all one nature, even as there is but one man (generic sense). As compared with his father, man is called son; as compared with his son, he is called father. Proceeding from this one may go on indefinitely, yet there is but one man and no more. Man should use his energy on his nature. If he is able to understand clearly the connotation of the word nature, he will be able to distinguish ten thousand principles.''

What is Included in Study

On a certain day I discussed studying. The Teacher said: ''In teaching anyone to study, prejudice should be avoided. When man begins to learn, the mind is like that of an ape, and the will is like that of a horse which cannot be tethered His thoughts are largely directed toward human desires He should be taught to sit quiet and cease his cares. After a while the desire of his heart will be somewhat fixed. (24) Merely to have him sit quiet in empty speculation, like a decayed tree which has crumbled to dust, is of no advantage. He should be taught to examine and control himself, and to allow none of the affairs of life to interrupt this task. If one wishes to drive out robbers and thieves, one must proceed with the determination of expelling them and of inaugurating a clean, clear state of things When one has leisure, salaciousness, covetousness, the desire for honor, and all like passions should be followed up and sought for individually. The root of evil must be pulled out, and never be allowed to appear again. Then first has a condition of joy been instituted. One should always be like a cat which is trying to catch a rat. When it sees or hears the rat, immediately a determination arises and it proceeds to catch the rat, persisting in spite of obstacles [12] One must not be lenient with the passions, conceal them, or give vent to them; for only thus may one be said to use his energy genuinely, and may succeed in expelling them and inaugurating a clear, clean state of affairs. When one reaches the condition in which there is no passion to control, naturally the time has arrived when one may sit upright with the hands before the breast and the thumbs coming together [13] Albeit it is said that the what of thinking and pondering is not the work of beginners The beginner must ponder on matters of self-investigation and self-control, and this means pondering upon sincerity He needs to think about heaven-given principles. When he reaches the condition in which his principles are pure, a pure state is the thing about which he should think and ponder.''

---

[12] Literally, ''cutting nails and gnawing through iron.''

[13] This implies that the task has been accomplished and one has come to a complete realization of one's self.

The Fear of Spirits and the Spirit of Fear

I made inquiry saying, "What do you say regarding the man who at night is afraid of spirits?"

The Teacher said: "This is due to the fact that in every-day life he is unable to assemble deeds of righteousness, and that his mind is timid about something. If his ordinary conduct is in harmony with the spirits, why should he be afraid of anything?"

Tzu-hsin said, "It is not necessary to be afraid of upright spirits, but perhaps the evil spirits will not differentiate between good and evil men. Consequently one cannot but be afraid."

The Teacher said: "Can an evil spirit delude and confuse an upright man? Only this one thing need be the object of fear: that the mind is depraved. Therefore, if anyone is deluded or confused, it is not that a spirit has deluded or confused him, but that his own mind has confused and deluded him. For instance, if a man is fond of women, it is the spirit of salaciousness that confuses; if he is covetous, it is the spirit of covetousness that deludes him; when a man is angry when he should not be angry, it is the spirit of anger that seduces him; and when a man is fearful at that which is not fearful, it is the spirit of fear that confuses and deludes him."

The Teacher said: "It is natural law that the mind in its original nature be fixed and established (self-possessed). This holds true of its activity as well as of its rest." (25)

The Great Learning and the Doctrine of the Mean Compared

I made inquiry as to whether the Great Learning and the Doctrine of the Mean were alike or different in doctrine. The Teacher said: "Tzu-ssu incorporated the fundamental idea of the Great Learning in the first chapter of the Doctrine of the Mean."

How Confucius Adjusted Mutual Relationships

I made inquiry saying: "Confucius corrected the mutual relationships of the people. Former scholars said. 'Upward one tells the emperor, downward one tells the financial commissioner, that Chê has been cast aside and Ying established.' What do you hold of this?"

The Teacher said. "It is perhaps as described. Can it be that a man who with the utmost respect exhausts propriety in waiting for me to take up official business would be the first discarded by me? Would this be reasonable and right? Since Confucius was willing to give the government to Chê, Chê certainly had thoroughly repented, restored the state to his father and obeyed the sage   Confucius, a man of staunch virtue and complete sincerity, had certainly brought Chê of the state of Wei to a realization that he who has no father cannot be counted a man, and that he must go and welcome his father speedily with tears. The love of father and son is in accordance with nature. In case Chê truly and thoroughly repented in this manner, could K'uai Wai fail to be influenced and satisfied? When K'uai Wai had returned, Chê would give him the state and ask to be executed. Since Wai would then have been influenced by his son, and the master, a man of complete sincerity, would have used his influence for peace in this matter, the father in turn would be unwilling to receive the state and would order Chê to rule   The body of ministers and the people would then also desire Chê to act as ruler. Chê, on the other hand, would confess his crime, request the emperor and tell the financial commissioner and all the noblemen that he wished to give the state to his father. Wai, the body of ministers, and the people would then publish the excellence of Chê's new awakening and unselfish filial piety, and would request the emperor and tell the financial commissioner and noblemen that they truly desired Chê to be the prince. Thereby the requests would center on Chê to cause him again to be the prince of the State of Wei. Chê would have no recourse except to do as in the story of a later emperor's father; that is, command the ministers and people to honor Wai as father of the duke, prepare the things necessary for the comfort of his father, and not till then step back and take up his position. In that way the prince would have carried out the doctrine of the prince, the minister that of the minister, the father that of the father, the son that of the son. The mutual relations would have been corrected, and conversation become filial. When once Chê had promoted this, he would be able to govern the Empire. The adjustment which Confucius made of the mutual relationships was perhaps of this kind.'' (26)

Sorrow as a Test of True Learning

While I was the official in charge of the granaries of the Court of Ceremonies, I unexpectedly received a letter from home saying that my son was dangerously ill. My mind was filled with unendurable sorrow.

The Teacher said: ''At this time you certainly should apply yourself to the truth (path of duty). If you allow this opportunity to slip by, of what advantage will it be for you to expound learning when you are in prosperity? You should gain experience now. The love of a father for his son is by nature the highest type of affection; but in accordance with natural law there is a state of equilibrium and harmony, which when exceeded leads to selfishness. If at this point men understand that the carrying out of natural law means love, then they will not realize that former sorrows and afflictions are examples of the saying, 'If the mind be under the influence of sorrow and distress, a man will be incorrect in his conduct.' The influence of the seven passions is in most people excessive; in a few only does it fail to reach its proper proportion. When it is excessive, it is not in accordance with the original nature of the mind. It must be adjusted to reach the mean, for then first is it right.   For instance, at the death of parents, is it not true that the son desires to mourn unto death because in that way his mind is put at rest?   But it is nevertheless said, 'The collapse should not injure the natural disposition.'   This does not imply that the sage is trying to quell it by force, but that nature has its limits which cannot be exceeded, and that everyone should recognize the nature of the mind   Nothing should be either added to or subtracted from this."

Many Fail to Reach the Ideal of the Classics

"Do not say that the equilibrium in which the passions are not manifested is kept by all men, that nature and its use have a common source, and that having nature, you also have its use.   If one keeps the equilibrium in which the seven passions have been suppressed, one also is in the state of harmony in which they are manifested in proper degree.   The present generation has been unable to acquire this harmony.   From this one must know that the equilibrium in which they are suppressed cannot have been completely acquired

"The restorative influence of the night is spoken of with reference to ordinary men; but the student, if he works diligently, may in the daytime, whether at work or at leisure, be the focus of the gathering and development of this restorative influence.   It is not necessary to speak of the influence of night with reference to the sage "

An Obscure Passage in Mencius Cleared Up

I made inquiry regarding the chapter, "Hold it (mind) fast and it remains with you, let it go and you lose it." [14]

He said: " 'Its outgoing and incoming cannot be defined as to time and place '   Though this is said of the common man, the student must certainly know that the nature of the mind is precisely of this type. (27) The task of

---

[14] Mencius, Book VI, Pt. I, Ch. 8, ¶ 4.

holding fast the mind is then free from any defects. One cannot say that the outgoing implies losing or the incoming means keeping, for the original nature (essence) has *ab initio* neither outgoing nor incoming. If, however, one refers to the outgoing and incoming, then its serious thought and its exercise would be the outgoing. However, the controlling power is continually manifested in these. Where has there been any outgoing; where has there been any incoming? The character *ch'iang* (breast or throat) used by the philosopher Ch'eng refers to nothing more than natural law. In case one entertains guests all day and does not depart from heaven-given principles, one remains within the idea of the character *ch'iang*. If one departs from natural law, he may`be spoken of as letting go and losing it (the mind's original nature)." He spoke again saying, "Outgoing and incoming also are really no more than action and rest. When action and rest are not right, how can there be a criterion?"

Wang Chia-hsiu Asks for an Explanation of the Investigation of Principles

Wang Chia-Hsiu made inquiry saying: "The Buddhists use Nirvana (to pass from life and leave death), and the Taoists use the idea of immortality (living long and seeing a long time), to induce men to believe their doctrines. Their expositions should not be construed as though they wished men to do evil. Investigate them to the very extreme and you will see a bit of the doctrine of the sage. However, this is not the true way of entering upon the path of duty. It may be compared to officials of the present day, some of whom have become high officials through examinations, some through offerings, some through the promulgation of service rendered or through similar means. In last analysis they have not become officials in the right way, for the superior man does not become an official through such methods.

"Taoists and Buddhists are somewhat like Confucianists in that they devote themselves to one thing only, but they do not know that this thing should be natural law (heaven-given principles). When they are occupied they cultivate empty contemplation. The Confucianists, whether occupied or unoccupied, devote themselves (their entire mind) to natural law alone.

"In consequence, the cherishing of reverence also implies a thorough examination of principles. The carrying out of the saying, 'to devote one's self particularly to the thorough examination of principles,' is what is called cherishing reverence. The carrying out of the saying, 'Cherish the very essence of reverence,' is what is called thoroughly examining principles This does not imply that in addition to the cherishing of reverence the mind also thoroughly examines principles, or that at the time of carrying on a thorough investigation of principles the mind also cherishes reverence Though the names are different, the task is the same. This is in accordance with the saying of the Book of Changes that reverence is for the purpose of rectifying the inner nature, while righteousness is for the purpose of correcting the external conduct Reverence is the righteousness of the time when one is unoccupied, while righteousness is the reverence of the time when one is occupied (28) When the two are harmonized, they are one.

"When Confucius, for example, said, 'In cultivating himself he uses reverence,' he did not need to speak of righteousness.[15] When Mencius spoke of 'the accumulation of righteousness,' he did not need to say reverence [16] At the time when they are brought together, though you discuss them from any angle, the task is the same If one dotes on literary style and expressions, and does not know the origin or arrangement separation and division of the doctrine ensue, and all the work is then left unsettled. I wish to ask

[15] Analects, Book XIV, Ch 45
[16] Mencius, Book II, Part I, Ch 2, ¶ 15

in what way the thorough investigation of principles means exhausting nature.''

The Teacher said: ''The original nature is the embodiment of natural law (heaven-given principles). He who thoroughly investigates the principles underlying benevolence, must be benevolent, very benevolent; he who thoroughly investigates the principles underlying righteousness, must be righteous, very righteous. Benevolence and righteousness are natural disposition. Therefore the thorough investigation of natural law implies the exhausting of righteousness. For instance, Mencius says, 'If a man gives full development to his natural sympathies he will attain more benevolence than can be used.'[17] This is what is called thorough investigation of natural principles.''

Jih-fu remarked: ''Former scholars said that a single blade of grass and a single tree also have underlying principles which must be examined. How is this to be construed?''

The Teacher said: ''Just now I have no leisure. Sir, first understand your own disposition. One should first be able to give full development to the natural disposition of mankind, and then one is in a position to give full development to the nature of things.'' Jih-fu was awed and understood fully.

Adaptability is Indispensable

Wei Ch'ien made inquiry regarding the saying of Mencius, ''By holding the medium without leaving room for the exigency of circumstances, it becomes like their holding their one point.''[18]

The Teacher said: ''The medium is merely natural law. And yet at any time it may change? How then can it be held? It certainly means that it must be suitably regu-

---

[17] Mencius, Book VII, Pt. II, Ch. 31, ¶ 2.

[18] *Ibid.*, Book VII, Pt. I, Ch. 26, ¶ 3.

lated in accordance with the occasion, and for that reason it would be difficult to establish a rule in advance. It would be as though later scholars through their expositions undertook to determine a pattern without leaving a loop-hole for any change. That would carry with it the idea of holding.''

T'ang Hsü made inquiry saying: ''Is it true that in fixing the determination one should constantly cherish good thoughts, do good, and expel evil?''

The Teacher said: ''The cherishing of good thoughts is in accordance with natural law. Such thoughts are themselves virtue. What other virtue shall one deliberate upon? They are not evil. What evil shall one expel? Thoughts are like the roots and rootlets of a tree He who is fixing his determination need only fix his thoughts for a long time. When one is able to follow the desire of the heart without overstepping propriety, one's determination has become habitual [19] (29)

''It is of first importance that mental and animal energy, virtue, words, and acts should for the most part be controlled (gathered together) That they will lack unity at times is inevitable. Heaven and earth, man and things, are all alike in this ''

The Character of Wen Chung-tzu

He (T'ang Hsü) made inquiry saying, ''What sort of a man was Wen Chung-tzu?''

The Teacher said. ''He had nearly all the characteristics, but in small proportion [20] Unfortunately he died young.''

He again asked, ''Why did he make the mistake of adding (by writing in a similar way) to the classics?''

The Teacher said · ''To add to the classics is not an unmitigated evil.''

He questioned the Teacher a long time The Teacher

---

[19] Analects, Book II, Ch 4, ¶ 6.

[20] Refers to the characteristics of a sage.

said: "You should the more realize that the mind of a good workman is distressed."

Selfishness is a Root of Evil

The Teacher said: "Pleasure, anger, sorrow, and joy are in their natural condition in the state of equilibrium and harmony. As soon as the individual adds a little of his own ideas, he oversteps and fails to maintain the state of equilibrium and harmony. This implies selfishness.

"In subduing one's self, one must clear out selfish desire completely, so that not a bit is left. If a little is left, all sorts of evil will be induced to make their entrance."

The Methods of Music are of Secondary Importance

He asked regarding the Lü Lü Hsin Shu.[21] The Teacher said: "Scholars should give their attention to the most urgent things. When these methods (referring to the music) have become familiar, they are perhaps of little value. It is important that the mind should first cherish the source from which ceremonies and music come. Moreover, the book (Lü Lü Hsin Shu) says, 'In the winter use a flageolet and wait till the wind blows out the dust from the reed. At the very time of the winter solstice the dust in the reed will be blown out.' Whether it be before or after, how can it be known that just at that time the reed has truly happened upon the winter solstice? It certainly is necessary that one's own mind should first know the time of the winter solstice. Thus there is an inconsistency. The scholar must first use his efforts upon the source of ceremonies and music."

The Mind May Be Compared to a Mirror

Yueh-jen said: "The mind may be compared to a mirror. The mind of the sage is like a bright mirror, the mind of the ordinary man like a dull mirror. The saying of

---

[21] Literally translated, "A New Book on Keyed Tones."

more recent natural philosophy may be compared to using it as a mirror to reflect things. If effort is expended in causing the mirror to reflect while the glass is still dull, how can one succeed? The natural philosophy of the Teacher is like a polished and brightened mirror. When after having been polished the mirror is bright, the power of reflecting has not been lost "

He asked regarding the general plan and the details (fineness and coarseness) of the doctrine.[22] The Teacher said "The doctrine has neither general plan nor detailed structure. What men consider the general plan and the details may be made clear in examining a house. (30) When one first enters it, one sees only the general plan. After a while one sees the supports and walls. Later still such things as the ornamental duckweed upon the supports become apparent. But all this is only a part of the same house."

Lack of Effort Involves Selfishness and Hinders Progress

The Teacher said: "Sirs, how is it that recently when you approach me you have so few questions to ask regarding the things about which you are in doubt? When a man fails to put forth effort, he invariably believes that he well knows how to devote himself to study, and that all that is necessary is to follow the order and act (*i.e* study). He certainly does not know that selfish desire increases every day like the dust of the earth. If one neglects to sweep for a day, another layer is added If one really works with determination one realizes that the doctrine is inexhaustible The more one searches, the profounder it becomes, until its essence and purity are fully comprehended "

Some one made inquiry saying: "After knowledge has been completed one can say that the thoughts are sincere.

---

[22] Translated literally. May perhaps be freely translated "minutiae."

At present neither moral law nor the passions of men are thoroughly understood.[23]   Under such circumstances how is anyone in a position to begin to subdue himself?''

The Teacher said: ''If a person unceasingly applies himself truly and earnestly, he will daily better comprehend the subtle essence of the moral principles of the mind, as well as the subtlety of selfish desires.   If he does not use his efforts in controlling himself, he will continually talk and yet never comprehend the meaning of moral principles or of selfish desire.   The situation may be likened to a man traveling.   When (by walking) he has covered a stage, he understands that stage.   When he reaches a fork in the road and is in doubt he makes inquiry, and having made inquiry he again proceeds.   In this way he gradually reaches his destination.   Men of today are unwilling to abide by the moral principles which they already know, and to expel the passions they have already recognized; but are downcast because they are unable to understand completely. They merely indulge in idle discussions.   Of what advantage is this?   They should wait until in the process of subduing and controlling themselves there are no more selfish motives to subdue, for then it would not be too late to sorrow because of their inability to understand fully.''

The Discussions of Truth Vary Because Truth is Inexhaustible

He made inquiry saying: ''Though there is but this one doctrine, yet the doctrinal discussions of the ancients were frequently not alike.   Are not some things more essential than others in seeking the path?''[24]

The Teacher said: ''Truth (the path) has no form; it cannot be grasped or felt.   (31)   To seek it in a bigoted and obstinate way in literary style or expression only, is far

---

[23] Moral law in its psychological aspects.   May be translated ''natural law.''

[24] May also be translated ''seeking the truth.''

from correct. It may be compared to men discussing heaven. As a matter of fact, when have they ever seen heaven? They say that sun, moon, wind, and thunder are heaven. They cannot say that men, things, grass, and trees are not heaven, while the doctrine is heaven. When the individual once comprehends, what is there that is not truth? People for the most part think that their little corner of experience determines the limits of truth, and in consequence there is no uniformity in their discussions If they realized that they need to seek within in order to understand the nature of the mind, there would be neither time nor place that would not be pregnant with truth Since from ancient times to the very present it is without beginning and without end, in what way would there be any likenesses or differences in truth? The mind is itself truth and truth is heaven. He who knows the mind thereby knows both truth and heaven."

Again he said: "Sirs, if you would truly comprehend truth, you must recognize it from your own minds. It is of no avail to seek it in external things"

The Development of the Original Nature of the Mind is of First Importance

He made inquiry saying: "Is it necessary first to investigate the mutual human relationships, the things of nature, measures, and numbers?"

The Teacher said: "It is necessary to develop the original nature of the mind; then its use will include the state of equilibrium. In case one nourishes the original nature of the mind and attains to the equilibrium in which there is no stirring of feelings, there surely is present the state of harmony which results when the feelings are stirred and act in due degree. Of course it must be exhibited If mind is lacking, the mutual human relationships, the things of nature, as well as measures and numbers, would have no relation to the self, though one explain them first; but would simply imply pretension and superficiality. When at times the feelings are displayed, the individual naturally does not maintain the equilibrium. I do not wish to say that the mutual relationships, the things of nature, measures, and numbers should be entirely left out of consideration. If the individual knows what is first and what is last, he will be near the truth."

He spoke again saying: "Man must develop in accordance with his capacity. Capacity constitutes his ability to accomplish things. For instance, the music of K'uei and the agriculture of Chi were noteworthy because they were in harmony with their natural endowment.[24] He who would complete himself need only preserve the nature of his mind guileless in natural law. When the occasions on which he acts all take their origin from nature itself, he may be said to have ability. When a person reaches the state in which he is completely in accord with natural law, he is no longer a mere utensil. Had K'uei and Chi been ordered to exchange professions and engage in them successfully, they would have been able to do so." (32)

Again he said: "In a position of wealth and honor to do what is proper to a position of wealth and honor, in a position of sorrow and difficulty to do what is proper to a position of sorrow and difficulty, implies that one is not a mere machine.[25] This can be accomplished only by the man who cultivates an upright mind."

The Teacher said: "To dig a pond several hundred *mu*[26] in size, but without a spring, is not equal to digging a well a few feet deep with a spring in it that runs without ceasing." The Teacher said this as he sat at the side of a pool near which there was a well. Subsequently he used this figure in elucidating learning.

---

[24] K'uei was an officer who acted as director of music at the request of Emperor Shun. Chi was Emperor Shun's minister of agriculture.

[25] The Doctrine of the Mean, Ch. 14, ¶ 2.

[26] The "mu" is about one-sixth of an acre.

The Mind Should Rule the Senses

He made inquiry saying, "In what way may the mind devote itself to things?"

The Teacher said: "When the people's prince is upright, reverent, and majestic, and the six boards distinguish their respective official duties, the Empire is well governed. In the same way the mind should govern the five senses. In our day when the eye wishes to see, the mind applies itself to color, and when the ear wishes to hear, the mind devotes itself to sound. It is as though the people's prince were himself to take a seat on the Board of Civil Offices, when he wishes to choose an official, or on the Board of War, when he wishes to move the troops. In this way the original character of the prince would be sacrificed and in addition the six boards also would be unable to perform their official duties."

The Manner of Thinking May Be Indicative of Selfishness

I said: "Love of lust, love of gain, love of fame, and similar dispositions of mind surely are selfish desires; but why should it also be called selfish desire when at a time of leisure one thinks anxiously and confusedly?"

The Teacher said: "For the reason that, after all, such thinking emerges out of love of lust, love of gain, love of fame, and similar roots. If you search for the roots, you will see. For instance, if you know that your mind is free from anxious thought about robbing, what does this imply? It means that you have had no such thoughts. If, as in the case of robbing, you also destroy the love of lust, fame, gain, and others, and the original character of the mind alone is left, what anxious thought will occupy your mind when you are at leisure? This implies being perfectly calm, and is the equilibrium of not manifesting the passions, and the open field without favoritism. Naturally it means to be influenced but at the same time to see clearly; to manifest the feelings but with moderation; and, of course, when affairs arise to respond properly.'' (33)

The Place of the Will in the Mental and Moral Life

I made inquiry regarding (the saying): ''The will is first and chief, and the passion nature is subordinate to it.'' [27]

The Teacher said: ''In whatsoever respect the will is great the passion nature may also be said to be great; and this does not imply that the will is chief and the passion nature is subordinate to it. Maintaining a firm will includes nourishing the passion nature, and doing no violence to the passion nature also includes maintaining a firm will. Mencius, in order to rescue Kao-tzu from his partiality, spoke thus to support him.''

A Virtuous Man Does Not Exalt Himself

I made inquiry saying: ''Former scholars said: 'The truths expressed by the sage show him forth as lowly and humble. The words of a virtuous man exhibit and exalt his personality.' Do you consider that true?''

The Teacher said: ''No. A statement such as that is false. The sage may be compared to heaven. There is no place where heaven is not present. Above the sun, moon and stars heaven is found, and below the nine divisions it is also found. How can heaven descend and make itself lowly? The implications here are greatness and the exercise of a transforming influence. The good man may be compared to a lofty mountain peak, maintaining his lofty height. Nevertheless, one a thousand feet high cannot stretch and become ten thousand feet high, and one ten thousand feet high cannot stretch and become a hundred thousand feet high. The good man does not exhibit and exalt himself. It is false to say, 'exhibits and exalts himself.' ''

---

[27] Mencius, Book II, Pt. I, Ch. 2, ¶ 9.

How the State of Equilibrium is to be Acquired

I made inquiry saying: "I-ch'uan said, 'One should not seek the state of equilibrium before pleasure, anger, sorrow, and joy have manifested themselves.' [28] Yen P'ing, on the other hand, taught the student to pay special attention to his bearing before the feelings have manifested themselves. What do you hold of this?"

The Teacher said: "Both are correct. I-ch'uan feared that the individual might seek the equilibrium before he had experienced the feelings, and thereby come to regard the equilibrium as a thing (rather than as an experience). This is in accord with my former statement that one acquires the equilibrium at the time of knowing how to bring the passion-nature to a proper state of control. It is for this reason that I enjoin upon you to expend your efforts in patient cultivation and close watching. Yen P'ing feared that the individual might lack a starting-point, and for that reason urged that he always seek the bearing of one who has not manifested his feelings. He influenced his followers to see and hear this only. This is what is meant by the task of being cautious with reference to that which is not seen, and fearful of that which has not been heard. These are sayings which the ancients were constrained to use to encourage the people."

I made inquiry saying: "An ordinary man surely is unable completely to attain the equilibrium and the harmonious development of pleasure, anger, sorrow, and joy. For instance, he who in some small thing should be either pleased or angry ordinarily has no inclination to be either pleased or angry, but when the time comes the feelings may be manifested in due degree. (34) May not this be called a state of equilibrium and harmony?"

The Teacher said: "At that time in that particular affair it certainly may be called a state of equilibrium and

---

[28] I-ch'uan is the name by which the philosopher Ch'eng was known — the brother of Ch'eng Ming-tao.

harmony, but it cannot be described as the great root or the universal path.[29]   The nature of all men is good.   The state of equilibrium and harmony is originally possessed by all men.   How, then, can they be said not to have it? However, the mind of the usual man has things that becloud, and therefore, though nature is manifested at times, the condition is such that it is sometimes manifested and sometimes extinguished.   It does not represent the functioning of the entire being.   When a condition has been reached in which there is a continuous state of equilibrium, it is designated as the great root (great fundamental virtue).   When a condition of continuous harmony has been acquired, it is designated as the universal way.   Only when a condition of the most complete sincerity under heaven is reached, is it possible for the individual' to establish himself in this great fundamental virtue of humanity.''

I further said: ''I do not yet clearly understand the meaning of the equilibrium.''

He said: ''You must recognize this from the nature of the mind itself, for it cannot be revealed by means of words.   The equilibrium is to be identified with heaven-given principles.''

I said, ''Why is it the same as heaven-given principles?''

The Teacher said, ''When passions have been cast out one understands heaven-given principles.''

I said, ''Why should heaven-given principles be designated as a state of equilibrium?''

He said, ''Because they are not prejudiced or selfish.''

I said, ''What kind of an attitude and bearing does this lack of selfishness give?''

He said, ''It may be compared to a bright mirror, all of which is perfectly clear and not spotted with a particle of dust.''

I said: ''Selfishness then implies being infected.   If one is infected with love of lust, love of gain, love of fame,

---

[29] *Vide* Doctrine of the Mean, Ch. I, ¶ 4.

and similar things, the selfishness is apparent. When they have not manifested themselves, when the lust, fame, and gain have not been experienced, how can one know that he is selfish?"

The Teacher said: "Though they may not have been experienced, yet ordinarily the individual has not been free from love of lust, gain, and fame. Since he has not been free from them, he may be said to have them; and since he may be said to have them, he cannot be free from leaning on them. It may be compared to a man who is sick with intermittent fever. Though at times the fever is not manifest, nevertheless as long as the root of the disease has not been extirpated he cannot be said to be free from the disease. It is necessary to sweep out and wash out the every-day love of lust, fame, and similar things — a lot of passions — so that not the least bit will be retained. Then the mind will be completely filled with unmixed heaven-given principles. (35) Thereupon it may be said to be in the state of equilibrium in which there are no stirrings of pleasure, anger, sorrow, and joy; and this is the great fundamental virtue of humanity."

Wang Eulogizes Yen-tzu

I made inquiry saying: "'Yen-tzu died and the learning of the sage perished.' This saying cannot be called in question."

The Teacher said: "Yen alone saw the perfection of the sage's doctrine. If you observe the sigh (of Yen in admiration of the sage's doctrine), you can see that only after having thoroughly realized it could he say, 'The Master, by orderly methods, skillfully leads men on. He enlarged my mind with learning and taught me the restraints of propriety.'[30] In what way is the enlarging of the mind with learning and the bringing of the individual under the restraint of propriety to be construed as skillfully leading

---

[30] Analects, Book IX, Ch. 10, ¶ 2

men on? The scholar should ponder on these things. It was difficult for the sage to explain the doctrine in every detail. The scholar must cultivate himself and bethink himself. Though Yen-tzu wished to carry out the doctrine of the sage, he found no way to do so.[31] Wen Wang (King Wen) turned his attention to the doctrine as though he had not understood it. That he did this really shows that he understood it. When Yen-tzu died, the idea running through the sage's doctrine could not be entirely transmitted to succeeding generations."

I made inquiry saying, "The mind is the master of the body; knowledge is the intelligence of the mind; purpose is the manifestation of knowledge; the place where the purpose is applied is called a thing. Is this correct?"

The Teacher said, "It is."

Wang's Idea of True Learning

The Teacher said: "It is only necessary to cherish the mind and see that it is continually present, for this is learning. What advantage is there in considering either that which is past or that which has not taken place? Such procedure implies needlessly losing one's mind."

The Unperturbed Mind of Mencius and Kao

Shang-ch'ien made inquiry as to whether there was a difference between the "unperturbed mind" of Mencius and that of Kao-tzu.

The Teacher said: "Kao-tzu forcefully controlled his mind because he wished it to be unperturbed. Mencius, on the other hand, gathered together righteousness until it naturally was unperturbed."

He spoke again saying, "It is natural for the mind to be unperturbed. Disposition should be construed as being the real nature of the mind, and as the embodiment of heaven-given principles. The disposition is originally unper-

---

[31] *Ibid.*, Book IX, Ch. 10, ¶ 3.

turbed; heaven-given principles are by nature unperturbed (not subject to alteration or open to influence). The gathering of righteousness means returning to the original nature of the mind."

The Teacher said: "When all nature is exuberant in growth, it is also peaceful, calm, and free from any thought for itself (*i.e.* without selfishness). This peace, calm, and lack of selfishness is the token of exuberant growth. Peace, calm, and lack of selfishness are the monitors of undividedness. (36) Exuberant growth is the matrix of discrimination. Undividedness includes discrimination and discrimination includes undividedness."

Wang Rebukes the Superficial Scholar

The Teacher said: "Very many of those whom I describe as students of philosophy merely allow it to circulate in their ears and mouth. Would that those mouth and ear students might reverse their procedure! If by continual use of effort the minutiæ of moral principles and of the passions of men are investigated and controlled, they may gradually be understood. Today at the very time they are discussing these principles, they do not realize that they already are subject to many selfish desires, which they are secretly and unwittingly manifesting. Though one make an effort to investigate them, it is difficult to understand them. Can it be that those who vainly speak about them are able to understand them completely? They pay attention only to the exposition of moral principles, and then lay them aside and do not act in accordance with them. They expound the meaning of passion, and then resting do not expel it from their minds. How can this be considered a type of learning which emphasizes the investigation of things for the purpose of extending knowledge? The literary accomplishment of later generations will at its best produce no more than superficial results." [32]

---

[32] Mencius, Book II, Pt. I, Ch. 2, ¶ 5.

Shang-ch'ien made inquiry saying: "Should one expend effort in the investigation of things at the point where the mind is stimulated?"

The Teacher said: "The difficulty of the task interrupts neither activity nor tranquility. Rest itself should be considered a thing. Mencius said, 'One must be occupied.' Whether at work or at rest, the mind is occupied."

Investigations Should Proceed for the Purpose of Developing the Intuitive Faculty

(The Teacher said): "The difficulty of the task rests wholly in investigating things for the purpose of developing the intuitive faculty to the utmost. It is really the task of making the purpose sincere. Since the purpose is sincere, the mind will in the main naturally be right, and the person regulated (controlled). Both rectifying the mind and regulating the body require specific effort. The regulating of the body has already manifested itself externally; the rectifying of the mind has not manifested itself externally. When the mind has been rectified, the state of equilibrium will have been attained; and when the person has been cultivated, the harmony of a proper use of the feelings will have been attained.

"From the investigation of things for the purpose of developing the intuitive faculty to the utmost, to the principles which underlie all things up to the point of making the world peaceful and happy, is all merely a matter of manifesting one's illustrious virtue.[33] Though loving the people is also illustrious virtue, the illustrious virtue here

___

[33] "Things being investigated, knowledge became complete. Their knowledge being complete, their thoughts were sincere. Their thoughts being sincere, their hearts were then rectified. Their hearts being rectified, their persons were cultivated. Their persons being cultivated, their families were regulated. Their families being regulated, their States were rightly governed. Their States being rightly governed, the whole kingdom was made tranquil and happy." — The Great Learning, Introduction, ¶ 5.

referred to is the original virtue of the mind—benevolence. (37) He who is benevolent considers heaven, earth and all things as an all-pervading unity. If one thing loses its relative place, benevolence has not been wholly achieved. To say that one manifests his original illustrious virtue, and yet not to say that he loves the people, is to be like the Taoists and Buddhists.''

Nature is the Highest Good

The Teacher said: ''Nature is the highest good. Nature is in its original condition devoid of all evil, and for this reason is called the highest good. To rest in the highest good implies returning to one's natural condition.''

He (Shang-ch'ien) made inquiry saying, ''Knowledge of the highest good is characteristic of my nature, and my nature is to be identified with my mind. My mind, however, is the place in which the highest good rests. In that case I should not, as of old, seek for the highest good confusedly in external things, but should fix my determination. When the determination has been fixed, it will not give trouble. Confusion will give place to quietude; quietude and absence of disorderly activity will usher in peace. When there is peace, both mind and will are interested in this alone. If in all planning and thinking I earnestly seek, I will surely get this highest good; but it can be acquired only after one is able to take serious thought for it. Is this manner of expounding the situation correct or not?''

The Teacher replied, ''In general, it is.''

Benevolence is the Principle of Continuous Creation and Growth

Shang-ch'ien made inquiry saying: ''The philosopher Ch'eng said, 'The benevolent person considers heaven, earth, and all nature as an all-pervading unity.' How, then, does it come that the philosopher Mo, who loved all things, said nothing about benevolence?''

The Teacher said: "It is very hard to give an adequate reason for this. You yourselves, Sirs, will need by means of introspection to investigate this thoroughly up to the point where you understand it, for then first will you get satisfaction. Benevolence is the fundamental principle of continuous creating and growth. Though these are boundless in extent and everywhere present, their progress and manifestation proceed gradually. For instance, at the winter solstice one Yang is brought forth, and from this one Yang later six other Yangs are gradually developed.[34] Were it not for the development of this one Yang, how could the six Yangs be generated? And the same holds true of the Yin. Because it is gradual in its operation, there is a beginning; and because there is a beginning, there is a bringing forth. Because it continues to bring forth, there is no ceasing. The tree begins by developing a bud. This is the point at which the tree's purpose to grow starts. After the bud has developed the trunk appears, and then the branches and leaves; and from that time it grows continually. (38) If it has no bud, how can it have trunk, branches, and leaves? Its ability to develop a bud surely depends upon the root underneath; for if there is a root there can be growth, and without the root it must die. From what shall the buds develop if there is no root? The love of father and son, elder brother and younger brother, is the point at which the purpose of man's mind to develop begins. Just as in the tree the buds shoot forth, thus from this love toward the people and love of things trunk, branches, and leaves develop. The man named Mo loved all things without difference of degree. He looked upon his own father, his own son, his own elder brother, and his own younger brother even as he did upon the stranger; and for that reason he lacked a point from which he might start to develop. Where there is no ability to grow a bud, there are no roots, and consequently no con-

---

[34] Yang and Yin are the two primeval forces.

tinuous development. How can such a condition be called benevolence? Filial piety and respectfulness toward the elder brother are the beginning of benevolence; benevolence, however, must be manifested from within.''

Action According to Moral Principles is Unselfish

Shang-ch'ien made inquiry saying: ''Yen P'ing said, 'He who acts in accordance with moral principles does not have a selfish mind.' In what way should I distinguish between moral principles and unselfishness?''

The Teacher said: ''The mind is to be identified with moral principles. When one's mind is freed from selfishness, acting in accordance with moral principles is a necessary accompaniment. If one does not act in accordance with moral principles, his mind is selfish. Perhaps it would be better not to distinguish between mind and moral principles in expounding this.''

He made further inquiry saying: ''The Buddhists are not infected by any of the selfishness of lust, and thus appear to have a mind free from selfishness. On the other hand, they outwardly disregard human relationships, and thus do not appear to be acting in accordance with moral principles.''

The Teacher said: ''This belongs to the same class of things. They all carry out the mind of a selfish personality.''

INSTRUCTIONS FOR PRACTICAL LIFE

PART III [1]

The Why and What of Learning are Important

I made inquiry saying: "To devote one's self to cherishing heaven-given principles and yet not energetically to seek them is apt to eventuate in identifying passion with heaven-given principles. How is this to be interpreted?"

The Teacher said: "The individual must know how to learn. (39) Seeking includes the idea of cherishing. Lack of seeking implies that one does not cherish one's purpose with determination."

I said, "What do you mean by saying that one must know how to learn?"

He said: "I meant to say that one should know why he is learning and what is to be learned."

I said, "I have frequently heard the Teacher giving instruction in learning how to cherish heaven-given principles. You said that the original nature of the mind is to be identified with heaven-given principles, and that knowledge of them means clearing selfish motives from one's mind."

The Teacher said: "In that case it is only necessary to prevail over selfish motives and to be solicitous lest some heaven-given principle or passion be not understood."

I said: "I am afraid that I do not truly understand selfish motives."

He said: "That would imply that you lack a will which is in full earnest. When the will is wholly sincere, the eyes will see it and the ears will attend to it. How can

---
[1] Recorded by Hsieh K'an.

there be the possibility of not truly understanding? The ability to distinguish between right and wrong is common to all men, so that it avails nothing to seek them in external things Investigation implies appreciation of that which one's own mind experiences. It will not do to go outside of the mind for this, as though there were additional possibility of understanding."

Growth in Virtue Should Not Be Forced Nor Should It Be Sought in External Things

The Teacher asked his friends who were seated with him how they were getting on in recent years with their task of learning. One of them spoke of the meaning of being emptied of selfishness and of understanding natural law. The Teacher said: "This refers to the circumstances in which one is " Another one spoke of the differences and similarities of the present and the past The Teacher said: "This refers to result " Two friends, not knowing exactly what to do, asked questions. The teacher said: "In our efforts at this time we need a mind earnest in doing good. When the mind which is truly in earnest sees virtue, it will advance toward it; and when it has erred, it will reform. When that condition has been attained, we have what is called devotion, in all earnest, to the task Then passion will daily decrease and natural law will be increasingly comprehended. He who merely seeks better circumstances, or speaks of results, fosters the development of the defect of forcing the growth and of going to external things. It should not be identified with pursuing the task."

The Student Should Not Criticise Hui-an

When his friends studied, there were many who selected Hui-an for criticism.[2] The Teacher said: "If you seek

---

[2] Chu Hui-an (Chu Hsi), commonly known as the philosopher Chu, was the well-known commentator of the Sung Dynasty He lived 1130-1200 A D

differences (between the philosopher Chu's exposition and mine), you are pursuing the wrong course. My exposition is at times different from what he has said. There are both small and great differences in the place and manner of beginning to study, so that I must of necessity distinguish between them. But, in all, there is no difference between my purpose and that of Hui-an. (40) If the rest of his ideas can be explained with a proper degree of clearness, why should a single character be changed?''

Wang Gives His Idea of What a Sage is

Hsi Yen made inquiry saying: ''The sage has been able to learn until he has attained. Po I and I Ying, however, never had the capacity of Confucius. How is it that they also are termed sages?''

The Teacher said: ''That the sage is a sage, is due solely to the fact that his mind is completely dominated by heaven-given principles, and not hampered by passion. As the gold is termed the finest when it has the quality and is free from brass and lead, so a man who has become fully dominated by heaven-given principles is a sage. When gold has the degree of quality required, it is the finest. The capacity of the sages varies just as the weight of gold may be light or heavy. Yao and Shun are as two hundred thousand ounces of gold; Wen Wang and Confucius as one hundred eighty thousand; Yü, T'ang, and Wu Wang as one hundred forty to sixty thousand; Po I and I Ying as eighty to one hundred thousand ounces. Their capacity varied, but in the matter of being dominated by a mind of pure heaven-given principles they were all alike. They may all be called sages. Though the weight varies, the quality is the same. They may be designated as the finest gold. That he who corresponds to one hundred thousand ounces may enter the class of two hundred thousand, is due to the fact that the quality is the same. To place I and Ying in the series of Yao and Confucius implies that all are completely dominated by heaven-given principles. It is because of quality and not quantity that they are compared to the finest gold. They are called sages not because of their capacity, but because of the fact that they are completely under the control of heaven-given principles.

"Albeit, whosoever is willing to devote himself to study may become a sage, provided he devotes his mind to heaven-given principles. It is as if an ounce of gold be compared with two hundred thousand ounces. Though there is great difference in weight, yet if the ounce has the quality it is without fault. I venture to say that every man can be as Yao or Shun; for in learning to be a sage, the student need only expel passion and cherish natural law. It may be compared to refining gold and striving for proper quality. If one does not strive much for the quality, the work of refining will be comparatively light and easy; but if the quality is too low, the work of refining will be made over-difficult. (41) The dispositions of men are bright and stupid, docile and contradictory. There are those who rank above the ordinary man, and those who fall below. As regards the truth, some are born with the knowledge of it; some practice it with natural ease; some know it by study, and practice it from a desire for advantage. The remaining ones surely belong among those who, if others succeed by one effort, must use a hundred efforts, and if others succeed by ten efforts, must use a thousand.[3] Nevertheless, when it comes to the matter of completing the task, the outcome is the same.

"Later generations did not know that the point of departure in becoming a sage is in being completely dominated by heaven-given principles, but devoted themselves to seeking to become sages by means of knowledge and power; for they thought that sages are all-knowing and all-powerful. Each said to himself: 'I must comprehend the

---

[3] Doctrine of the Mean, Ch. 20, ¶ 20.

exceedingly great knowledge and power of the sages, before I can rest.' For this reason they did not devote themselves energetically to moral principles, but vainly dulled their mental energies and exhausted their strength that they might worm it out of books, or search it out of nature, or surmise it from various signs left by the sages. With greater increase in knowledge there came greater increase in passion; and the greater the power they attained, the more they obscured moral principles. It may well be compared to a man who has two hundred thousand ounces of the finest gold and fails to use his energies in refining the quality. He seeks freedom from reproach in the matter of fineness, but absurdly places his hope in the weight. They use their energies as this man his hundred thousand ounces of gold. The more the weight increases, the lower is the quality, until at last there is no gold left.''

At that time Yüeh-jen (Ts'ü Ai) was near by and said: ''This comparison is sufficient to dispel the divergent doubts of present-day scholars regarding the Teacher. It represents a great achievement for later generations.''

The Teacher spoke again: ''We work for the sake of daily decreasing passion, and not for the purpose of increasing it. If we are able to decrease passion a little bit, we have thereby made another small advance in heaven-given principles. How comfortable and satisfying, how simple this work is!''

Wang Discusses Wen-kung's Strength and Weakness

Ssu Te made inquiry saying: ''The sayings regarding the investigation of things as taught by the Teacher are easily understood, so that everybody is able to comprehend them. How is it that Wen-kung, who was a paragon of wisdom, was unable to investigate the principles of philosophy?''

The Teacher said: ''Wen-kung's mental energy and vigor were great, so that he early adjusted himself to the principles of philosophy. (42) He desired to continue the things of the past and initiate things for the future, and for that reason devoted himself temporarily to investigation and writing If he had at the beginning earnestly renovated himself, he would not have had time for this, and after he had reached the state of abundant virtue he certainly would have been grieved because of inability to comprehend the doctrine. He would then have done as Confucius, who returned to his home and revised the Six Classics by correcting and expunging the text where there was too much, thereby making it terse and disclosing the meaning for later scholars What is more, he spent no great amount of time in carrying on investigation. Wenkung, on the contrary, wrote many books in his early years, and later repented because he had written them the reverse from what they should have been.''

Ssu Te said: ''The repentance of later years would seem to indicate that he had discovered the mistakes in his writings It would further indicate that though he studied the books, he had reaped no practical advantage. Or it would show that his study had no relation to preserving the contents of the books and bigoted discussions. When he reached the point where he deplored the mistakes of his former work, he earnestly proceeded to renovate himself.''

The Teacher said, ''Yes. This is the condition he was unable to attain in earlier years. However, his strength was great, for when he once repented he faced about. Unfortunately, he died soon after that Many of his ordinary mistakes he never really rectified ''

The Nature of Good and Evil

I (K'an) was pulling the weeds out from among the flowers, and for that reason said, ''How difficult it is to cultivate the good in heaven and on earth, and how hard it is to get rid of the evil!''

The Teacher said, ''You should neither cultivate the good

nor expel the evil." A little later he said, "This view of good and evil has its source in the body (is personal), and thus is probably mistaken."

I was not able to comprehend. The Teacher said: "The purpose of heaven and earth in bringing forth is even as in the instance of flowers and grass. In what way does it distinguish between good and evil? If you, my disciple, take delight in seeing the flowers, then you will consider flowers good and grass bad. If you desire to use the grass you will, in turn, consider the grass good. This type of good and evil has its source in the likes and dislikes of your mind. Therefore I know that you are mistaken."

I said, "In that case there is neither good nor evil, is there?" The Teacher said: "The tranquility resulting from the dominance of natural law is a state in which no discrimination is made between good and evil; while the stirring of the passion nature is a state in which both good and evil are present. If there are no stirrings of the passion nature, there is neither good nor evil, and this is what is called the highest good."

I said, "Buddhism also fails to discriminate between good and evil. In what way is it different from what you say?"

He said: "Buddhism gives attention to the lack of good and evil and then pays no attention to anything else, and for that reason cannot enter actively into matters of government. (43) The lack of good and evil in the case of the sage implies that he does neither that which he desires nor that which he does not desire. Having no stirring of the passion nature, he naturally carries out the doctrine of the kings (Yao and Shun). Having become most highly skilled in this, it transpires that in his compliance with natural law there is adaptation for the purpose of rendering mutual assistance."

I said, "Since the grass is not bad, it should not be pulled out."

He said, "That accords with the view held by the Buddhists and Taoists. If the grass impedes progress, what hinders you from plucking it out?"

I said, "In that case you again have action in accordance with likes and dislikes."

He said, "It is not action in accordance with likes and dislikes; but this does not mean that there is a complete lack of likes and dislikes, for a man without these would be devoid of consciousness Saying that one does not act in accordance with likes and dislikes means simply that in both likes and dislikes one follows the lead of natural law and does not act while one is harboring a single selfish purpose. Thus one is as though he had neither likes nor dislikes."

I said, "How can weeding be construed as obedience to natural law and as showing a lack of private motives?"

He said, "If the grass hinders progress, natural law demands that it be uprooted. It should be uprooted, and that is all Should one be unable to pull it out immediately, the mind should not be embarrassed. If one harbors the least selfish purpose, the very structure of the mind will be involved and there will be much stirring of the passion nature"

I said, "In that case good and evil are not at all present in things."

He said, 'They are only in your mind. Obedience to natural law is to be identified with good, and the stirring of the passion nature is evil."

I said, "After all, then, things are devoid of both good and evil"

He said, "As the mind is, so also are the things; but the ordinary scholar of today fails to realize this. He neglects the mind, strives for things, and in so doing makes a mistake in his view of the investigation of things. To the end they all eagerly search for the principle of things in external matters They are able to obtain it by incidental deeds of righteousness only. During their entire lives they act but without really manifesting it, and learn without investigating it.''

I said, ''How does this apply in the case of loving beauty and despising evil odors?''

He said, ''These are all in accordance with natural law. Natural law is in harmony with this, for originally there were no selfish motives manifested in carrying out likes or dislikes.''

I said, ''How can love of beauty and dislike of evil odors be other than selfish purposes?''

He said, ''On the contrary, they are sincere, not selfish, purposes; and sincere purposes are in accordance with natural law. Though they are in accordance with natural law, they must not contain the least trace of selfish purposes. If a person is under the influence of anger or of joy, he will not attain their true use (will not be correct in conduct). He must be open-minded and without favoritism, for then he is manifesting the original nature of the mind. (44) Know this and you know the state of equilibrium.''

Po Sheng said, ''The teacher has said that if the grass impedes progress, natural law demands that it be uprooted. Why, then, does he say that it is a thought emanating from the body (a purely personal affair)?''

He said, ''You must learn, from introspection, what manner of mind you harbor at the time you wish to pull the weeds. Chou Mei-shu did not pull up the grass in front of his own window. What was his state of mind?''

The Aim of Study Should Be Definite

The Teacher said to his disciples: ''When one devotes himself to study he needs a clue, for then he will have a definite thing on which to work. If interruptions must come, he should be as a boat with a rudder. The mere mentioning should cause him to rouse up. Otherwise, though he devotes himself to study, he will merely be able to do incidental deeds of righteousness. He will act without manifesting natural law, and practice it without investigating it. This is not the great root nor the universal path." Again he said: "When one comprehends it, it will be recognized no matter in what way it is mentioned. If one understands it in one aspect but fails in another, he has not really comprehended it."

Some one made inquiry saying, "Because of his parents, a student cannot avoid the embarrassment of writing the Chüjen's composition."[4]

The Teacher replied, "You say that for the sake of his parents the student becomes embarrassed in his study by the writing of the Chüjen's composition. Would this, then, imply that he who cultivates the field for the sake of his parents is thereby embarrassed in his study?"

Hsien Cheng said, "I fear lest the purpose be interrupted, but perhaps the purpose of the student is not really earnest."

Passion Causes Distraction

Ch'ung-i made inquiry saying, "What is your estimate of the following: One's purpose is ordinarily much distracted by care; when one is occupied it certainly is distracted by care; and when one is at leisure it is also distracted?"

The Teacher said: "The motions of heaven and earth are by nature ceaseless. Moreover, there is a Lord of all, and for that reason they are neither early nor late, fast nor slow. Though there be a thousand changes and ten thousand transmutations, all are determined by the Lord of all. Man partakes of this motion and lives, if the Lord determines the time. Just as heaven in its ceaseless motion, he, too, will not rest. Though his pledges change ten thousand times, he is continually dignified and at ease.[5] (45)

---

[4] This refers to the composition set for the examination leading to the second degree.

[5] His pledges as host and guest.

This is the condition described by the saying, 'The heavenly prince is exalted (majestic); all the members carry out his will.' If there is no Lord, the passion nature will be hurriedly released, and then how can there be anything but distraction?"

Love of Fame is a Great Defect of Students

The Teacher said: "The great defect of students is to be found in love of fame."

I said: "A few years ago I said to myself that this defect had become negligible. Since I have recently made a thorough examination, I have learned that the contrary prevails. It is due to the fact that I am energetic in external things for the sake of men. I need only hear praise to be delighted, and words of deprecation to be heavy at heart. These are manifestations of the defect."

The Teacher said: "They surely are, for devotion to fame and devotion to truth are contrary to one another. When devotion to truth is increased a little, devotion to fame is decreased a little. In case one is completely devoted to the truth, devotion to fame will be entirely absent. When the mind is devoted to truth — just as when one is hungry one seeks food, or when one is thirsty one seeks for a drink — how can one have time to love fame? 'The superior man dislikes the thought of his name not being mentioned after his death.'[6] The character *ch'en* (meaning "to mention") should be read in the fourth tone.[7] When he hears his reputation mentioned beyond the bounds of fact the superior man is ashamed; and if his name is not mentioned he may, if alive, still make amends, and if he is dead there is no help. Should a man at forty or fifty not have heard his name mentioned, it is because he has not heard the truth, and not because he has no reputation which

[6] Analects, Book XV, Ch. 19.

[7] The tone, of which there are four in parts of China, to some extent determines the meaning of the character.

may be heard. Confucius said, 'This is notoriety and not distinction.' [8] How can anyone be willing to place in others his hope for this?"

Repentance is a Remedy for Disease

I was often repentant. The Teacher said: "Repentance is a remedy for disease. However, it is well that it should cure the defect. In case repentance persists, you have a condition in which disease arises because of the remedy."

The Sage May Be Compared to the Finest Gold

Te Chang said: "I have heard the Teacher compare the sage to the finest gold, the sage's rank to the weight of the finest gold, and the task of the scholar to the refining of the gold. I consider such a comparison very profound. It was only when you said that Yao and Shun stood for two hundred thousand ounces of gold and Confucius for only one hundred eighty thousand that I was in doubt as to the propriety of the remark"

The Teacher said· "This is a thought that is superficial and personal. Because of that you contend about the weight of the sage (Confucius). Were it not private and superficial, you would not consider two hundred thousand ounces too much for Yao and Shun, nor one hundred eighty thousand too little for Confucius (46) The two hundred thousand of Yao and Shun belong to Confucius, and the one hundred eighty thousand of Confucius belong to Yao and Shun. There is *ab initio* no distinction between them It is for this reason that they are designated sages One speaks in this connection of the discrimination and undividedness, and not of the quantity That they are called sages means only that there is agreement in the matter of complete devotion to natural law How can there be exact agreement in the matter of strength and faculties? Later scholars have instituted comparisons of weight only,

---

[8] Analects, Book XII, Ch 20, ¶ 4.

and for that reason have drifted into discussions regarding merit and gain. If everyone could expel the idea of comparison by weight, and in proportion to his strength and mental energy use his efforts in devoting his mind wholly to natural law, all might themselves reach the rank of sage — yes, completely reach it. Those with great capability could become great sages, and those with small ability small sages. That one does not avail one's self of desire for external things and is thoroughly satisfied in himself, is a matter which requires a knowledge of the good and a sincere (guileless) personality. Later scholars did not understand the learning of the sage, nor know that in making use of the intuitive knowledge and innate ability of their own minds they could learn how to appreciate and fulfil them. On the contrary, they sought to know that which they could not know, and to do that which they could not do. They hoped only for exalted position, and desired greatness. They did not know that they had the evil mind of Chê and Chou, and attempted to act as Yao and Shun. How could they succeed? They were unwearied year after year, until they died in old age; and yet who knows that they accomplished anything? How lamentable this is!"

The Mind is Both Tranquil and Active

I made inquiry saying: "Former scholars considered the tranquility of the mind as its natural condition, and its activity as its functioning. What do you think of this?"

The Teacher said: "The tranquility and activity of the mind should not be considered as the natural condition of the mind and as its functioning. Whether active or at rest, if one speaks of the natural condition of the mind, its functioning is included; and if one speaks of its functioning, the natural condition is included therein. The import of this is that structure and natural condition have a common source. It creates no special difficulty to say that the natural condition of the mind is seen when it is at rest, and its use when it is in action.''

I made inquiry saying, ''Why is it impossible to change the wise of the highest class and the stupid of the lowest?''[9]

The Teacher said, ''It is not that they cannot be changed, but that they are unwilling to change.'' (47)

I made inquiry saying, ''The disciples of Tzu-hsia made inquiry regarding the chapter which discusses the principles of mutual intercourse.''[10]

The Teacher said, ''Tzu-hsia discussed the principles of mutual intercourse as pertaining to children, while Tzu-chang referred to adults. If you apply the ideas of both carefully, you will find that each is correct.''

The Truly Educated Man Expels Passion and Cherishes Natural Law

Tzu Jen made inquiry saying: ''The Master said, 'Is it not pleasant to learn with a constant perseverance and application?'[11] A former scholar held that education implied imitating the things those before us understood.[12] How do you interpret this?''

The Teacher said: ''Education means learning to expel passion and harbor natural law. If one occupies himself

---

[9] *Vide* Analects, Book XVII, Ch. 3.

[10] ''The disciples of Tsze-hsia asked Tsze-chang about the principles that should characterize mutual intercourse. Tsze-chang asked, 'What does Tsze-hsia say on the subject?' They replied, 'Tsze-hsia says:—''Associate with those who can advantage you. Put away from you those who cannot do so.''' Tsze-chang observed, 'This is different from what I have learned. The superior man honors the talented and virtuous, and bears with all. He praises the good, and pities the incompetent. Am I possessed of great talents and virtue? —who is there among men whom I will not bear with? Am I devoid of talents and virtue?—men will put me away from them. What have we to do with the putting away of others?' ''—Confucian Analects, Book XIX, Ch. 3.

[11] *Ibid.*, Book I, Ch. 1, ¶ 1.

[12] Refers to the philosopher Chu.

with expelling passion and cherishing natural law, he will rectify all that which those before him understood, and will test all admonitions of the ancients. He will in all his efforts of inquiry and criticism, deep meditation and comprehension, preservation and examination, subduing and governing himself, not go beyond a desire to get rid of passion and cherish natural law. If it should be said that imitation of the actions of those who have gone before refers only to the matter of learning the state of equilibrium, this, too, would appear to be seeking for culture in external things. He who learns with constant application how to sit as the image of an ancestor, applies himself not only to practicing how to sit, but at the same time to cultivating the correct attitude of mind; or he who stands as though he were respectful, applies himself not merely to standing, but while standing to practicing this attitude of mind.[13] Pleasure here implies the pleasure arising out of righteous principles — the pleasure of the mind. The human mind naturally finds pleasure in the principles of righteousness, just as the eyes take pleasure in color and the ears in sound. He alone who is obscured and embarrassed by passion does not at first take pleasure in these principles. If the individual daily expels passion, he will daily be more imbued with the principles of righteousness. How can he then do otherwise than take pleasure in them?"

The Philosopher Tseng's Study of Himself Did Not Proceed Far Enough

Kuo Ying made inquiry saying: "Although the philosopher Tseng was earnest in daily examining himself in three respects, he had at that time perhaps not heard of the task of connecting them all into an all-pervading unity."[14]

---

[13] In ancient times at the time of sacrifice to deceased parents, the youngest son sat at the table dressed in the clothes of the deceased. Hence the expression, "to sit as the corpse."

[14] "The philosopher Tseng said, 'I daily examine myself on three

The Teacher said: "Connecting them all into an all-pervading unity implies that the Master saw that the philosopher Tseng had not mastered the essentials of application Therefore he told him. If the scholar really is able to be loyal and humane, does not this imply unification? It may be compared to the roots of a tree, which are connected with its branches and leaves If the roots have not been cultivated, how can there be branches and leaves? The structure of the tree and its function have a common source If the structure has not been established, from whence shall its function proceed? This means that the philosopher Tseng in the matter of his own service had already made most careful investigation and had used effort in rendering it, but did not understand the character of his native disposition. Perhaps he had not fully realized this " (48)

Interesting Facts Regarding Some of the Disciples of Confucius

Huang Ch'eng-fu made inquiry regarding the chapter which begins: "Which do you consider superior, yourself or Hui?" [15] The Teacher said: "Tzu-kung learned much and remembered. He applied himself to carrying out that which he heard and saw Yen-tzu applied himself to the mind. Therefore the sage (Confucius) made inquiry in order to inform him. The reply of Tzu-kung referred only to knowledge and observation. For this reason the sage sighed and did not agree (that he was equal to Hui)."

points: — whether, in transacting business for others, I may have been not faithful; — whether, in intercourse with friends, I may have been not sincere; — whether I may have not mastered and practiced the instructions of my teacher.' " — Analects, Book I, Ch. 4

[15] "The Master said to Tsze-kung, 'Which do you consider superior, yourself or Hui?' Tsze-kung replied, 'How dare I compare myself with Hui? Hui hears one point and knows all about a subject; I hear one point and know a second.' The Master said, 'You are not equal to him. I grant you, you are not equal to him.' " — Analects, Book V, Ch 8.

(The Teacher said): "Yen-tzu did not transfer his anger nor repeat his faults. This implies that he had the initial capacity of the equilibrium in which there is no stirring of passion."

Growth in Virtue Depends Upon Developing the Mind

(The Teacher said): "As he who grows a tree should not neglect to cultivate the roots, so he who desires to grow in virtue should develop his mind. If the tree is to grow, the branches must be reduced when they first appear in great number. If virtue is to flourish, love of external things must be expelled when the student first begins to learn. If he dotes on poetry and style, his mental energy will gradually be expended on poetry and style. The same holds true of all love of external things." He spoke again saying, "That I discuss learning in this way carries with it the task of begetting the equilibrium in a mind that does not have it. This it will be necessary for you to believe, Sirs. You will need to fix your purpose — the purpose of the scholar to consider doing good. The seed of the tree should neither be helped nor forgotten, but banked up. Then it will naturally grow larger, and its growth will daily be more complete and its leaves more luxuriant. When the tree first begins to grow, it shoots forth many branches which must be cut off, in order that the roots and trunk may grow large. Thus it is when one begins to learn. Therefore in fixing the determination it is important to devote one's self to that one thing."

The Different Attitudes of Wang's Disciples

Ying spoke about the disciples of the Teacher. "One," he said, "applies himself to cherishing natural law; another devotes himself to knowledge."

The Teacher replied: "The one who devotes himself completely to cherishing natural law daily realizes his insufficiency, while he who devotes himself to knowledge daily holds himself to have a superabundance. He who daily deems himself insufficient daily has a superabundance, while he who deems himself to have a superabundance is daily suffering from insufficiency." (49)

Cherishing a Reverent Mind and Investigating Principles Are One and the Same

Liang Jih-fu made inquiry saying: "Cherishing a reverent mind and thoroughly investigating the principles of things are really two distinct things. How does it come that the Teacher identifies them?"

The Teacher replied: "In heaven and on earth there is but one thing. How can there be two? If you say that there are innumerable differences, three hundred rules of ceremony, and three thousand rules of demeanor, how can there be two only? You, Sir, tell me what cherishing a reverent mind and thoroughly investigating the principles of things mean."

Liang said, "Cherishing a reverent mind implies devoting one's self to harboring and nourishing; thoroughly investigating the principles means a thorough investigation of the principles of events and things."

The Teacher said, "Harboring and nourishing what?"

Liang said, "Harboring and nourishing the heaven-given principles of the mind."

The Teacher said, "In that case it also implies a thorough investigation of the principles. Moreover, tell me what is meant by a thorough investigation of events and things."

Liang said, "It would imply that in caring for one's parents one must thoroughly investigate the principles of filial piety, or in serving one's prince one must thoroughly investigate the principles of loyalty."

The Teacher said, "Are the principles of loyalty and filial piety to be investigated on the bodies of the prince and parents or in the mind of the individual himself? If they are to be investigated in the mind, that would imply a thorough investigation of the principles of the mind. Moreover, tell me, what does 'cherishing a reverent mind' mean?''

Liang said, "It means complete devotion to one thing."

The Teacher said, "What do you mean by complete devotion to one thing?"

Liang said, "When one studies he should devote himself entirely to study; when one takes charge of any affair he should devote his entire mind to that one thing."

The Teacher said: "In that case, one should give his entire mind to drinking when one drinks wine, or to lust when one gives one's self over to lust; but that is striving for things. How can anyone in that way carry out to completion the cherishing of a reverent mind?"

Jih-fu asked for further information.

The Teacher said, "The 'one thing' must refer to heaven-given principles. To devote one's self to one thing implies giving the entire mind to heaven-given principles. Whenever intelligence is able to prevent its being obscured by passion, and satisfies and improves itself completely, it is perfectly true to its original nature and is in harmony with the virtue of heaven and earth. The sage alone is able to prevent the obscuration of his mind. Therefore the investigation of things is necessary for the purpose of developing the intuitive faculty."

Wang Explains What is Meant by Rectifying the Mind

Shou Heng made inquiry saying, "The principal task of the Great Learning is that of making the purpose sincere. Making the purpose sincere implies the investigation of things (philosophy). When the person has been cultivated, the family regulated, the state governed and the kingdom made tranquil, sincerity of purpose is present in the highest degree.[16] In addition to this there is the task of rectifying the mind. If one is under the influence of

---

[16] Great Learning, Introduction, ¶ 5.

passion or of joy, his conduct is not correct. What have you to say regarding this?"

The Teacher said: "This must be acquired by the individual himself through careful deliberation. (50) If one knows this, he understands the equilibrium in which there is no stirring of feelings."

Shou Heng asked him for information two or three times.

The Teacher said, "There are grades in application to study. If, when one first studies, one does not zealously and truly use his will in expelling love of the good and hate of the evil, how will he be able to do the good and expel the evil? Zealous and true use of one's will is what is meant by a sincere purpose. Moreover, if one does not realize that the mind is in its original character devoid of all things, and continues to add private purpose to one's effort in expelling love of the good and hate of the evil, there is just that particle of selfish purpose too much, and consequently the mind does not present a fair and open field. What the Shu-ching describes as a state in which the individual does not carry out his likes and dislikes is really the original nature of the mind.[17] Therefore, if one is under the influence of passion or of joy, he has not acquired a rectified mind. Rectifying the mind involves the task of making the purpose sincere. In this, one must properly appreciate the real nature of one's mind and maintain it with power and equity, for this is the equilibrium."

Apprehensiveness and Watchfulness Both Imply Thought

Cheng-chih made inquiry saying, "Apprehensiveness is present as the result of one's ignorance; watchfulness over one's self as the result of what one is alone aware of. What do you think of this?"

The Teacher said: "The two are really one task. When

---

[17] The Shu-ching, or Book of History, is one of the Classics. References in the footnotes usually read Shooking.

one is unoccupied one alone knows, and when one is occupied one also alone knows. If the individual does not know how to use his energy at the point where he alone has knowledge, but confines his work to that of which everybody knows, this is to act hypocritically and to disguise himself when he sees a superior man. The point at which one alone knows is the point where sincerity puts forth shoots and where there is no hypocrisy either about good or evil thoughts, so that if one thing is correct a hundred will be correct, and if one is wrong a hundred will be wrong. This is the dividing-place (boundary) between right and might, justice and gain, sincerity and hypocrisy, good and evil. If at this point the determination is firmly fixed, the foundation will be correct and the source clear; and that means that sincerity has been established. The ancients permitted the expending of much effort in making the person sincere, so that mental power and vital energy were applied with full force at this point. Surely this has the implication that this task belongs to that which is invisible and not subject to the categories of time and place. If you distinguish between this and being apprehensive with reference to that of which one has no knowledge, the task will not be clearly defined and there will be interruption. (51) Since one is apprehensive one really knows. If the person himself does not realize it, who is it that is apprehensive? Interpreted in this way, it means that one must break off the habit of determining things through abstraction.''

Cheng-chih said, ''Does this mean that the more good and evil thoughts are devoid of hypocrisy, the more he who alone knows will be without an occasion in which he does not think?''

The Teacher said, ''Apprehensiveness also implies thought. The thoughts which occasion apprehension never cease. He who fails in any way to cherish an apprehensive mind is not dim-sighted, but has already begun to think evil thoughts. He who wishes to be without thought from morning to evening and from youth to old age fails to realize this, unless, perchance, it be that he is sound asleep or dead, or that he is a worthless fellow.''

Sincerity Has an Important Place in the True Culture of the Mind

Chih Tao made inquiry saying, ''The philosopher Hsün said, 'In cultivating the heart there is nothing as good as sincerity.' Former scholars did not agree with this. What construction do you put on it?''

The Teacher said: ''His saying cannot be construed as false. Sincerity can be made to have reference to the task, for sincerity is original to the mind. Seeking to return to the original nature of the mind implies application in reflecting upon sincerity. The saying of Ming-tao, 'Cherish sincerity and reverence', also has this meaning.[18] The Great Learning also says, 'Wishing to rectify their minds they first made their thoughts sincere.'[19] Though the sayings of the philosopher Hsün have many mistakes, one should not go out of one's way to find weak points. In general, if in examining the sayings of anyone one has arbitrary predeterminations, there is excess of criticism. The saying, 'He who seeks to become rich will not be benevolent', was taken by Mencius from the sayings of Yang Hu. Here one can see the great justice of the mind of the sage and virtuous man.''

The Strong Man Controls His Passions and Devotes Himself to the True Self

Hsiao Hui made inquiry saying: ''One's own passion is hard to control. What remedy is there for this?''

The Teacher said, ''You must take your own passion and control it for yourself.'' He further said, ''The individual

---

[18] Ming-tao was the elder philosopher Ch'eng. The philosopher Ch'eng I-ch'uan was his brother.

[19] Great Learning, Ch. I. ¶ 4.

must have a mind which devotes itself to self, for then he can control himself. Being able to control himself, he can complete himself.''

Hsiao Hui said, ''I have a mind greatly devoted to myself, but I do not know why I am unable to control myself.''

The Teacher said, ''Tell me what sort of devotion to self your mind manifests.''

After a long time Hui said, ''With my whole mind I desire to be a good man. (52) Therefore I say that I have a mind greatly devoted to self. As I think of it, I realize that this devotion is to the bodily self alone and that it has not been devotion to the true self.''

The Teacher said: ''Has it, then, been the case that your true self has been separated from your bodily self? I fear lest perhaps you have even failed to devote yourself to the bodily self. Tell me, is not what you call the bodily self to be identified with your ears, eyes, nose, hands, and feet?''

Hui said, ''It is just as you say. The eyes desire beauty, the ears music, the mouth tasty morsels, and the four members idleness and pleasure. In consequence of this I am unable to control myself.''

The Teacher said: ''Lust causes one's eyes to become blind, licentious music causes his ears to become deaf, gluttony causes his taste to fail him, wild pursuit on the hunt causes him to become violent. All these things are harmful to your ears, eyes, mouth, nose, hands, and feet. How can this be construed as devotion to them? If you are truly devoted to them, you must reflect upon the manner in which the ears, eyes, mouth, and four members are to be used, and if the situation is not in accordance with propriety, you should not see, hear, speak, or act. Then first are you able fully to realize the true function of ears, eyes, mouth, nose, and the four members, and can be said to have true devotion to ears, eyes, mouth, nose and the four members. At present you constantly strive wildly for external things, and devote yourself to fame and gain. These are all things external to the body itself. When you devote yourself to your ears, eyes, mouth, nose, and four members, so that you do not see, hear, speak, or act that which is contrary to propriety, does this imply that your ears, eyes, mouth, nose, and four members have the ability in themselves not to see, or hear, or speak, or act? That ability must come from the mind. Seeing, hearing, speaking, and acting are to be identified with the mind. The sight of the mind manifests itself in the eyes; its hearing in the ears; its speech through the mouth; and its activity by means of the hands and feet. When your mind is absent there are no ears, eyes, mouth, or nose. The mind is not merely to be identified with flesh and blood. If it were, how does it come that though flesh and blood are still present the dead man cannot see, hear, speak, or act? (53) It is the mind that is able to see, hear, speak, and act. It is nature, it is heaven-given principles. If one has this nature, he is able to develop the principle of the growth of nature — benevolence (the highest virtue). If the growth of the mind manifests itself in sight, one is able to see; if in audition, one is able to hear; if in speech, one is able to speak; if in the four members, one is able to act. All are a development of natural law. In the capacity of ruler of the person it is called mind. The original character of the mind thus is in complete harmony with natural law and in complete accord with propriety. This is your true self, and this true self is the master of the body. If there is no true self, there is also no body. The true self is born from the body; and without it, it is dead. If you devote yourself truly to the bodily self, you must protect and maintain the original nature of the true self. You must be cautious with reference to that which you have not seen, and apprehensive of that which you have not heard. You need only fear lest perchance you have injured the true self and are in danger of acting counter to the rules of propriety. It is as though one were being cut with a knife or stuck with a needle until one cannot endure it. The knife and the needle must be taken out of the wound, before one can have a mind devoted to self and be able to control one's self.[20] Since you frankly admit that you have a thief as a son (admit your shame), why do you say that you have a mind devoted to self and yet cannot control yourself?''

One of the students had sore eyes, and was exceedingly melancholy about it. The Teacher said, ''You evaluate your eyes too high and your mind too low.''

Wang Warns Hsiao Hui Against Taoism and Buddhism

Hsiao Hui was very fond of Taoist and Buddhist doctrines.

The Teacher cautioned him saying: ''From youth I also was generously inclined toward the two religions. I said to myself, 'I have acquired their learning,' implying thereby that the doctrines of Confucius are not fully adequate. Later, while I lived in a distant part of the Empire among barbarous tribes for three years, I realized that though the learning of the sage is simple it is nevertheless profound. Sighing, I then regretted that I had wasted my energy for thirty years. In general, it may be said that the excellences of the learning of the two religions constitute but a small portion of those of the sage. What you have learned up to the present is but an effigy, but you believe in it and have become fond of it. It may be compared to an owl stealing a decayed rat.''

Hui made inquiry regarding the excellences of the two religions.

The Teacher said: ''When I speak to you about the simplicity and profundity of the learning of the sage, you do not care to make inquiry regarding the doctrine to a real-

---

[20] Action that is indecent and indecorous must be put aside.

ization of which I have come, but merely ask regarding that of which I have repented.''

Hui was ashamed and thanked. He then made inquiry regarding the learning of the sage.

The Teacher said: ''Now you have made inquiry as to how the affairs of men may be accomplished. I will explain this to you when you come seeking to acquire the mind of the sage.'' Hui asked him a third time.

The Teacher said, ''I have finished telling you one thing, but you have not been able to comprehend it.''

Liu Kuan-shih made inquiry as to the meaning of the state of equilibrium in which there is no stirring of the feelings.

The Teacher said: ''You need only be cautious regarding that which you do not see, apprehensive regarding that which you do not hear, and cultivate the mind until it is completely devoted to natural law. Then you will naturally understand.''

Kuan-shih asked that he might explain it somewhat more fully.

The Teacher said: ''When a dumb man eats a bitter melon, he is unable to tell you. If you wish to become aware of the bitterness you must eat of it yourself.''

At that time Yüeh-jen, who was near by, said, ''That is true knowledge; it can forthwith be carried out.'' On this occasion all the friends who were sitting there came to a realization of the truth.

What Death and Life Meant to Wang

Hsiao Hui made inquiry regarding death and life.

The Teacher said: ''If you understand day and night, you know death and life.''

He then made inquiry regarding day and night.

The Teacher said: ''If you understand the day, you also know the night.''

Hsiao Hui said, "Perhaps I do not fully understand the day."

The Teacher said, "You are able to understand the day. Stupid yet arising, foolish yet eating, acting yet not manifesting natural law, practicing yet not investigating principles, fuddled all day long, this is dreaming during the day. When one cultivates natural law at every breath, and harbors it at every glance of the eye; when the mind is intelligent and clear, and natural law is not interrupted for a moment, then one is able to understand the day. This is the virtue of Heaven. This implies that one perceives and understands the path of duty by day and by night. How can there, then, be death and life any more?"

The Fundamental Principles of Conduct Are Innate

Ma Tzu-hsin made inquiry saying: "Referring to regulating the path of duty, the old saying is that the fundamental principles of the conduct of the sages are native to the individual. How would it be if this view were adopted in the Empire in regulating ceremony, music, and punishments?" (55)

The Teacher said: "The path (doctrine) is nature and the decree of Heaven. Originally it is perfect, and should not be increased or decreased, nor need it be regulated. Why, then, should the sage's conduct be regulated, as though it were not a perfect thing? Since ceremony, music, and punishment are methods of governing the Empire, they surely can be designated as instruction. But this is not the original purpose of Tzu-ssu. If, as former scholars say, he in the following section passes from instruction to doctrine, why does he neglect the sage's instruction regarding ceremony, music, and punishment, and emphasize the state of being cautious and apprehensive? That would imply that the instruction of the sage had been devised in vain."

Tzu-hsin asked for an explanation. The Teacher said:

"Tzu-ssu's discussions of nature, the path of duty (truth), and instruction all come from the same source (the order of Heaven). When the decree of Heaven settles upon man it is called nature; when one acts in accordance with this nature it is called the path of duty. The regulating of the path, accompanied by learning, is called instruction. Obedience to nature is the outstanding characteristic of a sincere man, which is in full accord with the saying, 'When intelligence results from sincerity, we have a condition which is true to nature.' [21] The regulation of the path of conduct is characteristic of a sincere man and is in accordance with the saying, 'When sincerity results from intelligence, this is to be ascribed to instruction.' When the sage follows his nature in his actions, he is on the path of duty. Those below the sage in qualities of character are unable to obey the natural disposition. Because some go too far and others not far enough, it is necessary to regulate the path of conduct so that the good and wise cannot go too far and the stupid and degenerate cannot fail to reach it. They all must follow it, and thus the path of conduct becomes instruction. This word *chiao* (meaning "instruction") is in every way the same as the *chiao* of 'the highest instruction of the laws of Heaven'; viz., of wind, rain, frost, and dew. The words *hsiu tao* (meaning "to regulate the path of conduct") have the same meaning as *hsiu tao i jen* (meaning "the path of conduct is to be regulated by means of benevolence").[22] After the individual is able to regulate his path of conduct, he will be able to keep from trespassing. Because he has returned to this original nature, he is on the path of the sage, who obeys his nature. Exercising caution and apprehensiveness, as mentioned below, implies using one's energy in regulating the path of conduct.[23] The state of equilibrium and har-

---

[21] Doctrine of the Mean, Ch. 21, ¶ 1.

[22] *Ibid.*, Ch. 20, ¶ 4. 修道以仁

[23] Refers to the Doctrine of the Mean, Ch. 1.

mony means that the individual has returned to his original nature. It is in accordance with the saying of the Book of Changes, 'Use investigation of principles and completion of your nature, in order to attain to the decrees of Heaven.' The saying, 'Let the states of equilibrium and harmony exist in perfection, and a happy order will prevail throughout heaven and earth and all things will be nourished and flourish', implies completing one's nature in order to attain the decree of Heaven.''[24] (56)

The Tenth Chapter of the Fifteenth Book of the Analects Does Not Give Full Instructions on Methods of Government

Huang Ch'eng-fu made inquiry saying: ''Former scholars held that the instructions regarding the method of governing a country given by Confucius to the philosopher Yen are laws for all succeeding generations.[25] How do you view this?''

The Teacher said: ''The philosopher Yen was a perfect sage, so that in the matter of governing a country he was already prepared on the essential points. The Master knew that his learning was profound and thus did not need to speak about them, but confined himself to organization and ceremonial acts. These points can not be neglected, for thus alone can the good be fully realized. Nor would it do, because his own natural skill was sufficient, to become neglectful about being on his guard. It was necessary to do away with the songs of Cheng and send away specious talkers.[26] The philosopher Yen was a man who controlled himself, and who devoted himself to internal rightness. Confucius was afraid lest his external conduct would be regulated last or entirely forgotten, and for that reason he talked about things that would be of help to him. Had

---

[24] Analects, Book XV, Ch. 10, ¶ 5.

[25] *Ibid.*, ¶ 1.

[26] *Ibid.*, ¶ 6.

it been some other individual, he certainly would have told him that the administration of government depends upon getting the men; that men are gotten by means of character; that character is cultivated by treading in the path of duty; that the path of duty is to be regulated by means of benevolence.[27] He would have said that when the individual is able to carry out the duties of universal obligation and the nine standard rules up to the point where character is sincere, then he is really able to govern the country.[28] At this point laws for all succeeding generations emerge. But it was not thus in the case of the philosopher Yen. He needed only to follow the seasons of Hsia, ride in the state carriage of Yin, wear the ceremonial cap of Chou, and provide for the music, Shao, with its pantomimes, in order to rule the Empire. Later generations merely see that the philosopher Yen was the first of the disciples of Confucius and that he made inquiry regarding the ruling of the country, and in consequence consider this one of the most important things under heaven.''

Sincerity of Purpose is the Best Point of Departure for the Investigation of Things

Ts'ai Hsi-yüan made inquiry saying: ''In the later

[27] Doctrine of the Mean, Ch. 20, ¶ 4.

[28] ''The duties are those between sovereign and minister, between father and son, between husband and wife, between elder brother and younger, and those belonging to the intercourse of friends.'' — Doctrine of the Mean, Ch. 20, ¶ 8.

''All who have the government of the kingdom with its States and families have nine standard rules to follow; — viz. the cultivation of their own characters; the honouring of men of virtue and talents; affection towards their relatives; respect towards the great ministers; kind and considerate treatment of the whole body of officers; dealing with the mass of the people as children; encouraging the resort of all classes of artisans; indulgent treatment of men from a distance; and the kindly cherishing of the princes of the States.'' — Doctrine of the Mean, Ch. 20, ¶ 12.

edition of the Great Learning, according to Wen-kung (the philosopher Chu), the extension of knowledge through investigation of things precedes the task of making the purpose sincere. It seems as though this were in accordance with the order given in the first chapter. According to the sayings of the Teacher, which take the original as the authority, the task of making the purpose sincere precedes that of extending knowledge through investigation of things. I am not clear about this matter.''

The Teacher said: ''The fundamental task according to the Great Learning is to manifest illustrious virtue. The manifesting of illustrious virtue implies a sincere purpose. Making one's purpose sincere implies the investigation of things for the purpose of extending knowledge. If the individual uses the making sincere of the purpose as the controlling motive and thus proceeds to devote himself to the investigation of things, he has a point of departure. One cannot do good and expel evil without having a sincere purpose. (57) If one follows the revised edition and first investigates the underlying principles of things, the situation is so vast and incomprehensible that there is no point of departure. It is necessary first to add the feeling of self-respect and a due regard for all positions before the investigation of things can be related to one's person and mind. But even then there is no real foundation. If it is really necessary to add the word *ching* (meaning ''reverence''), why did Confucianists leave out so very important a word, so that the world had to wait more than a thousand years until some one added it?

''If a sincere purpose is used as controlling impulse, it is not necessary to add the feeling of self-respect and a due regard for all positions. Consequently, it is true that when one has selected sincerity of purpose as the starting-point of the exposition, one has begun at the very foundation of learning. If investigation does not start at this point, a small mistake will eventuate in a great error. Speaking in a general way, it may be said that according to the Doctrine of the Mean the task consists in making the person sincere, which, when it has reached its highest point, implies the highest degree of sincerity. The fundamental task of the Great Learning is that of making the purpose sincere, which, when it has reached its maximum, implies the highest virtue (good). The task, notwithstanding, is one. To say at this time that reverence needs to be added here and sincerity there, makes an exaggeration inevitable."

Self-righteousness and Love of Fame Are Great Defects

Meng Yüan had the defects of considering himself always in the right and of loving fame.

The Teacher reprimanded him a number of times. One day after he had warned him and reprimanded him, a friend asked the Teacher kindly to correct his recent actions.

Yüan said at one side, "This implies that you are trying to search out my former condition."

The Teacher said to Yüan, "Your old trouble has reappeared." Yüan blushed and proposed something which he wished to dispute. The teacher said, "Your old trouble has returned." Therefore he used a comparison saying, "This is the root of all your defects. It may be compared to growing a large tree within an area ten feet square. The moisture of rains and dew, the growing power of the soil (the water courses of the earth), are made to nourish only the roots of that tree. Even if grain should be planted on the four sides, it would be covered and shaded by the leaves of the tree on top and strangled by its roots below. How could it grow to fruition? It will be necessary to cut down the tree and not leave a particle of the roots, before it will be possible to grow good seeds. If not, you may cultivate the soil, remove the grass, and bank up the earth around the root, and yet you will be able to grow only this one tree."

BOOK II

RECORD OF DISCOURSES

Chiu-ch'uan Makes the Acquaintance of Wang and Becomes His Disciple

In the tenth year of the emperor Cheng Te, Chiu-ch'uan first saw the Teacher at Lungchiang.[1] The Teacher was at that time discussing the investigation of things with Kan-ch'üan, who was holding to the old sayings.[2] The Teacher said: "This means that you are seeking for principles in external things."

Kan-ch'üan said, "If you consider the principles underlying the investigation of things as external, this minimizes the function of the mind."

Chiu-ch'uan was much delighted to have the old sayings defended as correct. The Teacher also discussed the chapter in Mencius which treats of exhausting one's mental constitution.[3] When Chiu-ch'uan heard this he no longer doubted.

Later when at home he again made inquiry by letter about the investigation of things and the Teacher answered: "You need only use your energies in a true way, for then you will soon understand." Thereupon Chiu-ch'uan went into retirement in the mountains, and having made a record

---

[1] Chen Chiu-ch'uan was one of the disciples of Wang Yang-ming. Lungchiang is at Nanking and is now called Hsiakwan.

[2] Kan-ch'üan was also one of Wang's disciples.

[3] "He who has exhausted all his mental constitution knows his nature. Knowing his nature, he knows Heaven. To preserve one's mental constitution, and nourish one's nature, is the way to serve Heaven. When neither premature death nor long life causes a man any double-mindedness but he waits in the cultivation of his personal character for whatever issue, — this is the way in which he establishes his heaven-ordained being." — Mencius, Book VII, Pt. I, Ch. 1.

of the original copy of the Great Learning he studied it carefully. He then realized that the philosopher Chu was mistaken in his discussion of the investigation of things. But he also questioned the Teacher's position that a thing is identical with the presence of an idea or a purpose. He felt that he himself did not understand the meaning of the word "thing."

Chiu-ch'uan Relates His Experience as a Beginner

In the fourteenth year of Cheng Te, when he returned from the capital, he met the Teacher at Nanchang (in the province of Kiangsi). At the time, Wang was much pressed with military matters, so that he was able to confer with him only when he had a moment's leisure. The first question Wang asked was regarding the progress he had made in his studies in recent years. Chiu-ch'uan said that he had thoroughly investigated the fact that the manifesting of illustrious virtue really consisted in making one's purpose sincere.

"From the point of manifesting illustrious virtue throughout the Empire," he said, "I have pushed forward step by step into fundamental virtues, until I reached the point of making the purpose sincere. From this point I could proceed no further, for how could it be that preceding this there is the task of thoroughly investigating things for the purpose of extending knowledge? Later I pushed my investigation further and realized that it was first necessary to become conscious of the distinction between a sincere and a hypocritical purpose. In confirmation of this I used the case of the philosopher Yen, who, when he had done wrong, not only knew it but also used this knowledge in not repeating the act.[4] (2) When I understood this beyond all doubt, there remained the matter of thoroughly investigating things. Again I

---

[4] Yen was one of the disciples of Confucius. Also is written Yen-tzu.

thought: How is it that my cognitive powers did not know the good and evil of my purpose? Surely this was due to the fact that they had been obscured by a desire for things. I realized that it was necessary to get rid by investigation of this desire for things, if I would be like the philosopher Yen and distinguish the good and evil in my purpose. Moreover, I feared that my efforts were wrongly directed and would not fit in with a sincere purpose.

Since Body, Mind, Purpose, Knowledge, and Things Are a Unit, the Purpose Must Be Sincere

Thereupon I made inquiry of Hsi Yen and he said, 'The Teacher says that the investigation of things for the purpose of extending knowledge is the highest type of devotion to making one's purpose sincere.' I said, 'In what way is it devotion to making the purpose sincere?' Hsi Yen urged me to think once more and look carefully at the original nature of a sincere purpose."

To the end Chiu-ch'uan did not fully understand, and asked for an explanation.

The Teacher said, "Alas! At one saying you should fully understand. What Wei-chün said about this concerning the philosopher Yen is true — it is only necessary that one know that the person, mind, purpose, knowledge, and things are, in last analysis, one thing."

Chiu-ch'uan doubted and said, "Since things are external, how can they be a unit with body, mind, purpose, and knowledge?"

The Teacher said: "The ears, eyes, mouth, nose and four members constitute the body, yet without the mind how can the body see, hear, speak, or move? On the other hand, if the mind wishes to see, hear, speak, or move, it is unable to do so without the use of ears, eyes, mouth, nose, and the four members. From this it follows that if there is no mind there is no body, and if there is no body there is no mind. If one refers only to the place it occupies, it is called body; if one refers to the matter of control, it is called mind; if one refers to the activities of the mind, it is called purpose; if one refers to the intelligence of the purpose, it is called understanding; if one refers to the relations of the purpose, it is called things. Yet it is all one. The purpose is not suspended in empty space, but is placed in some thing. Therefore, if one wishes to make the purpose sincere, it is necessary to correct the purpose, expel passion, and revert to natural law with special reference to the matter on which the purpose is fixed. He whose unobscured natural ability is devoted to this will develop it. This is what is meant by making the purpose sincere.''

Investigating Things Means Investigating and Recognizing Natural Law in One's Own Person

Chiu-ch'uan at the time understood thoroughly and dispelled the doubt of many years. He again asked Kan-ch'üan whether he, too, believed in the use of the original text of the Great Learning.

Kan-ch'üan said, ''This means that the investigation of things is an act of creating doctrines, and is like the investigating which one does when examining a den. One must go into it in person. It is clear, then, that the investigation of things is merely a task of investigating and recognizing natural law in any place or condition, and that it is in practical conformity with the sayings of the Teacher.'' (3)

The Teacher said: ''Kan-ch'üan has expended effort on this matter and accordingly has changed his view. At the time when I told him that it was not necessary to change the character *ch'in* (meaning ''love''), he did not believe.[5] In the matter of investigating things he also is nearly correct, but it is not necessary to change the word *wu* (物, meaning ''thing'') to the word *li* (理, meaning ''principles''). Let it continue to be the character for 'thing.' ''

---

[5] For a discussion of *ch'in* the reader is referred to pages 48 ff. of ''Instructions for Practical Life.''

Later some one made inquiry of Chiu-ch'uan saying, "Why do you now no longer stand in doubt regarding the word *wu* (meaning "thing")?"

He said, "The Doctrine of the Mean says, 'Without sincerity there would be nothing.'[6] The philosopher Ch'eng said, 'If things come in a propitious way one should respond.' At another time he said, 'If all things are put into the class of external things, there will be no things within the personality.' These are words in constant use among the ancients." On that day the Teacher assented.

Mental Activity is Always Present

Chiu-ch'uan made inquiry saying, "In recent years because of a dislike for excessive study I find that whenever I try to sit perfectly tranquil and put aside troublesome thoughts, I not only am unable to do so, but am the more troubled. How is this to be explained?"

The Teacher said, "How can thinking cease? The thoughts should be correct."

Chiu-ch'uan said, "Should there not be times when thoughts are absent?"

The Teacher said, "Thoughts are present all the time."

Chiu-ch'uan said, "In that case, how can one speak of tranquility?"

The Teacher said: "When the individual is tranquil, he does not of necessity fail to evince activity, nor is he who is in a state of motion by virtue of that of necessity not in a state of tranquility. To be cautious and apprehensive also implies thinking. Why should you distinguish between motion and rest in this matter?"

Chiu-ch'uan said, "Why did the philosopher Chou say, 'In fixing the determination one should use the state of equilibrium and harmony, benevolence and righteousness, to regulate tranquility'?"

The Teacher said, "Being without desire, the mind is

---

[6] Doctrine of the Mean, Ch. 25, ¶ 2.

tranquil. Whether one is at rest or in motion, the word used for 'fixing the determination' is the same. One must make the original nature of the mind the master. Cautious thoughts are the point of activity at which the mind naturally never is at rest. It is in harmony with the saying, 'The ordinances of Heaven, how profound are they and unceasing! When once they stop, death ensues.' If the thoughts are not the product of the mind's original nature, they are selfish.''

Desire Should Not Go Out for External Things

Chiu-ch'uan made further inquiry saying, "If at the time when the individual is guarding his mind with diligence, there is such music and show of color present as he is accustomed to hear and see, there is danger that he will not be able to devote himself completely to the one thing."

The Teacher said, "Why should one wish not to hear or to see them? Except for a person devoid of all life or a man deaf and blind, it is not possible. However, though one hears and sees, the desire should not go out after the external thing."

Chiu-ch'uan said, "Formerly there was a man who sat in tranquility while his son was studying on the other side of the wall, and yet did not know whether his son was diligent or slothful. The philosopher Ch'eng said that this man watched himself exceedingly well. How do you interpret this?"

The Teacher said, "Perhaps the philosopher Ch'eng was ridiculing him." (4)

Mind Can Have No Internal and External

Chiu-ch'uan made further inquiry saying, "If I try while sitting quietly, I become fully aware that my mind is concentrated; but when I meet with the affairs of life this concentration is interrupted. I then make a new resolution, to carry on my investigation in the affairs of life. When, however, the affair under consideration has passed and I resume my effort, I still realize that experience has subjective and objective aspects, and that they cannot be blended into one.''

The Teacher said, ''You have not yet arrived at a full understanding of the principles underlying the investigation of things. How can the mind have an internal and an external? For instance, when Wei-chün (Ch'ien Te-hung) expounds, is it necessary that he have a mind within to manage attention to his words? When you hear his exposition and devote yourself respectfully to this, that is the mind of the time when one sits quietly. The task is a unified, connected one. Why must you bring up new thoughts? Man must be polished and refined by the affairs of life, that the energy expended at work may be of advantage. If one stops at love of tranquility, is distressed and confused when one meets the affairs of life, and to the end makes no progress, the energy expended while in the state of tranquility is misapplied. It is as though one were striving for concentration, while in reality the mind remained scattered and sunk in excess.''

Later Chiu-ch'uan again discussed the different opinions regarding the internal (subjective) and the external (objective) at Nanchang with Yü Chung and Kuo-shang. They all said that with reference to things there naturally is an internal and an external, but that the internal and external should be united and not separated. They used this point of view in asking the Teacher.

He said: ''The task is confined to the original nature, and this is *ab initio* devoid of internal and external. The distinction between the internal and external was made later for the sake of students, and in that way the original nature was lost. If you wish truly to explain the task, you should not distinguish between external and internal, for it is in reality a task of the original nature.'' That day they all realized the situation.

How Knowledge May Be Extended to the Utmost

In the fifteenth year of the emperor Cheng Te, Chiu-ch'uan went to Ch'ienchou and there again met the Teacher and made inquiry. "Though in my recent efforts," he said, "I have reached the point where I understand in a measure the point of departure, I have little confidence and joy."

The Teacher said, "You are searching for natural law in the mind, whereas it comes without search. This is truly an instance where natural law becomes a hindrance and an obstruction. There is a secret in this."

Chiu-ch'uan asked for an explanation. The Teacher said, "It is to extend knowledge to the utmost."

Chiu-ch'uan said, "Extend it in what way?"

The Teacher said, "The little intuitive knowledge of good you have is your own standard. If your thoughts are right it is aware of it, and if they are wrong it also knows. You must not blind it nor impose upon it, but must truly follow its lead. (5) Whatever is good should be cherished; whatever is evil should be discarded. What confidence and joy there is in this! This is the true secret of the investigation of things, and the real method of extending knowledge to the utmost. If you do not depend upon these true secrets, how will you carry on an investigation of things? I, too, have appreciated only in the past few years that this is the explanation. At first I doubted that a simple obedience to the intuitive faculty would be sufficient, but when I had very carefully examined it I found that it is deficient at no point whatsoever."

Extension of Knowledge to the Utmost is Progressive

Ch'ung-i said, "If the Teacher's idea regarding the extension of knowledge to the utmost is exhibited, it is exceedingly subtle and recondite. Once view it, and there is no possibility of further advance."

The Teacher said, "Why do I speak of its simplicity?

Apply yourself a further half-year, and see what the outcome is; and then apply yourself for another year and see. The longer you apply yourself, the more you will realize that the application makes advance. This is difficult to explain."

The Highest Type of Knowledge

The Teacher asked Chiu-ch'uan what progress he was making in his investigation of the extension of knowledge to the utmost.

Chiu-ch'uan said, "I realize myself that there is a difference in my application. Formerly when I experimented I was never able to get what seemed to me to be just the thing, but now I am more fortunate."

The Teacher said, "You now know that knowledge that comes from appreciation of nature itself is different from that which comes from hearing expositions. When I first expounded the meaning to you, I knew that you were careless and not at all interested. It was only when you had investigated to the extreme this its exceeding wonderfulness, that you saw that there daily was a difference, and that it is inexhaustible." He further said, "Those two characters, *chih chih* (致知 , meaning "to extend knowledge to the utmost") are truly a secret that has been transmitted from the sages of thousands of years ago.[7] When one has reached this point of view, he is prepared to wait for the rise of a sage a hundred years hence, and has no misgivings."

The Teacher said, "In general it may be said that friends should seldom admonish and warn one another, but should lead, support, exhort, and encourage one another." Later he warned Chiu-ch'uan saying, "When you discuss learning with your friends, you should be long-suffering, unassuming, and magnanimous."

Chiu-ch'uan was sick abed at Ch'ienchou. The Teacher

---

[7] To extend knowledge to the utmost means progressively to develop the intuitive faculty.

said, "It is hard to investigate disease and realize just what it is."

Chiu-ch'uan answered, "It is a very difficult task."

The Teacher said, "It is the task of always being cheerful." (6)

Learning is Increased by Earnest Application to the Affairs of Life

A subordinate official having for a long time heard the expositions of the Teacher regarding learning said, "This is very good, but unfortunately I am not able to devote myself to learning, because of its difficulty and the number of my duties connected with accounts, letters, and litigation."

When the Teacher heard this he said, "When did I teach you to drop these things and devote yourself only to the exposition of learning? Since you are engaged in trying law cases, you should devote yourself to learning in connection with these law cases, for thereby you will really be engaged in the investigation of things. For instance, when you judge an accused person, you should not become angry because his replies are disorderly, nor should you be glad because his arguments are well arranged; you should not despise those to whom he has entrusted his case, and impose your own will in administering sentence; you should not, because of his beseechings, bend your will and be influenced in favor of him; you should not, because of your own annoying and scattered affairs, judge him arbitrarily and carelessly; you should not, because of the praise, slander, and scheming of others, manage the case in accordance with the ideas of others. All these ideas are selfish. You need only know yourself. You should most carefully examine yourself and control yourself, lest your mind be prejudiced and misjudge the right or wrong of anyone. Then you will be investigating things for the purpose of extending your intuitive knowledge to the utmost. Though it is done while the duties of registering, writing, and litigation are pressing, it is real learning. If you leave your daily affairs in order to devote yourself to study, it will be in vain.''

Yü Chung and Kuo-shang were feasting with the Teacher, who said: ''We drink and eat only in order to nourish the body. The food which has been eaten must be digested; for if it collects in the stomach it causes dyspepsia. How can it under such circumstances become muscle? Later scholars read extensively and know much, but what they read and know remains undigested. They all have dyspepsia.''

Intuitive Knowledge of Good is Characteristic of All Men

The Teacher said: ''The sages, also, have first devoted themselves to study, and thus know the truth. The common people, also, have knowledge of it from birth.''

Some one asked, ''How can that be?''

He replied: ''Intuitive knowledge of good is characteristic of all men. (7) The sage, however, guards and protects it so that nothing obscures it. His contending and anxiety do not cease, and he is indefatigable and energetic in his efforts to guard his intuitive knowledge of the good. This also involves learning. However, his native ability is greater, so that it is said of him that he is born with knowledge of the five duties and practices them with ease. There is nobody who does not in the period from his infancy to his boyhood develop this intuition of good, but it is often obscured. Nevertheless, this original knowledge of good is naturally hard to obliterate. Study and self-control should follow the lead of intuitive knowledge. Only when the capacity for learning is great does the saying apply, 'Some know them from study and practice them from a desire of advantage or gain.' ''[8]

---

[8] Doctrine of the Mean, Ch. 20, ¶ 9.

Man's Original Nature is All-inclusive

Huang I-fang made inquiry regarding the Teacher's discussion of the investigation of things to extend knowledge to the utmost. "At whatever time," he said, "one engages in the investigation of things in order to extend one's knowledge to the utmost, one realizes that it refers merely to knowledge in some specific instance and not to knowledge as a whole. How, then, can the sage reach the condition in which it is said of him, 'All-embracing and vast he is like heaven; deep and active like a fountain he is like the abyss'?" [9]

The Teacher said, "The mind of man is heaven and it is the abyss, for there is nothing that does not belong to the original nature of the mind. There is *ab initio* this one heaven, but it is obscured by means of selfishness, and therefore its original character is lost. The principles of the mind are inexhaustible. The mind is *ab initio* an abyss, but it has been stopped up by selfishness, and thus its original nature has been lost. If you really contemplate extending the use of your intuitive knowledge of good to the utmost, you will need to clear away all the things that obscure and obstruct. Then nature will reassert itself and will be both heaven and the abyss."

He then pointed to heaven in order to make it clear and said, "It may be compared to your seeing heaven before your eyes, — luminous, refulgent heaven. Though you see it from four sides, it is only the luminous, refulgent heaven. But because the walls of many houses obstruct your vision you cannot see the whole heaven. If you tear down the walls there is but one heaven. You cannot say that the visible heaven partly displays heaven, while that outside of your range does not. In this way you can see that one section of intuitive knowledge of good is complete intuitive knowledge of good, and that the latter includes the former. There is but this one nature." (8)

---

[9] Op. cit., Ch. 31, ¶ 3.

Necessary Qualities of Character of the Sage

The Teacher said,[10] "Sages and good men serve their fellowmen and regulate their passions. When they render obedience to natural law, this is the path of duty; but their service and self-control should not be made the foundation of their reputation."

The Teacher said: "The purpose of the sage is to be a man who in his eager pursuit forgets his food.[11] Men of this type never cease in their pursuit of knowledge. The practice of the sage is to be a man who in the joy of its attainment forgets his sorrows. Men of this type are never distressed. Perhaps it is not necessary to say whether he has been successful or not in his pursuit."[12]

Thoughts Are Incipient Acts

I asked the Teacher regarding the union of knowledge and practice. He replied: "You need to understand the purport of my sayings. Since in study and inquiry present-day men distinguish between knowledge and practice, they do not check their debased thoughts which have not been expressed in action. When I say that knowledge and practice are one, I wish others to know that at the very point at which thoughts are manifested, there is incipient action. If the inception is evil, the evil thought should be subdued. It is necessary to get at the root, to go to the bottom, and not allow evil thoughts to lurk in the breast. This is the purport of my dicta."

---

10 From this point Huang Chih took up the record.

11 *Vide* Analects, Book VII, Ch. 18, ¶ 2.

12 The philosopher Chu in his exposition of this passage, which refers to Confucius, says that he was a man who forgot his food when he was not successful in his pursuit of knowledge, and on the other hand his sorrows when he was successful. Wang's idea is that the sage is constantly pursuing and constantly attaining and that he consequently keeps his mind free from thoughts of food and sorrow.

The Sage Does Not Need to Know the Details of Everything

The Teacher said: "The omniscience of the sage has reference to natural law only; his omnipotence has reference to natural law alone. The mind of the sage is clear and intelligent; therefore in all things he knows the place of natural law and carries it out fully in practice. It is not that after the mind in its original nature is enlightened, he needs first to acquire knowledge with reference to the things of earth, before he can act. The things of the earth — sacred utensils, measures, numbers, grasses, trees, birds, and animals without number — the sage understands by nature. Why should he be able to know them completely? That which need not be known, the sage need not seek to know. About that which he needs to know he is able to make inquiry. For instance, when the Master (Confucius) entered the grand temple he made inquiry about everything. Former scholars said that one should ask even though one knows, for this shows reverence and caution in the highest degree. (9) But that saying cannot be made universal. The sages did not need to know everything about ceremonies, music, and the sacred utensils; but they did understand natural law, and out of this arose many things, such as moderation, measures and numbers. To ask when one does not know also shows that principles and moderation are present."

Wang Again Discusses the Problem of Good and Evil

I made inquiry saying: "The Teacher frequently says that good and evil are one thing, and yet these two things are as opposed to one another as ice and burning coal. How can they be said to be one and the same thing?"

The Teacher said: "The highest excellence is from the beginning characteristic of the mind. When the individual has exceeded this, we have evil. This does not mean that we have virtue and evil standing in opposition to one another. Therefore good and evil are one thing."

Because I had heard the Teacher's exposition I understood what the philosopher Ch'eng meant by saying that virtue is surely nature, and that evil also must be viewed as nature.

The Teacher further said: "Good and evil are both an outgrowth of natural law. That which is called evil is originally not evil, but consists in exceeding or in failing to realize nature." His exposition is not to be doubted.

How to Become a Sage

The Teacher frequently said: "To be a sage, a man need only love and desire virtue as men love and desire beautiful colors; he need only despise and shun evil as one despises and avoids an evil odor." When first I heard this, I felt that it was an easy matter. Later, when I had investigated and tried this task, I realized that it really was difficult. For instance, as regards thought, though I understood how to love and desire virtue and to despise and shun evil, yet without knowing it I mixed the two; and as soon as I mixed them I did not love virtue as men love and desire beautiful colors nor hate and shun evil as one despises and shuns an evil odor. When one really loves and desires virtue, all one's thoughts are virtuous; and when one really hates evil, no thoughts are evil. Why should such a man not be a sage? From this it is clear that the learning of the sage implies full sincerity.

Wang Comments on the First Chapter of the Doctrine of the Mean

I inquired about the chapter in the Doctrine of the Mean which refers to regulating the path, "Does the saying, 'An accordance with the native disposition is called the path,' refer to the sages, while the saying, 'The regulation of this path is called instruction,' refers to the affairs of virtuous people?" [13] (10)

The Teacher said: "The ordinary man also lives in ac-

---

[13] Doctrine of the Mean, Ch. 1, ¶ 1.

cordance with nature; but it is carried out by the sage to a greater extent, and therefore the saying, 'An accordance with nature is called the path,' refers to the affairs of the sage. The sage also regulates the path; but the regulation of the path refers more especially to virtuous men, and therefore the saying, 'The regulation of the path is called instruction,' refers to the affairs of virtuous men."

He further said: "The entire Doctrine of the Mean gives an exposition of regulating the path of duty. Consequently, whenever it later describes the superior man, it calls attention to the fact that Yen Yen (Yen Hui) and Tzu-lu were able to regulate the path; and when it mentions the inferior or mean man, it says that the good man knows and the foolish does not. When it discusses the common people, it says that they are not able to regulate the path. For the rest, it says that Shun, Wen, Chou Kung, and Chung-ni (Confucius) — men belonging to the class the most sincere and holy — had the sage's ability to regulate the path."

The Buddhist Priest and the Confucian Scholar Compared

I made inquiry saying: "In the third watch the Confucian scholar banishes all care from his mind.[14] Empty in thought and resting, he is just like the Buddhist. Both the scholar and the Buddhist priest are free from care. What is the difference between them at that time?"

The Teacher said: "Activity and tranquility are a unit. When the mind is empty and at rest in the third watch, it harbors heaven-given principles; and it is this same mind which today follows its work and takes charge of affairs. The mind which today follows its work and takes charge of affairs, also complies with heaven-given principles, and is

---

[14] The Chinese have five night watches of two hours each, from 7 P.M. to 5 A.M. "In each watch, the watchman makes five rounds beating his wooden rattle to warn off thieves, in each case with as many strokes as denote the number of the watch." (Giles, Herbert A.: Chinese Dictionary, Shanghai, Kelly and Walsh, 1892.)

the same mind which is empty and at rest in the third watch. Therefore, whether it is active or tranquil you should make no distinction between the states in which it is, but know that they are a unity. The minute mistakes of the Buddhists you should, of course, not conceal.''

Over-preciseness is Indicative of Some Moral Defect

While the disciples were sitting in the presence of the Teacher, some were exceedingly precise in their manners. The Teacher said: "If a man is too precise, he surely has some defect."

I said, "Why should an excess of precision imply some defect?"

He said, "The individual has a great deal of mental and physical energy. If he pays attention only to his external appearance, he will lack greatly in the matter of guarding his mind."

One of the disciples was too forward. The Teacher said, "As I now make my exposition of learning, you do not keep yourself in check even as to appearance, and thus make the mind a thing distinct and separate from affairs."

(11)

Buddhists Do Not Have Complete Success in Expelling Desire

The Teacher frequently said that though the Buddhists do not emphasize the matter of watching mutual relationships and circumstances, still, as a matter of fact, they do pay attention to them. We scholars emphasize the matter of watching the circumstances, and yet in actual fact we are not influenced by them.

I asked for an explanation and the Teacher said: "The Buddhists are afraid of the responsibilities of father and son, and hence avoid such responsibility. They are afraid of the perplexities of prince and minister, and avoid becoming prince or minister. They are afraid of the responsibility of husband and wife, and hence avoid becoming husband and wife. This is due to the fact that they pay attention to the circumstances involved in being prince, minister, father, son, husband, and wife, and hence avoid such responsibilities. If we scholars have a father or a son, we recompense them with affection; if we have a prince or a minister, we use righteousness in dealing with them; if we have a husband or a wife we pay attention to differences. Have we then been influenced by the relationships of father, son, prince, minister, husband and wife?"

Huang Mien-shu made inquiry saying, "I do not know whether the mind need harbor good thoughts when it has no evil thoughts and at the same time is empty and vast."

The Teacher said, "Since evil thoughts have been expelled, there must be good thoughts present, and thereby the original nature of the mind has been reinstated. It may be compared to the obscuring of the sunlight by the clouds. When the clouds are gone the light has returned. In case evil thoughts have been expelled and you then attempt to cherish good thoughts, it is as though you lighted a lamp in the sunlight." [15]

The Will Must Be Fixed Definitely on the Truth

I made inquiry regarding the chapter which treats of fixing the will on the path of duty. [16]

The Teacher said: "The statement, 'Let the will be set on the path of duty,' is embodied with those that follow into the same chapter. The task thereby is continuous. For instance, in building this house, if the will is fixed on the path the individual must think of selecting a plot of land, collecting the materials, marking out, and completing the house. Grasping firmly every virtue, means that when the making of the plan is completed, it can be firmly grasped. The sentence, 'Let every virtue be accorded with,' implies that one should constantly live in the house

---

[15] At this point Huang Hsui-i (Huang Mien-shu) begins to write.
[16] Analects, Book VII, Ch. 6.

and not leave it. The sentence, 'Let relaxation and enjoyment be found in the polite arts,' means that one is decorating and beautifying the house with colors. The idea conveyed by the polite arts is in accordance with natural law. For instance, singing songs, reading books, playing on stringed instruments, practicing with archery, and the like, regulate the mind and give it skill. They make it familiar with the path of duty. If the will is not fixed on the path and one finds enjoyment in the arts, one is like an ill-behaved child that does not first build the house, but attends only to buying pictures to hang up for show without knowing where it is going to hang them.'' (12)

Kao Lacked Care in His Interpretation of Nature

I made inquiry saying, ''The philosopher Kao also said, 'Life is what is called nature.' [17] Why did Mencius disagree with him in this?''

The Teacher said: ''Surely it is nature, but the philosopher Kao understood only in part, and did not know the point of departure. Had he known this, to speak as he did would have been correct. Mencius has also said that 'the bodily organs with their functions belong to our heaven-conferred nature.' [18] This, too, was said with reference to the passion nature.''

The Teacher further said: ''Whenever men say what comes uppermost in their minds or act in accordance with their own ideas, they all say that it happened in accordance with the nature of their minds. This is what is meant by 'Life is to be understood as nature.' But under such circumstances mistakes will creep in. If one knows where to begin to speak, and acts in accordance with his intuitive knowledge of good, the affairs of life will be satisfactorily settled and arranged. Nevertheless, intuitive knowledge of good also depends in its application upon using one's

[17] Mencius, Book VI, Pt. I, Ch. 3, ¶ 1.
[18] *Ibid.*, Book VII, Pt. I, Ch. 38.

speech and one's body. When the body acts, does it acquire vital force from the external environment? Is there any other way of acting or of speaking (than that of using the intuitive knowledge)? Therefore I say that to discuss nature without discussing temperament is incomplete, and to discuss temperament without discussing nature lacks clearness. Temperament is to be identified with nature, and nature with temperament. But the point of departure must be understood.''

The Development of Nature Should Not Be Forced Nor Should It Be Hindered

The Teacher spoke again saying: ''Sirs, in your task (of internal development), you must not in the least hinder or force the development, for the highest type of wisdom is seldom met with. The student cannot leap over into the principles of the sage. Rising, falling, advancing, receding are the order of the task. The individual should not pose as being free from faults or blemishes on the strength of former efforts, while at the time he falls short of the mark. That would be a case of assisting the development, and thereby former efforts would be vitiated. This is not a small mistake. For example, when a traveler happens to stumble and fall and gets up and proceeds, he should not deceive others by acting as though he had not fallen. Sirs, you should cherish a mind which desires to leave the world without regret and which, when it does not see things coming its own way, is not melancholy. (13) You should patiently act in accordance with your intuitive knowledge of good and give no heed to ridicule, slander, prosperity, or adversity. 'In accordance with the stage of the task, whether it be advancing or receding,' you should say, 'I will not cease in the matter of controlling and regulating my intuitive knowledge to the utmost.' After a while you certainly will gain strength, and no external things will be able to influence you.''

He further said: "If the individual devotes himself earnestly to his task — let men slander or let them insult — in all things he will gain advantage, in all things he will gain the advantage of progress in virtue. On the other hand, if he does not devote himself to the task, he is only a worthless fellow and will ultimately be ruined."

Genuine Study Includes Introspection

One of his friends easily became annoyed and upbraided others. The Teacher admonished him saying, "When you study you must introspect. If you merely reprove others, you see only the faults of others and do not come to a realization of your own mistakes. If you bring your study to bear upon yourself, you will realize that you are in many respects imperfect. How will you find time to reprove others? Shun was able to change the pride and arrogance of Hsiang.[19] The ingenious method by which he contrived to do this was by not noticing the mistakes of Hsiang. If Shun had wished only to correct his wickedness, he would have seen only the mistakes of Hsiang; and since the latter was a proud, arrogant man he would have been unwilling to comply. Then how could he have influenced him?"

The friend was influenced and repented. The Teacher said: "You should from this day on never discuss the right and wrong of others. Whenever anybody needs to be reproved or criticised you should expel the selfish desire to be the big man."

Wang Discusses Divination

I made inquiry regarding the Book of Changes saying, "The philosopher Chu depended upon divination by means of the tortoise shell and the stalks of plants, while the philosopher Ch'eng proclaimed that heaven-given principles should be in control. How do you construe this?"

The Teacher said: "Divination by means of the tortoise

---

19 Hsiang was the half-brother of Shun.

shell or plants is in accordance with the principles bestowed by Heaven, for these principles include divination by those methods Of the principles of the earth who has any greater than these? But because later generations referred these types of divination only to fortune-telling, they have become a profession. They do not know that the questioning and answering of teacher and friend, extensive study, accurate inquiry about it, careful reflection on it, clear discrimination of it, earnest practice of it, and so forth, are all divination. He who practices divination by means of the tortoise shell and stalks of plants merely seeks to determine his suspicions and to understand as the gods do The Book of Changes inculcates asking of Heaven If anyone is in doubt, if his faith is insufficient, he may use the Book of Changes to ask Heaven. (14) It means that Heaven will not endure the false in anything that concerns the mind.'' [20]

The Importance of the Phrase, ''Having No Depraved Thoughts''

I made inquiry saying· ''How does it come that the phrase, 'having no depraved thoughts,' covers the meaning of three hundred pieces in the Book of Poetry?'' [21]

The Teacher said: ''Is it true that it covers only three hundred poems? This phrase includes and connects the Six Classics, as well as all the sayings of sages and virtuous men in the past and the present. What more is to be said? When this is said, provision has been made for a hundred other things ''

The Path of Duty Explained

I made inquiry regarding the mind which is devoted to the path of duty and the mind which is given over to selfishness and passion.

---

[20] From this point on the record was written by Huang Tseng-hsing, also called Huang Mien-chih.

[21] Analects, Book II, Ch. 2.

The Teacher said: "Living in accordance with nature is what is to be understood by the path of duty, and this is what is meant by a mind devoted to the path. But as soon as a little selfish purpose is superimposed, it becomes a mind which is given over to selfishness and passion. The mind which is devoted to the path of duty is not subject to the influence of the senses. Therefore it is said that when one acts in the least in accordance with a selfish mind, there forthwith are many insecure, unsteady places. For this reason it is said to be dangerous."

Wang Emphasizes a Clear Grasp of What is Read

One of his friends asked him why it was that he did not remember what he read and studied.

The Teacher said: "You need only understand. Why should you remember? In wishing to understand, you have already passed on to another purpose. You need to understand your own original nature. If you merely wish to remember you will not understand. If you wish to understand merely what you have read, you will not be able to understand your own original nature."

Self-preservation is of Less Value than the Preservation of One's Virtue

I made inquiry regarding the chapter which reads: "The determined man and the man of virtue will not seek to live at the expense of injuring their virtue. They will even sacrifice their lives to preserve their virtue complete." [22]

The Teacher said: "Because the people of the world all think too highly of their physical being and do not ask whether it behooves it to die or not, but determine that whatever may happen they will preserve it, therefore they cast aside heaven-given principles, and giving way to their feelings violate these principles. What is there that they are not capable of doing? Since they disregard these prin-

---

[22] *Ibid.*, Book XV, Ch. 8.

ciples there is no difference between them and animals.
Should they live on earth for one hundred thousand years,
they would be animals for that many years (15)
The student should have a clear understanding of this. Pi
Kan and Lung Feng, because they fully realized and under-
stood, became complete men.''

The Teacher said to Lu Yüan-ching: ''Yüan-ching,
when you were young, you wished to explain the Five
Classics, and your purpose was that of loving learning.
The sages in instructing people were afraid that others
would not simplify as they should   The rules which they
gave had all been simplified   As those of the present day
who find great pleasure in extending the range of the
mind's observation view it, it would appear that the sages
had made mistakes in their instruction.''

The Intuitive Faculty Does Not Sleep

I made inquiry with reference to understanding day and
night.

The Teacher said: ''Intuitive knowledge of good includes knowledge of day and night.''

I made further inquiry saying, ''When the individual is
in a deep sleep, is not the intuitive faculty also unconscious?''

The Teacher said: ''If it is unconscious, how does it
come that when the individual is called he answers?''

I said, ''If the intuitive faculty is always conscious, how
can it at times be asleep?''

The Teacher said: ''Rest at night has always been a
period of building up and creating   When night comes,
heaven and earth are confused and hard to distinguish,
form and color are obliterated, and man's eyes see nothing
and his ears hear nothing, and all the channels of the mind
are closed.   This is the time when the intuitive faculty is
renewed.   When day returns and multitudinous things are
disclosed, and man's eyes can see and his ears can hear and

all the channels of the mind are open, the wonderful use of intuition is revealed. From this you can see that man's mind is a unity with heaven and earth, for its (mind's) manifestations follow the movements of heaven and earth. The people of this generation do not know how to repose. If they do not sleep stupidly they forthwith think wildly and have bad dreams."

I said, "How can one use his efforts when asleep?"

The Teacher said, "If you know day, you know night. In the day one's intuitive knowledge is free, graceful, and devoid of obscuration in its response to heaven-given principles; while in the night it is collected and consolidated. Before one dreams there is some omen."

The Contemplation of the Taoists and Buddhists Obscures the Mind

The Teacher said: "In so far as the Taoists speak of the contemplative condition of the mind, is the sage able to add anything of real value to what they say? When the Buddhists say that they are free from desire, is the sage able to add anything to this? (16) The contemplation of which the Taoists speak comes from their attempt to preserve life, and the absence of desire of which the Buddhists speak comes from their attempt to escape the bitterness and pain of life and death. But if such ideas are inflicted on the original nature, the original meaning of contemplation and lack of desire has been abandoned and thereby nature has been obscured. The sage returns to the original condition of his intuitive knowledge, and thus the more refrains from superimposing his own ideas. The contemplation (emptiness) of intuitive knowledge is the great emptiness of heaven, and the absence of desire in intuition is the lack of form of heaven. Sun, moon, wind, thunder, mountains, rivers, men, and things — in fact, all things that have figure and form — are manifested, used, and themselves live and move within this formless, great emptiness

called heaven. How can they obstruct and hinder heaven?
The sage complies with the manifestations and use of his intuitive faculty. Heaven, earth, and all things are within the
manifestations, use, and activities of my intuitive faculty.
How can anything arise outside of my intuitive knowledge
and obstruct or hinder it?''

Nourishing the Mind Does Not Include Asceticism

Some one made inquiry saying, ''The Buddhists also devote themselves to preserving and nurturing the mind.
But if one desires to do this he cannot act in official capacity in the state. How do you interpret this?''

The Teacher said: ''When we scholars preserve and
nourish the mind, we do not leave affairs and things. We
need only comply with Heaven's mandates in order to carry
out the task. In contrast to this, the Buddhists desire to
cast aside and abnegate all things, and view the mind as
subject to metempsychosis and as gradually entering the
state of Nirvana. Since this has no relation to this earth,
they cannot govern and rule the Empire.''

Some one made inquiry regarding heterodoxy. The
Teacher said: ''He who is like a simple husband or wife
is said to be like them in virtue. He who differs from
them is said to be heterodox.''

Plants and Inanimate Objects Have Intuitive Knowledge

Chu Pen-ssu made inquiry saying, ''When the mind is
emptied of desire, the individual has intuitive knowledge of
good. Have, then, such things as plants and stones intuitive knowledge of good?''

The Teacher said: ''The intuitive knowledge of man is
the intuitive knowledge of plants and stones. If plants and
inanimate things lack the intuitive knowledge of man, they
cannot be plants and inanimate things. (17) And is this
true of plants and inanimate objects only? If heaven and
earth lack the intuitive knowledge of good which man has,

they cannot exist. But heaven, earth, and all things are *ab initio* one with man. The point at which this great unity (the absolute) manifests intelligence in its highest and best form is called the little intelligence and cleverness of man's mind. Wind, rain, dew, thunder, sun, moon, heavenly bodies, animals, plants, mountains, rivers, earth, and stones, are of one structure with man. It is for this reason that the grains, animals, and other things are able to nourish man, and the various medicines can heal diseases. Since they share the same vital principle they are similar.''

Wang Shows that Flowers Are Not External to the Mind

The Teacher was taking recreation at Nanchen.[23] One of his friends pointed to the flowers and trees on a cliff and said: ''You say that there is nothing under heaven external to the mind. What relation to my mind have these flowers and trees on the high mountains, which blossom and drop of themselves?''

The Teacher said: ''When you cease regarding these flowers, they become quiet with your mind.[24] When you see them, their colors at once become clear. From this you can know that these flowers are not external to your mind.''

He further said: ''Perception has no structure upon which it depends: it uses the color of all things as its structure. The ear has no structure upon which it depends: it uses the sounds of things as its structure. The nose has no structure: it uses the odors of things as its structure. The mouth has no structure: it uses the taste of things as its structure. The mind has no structure: it uses the right and wrong influences of heaven, earth and things as structure.''

---

[23] A village in the Chekiang Province.

[24] This would appear to imply that when the mind stops thinking about them they *ipso facto* are no more.

The Sage Manifests Ability in the Use of His Intuitive Faculty

The Teacher said: "He alone is possessed of the highest sagely qualities under heaven, who shows himself quick of apprehension, clear in discernment, far-reaching in intelligence, and all-embracing in knowledge.[25] How very mysterious this formerly seemed; but as I examine it today, I realize that all men originally have these characteristics. The ears are by nature quick in apprehension, the eyes clear in discernment, and the mind far-reaching in intelligence and all-embracing in knowledge. The sage is a man of unified ability. The point of his ability is just his intuitive faculty. The inability of the common people is due to a lack of extending knowledge to the utmost. How clear and simple this is!"

Strength and Wisdom Are Indicative of Sageness and Wisdom

Chu Pen-ssu made inquiry regarding the saying of Mencius: "As a comparison of wisdom, we may liken it to skill, and as a comparison of sageness we may liken it to strength."[26] "The philosopher Chu said that the three philosophers had more strength than they needed, but lacked skill.[27] What do you hold of this?"

The Teacher said: "The three disciples surely had both strength and skill. (18) Skill and strength are really not two separate things. Skill is found only where strength is applied, and strength without skill is useless and vain. The three philosophers may be compared to archers. One is able to shoot an arrow while walking, another is able to shoot while riding a horse, and the third is able to shoot and hit from afar. In case the archer is able to reach the mark, he is said to have strength; if he hits the mark, all

[25] Doctrine of the Mean, Ch. 31, ¶ 1.
[26] Mencius, Book V, Pt. II, Ch. 1, ¶ 7.
[27] Disciples of Confucius, named Po I, I Ying, and Liu Hsia-hui.

say that he has skill. Nevertheless, he who is able to do so while walking may be unable to do so while riding, and he who is able to do so while riding a horse may be unable to do so at a distance. Each has his advantages, so that the portion of their capacity and strength varies. Confucius had advantages over all three. However, the kindly, accommodating character of Confucius reached only to the highest kindliness of Liu Hsia-hui. His purity reached only to the highest purity of Po I; his inclination to take office reached only to the greatest inclination of I Ying to take office. Why then should anything be added as though there were any insufficiency? If one says that the three philosophers had more strength than they needed while they lacked skill, it implies that their strength went beyond that of Confucius. Skill and strength merely illustrate the high character of sageness and wisdom. If one knows the real nature of sageness and wisdom, one will naturally understand.''

Intuitive Knowledge May Be Compared to the Sun, and Desire to the Clouds

He (Chu) made inquiry saying, ''Intuitive knowledge should be compared to the sun and desire to clouds. Though the clouds may obscure the sun, they nevertheless have their origin in the condensation of the vapors of heaven. Does not desire also originate from a fusion of the thoughts of the mind?''

The Teacher said: ''The seven passions — joy, anger, sorrow, fear, love, hatred, and desire — all have their origin from combinations within the mind. But you should understand intuitive knowledge clearly. It may be compared to the light of the sun. One cannot point out its location. Even when a little chink has been penetrated by the brightness of the sun, the light of the sun is located there. Although the fog of the clouds may come from all four sides, color and form can be distinguished. This, also, implies that at that point the light of the sun has not been destroyed. One cannot, for the simple reason that the clouds may obscure the sun, order heaven to desist from forming clouds. If the seven passions follow their natural courses, they all are functions of the intuitive faculty. They cannot be distinguished as good and evil. However, nothing should be added to them. When something has been added to the seven passions, desire results, and this obscures intuitive knowledge. Still, at the time that something is superimposed, the intuitive faculty is conscious thereof; and since it knows, it should repress it, and return to its original state. If at this point one is able to investigate carefully, the task is easily and thoroughly understood." (19)

The Mind is by Nature Joyous

Chu made inquiry saying: "Joy is by nature characteristic of the mind, but I do not know whether this joy is still present when, because of some great and adequate reason, I weep from grief."

The Teacher said: "Certainly; for when the period of great weeping and grief is past, you are filled with joy. If you do not weep you will not rejoice. Though you weep, the point at which the mind is at rest should be considered as joy. The original nature of the mind has not been influenced."

Wang Judges a Litigation Between Father and Son

Among the country people a father and son engaged in litigation, bringing it before the Teacher. His underlings desired to stop them, but the Teacher heard their case. He had not ceased speaking when father and son embraced one another and left weeping. Ch'ai Ming-chih entered and made inquiry saying, "What did the Teacher say that they should be influenced to repent so quickly?"

The Teacher said: "I said that Shun was the most unfilial son of all times, and that Ku Sou was the most loving of all fathers."

This alarmed Ming-chih and he asked for an explanation. The Teacher said: "Shun always viewed himself as a most unfilial son, and for that reason was able to be filial. Ku Sou always considered himself as being very kind, and therefore could not be kind. He was able to remember only that Shun was a child whom he had raised. 'Why has he not appeared to love me?' he said. He did not know that his own mind had been influenced by his second wife. As he insisted that he himself was able to love, he was the more unable to do so. Shun only thought of how his father had loved him when he raised him. 'That he does not love me now is due to the fact that I am not fully filial,' he said. Since he daily thought that he was not completely filial, he became the more filial. Even at the time when Ku Sou was fully and finally pleased with his son, he (Ku Sou) did no more than revert to the love which is native to the mind. For that reason later generations have called Shun the most filial of all sons both of past and present, and Ku Sou a loving father."

The Virtuous Shun Overcame the Evil in His Half-brother

The Teacher said: "If one gradually makes progress in self-government, one will not drift into wickedness. The original commentary says that Hsiang had already entered upon a righteous course and hence could not drift seriously into doing evil. After Shun had been asked for and employed (by Yao), Hsiang still sought daily to kill Shun. But while Hsiang was so wicked, Shun controlled himself, and by his self-control caused his advances to have a sweet savor. He did not go and attempt to correct his brother's wickedness. (20) The tendency of the evil man is always that of glossing over and mitigating his own mistakes and covering his own evil. If anybody wishes to point out the right and wrong of his conduct, he should influence the evil nature of the other person. When Shun first learned that Hsiang wished to kill him, he was over-anxious to get the good will of Hsiang, and that was his mistake. When it was past he realized that the real task rested with himself and that he should not reprove his brother. For that reason a state of harmony was reached. This implies that Shun's patience, when he was in a state of excitement, brought the advantage to him where he had been unable to realize his purpose. The sayings of the ancients all refer to things which they themselves experienced, and for that reason seem personal and sincere. Transmitted to later generations, they conform to the passions of men of this day. Had they not themselves experienced these things, how could they have touched upon so much of the sorrow and bitterness of the mind?''

The Teacher said: ''The wisdom of Su Ch'in and Chang I had the essential characteristics of that of the sage. In later generations, a great many heroic, renowned and well-known men studied the methods they employed in their occupations and essay writing. The plans and methods of the learning of I and Ch'in estimate well and accurately the passions of men. For this reason their dicta are inexhaustible. I and Ch'in had also detected the wonderful function of the intuitive faculty, but they failed to make good use of it.''

Some one made inquiry regarding the state in which there are no stirrings of the feelings, and the state in which these have manifested themselves. The Teacher said: ''Because later scholars separated the two states in explaining them, I boldly said that they should not be separated, so that others might think and understand. If I should say that there is a state in which the feelings have been manifested and a state in which they have not been manifested, those who hear would follow their old ideas and fall into the exposition of later scholars. If they truly understand that there are not two separate states, it will do no harm to speak of the two states — that in which there is no stirring of feeling and that in which there has been. These ideas are present from the beginning.''

He made inquiry saying, ''Does this mean that he who has not experienced the stirring of feelings is not in a state of harmony, and he who has the same stirring of feelings is not in the state of equilibrium? For instance, in the case of the sound of a bell, if the bell has not been struck one cannot say that it has no sound. And having been struck one cannot say that it has a sound. After all, there is the matter of striking or not striking the bell. What do you say to this?''

The Teacher said: ''The state in which it is not struck is inherently one to startle and surprise the world, and the state in which it has been struck is the state of a quiet, silent heaven and earth.'' (21)

The Teacher's Words Had a Refining Influence

In refining and perfecting anyone, a word from the Teacher had a profound influence. One day when Wang Ju-chih returned from taking recreation the Teacher asked, ''What did you see?''

He answered, ''I saw that all the people on the entire street were sages.''

The Teacher said, ''If you saw that all on the street were sages, the people on the street all viewed you as a sage.''

Another day Tung Lo-shih returned from walking about. When he saw the Teacher he said, ''Today I saw a strange thing.''

The Teacher said, ''What was it?''

He answered, ''I saw that all the people on the entire street were sages.''

The Teacher said, ''This is a frequent occurrence. Why should it be considered strange?''

Since Ju-chih was not perfectly correct in his conduct, and Lo-shih was disturbed and aroused to a sense of his condition, the answer given to each was different though the questions were the same. He changed their words and proceeded.

Hung Yü, Huang Cheng-chih, Chang Shuh-ch'ien, and Ju Chung returned from the examination, in the fifth year of Cheng Te, and on the way expounded the teacher's doctrines. Some believed them; others did not.

The Teacher said: "You assume the bearing of a sage and expound learning to the people. When they see a sage coming they are all afraid and leave. How can you expound under such circumstances? You must be like a simple husband or wife; then you will be able to discuss learning with others."

Hung replied, "If one wishes to see the height and depth of anyone's character today, it is very easy."

The Teacher said, "How can it be seen?"

Hung answered, "The Teacher may be compared to one's having the T'ai Shan in front of him.[28] He who does not look up to him with respect must be blind."

The Teacher said, "The T'ai Shan is not as large as the level ground. How can the level ground be seen?" This one word of the Teacher's cut and laid open the perennial defect of striving for external things and desiring exalted position. All that were sitting in his presence were struck with fear and trembling.[29] (22)

I (Huang I-fang) made inquiry saying, "'Extensively studying all learning,' whatever thing you may be doing learn to cherish heaven-given principles.[30] Then there is the saying, 'If he has strength in excess of requirements, he should employ it in the fine arts.'[31] These two sayings do not seem to be in harmony one with the other."

The Teacher said: "The Book of Poetry, the Book of History, and the six liberal arts are all manifestations of

---

[28] The T'ai Shan is a sacred mountain.
[29] From this point Huang I-fang takes up the record.
[30] Analects, Book VI, Ch. 25.
[31] *Ibid.*, Book I, Ch. 6.

heaven-given principles. The character *wen* (meaning "literature") is included in this. In carefully studying the Books of Poetry and History and the six liberal arts, one is learning how to cherish heaven-given principles, for they do not manifest themselves peculiarly in affairs. Then first can one be said to be devoting one's self to learning. The matter of using excess strength in the fine arts also is included in extensively studying all learning."

Wang Comments on the Analects, Book II, Chapter 15

Some one made inquiry regarding the two sayings, "Learning without thought is labor lost," and "Thoughts without learning are perilous." [32]

The Teacher said, "This was also said in response to some definite situation. The real meaning is that thought implies learning. If in studying any doubt arises, one must give thought. Referring to 'thought without learning,' it is true that there are individuals who merely think. They desire to discover principles through thought, but do not really use their strength upon their own bodies and minds in order to learn how to cherish heaven-given principles. They make thought and learning two distinct things, and therefore have the defects of losing their labor and of being in a perilous state. The real meaning of the two sayings is that thought is to be given to that which is being learned. They do not have reference to two things."

Through Actual Test Wang Found that Some of the Philosopher Chu's Sayings Are Impracticable

The Teacher said: "The common people say that in investigating things one should follow Hui (the philosopher Chu), but where is there anyone who has been able to carry out his teachings in practice? I myself have tried to do so. In former years I discussed this with my friend Ch'ien saying, 'If to be a sage or a virtuous man one must investi-

---

[32] *Ibid.*, Book II, Ch. 15.

gate everything under heaven, how can at present anyone acquire such tremendous strength?' Pointing to some bamboos in front of the pavilion, I asked him to investigate them and see. Both day and night Ch'ien entered into an investigation of the principles of the bamboo. For three days he exhausted his mind and thought, until his mental energy was tired out and he took sick. At first I said that it was because his energy and strength were insufficient. Therefore I myself undertook to carry on the investigation. Day and night I was unable to understand the principles of the bamboo, until after seven days I also became ill because of having wearied and burdened my thoughts. In consequence we mutually sighed and said, "We cannot be either sages or virtuous men, for we lack the great strength required to carry on the investigation of things." When, while living among the savage tribes for three years, I clearly saw through this idea, I knew that there was really no one who could investigate the things under heaven. The task of investigating things can only be carried out in and with reference to one's body and mind (23) If it is actually true that all men can reach the state of sage, there naturally is responsibility connected with this The purpose therein contained I wish to explain so that you, Sirs, may understand "

A Boy of Sixteen Can Engage in the Investigation of Things

One of the desciples said, "Shao Tuan-feng argues that a boy under sixteen is unable to investigate things. He should be taught to sprinkle, sweep, answer, and reply."

The Teacher said: "Sprinkling, sweeping, and replying are also things. The intuitive knowledge of the boy reaches only to this point; therefore if he is taught to do these things, this small part of his intuitive knowledge is extended to the utmost. Again, if the boy knows enough to stand in awe of his teachers and elders, this also is making contact with his intuitive knowledge. If while at play he happens to see his teacher or elder, he will bow and be reverent. This shows that he is able to investigate things so as to extend to the utmost his knowledge of reverencing his teachers and elders. The boy naturally has the boy's ability to investigate things in order to extend his knowledge to the utmost."

He further said: "My instruction regarding philosophy implies that from the boy to the sage there is just this sort of application. Nevertheless, the sage is more familiar with it, so that he does not need to exert his strength in order thus to investigate. Though he be a vender of kitchen fuel, he may investigate things; and though they be princes and high officials or even the Son of Heaven (emperor) himself, all must do this."

Wang Discusses Knowledge and Practice

One of the disciples made inquiry saying, "In what way do knowledge and practice become a unity? The Doctrine of the Mean says 'extensive study,' and in addition speaks of 'earnest practice'.[33] This would clearly distinguish knowledge and practice as two distinct things."

The Teacher said: "Extensive learning implies that in all things one should learn how to cherish natural law, while earnest practice carries with it the idea of learning without ceasing."

He made further inquiry about the saying of the Book of Changes: "He studies that he may bring together (combine) all learning in his mind," and the further saying, "He is benevolent in order that he may practice it." "How is this to be interpreted?" he asked.

The Teacher said: "This, also, implies that in all things one should learn to harbor natural law. In that case the mind will the more never lose it. It is for this reason that the Book of Changes says, 'He studies in order that he may

---

33 Doctrine of the Mean, Ch. 20, ¶ 19.

combine all.' Moreover, if the individual continually cherishes this natural law, selfishness will the less be able to interrupt the task. (24) This is the point at which the mind does not rest, and therefore the book says, 'He is benevolent in order that he may practice it.' "

He made further inquiry saying, "There is the saying of Confucius, 'When a man's knowledge is sufficient to attain, but his virtue is not sufficient to enable him to hold, whatever he may have gained he will lose again.' [34] According to this, knowledge and practice are two."

The Teacher said: "The saying, 'to attain it,' implies that he already has practiced it continually. Because selfish desires intervene, his virtue does not enable him to hold it."

He made further inquiry saying, "There is the saying, 'The mind is itself heaven-given principles,' while the philosopher Ch'eng said, 'Principles are to be found in things.' How can it be said that the mind is these principles?"

The Teacher said· "In the saying of the philosopher Chu the word 'mind' should be added so that it would be, 'When the mind is engaged with things, that is principles.' In this way, when the individual's mind is engaged in serving his prince, he is loyal."

Accordingly the Teacher said to them· "Sirs, if you wish to know the original purport of my dicta, I will now explain what I mean by saying that the mind is heaven-given principles. It is only because people make a distinction between mind and principles that there are so many diseases (evils) For instance, that the five famous rulers (of the sixth century B.C.) drove out the barbarians and dignified the Chou dynasty was entirely due to selfishness, and thus was not in accordance with heaven-given principles. People say that they acted in accordance with principles, but that their minds were not unaffected by selfishness. They always found joy in desiring what they

[34] Analects, Book XV, Ch. 32, ¶ 1

themselves accomplished. People further say that their desire to make external things appear propitious had no relation at all to their minds. In this way they distinguish between mind and heaven-given principles. They drifted into the false condition of ruling by might and did not know themselves. Therefore, when I say that the mind is principles, I wish you to understand that mind and principles are one and the same thing. Then you will come to use your efforts on your minds and will not steal into righteousness with external things. This is the truth of ruling by law or right. This is the original purport of my dicta.''

He made further inquiry saying: ''There are a great many sayings of sages and good men. Why should they be combined into one dictum?''

The Teacher said, ''Not because I wish to combine them into one; for it has been said, 'The path is one and one only.' [35] Further it has been said, 'They are without any doubleness, and so they produce things in a manner that is unfathomable.' [36] Heaven and earth and sages are all one. How can there be any distinction between them?'' (25)

One Honors One's Virtuous Nature in Maintaining Constant Inquiry and Study

I made inquiry regarding the section, ''He honors his virtuous nature.'' [37]

The Teacher said: '' 'He maintains constant inquiry and study,' and therefore honors his virtuous nature. Hui (the philosopher Chu) spoke of the sage's pondering in order to admonish the people to honor their virtuous nature. Do I in instructing others add anything to the maintaining of constant inquiry and study and thus separate 'honoring' one's virtuous nature' and 'maintaining constant inquiry

---

[35] Mencius, Book III, Pt. I, Ch. 1, ¶ 3.

[36] Doctrine of the Mean, Ch. 26, ¶ 7.

[37] *Ibid.*, Ch. 27, ¶ 6.

and study' into two? That I now explain, practice, seek, and-discuss these many tasks, means nothing more than cherishing the mind so that it does not lose its virtuous nature Is there such a thing as merely honoring one's virtuous nature, and not engaging in inquiry and study? Is there such a thing as merely inquiring and studying with no relation to one's virtuous nature? In that case I do not know what those who are making use of explanation, practice, inquiry, and discussion are really learning."

I made inquiry regarding the two sentences, "He seeks to carry it out to its breadth and greatness, so as to omit none of the more exquisite and minute points which it embraces, and to raise it to its greatest height and brilliancy, so as to pursue the course of the mean." [38]

The Teacher said: "He overlooks none of its finest points and therefore carries it out to its breadth and greatness. He pursues the course of the mean and therefore raises it to its greatest brilliancy, for the original nature of the mind is extremely broad and great (inclusive). If the individual is not able to reach the state in which he omits none of its most excellent and minute points, his mind has been obscured and obstructed by selfish desires, the least of which he has not been able to overcome. If the individual overlooks none of the smallest and most involved points, selfish desire cannot obstruct his mind, and thus there naturally cannot be a great many points at which it is obstructed and obscured Why should he not carry it out to its greatest breadth and greatness?"

The Minutiæ of Thought Are the Minutiæ of Principles

I made further inquiry saying, "Are these excellent and minute points of thought and experience, or do they refer to the principles of things?"

The Teacher said "The excellency and minutiæ of

---

[38] Op cit

thought are the excellency and minutiæ of the principles of affairs.''

The Teacher said: ''Those who in this day discuss nature are numerous and have various points of view, but none realize what it is. Those who understand nature do not represent various points of view in their discussion.''

Wang Explains a Typical Practice of the Buddhists

One of Yang-ming's friends mentioned the practice of the Buddhist when he displays his fingers to explain his point of view, while saying, ''Have you all seen them?'' They say, ''Yes,'' and he then draws his fingers back into his sleeve again, saying, ''Do you all still see them?'' They say, ''We do not.'' The Buddhist says, ''You have not yet seen nature.'' ''I do not understand this,'' the friend said.

The Teacher said: ''The fingers at times may be visible and at other times not. (26) You see the mind continually in the mind and intelligence of others, but you lose yourself in matters that can be seen and heard and do not use your energies in that which cannot be seen and heard. Since the original nature of our intuitive faculty cannot be seen, cautiousness and apprehensiveness are conditions that extend intuitive knowledge to the utmost. When the student at all times sees what they do not see and hears what they do not hear, his efforts have a true point of departure. When after a time he becomes thoroughly familiar, he does not need to exert any strength nor wait until he may take his ease. His true nature does not rest. Can he allow the external seeing and hearing to embarrass him?''

Heaven, Earth, Spirits, Gods, and Man Are a Unity

I made inquiry saying: ''The mind of man, and things, have a common structure. It may be compared to my body, in which blood and the vital force flow together. Therefore it may be said that they have a common structure If they have a different structure from man, animals and plants are still more distinct. Why should they all be said to have a common structure?''

The Teacher said: ''You should judge this matter from subtleness of cause and effect, of stimulation and response. And does this refer only to animals and plants? Heaven and earth are one structure with me; spirits and gods are in one all-pervading unity with me.''

I asked that the Teacher kindly explain it further.

Whereupon he said: ''What do you consider the mind of heaven and earth to be?''

I answered, ''I have often heard that man is the mind of heaven and earth.''

The Teacher said: ''What has man that may be called mind?''

I answered, ''There is only his intelligence that can know how to fill heaven and earth In the midst of heaven and earth there is only this intelligence. It is only because of his form and body that man is separated into body and mind. My intelligence is the ruler of heaven and earth, of spirits and gods. If heaven is deprived of my intelligence, who will respect its eminence? If the earth lacks my intelligence, who will look into its depths? If spirits and gods lack my intelligence, who will distinguish between their happiness and their misfortunes? If heaven, earth, spirits, gods, and things separate themselves from my intelligence, then there will be neither heaven, nor earth, nor spirits, nor gods, nor things If my intelligence departs from these things, it also will exist no more. Thus they are combined in one structure or substance Why should they be separated?'' (27)

I made further inquiry saying, ''Heaven, earth, spirits, gods, and things have existed for thousands of years. Why should it be that when my intelligence is gone they all exist no longer?''

The Teacher said· ''Consider the dead man. His energy and intelligence have been separated. Where are his heaven, earth, and things?"

Pride is a Great Disease

The Teacher said: "The great disease of mankind is all expressed in the word *nao* (meaning "pride" or "haughtiness"). The proud son certainly is not filial, nor the haughty minister loyal, nor the proud father loving, nor the proud friend sincere. The reason why Hsiang and Tan Chu were both degenerate was their pride. Sirs, you should appreciate that the mind of man is *ab initio* natural law. It is discriminating, clear and without the least spot of selfishness. Selfishness should not be cherished in one's breast, for its presence engenders pride. The many good characteristics of the sages of most ancient times were due to a selfless mind. Being selfless they were naturally humble. Humility is the foundation of all virtue; pride is the chief of vices."

Tsou Ch'ien-chih often spoke to Te-hung (Ch'ien Te-hung) saying, "Shuh Kuo-shang took a sheet of paper and asked the Teacher to write the following chapter: 'Anybody who wishes to cultivate the *t'ung* or the *tsze*, which may be grasped with both hands, perhaps with one, knows by what means to nourish them. Is it to be supposed that their regard of their own persons is inferior to their regard for a *t'ung* or a *tsze?* Their want of reflection is extreme.' [39]

"The Teacher took the pen and wrote it for him up to and including, 'In the case of their own persons, men do not know by what means to nourish them.' He looked at him and laughing said, 'Kuo-shang, you have through study acquired the title of Chuang Yüan.[40] Can it really be that

---

[39] Mencius, Book VI, Pt. I, Ch. 13, ¶ 1.

[40] The title of the candidate who wins the first place at the Triennial Palace Examination which is the final test of the already successful graduates of the third degree. The holder is thus, popularly

you do not know by what means to nourish your person and still need to recite this in order to seek to warn yourself?' At that time all the friends that stood there were awed.''

Wang Advises Chiu-ch'uan to Devote His Energies on His Intuitive Faculty

Chiu-ch'uan made inquiry saying, ''I examine my thoughts to find whether they are connected with depraved and wrong things or are ready to grapple with the affairs of earth. When my thoughts are most intense and, being arranged in regular order, awaken interest, love of lust is difficult to expel I realize that if I attempt to expel it early, it is readily done; but if late, it is difficult. If I use effort in controlling myself, I realize its obstructing powers the more. Only when I gradually shift my thoughts to some other affair, does it give way and I forget. This method of making my thoughts magnanimous and pure also seems to do no harm.''

The Teacher said: ''Why do you need to pursue that course? You need only earnestly devote your energies upon your own intuitive faculty.'' (28)

Chiu-ch'uan said, ''I may truly say that at such times I am not aware of its presence.''

The Teacher said: ''If you devote yourself to the intuitive faculty, why should evil thoughts come? Your intuitive faculty is obscured because your task is interrupted. You should connect up present endeavor with your former task Why should you use the method you suggest?''

Chiu-ch'uan said: ''Lust is very difficult to exterminate. Though I know that it should be put aside, it does not leave me.''

The Teacher said: ''You need to be courageous. If you devote yourself to this for a long time, you will naturally

---

speaking, the best man of his year. (Giles, Herbert A.· Chinese Eng. Dictionary, Kelly & Walsh, Shanghai, 1892, p. 284.)

have moral courage. Therefore it is said, 'It is produced by the accumulation of righteous deeds.' [41] He who overcomes easily is a man of great virtue.''

Chiu-ch'uan made inquiry saying: ''When I study, the idea of a literary degree comes up. I do not know how this can be avoided. I have privately heard that abject poverty and prosperity are fated, and that men of superior wisdom will perhaps not condescend to this. The degenerate who is bound by a desire for fame and gain gladly undergoes futile painstaking work. If he seeks to drive out any desire for fame and gain, his parents restrain him. What do you think about this?''

The Teacher said: ''Many attribute this to their parents, but as a matter of fact they themselves lack purpose; for when the purpose is fixed, all things whatsoever are unified. How can study and the writing of essays embarrass such an individual? That he is embarrassed is owing to the fact that his mind is perplexed with getting or losing.'' Therefore the Teacher sighed and said, ''They do not understand this learning. They do not know how many men of ability have wasted their time at this point.''

The Intuitive Faculty is Discriminating in Its Application of Principles

Pen-ssu made inquiry saying, ''If the sage and things have a common structure, why does the Great Learning mention things of great importance and things of slight importance?'' [42]

The Teacher said: ''Referring to the path of duty, there naturally are things of great importance and things of minor importance. The body, for instance, is a unity. When one uses the hands or feet to defend and protect the head and eyes, does not this imply that one is inclined to consider his hands and feet of slight importance? Prin-

[41] Mencius, Book II, Pt. I, Ch. 2, ¶ 15.
[42] *Vide* Great Learning, Introduction, ¶ 7.

ciples manifest themselves in the same way. Though animals and plants are both objects of regard for man, he gives plants to feed and nourish animals, and is able to endure it. Men and animals are objects of affection, yet one butchers the animals in order to feed one's parents, to offer sacrifice, or to entertain guests, and the mind endures it. Nearest parents and traveling companions (passing acquaintances) are both objects of regard and affection. But suppose that there is only one dish to eat and one bowl of soup, and that if the individual gets this he will live, otherwise not. (29) It is not possible to carry out both ideas. Under such circumstances it is better to save one's nearest relative and not the passing stranger — a fact which the mind allows. All this is in harmony with the doctrine. When comparing one's own body with that of one's parents, one should not distinguish between what is of great or slight importance in either case, for benevolence toward the people and regard for things have sprung from this. At this point one should be patient — patient in everything. The things of great importance and slight importance mentioned in the Great Learning are natural principles within the realm of intuitive knowledge. To be unable to transgress them is called righteousness; to render obedience to them is called propriety; to know them is called wisdom; at all times and in all things to use them is called integrity and loyalty.''

The Result is of Less Importance than the Process

I made inquiry saying: ''I realize that I have recently had less evil thoughts and that I have given less attention to the exact way in which I must apply myself; but I do not know whether this is working in the right direction or not.''

The Teacher said: ''Go and apply yourself truly and earnestly. Then the matter of having these additional moments of giving thought will not interfere. After a while you will be on a secure basis. If, when you attain genuine application, you speak of results, how can this be deemed sufficient to rely upon?"

Inquiry on the Part of Others Stimulates the Sage to Greater Mental Activity

I made inquiry saying, "Confucius said, 'Hui is not a man who helps me.'[43] Does this imply that the sage really hoped that his disciple might help him?"

The Teacher said: "It is true. The truth is by nature inexhaustible. The more inquiry is made about its difficulties, the more its fineness and its minutiæ will be apparent. The words of the sage naturally are all-inclusive. But if anyone whose mind is obscured makes inquiry regarding some difficulty, the sage will be moved (animated) by the difficulty and will thus increase his mental energy. If the philosopher Yen heard one thing he understood ten, for his mind was clear. Why should he make inquiry regarding difficulties? Therefore the sage was quiet in mind and not animated. Since there was nothing to influence him, he said that he received no assistance."

The Teacher said: "In case the individual knows the secret of intuitive knowledge, no matter how many thoughts he has that are depraved, corrupting, and useless, they will all be dissipated when intuitive knowledge becomes aware of them. (30) Truly this is an efficacious pellet, which changes iron into gold."

The Beginning of Learning is to be Found in Extending Intuitive Knowledge

One of Wang's friends sitting quietly came to a realization, and forthwith ran to make inquiry of the Teacher, who answered him thus: "When formerly I lived at Ch'u, I saw that all my disciples were earnestly devoted to the interpretation of learning.[44] What they said and heard

---

[43] Analects, Book XI, Ch. 3.

[44] Ch'u is a city in Anhui.

was inconsistent one with the other, and they received no advantage. It was for that reason that I told them to sit quietly a while, so that they might get a glimpse of their condition and thereby gain ample results. After a while there were some who found delight in tranquility and had aversion to activity. They became dead and lifeless. Others of the disciples devoted themselves to profound explanations of wonderful experiences which moved men when they heard them. As a result, I have recently discussed only the matter of extending intuitive knowledge to the utmost. When your intuitive knowledge is clear, it is well for you to sit and examine your mind and come to a state of realization; and it is also well to be polished and refined in the affairs of life. The intuitive faculty originally is neither active nor tranquil. It is the starting-point of learning. This saying I have explained through comparison seven times since I lived at Ch'uchou. The three words, *chih liang chih* (meaning "to extend intuitive knowledge of the good to the utmost"), have no defect. After the doctor has had experience with a broken arm, he can investigate the principles underlying disease.

There Are Various Degrees of Knowledge

"The knowledge of the sage may be compared to the sun on a clear day; that of the virtuous man to the sun on a day of floating clouds; that of a simple-minded, rustic man to the sun on a dark, foggy day. Though the darkness and clearness vary, they may all equally distinguish between black and white. Though there be the confusion and darkness of night, they may indistinctly distinguish black and white. This implies that the light of the sun is not completely exhausted. Even study as a result of being distressed because of ignorance proceeds only from careful examination at the point where there is a little light and clearness."

I made inquiry saying, "If it is self-evident that the

sage is born with knowledge of the truth and practices it with ease, what task remains for him to do?"

The Teacher said: "Knowledge and practice are the task."

Ancient Music Had a Vital Relation to Public Morals

The Teacher said: "For many years the music of the ancients has not been used."

Someone asked, "Is the purpose of the present-day actors inconsistent with that of ancient music or not?"

The Teacher said, "The nine chapters of the music of Shun constituted the book of the actors of his time, and the nine sections of the music of Wu constituted the book of the actors of Wu's time. (31) The important affairs from the life of the sages were all exhibited in the music. When virtuous men heard it, they understood the exceeding goodness and beauty of the music of Shun and the exceeding beauty of the music of Wu, as well as the points at which it was not perfectly good. When later generations compose music, they merely produce harmonized poetical compositions which have no relation to changing public morals. How can they bring about good customs?

"Most of the men who have faults spend their efforts on their faults — that is to say, in mending the rice-boiler. The direction of their efforts lies in glossing over the fault. Present-day people while eating, though they have nothing further to do, employ their minds and are not in a state of tranquility. For this reason the mind is habitually distracted with care, and consequently they cannot control it."

Nature May Be Discussed from Many Standpoints

I made inquiry saying, "The discussions of the ancients regarding nature are various. Whose shall be accepted as the criterion?"

The Teacher said: "Nature has no fixed form, and the discussion of nature also takes no fixed form. There were

those who discussed it from the point of its underlying substance; there were those who based their discussions on its
manifestations; there were those who proceeded from its
source; there were those who proceeded from its defects
and corruptions. Taking it all together, they all referred
to this one nature, but there were degrees of depth in what
they saw. Insisting on any one aspect involves mistakes.
Nature is *ab initio* characterized neither by good nor evil;
but its impulses may fix upon either good or evil. It may
be compared to the eyes. There are the eyes of one who is
joyous, and the eyes of the one who is angered. When one
sees direct and exactly, they are the eyes of one who sees.
When one peeps with his eyes, the eyes are near-sighted.
Taking it all together, they are eyes. If one sees the eyes
of an angry person, one says he does not have eyes which
express delight. If one sees eyes at the time they perceive,
one says they are not peeping. This all implies an in-
sistence on a fixed condition, and from this we know that
there is a mistake. Mencius in discussing nature discussed
it directly from the point of view of its source and thus
spoke of it in this general way. The philosopher Hsün's
discussion of the evil of nature proceeded from its impulses toward evil. One cannot say that he was wrong.
Nevertheless, he did not view the situation with discrimination.'' (32)

Wang's Disciples Discuss His Unpopularity

Hsieh Shang-ch'ien, Ts'ou Ch'ien-chih, Ma Tzu-hsin,
and Wang Ju-chih sat near the Teacher. They deplored
the fact that from the time the Teacher had reduced Ningfan to submission he had been slandered and criticised by
many, and therefore requested that each in turn give his
version of the reason. One said it was due to the fact that
his merit and his power were daily increasing and the
number of those who were envious of him in the state was
also increasing. One said that the Teacher's learning was

daily becoming clearer, and that therefore the scholars who defended the philosopher (Chu) of the Sung dynasty were daily becoming more numerous. One said that after the Teacher had been at Nanchang, those who had the same purpose and followed him, daily congregated the more; while those who had been delegated from all sides to hinder him, daily exerted themselves the more.

The Teacher said: "What you have said, Sirs, I believe is all true. However, the fact that I myself have come to self-realization, you, Sirs, have entirely overlooked. Before I came to Nanchang, I harbored the purpose of the 'good, careful people of the villages,' but today I believe that I reach what is right and wrong by means of the intuitive faculty.[45] I do what comes uppermost, and not being involved in dissimulating, I present the front of one who is ardent. Therefore the people all say that my actions do not cover my assertions."[46]

"Your Good, Careful People of the Village" Are Not Superior Men

The disciples asked him to explain the difference between "your good, careful people of the village" and the "ardent man."

The Teacher said: "Your good, careful people of the village, because their principles have a semblance of right-mindedness and their conduct of disinterestedness, are taken for superior men. They agree with current customs, conspire with an impure age, and are not firm in holding their views in the presence of mean men. Therefore, if you blame them, you find nothing to allege; and if you would criticise them you have nothing to criticise. However, if you examine their minds you will know that in their right-mindedness and truth, and in their disinterestedness, they flatter the superior man; and that in their agree-

---

[45] Mencius, Book VII, Pt. II, Ch. 37, ¶ 8.

[46] Meaning that he does not carry out what he says.

ment with custom, and in their conspiracy with an impure age, they flatter the mean man. Their minds have been ruined, and therefore they are unable to enter upon the path of Yao and Shun. The will of the ardent, ambitious man cherishes the institutions of the ancients.[47] Neither the confused murmur of others nor the influence of custom are sufficient to embarrass his mind. He truly represents the phœnix soaring eight thousand feet in the air. When once he is able to control his thoughts, he forthwith becomes a sage. Only because he is unable to control his thoughts is he perverse and offensive in affairs. But what he does he never covers up. Since he does not cover his actions, his mind is not ruined and may perhaps be regulated.''

The disciples asked: ''Why give judgment that 'your good, careful people of the village' flatter and love the world (of people)?''

The Teacher said: ''I know this from the fact that they ridicule the ardent and the cautiously-decided. Moreover, they say of them: 'Why do they act so peculiarly and are so cold and distant? Born in this age, we should be of this age; to be good is all that is needed.'[48] Therefore, whatsoever they do is mere form and never fixed. (33) Consequently they are said to have a semblance. Moreover, since the time of the Three Dynasties, the scholars who have acquired fame have attained no more than the semblance of 'your good people of the villages.' If the loyalty, faithfulness, and disinterestedness of such an individual is investigated, it is perhaps not possible to avoid his being suspected by his wife. Though one desires to be in the fullest sense one of these good country people, this also is not easy. And how much more is this true of the path of the sage!''

The disciples said, ''Confucius had thoughts of the am-

---

[47] Mencius, Book VII, Pt. II, Ch. 37, ¶ 5 and 6.

[48] *Ibid.*, Book VII, Pt. II, Ch. 37, ¶ 9.

bitious ones and the cautious ones, but when it came to the matter of expounding the truth, why did he explain it to the philosopher Tseng and not to Ch'in and Chang and their class? Was it because the philosopher Tseng was cautious and decided?''

The Teacher said: "No. Ch'in, Chang, and their companions were by disposition ardent and ambitious. Though they attained what they wanted, they remained ardent and ambitious to the end. The philosopher Tseng was a man who naturally acted in accordance with the mean, and for that reason was able to come to a state of realization and to enter the path of the sage.''

Te-hung and Ju-chung Discuss Learning

In the sixth year of Chia Ching, in the ninth month, the Teacher was again in official position. As he was starting out to subdue Ssut'ien, Te-hung and Ju-chung were discussing learning. Ju-chung spoke of the instruction of the Teacher as follows: "Being without virtue and without evil is the original nature of the mind, while the presence of virtue and vice is due to the activity of the purpose (will). Knowledge of good and evil is due to the intuitive faculty. To do good and abhor evil implies the investigation of things.''

Te-hung said: "What do you think of it?''

Ju-chung said: "This perhaps is not the final word. If you say that the mind is characterized neither by virtue nor by vice, the will, knowledge, and things are all free from virtue or vice. If you say that the will is characterized by virtue and vice, it is finally a fact that there still is good and evil in the original nature of the mind.''

Te-hung said: "The mind is heaven-decreed nature, and thus is *ab initio* neither good nor evil. But in one aspect the mind is the result of habit. In will and thought you can see that there is good and evil. Investigating things for the purpose of extending knowledge to the utmost, making the purpose sincere, rectifying the mind, cultivating the person, and regulating the families, imply a return to nature. If there is originally neither good nor evil, it is not necessary to speak of these tasks."

The Teacher Instructs Them

That evening they sat near the Teacher at the T'ien-ch'üan-ch'iao and both asked that he might correct them. The Teacher said: "As I am about to leave, I really want you two men to disclose the purport of your ideas. Sirs, both points of view may render you some mutual assistance, but neither one of you should insist upon one aspect. (34) I originally welcome both types of men. The man who is by nature clever is able to comprehend immediately from the source. The mind in its original nature is clear and unobstructed, and is in a condition of equilibrium in which there is no stirring of passion. As soon as the clever man fully realizes the nature of the mind, he forthwith enters upon the task and understands everything — others, himself, things internal, and things external. On the other hand, there necessarily are those whose mind, by habit, takes definite grooves. Nature has been obscured. I gently instruct them to do good and to abhor evil in their thoughts. When they have mastered this task and have entirely removed all feculence, nature is completely clear.

"The point of view of Ju-chung is the one by means of which I receive those who are naturally clever. The point of view of Te-hung is the one I use in the second instance. If I use your two points of view, Sirs, I am able to lead individuals of the upper, middle, and lower classes upon the path. If each insists upon one aspect, you will lose men in your very presence."

After a while he spoke again, saying: "When after this you discuss learning with your friends, you must not lose sight of my real purpose: 'To be free from good and evil is the nature of the mind, while good and evil are due to the activity of the thoughts (purpose). It is the intuitive knowledge of good that gives knowledge of good and evil. To do good and expel evil is what is meant by investigation of things.' Following my words you should adapt yourselves to the individual when offering instruction, and then there will be no defects. This is a method whereby I reach both the upper and the lower classes. Men who are naturally clever are few. When once they realize what the task is they understand it fully. This Yen-tzu and Ming-tao did not dare to assume. Is it an easy matter to espy men from afar? If the individual has a mind fixed by habit, and is not taught to devote himself earnestly to furthering the good and keeping out the evil in his intuitive faculty, but vainly thinks of reverting to nature while all his acts are not genuine, he will do no more than cultivate an empty, false tranquility. This is not a minute defect. I must dissipate such notions at the earliest opportunity.''

Wang's Ideal for His Disciples

The Teacher said: ''Sirs, you should fix your minds upon definitely becoming sages. Whenever you strike, there should be a mark; and whenever you hit there should be blood on the hand; for not until then will you hear me speak and get virtue out of every sentence. (35) If you spend your days in a dazed and vague fashion, you may be compared to a lifeless piece of flesh that neither feels pain nor itches, though it is struck. I fear that under such circumstances you will not be of any use. When you return home you will be able to measure up only to the ability of former times. Would not that be unfortunate?

His Idea of Recapitulation

''During a single day the individual experiences the world from the ancients up to the present time. Nevertheless, people do not realize this. In the night when the night air is pure and clear, when nothing is seen or heard, and man neither thinks nor works, and is indifferent and undisturbed, this is the age of Emperor Hsi.[49] In the morning when the air is transparent, peaceful and inspiring, this is the age of Yao and Shun. Just before the middle of the day, when the vital forces are blended and the various forms are regular and clear, this is the time of the Three Dynasties.[50] After the middle of the day, when the air gradually becomes unclear and moves confusedly, this is the time of the contending states in feudal times. When the day gradually becomes confused and dark, nature rests, and forms are lonely and solitary, this is the age when man and things are done away with. If the student has had faith in his intuitive knowledge of good he will not be disturbed by the passion nature, and thus will become an individual, as it were, belonging to the period before Emperor Hsi.''

He Inculcates Humility

From the time when he was at Nanchang, the Teacher, whenever he made any explanation to the students, always urged them to cherish natural law and expel desire, as being the very foundation of the truth. When anyone made inquiry regarding what he said, he ordered him to seek for himself. He had not yet explained or shown what natural law is. Kuo Shan-fu from Kuangkang helped his follower Liang Chi to go to Yüeh to receive instruction. On the way they had a discussion without coming to an agreement, but, having arrived, they made inquiry of the Teacher.

At that time he was in a pavilion eating congee. He did not answer their inquiry, but inspected Liang Chi several times. Pointing to his congee bowl, he said, "This bowl when underneath is able to contain this rice. This

---

[49] Fu Hsi was the legendary monarch who is said to have discovered the diagrams on the back of a tortoise. (Giles.)

[50] Vide footnote 28, p. 69.

table is able to hold this bowl from below. This pavilion is able to contain this table. The earth is able to carry this pavilion. Only by descending (being humble) is one truly great.''

A Quarrel Diagnosed

One day there was the noise of fighting and angry speech on the street. One man said, ''You are lacking in moral principles.'' The other said, ''You are lacking in moral principles.'' The first one said, ''You have a deceptive mind.'' The second one answered, ''You have a deceptive mind.'' (36)

The Teacher heard them, and calling his disciples said, ''Hear them — these men that are screaming at one another — for they are discussing learning.''

His disciples answered, ''They are scolding. How can it be learning that they are discussing?''

The Teacher said, ''Do you not hear that they are speaking of moral principles and the mind? If this is not discussing learning, what is it?''

The disciples said, ''Since it is learning, why do they speak angrily?''

He said, ''It is because these men know only how to reprove others and do not know how to apply it to themselves.''

Wang Relates His Experience in Acquiring a Full Understanding of the Meaning of Intuitive Knowledge of Good

The Teacher often said, ''After I had been at Lungch'ang I did not discuss the meaning of the intuitive knowledge of good, for I was not able to interpret it. When I spoke with the students, I wasted a great many words. Fortunately I now comprehend the meaning. In one sentence I fully comprehended it at the time and was truly extremely happy. Unconsciously I gesticulated with hands and feet. When the students heard it, they also were saved a great deal of troublesome work. Place the starting-point of learning there, and one is able to discuss it very definitely. Yet there is danger that the students are unwilling directly to assume the responsibility involved.''

He further said, ''My teachings regarding intuitive knowledge of good have been acquired with extreme difficulty. It has not been easy to reach my standpoint. Since this is the ultimate subject which the student gets, I cannot help discussing it fully with others at one time. But there is danger that if the students get this easily, they will consider it as a thing to trifle with, and thereby neglect it.''

He spoke to his friends saying, ''For some time I desired to publish this, but I knew that there was one expression which I was unable to give, though I held it moistened in my mouth.'' Soon after, however, he said, ''Of late I realize that there is no other learning but this.''

Near by there was one who strongly desired to understand but did not. Accordingly the Teacher spoke again, ''Even this did not give satisfaction. It was after I had changed at this point that I came forward with my teachings regarding the intuitive faculty.''

One of his friends stood near. His eyebrows indicated that he was troubled in thought. The Teacher noticed him and said to another friend, ''The intuitive faculty unquestionably penetrates heaven and earth. Near us it is penetrating a person. (37) When a man's person is not cheerful, it does not necessarily imply anything very serious. If only a hair falls from the head, the entire person is forthwith sorry. How can anything (selfishness) be allowed within it?''

Wang Recognizes the Mistakes of His Youth

When the Teacher first became a Chinshih, he sent in a memorial regarding eight essential things (pertaining to the border of the Empire). Shih Yen admired and praised him. When in later life someone used this memorial in asking the Teacher a question, the Teacher said: ''This is one of the affairs of my early life. It manifests a great deal of the spirit of opposition and oppression. If such a spirit is not expelled while one wishes to hold office in the state, how can one measure up to the requirements?''

Someone made further inquiry regarding the pacifying of Ningfan. The Teacher said: ''At that time I acted in accordance with that standpoint, but now I realize that I formerly had this extravagance. Were I ordered to do it now, there would be a change.''

Wang Did Not Desire to Contrast His Standpoint in a Hostile Way with That of the Philosopher Chu

Because of the judgment of others that the learning of the Teacher was different from that of the philosopher Chu, doubt was raised in the minds of men concerning its correctness. The simple-minded thought there really was no difference between them. They held that though the sayings of the two teachers were different, the two men were alike in the matter of defending the doctrine and understanding the world. This was not due to the fact that the simple-minded ventured to use their own private ideas to observe them on the sly, but rather to the fact that they erroneously harmonized their sayings. I still made inquiry regarding the sayings of the two teachers. Wen-ch'eng (Yang-ming) said, ''My sayings are sometimes different from those of Hui-an.[51] Since in the matter of beginning the task there are both small and great differences, I cannot but explain them. Nevertheless, my mind has not been different from his. Mencius loved to dispute only because he wished to rectify the minds of men. Since my mind and that of Hui-an are alike, why should there be any dispute?''

[51] Wen-ch'eng was Wang's posthumous title; Hui-an was the philosopher Chu.

Wang's Standpoint is Completely Idealistic

From this one can know that the Teacher did not argue regarding the learning of Hui-an. He disputed because he feared that there were those who studied Hui-an but lost the truth he taught. Hui-an's writings say, "My learning is not of the kind that seeks without the mind and not within." The sage established his teachings (Confucianism) in order that one might silently treasure knowledge of the intelligence of the mind, and be dignified and peaceful, and further that one might consider these as the root of investigating principles. He caused the individual to know the wonderfulness of all principles, to study extensively, to make accurate inquiry, to reflect carefully, and to use clear discrimination, for the purpose of extending to the utmost the task of exhausting his mental constitution.[52] Thus in the mutual nourishing of the great and the small, in activity and tranquility, he will not choose between the inner and the outer, nor between the fine and the coarse. (38) He will consider these as superficial and will desire that which is invisible. Further, he will desire to devote himself to that which is hidden and profound. This is comparable to saying that difficulty will hinder and exterminate any choice between the inner and the outer, the fine and the coarse. To cause the student heedlessly to place his mind on words and literary style implies falling into the one-sidedness, extravagance, depravity, and evasiveness of the Buddhists. How deep and how far-reaching is the anxiety which Hui-an has beforehand displayed regarding future scholars!

Both Chu and Wang Wrote for Their Respective Ages

In order to push inquiry into the reasons for the sayings of the two teachers one must realize that Hui-an lived after the five dynasties. At that time Buddhism and Taoism had spread over the Empire and precipitated it into dense ignorance of the true investigation of principles.

---

[52] *Vide* Doctrine of the Mean, Ch. 20, ¶ 19.

Therefore he turned toward the learning of the philosopher Ch'eng. He bore in mind and made known the learning (Confucianism) which advocated a reverent investigation of principles, and caused the people to have a fixed guide. Wen-ch'eng lived after Hui-an. At that time the writing of verbose essays and the practice of making comments on the classics had ruined the minds of men and precipitated them into a condition in which they saw and heard vain things. Therefore Wen-ch'eng illustrated the learning of Lu and made known the purport of combining knowledge and practice into one, so that they might know that it is necessary to return to nature. The solicitous mind of the two teachers in behalf of the doctrine was for no other purpose than to be a little factor in correcting one-sidedness and saving men from defects. It was not that Wen-ch'eng understood the inner and did not understand the outer, and that Hui-an understood the outer but not the inner. How could there have been any disagreement between them? The path is one only. If it is observed from within, one does not see or hear it. It is the principle which contains, and is as vast as, heaven, earth, and all things. If it is viewed from without, it is the five human relations, things, and change. The mystery of wonder of having its roots in the person, mind, and life, is what is called virtue by natural disposition. This is the path of uniting the external and the internal. The superior man devotes himself to studying it, inquiring about it, reflecting on it, clearly discriminating it, and earnestly practicing it, in order to exhaust his nature. The two teachers are both my models. Inquiry should not be made into their differences and agreements. If students do not emphasize their likeness of purpose, but vainly take the differences in their sayings and argue and wrangle about them, the two teachers will certainly be grieved in the corridors of the temple. The simple and unintelligent are not able to understand them. I venture to ask those who have the same purpose whether I am not correct. (39)

INQUIRY REGARDING THE GREAT LEARNING [1]

The Great Learning is Adapted to the Adult Mind

Referring to the Great Learning, a former scholar held that it is adapted to adults.[2] I ventured to ask why learning adapted to adults should consist in illustrating illustrious virtue.[3]

Wang said: "The adult is an all-pervading unity — one substance — with heaven, earth, and things. He views the earth as one family and his country as one man. The youth makes a cleavage between things, and distinguishes between himself and others, while the adult's ability consists in considering heaven, earth, and all things as one substance. This is not because his own purpose is of that kind, but because the benevolent nature of the mind is of that type. It is one with heaven, earth, and things. But is this true only of adults? The mind of a youth is also of this type, but he views himself as small. When he sees a child fall into a well, he certainly will experience a feeling of alarm and distress, which implies that his kindly nature is of the same sort as that of the child and that the child belongs to the same class as he. When he hears the pitiful cry and sees the frightened appearance of a bird or an animal that is about to be slaughtered, his mind surely cannot endure it; and this implies that his kindly nature is one with that of birds and animals, and that birds and animals may be said to be conscious and have feelings. If he sees plants destroyed, he surely feels sympathetic. This

---

[1] Written by Ts'ü Ai.

[2] This refers to the interpretation of the philosopher Chu.

[3] Great Learning, Introduction, ¶ 1.

implies that his benevolence includes plants, and that plants may be said to have life. When he sees tiles and stones being broken, he surely will have regard for them. This implies that his benevolence is one with inanimate things. They are all the benevolence of the same body (substance). Even a youth will have this type of a mind, which means that the source is in the heaven-given nature. But of course his intelligence must not be obscured. For this reason it is called illustrious virtue. Though the young man's mind is divided, hampered, and vile, his benevolence may not be obscured and darkened, for he may have had no stirrings of desire; and his mind may not be obstructed with selfishness. As soon as he has stirrings of desire and his mind is obscured because of selfishness, and these (desires) contend severely among themselves and angrily impede one another, then will he kill and destroy living things and will be equal to anything. (40) This may easily reach the place where brothers desire to kill one another; but thereby benevolence is completely destroyed. For this reason if the youth is free from the obscuration of selfish desire, his benevolence is as that of the adult, even though he is but a youth. When once the individual has been obscured by selfish desire, he is as divided and ignorant as the youth, even though he be an adult. Thus it is evident that learning adapted to adults merely clears away the obscuration of selfish desire from the mind so as to illustrate the mind's illustrious virtue and to cause it to revert to the original all-pervading unity of heaven, earth, and things. It is not possible to add anything to this original substance.''

I said: ''I venture to ask why learning for adults should consist in loving the people.'' [4]

He said: ''He who manifests illustrious virtue estab-

---

[4] *Ibid.* Wang keeps the original *ch'in*, meaning ''to love.'' He refuses to accept the philosopher Chu's *hsin*, meaning ''to renovate.''

lishes himself in the proper place in the great all of heaven, earth, and things. He who loves the people perceives and understands the use of his nature (common to heaven, earth, and things). The manifesting of illustrious virtue consists in loving the people, and loving the people in manifesting illustrious virtue. For this reason, if I love my own father, the fathers of others, and even the fathers of all men, my benevolence will truly be one with that of my father, the fathers of others, and even with that of the fathers of all men. When they are truly one, then first will the illustrious virtue of filial piety be illustrated. When I love my elder brother, the elder brothers of others, and even the elder brothers of all men, my benevolence will be one with them. When it is truly one with them, then the illustrious virtue of a younger brother will first be illustrated. Everything, from prince, minister, husband, wife, friends, up to mountains, rivers, spirits, gods, birds, animals, and plants, should be truly loved in order to promote my natural benevolence; then there will be nothing left unmanifested by my illustrious virtue, and I will be truly one with heaven, earth, and all things. This is what is called illustrating illustrious virtue throughout the kingdom. This is what is meant by, 'Their families being regulated, their states were rightly governed and the whole Empire was made tranquil.'[5] It is called 'exhausting nature.'" (41)

I said: "I venture to ask in what way learning for adults consists in the individual's 'resting in the highest excellence.'"[6]

The Teacher said: "Resting in the highest excellence implies manifesting illustrious virtue and loving the people in the highest degree. When the heaven-given nature reaches a condition of complete excellence, its intelligence will not be darkened. This is a manifestation of highest

[5] Great Learning, Introduction, ¶ 5.
[6] *Ibid.*, ¶ 1.

excellence. It is really the original form of illustrious virtue, and is called intuitive knowledge of good. When the highest excellence manifests itself, right is right and wrong is wrong. Things of less and greater importance come and go as they will without ceasing, but none of this change is other than natural. This, moreover, implies that mankind holds fast to its natural disposition and has its various faculties and relations with their specific laws. However, it is not allowable that there be the least purpose to add to or subtract from them. If there is the least disposition to add to or diminish them, this implies self-ishness and shallow wisdom, and cannot be said to be the highest virtue. Naturally, one who does this does not attain to the condition of watching over himself when he is alone. How can he who is discriminating and undivided be like that? Later generations fail to realize that the highest excellence is in their own minds, but use their selfish wisdom to estimate and calculate how they may find it in things external to themselves. They hold that every affair and every thing has its own definite principles. This is due to the darkening of their ability to estimate right and wrong. They branch off from, and are at variance with, their heaven-given nature. Passion is excessive, while moral principles perish. Thus the learning which inculcates illustrious virtue and love of the people becomes greatly confused in the Empire. Among former scholars there were some who desired to manifest their illustrious virtue, but who did not know how to rest in the highest excellence. They used their selfish purposes to excess and lost the mind in vacuous, lifeless, and lonely contemplation. They did not regulate their families, govern their states, nor make the kingdom happy and tranquil. This means that they drifted into Buddhism and Taoism. Certainly some wished to love the people, but they did not know how to rest in the highest excellence. They sank their selfish minds into base and trifling things. This implies that they lost their power, strategy, wisdom, and craft, and that they did not have the sincerity of real benevolence and sympathy. Thus they became followers of the five rulers, devoting themselves to might, merit, and gain, and all failed to realize their mistake in not resting in the highest virtue. Therefore resting in the highest excellence is to the manifesting of illustrious virtue and loving the people as a pair of compasses and square are to the square and the circle, or rule and measure are to length, or the balances are to weight. (42) If the square and the circle do not correspond with the compasses and the square, they will be defective; if the length and shortness fail to coincide with the rule and the measure, they lose their adjustment; if the weight is not true to the balances, it loses its accuracy. If manifestation of illustrious virtue and love of the people do not rest in the highest excellence, they lose their original character. Therefore, resting in the highest excellence requires the previous use of loving the people and illustrating illustrious virtue. This is what is meant by saying that learning is adapted to adults.''

The Mind is Possessed of the Highest Excellence

I said: ''How is the following saying to be interpreted? 'The point where to rest (in the highest excellence) being known, the object of pursuit is then determined, and that being determined, a calm unperturbedness may be attained to. To that calmness there will succeed a tranquil repose. In that repose there may be careful deliberation and that deliberation will be followed by the attainment (of the highest excellence).' '' [7]

The Teacher said: ''People fail to understand that the highest excellence is in their mind and seek it in external things. They believe that all affairs and all things have definite principles, and seek the highest excellence in the midst of affairs and things. This shows that their heaven-

---

[7] Great Learning, Introduction, ¶ 2.

given nature has branched off and been disrupted. They are mixed up and confused, and do not know that there is a definite direction which they ought to take. Since you know that the highest excellence is in the mind and that there is no need of seeking it in external things, your purpose has taken a definite direction and you are not precipitated into a condition in which nature branches off, is disrupted, or is all mixed up and confused. Moreover, if you are in that condition, your mind will not make mistakes, but will be quiet and calm. If the mind does not make mistakes but is able to rest, then in its daily use, whenever it gets a moment's rest, it will be in tranquil repose. If the mind is in tranquil repose, your intuitive faculty — whenever thought manifests itself or an affair influences the mind — will naturally carefully inquire, minutely investigate, and thus be able earnestly to deliberate, whether the thing under consideration is in accordance with the highest excellence. If it is able to deliberate carefully, it will choose only the finest, and do only what is proper. But in this the highest excellence is attained.''

As Roots and Branches are One Thing, thus Manifesting Virtue and Loving the People are One

I said: '' 'Things have their roots and their branches.' [8] A former scholar (the philosopher Chu) considered illustrious virtue as the root and 'renovating the people' as the branches. But these two, the one being within and the other without, are really opposed to one another. 'Affairs have their end and their beginning.' A former scholar held that knowing where to rest in the highest excellence was the beginning, and ability to attain (the highest excellence) was the end. Every affair has its beginning and its end, and these are mutually connected. According to the teaching of the Master (Wang) one should change the character *hsin* (新, of the philosopher Chu's commentary

---

[8] *Ibid.*, ¶ 3.

on the Great Learning (meaning "to renovate") to the character ch'in (親 , meaning "to love") Would not this be at variance with the saying regarding the roots and the branches?" (43).

The Teacher said· "What has been said regarding the end and the beginning is, in general, correct. To use the original, 'love,' in place of 'renovate,' and then to say that the manifesting of illustrious virtue is the root and loving the people the branches, is also a legitimate method of procedure. But root and branches should not be distinguished as being two different things. The trunk of this tree is called the root (source), and its twigs are called branches, but the whole is but one thing. If root and branches are two things, they should have been considered as two things. How, then, are they connected in the saying, 'Things have roots and branches'? If the idea expressed in 'renovating the people' is different from that of loving the people, then the task of illustrating virtue is naturally an entirely different thing from renovating the people. If one understands that illustrious virtue is manifested by loving the people, and on the other hand that one loves the people in manifesting illustrious virtue, what occasion is there for separating them? The former scholar's exposition is due to his ignorance of the fact that manifesting virtue and loving the people are *ab initio* one thing, whereas he considered them as two. This means that though he knew that root and branches ought to be considered as one thing, he could but distinguish them as two."

Wang Offers Comments on the Great Learning, Introduction, ¶ 4

I said: " 'The ancients who wished to illustrate illustrious virtue throughout the kingdom first ordered well their own states. Wishing to order well their states, they first regulated their families. Wishing to regulate their families, they first cultivated their persons.'⁹ In using the Master's idea of understanding the expressions, 'manifesting virtue' and 'loving the people,' I have been able to understand this. May I venture to ask regarding the arrangement of the task, and the way in which one should proceed, as implied in the following passage from the Great Learning? 'Wishing to cultivate their persons, they first rectified their hearts. Wishing to rectify their hearts, they first sought to be sincere in their thoughts. Wishing to be sincere in their thoughts, they first extended their knowledge to the utmost. Such extension of knowledge lay in the investigation of things.' "

The Teacher said: "This saying is merely giving in detail the order of the task from the 'manifesting of illustrious virtue' on to 'resting in the highest excellence.' The person, the mind, thought, knowledge, and things constitute the logical order of the task. Though each has its particular place, they are in reality one thing. Investigating, extending, being sincere, rectifying, and cultivating are the task in its logical sequence. Though each has its name, in reality it is only one affair. What is it that is called the person? The form and body in its various exercises. What is it that is called mind? The intelligence of the person, which is called lord or master. What is meant by cultivating the person? That which is described by saying, 'Do good and expel evil.' (44) That my person is able to do good and abhor evil is due to the fact that its master — the will — desires to do good and abhor evil. After that the body in its various exercises is able to do good and abhor evil. Therefore he who desires to cultivate his person must first rectify his heart. Moreover, the mind in its original form is what is called nature. If nature is virtuous in everything, then the mind in its original form is at all times characterized by rectitude. From whence, then, the

⁹ Op. cit., Introduction, ¶ 4.

use of effort in rectifying it? The mind is originally in a condition of perfect rectitude, it is only after there has been a stirring of its purposes and thoughts that it is wrong Therefore he who wishes to rectify his mind will correct that which his will and thought bring forth Whenever he manifests a virtuous thought, he will love it as one loves a beautiful color; when he thinks an evil thought, he will hate it as one despises an evil odor Since his purpose is perfectly sincere, he will be able to rectify his heart. The purpose manifests both that which is virtuous and that which is evil, and has no knowledge of the difference between good and evil. It confuses and mixes the right and the wrong. Though the individual desires to make his purpose sincere, he is unable to do so Therefore he who wishes to make his purpose sincere must extend his knowledge of the good to the utmost by developing his intuitive faculty to the utmost. The utmost here is like the utmost of the saying, 'When mourning has been carried to the utmost degree of grief, it should cease ' [10]

"The Book of Changes says, 'Knowing the utmost one should reach it. He who knows the utmost really knows. He who reaches it, reaches the utmost' This signifies extending knowledge to the utmost. It is not what later scholars call filling and extending knowledge, but extending to the utmost the mind's intuitive knowledge of good, — the knowledge of good which Mencius calls the good-evil mind and which all people have. The good-evil mind does not need to deliberate in order to know, nor does it need to learn in order to be able to act. It is for this reason that it is called intuitive knowledge of good It is the heaven-given nature — the original character of the mind. It is naturally intelligent and clearly conscious Whenever any purposes or thoughts are manifested, they are all known and recognized by the intuitive faculty. If they be good, the intuitive faculty naturally knows. Are they

---

[10] Analects, Book XIX, Ch. 14

evil? This, too, the intuitive faculty naturally knows. This shows that it is no concern of others. (45) Therefore, though there is no evil to which the mean man will not proceed, yet when he sees a superior man, he will certainly disguise himself, conceal his evil, and display his virtue.[11] In this it is manifest that his intuitive faculty does not leave him unenlightened. If he desires to distinguish between good and evil in order to rectify his purpose, there is but the one way, that of extending the knowledge of his intuitive faculty to the utmost. How is it that when a purpose manifests itself, the intuitive faculty already knows whether it is good or not? Nevertheless, if the individual is not able to love the good sincerely, but rather turns his back on it and expels it, he uses the good to do evil and obscures his intuitive faculty, which knows the good. How is it that when the intuitive faculty knows that what the purpose has manifested is evil, nevertheless, if the individual does not sincerely hate the evil, he violates the good and does the evil, and thus uses the evil to do evil and thereby obscures his intuitive faculty, which knows the evil? If this is true, then, though it is said that he knows, he is as though he did not know. How can his purpose be made sincere under such circumstances? If, in that which the intuitive faculty understands to be good and evil, there is nothing that is not sincerely loved and sincerely hated, then the individual does not deceive his own intuitive faculty and his purpose can be made sincere.

"Again, if the individual wishes to extend his intuitive knowledge to the utmost, shall it be said that he, like a shadow and an echo, is vain and lacks genuineness? If in reality there is such an extension of intuitive knowledge, it must consist in investigating things. Things are affairs (experience). Whenever a purpose is manifested it certainly is relative to some affair and the affair toward which it is directed is called a thing. Investigating means

---

[11] Great Learning, Ch. 6, ¶ 2.

rectifying — rectifying that which is not correct, that it may belong to the things that are correct, rectifying that which is not true, and expelling evil. It implies that turning to the true and the right is what is meant by doing good This is called investigating.

"The Book of History says, 'He (Yao) investigated heaven above and the earth beneath [12] He (Shun) investigated (in the temple of) the accomplished ancestors.' [13] The individual investigates the evil of his heart The 'investigating' of 'investigating things' truly combines all of the above ideas. If one sincerely wishes to love the good which the intuitive faculty knows, but in reality fails to act with regard to the thing on which his purpose is fixed, this implies that the thing has not been investigated, and that the determination to love good is not sincere (46) If one sincerely wishes to despise the evil which the intuitive faculty recognizes, but fails really to expel the thing upon which the purpose is fixed, this implies that the thing has not been investigated and that the purpose of despising the evil is not sincere If the individual wishes the good which his intuitive faculty knows and he really does that upon which his purpose is fixed, is there anything which he may not accomplish? If in the matter of the evil which his intuitive faculty knows he really expels that upon which his purpose is fixed, is there anything which he may not complete? After that there is nothing that he does not thoroughly investigate. In that which the intuitive faculty knows, there will be no deficiency nor anything that is obscure, and it will have been extended to the utmost. After that the mind will be joyous, without remorse or regret, but modest and humble, and all the manifestations of

---

[12] The expression referred to is found in the Shooking, Pt I, The Book of T'ang, The Canon of Yao, ¶ 1. The translation here given does not agree with Legge's but fits much better into Wang's discussion The whole paragraph is suggestive.

[13] Shooking, Pt. II, The Books of Yu, Book I, The Canon of Shun, ¶ 14.

the purpose will be free from self-deceit, so that the individual may be said to be sincere in thought. Therefore it is said, 'Things being investigated, knowledge became complete. Their knowledge being complete, their thoughts were sincere; and their hearts being rectified, their persons were cultivated.'[14] These are the principles of the task. Though there may be said to be an order of first and last in this, it is in reality one connected whole and there is no distinction between first and last. Though the task for which these principles stand is not to be divided in an order of first and last, its use nevertheless implies great discrimination. Assuredly, there cannot be the least bit lacking. This is the correct exposition of investigating things, extending knowledge, making the thoughts sincere, and rectifying the mind. Therefore making known the true precepts of Yao and Shun is made the Confucian heart-seal.''

The Investigation of Things is the Real Starting-point of the Task Outlined in the Great Learning [15]

If from the Great Learning the idea contained in "investigating things" is expunged, there will be no real starting-point. There must be genuine investigation, before this can be appreciated. From the opening (creation) of heaven and earth, in heaven above and the earth beneath everywhere there are things. Even the person who seeks for the path is a thing. Taken together they have coherent principles, namely in what is called the source of the doctrine. Since the high and the low, altitude and depth, together constitute the great round, unmoved stillness, from what other point can knowledge of the doctrine be gained? If the individual wishes to investigate conditions previous to heaven and earth, he will find it in the Taoist abstract learning of Lao-tzu and Chuang-tzu. This thing can be seen from the manifestations of the doctrine. This

14 Great Learning, Introduction, ¶ 5.

15 At this point Ts'ü Ai offers comments.

is in conformity with the saying of the Book of Changes: "When the form is directed upward it is called the doctrine; when it points downward it is called a finished vessel." If you cast aside the vessel, there is the more nothing that can be called the doctrine. (47) The thing referred to is my nature, my heaven-decreed nature. It is in accordance with the saying of Mencius that "all things are already complete in us." [16]

Man alone knows what is meant by being enticed by the influence of things, but is unable to carry on self-investigation with full sincerity or to carry out vigorously the law of reciprocity. He stops with recognizing his body as the person and external objects as things, and forthwith separates things and himself into two distinct realms, so that in last analysis his person represents but one thing among ten thousand. How, then, can he extend his knowledge to the utmost, be sincere in purpose, rectify his mind, cultivate his person, regulate his family, govern the kingdom, and tranquilize the empire, in order to complete and exhaust the doctrine of the Great Learning? Therefore it is said that the task is exhausted in extending knowledge to the utmost through the investigation of things.

What is called investigating, does not consist in seeking within the realm of so-called external things. This excellency should be sought in extensive study of what is good, accurate inquiry about it, careful reflection upon it, clear discrimination of it, and earnest practice of it. This excellency is sincerity. In this way, these things may be considered as things. The manifesting of this excellency consists in knowing how to rest in the highest virtue. If one knows how to rest in the highest virtue, he will be able to attain the desired end. If thus understood, all nature will be comprehended in this. It is for this reason that the Doctrine of the Mean says: "Sincerity is the end and the beginning of things. The superior man regards the attain-

---

[16] Mencius, Book VII, Pt. I, Ch. 4.

ment of sincerity as the most excellent thing."[17] Naturally he completes himself and things also. Once mentioned he employs them and does nothing that is not proper. The task of investigating things having been completed, all other things will be adjusted. Therefore, when the philosopher Chu in giving instruction regarding the investigation of things, said "to the utmost," he did that which was exceedingly proper.

Whatever falls into the class of speculation or mere abstract thinking, as in considering extreme height, cannot be said to be to the utmost. What is here called the utmost means that the personality has developed to the utmost degree. Knowledge and practice also should be called activity and tranquility. This is what the Teacher refers to in the saying of the Book of Changes: "If you know the highest (utmost), attain to it." To attain to the utmost is the essence of staunch virtue. Beyond this there is no task which has reference to the essence, or is wonderful and godlike. But the people find too shallow a meaning in the "utmost" of the philosopher Chu and thus say: "When you take up anything, investigate it." This is the practice whereby the latest scholars branch off, though the philosopher Chu from the first gave no such explanation. Having received the plain exposition of the Teacher, I use it to explain the incomplete idea of the philosopher Chu.

---

[17] Doctrine of the Mean, Ch. 25, ¶ 2 and 3.

BOOK III

王陽明先生遺像

A Picture of Wang Yang-ming, reproduced from the Chinese edition of his Philosophy

The Chinese characters may be translated: A transmitted picture of the Teacher, Wang Yang-ming

LETTERS WRITTEN BY WANG YANG-MING

Answer to Wang T'ien-yü's Letter (First Letter)

Written in the ninth year of Emperor Cheng Te

Wang Asks for More Explicit Information Regarding Wang T'ien-yü's Difficulties

Your letter has been received. From it I note the experimental efforts you make in your study, and am exceedingly pleased and comforted. At present there are not many who, even to a limited extent, have fixed their purpose on the learning of sages and virtuous men. How much more difficult is it to find anyone who really uses his energies! You have honored me beyond what you really should. I do not venture to claim the degree of attainment you ascribe to me. Referring to your inquiry about virtue in order that you may get some real advantage from it, I must confess that my own mind has not been as serious and earnest as it should have been. That I have also gained you as a friend is more fortunate than words can express. Since your kindly feeling toward me has come to my knowledge, I dare not be false. Moreover, I admire and love you, but am unable really to help you.

Perhaps there are a few things in your letter about which we may critically consult. You say that you have the purpose, but cannot make it earnest. I do not know to what sort of a purpose you refer, nor with reference to what particular things you are not able to be earnest. You say that the learning of the sages and virtuous men can utilize the quiescence and repose of the mind to control its stirrings. I do not know what you mean by being able to be in a state of tranquility. Is the mind when tranquil and the mind when stimulated to be considered as two minds? You say that when you make a decision while transacting official business, you force the mind to follow the path of duty. Truly there are things here that should not be! I do not know in what way cleaving to virtue in moments of haste and in seasons of danger is to be considered as application to the task. You say that when you open a book to study, you gain something from it; and that when you entertain virtuous and superior men, you are influenced. If you rely upon these two things and are influenced thereby, what do you earnestly do in addition to them? At the time when you do these things, toward what is the purpose, of which you have spoken, directed? Unless you had truly used your energies, you could not have attained to the numerous things you have mentioned in your letter. (2) But they suffice to show that you have not been clear in the discussion of learning, and thus still have these defects. If there are things which you have attained to through reflection, do not hesitate to tell me.

Second Letter to Wang T'ien-yü

Written in the ninth year of Emperor Cheng Te

Thank you for your favor! You make inquiry regarding the meaning of study, and are sufficiently more in earnest than formerly that I am able to know that you have entered the path. How fortunate this is! Yet in your progress you have not fully carried out some of my suggestions. Since I have been honored with your questions, how can I fail to respond? Nevertheless, I hope that you will make a thorough investigation with a view to finding out whether there may not perhaps be something that will exhibit this truth.

Your letter says: "When first I read that I should use the investigating of things for the purpose of making my person sincere, I had strong doubts. Later, having carefully asked Hsi Yen, I understood its exposition."

Wang Replies to T'ien-yü that Investigation of Things Signifies Making the Purpose Sincere

I have not suggested that anyone should use the investigation of things as the correct method of making the person sincere. Has not this come from Hsi Yen? I say that in acquiring knowledge the superior man uses sincerity of purpose as the controlling factor. The investigation of things to extend knowledge to the utmost signifies making the purpose sincere; just as the hungry man makes it his business to become satisfied, and food has the function of satisfying hunger. Hsi Yen knows my idea very well; he should not give that interpretation, but perhaps at the time he was not clear. It is fortunate that you are carrying the investigation further.

Your letter also says: "The ancients held that the Great Learning gave the order and method of learning. The philosopher Chu said: 'After investigating fundamental principles to the utmost, the purpose will be sincere.' This appears to contradict the saying, 'Reverently investigate fundamental principles. Unless you thus maintain your mind, you are not able to extend knowledge to the utmost.' (3) The saying, 'Reverently maintain your mind,' is supplied in the commentary, while the teaching of the classics themselves distinctly says: 'Fundamental principles having been investigated, the mind was rectified.' If he who is beginning to learn holds himself to the classic text alone and does not investigate the comments, how can he prevent mistakes?"

Later Scholars Do Not Emphasize the Classic Text Sufficiently and Neglect a Careful Study of Their Own Persons

The order as given in the Great Learning is as follows: "Things being investigated, knowledge became complete. Their knowledge being complete, their thoughts were sincere." If it is true that when fundamental principles have been investigated to the utmost, the thoughts are sincere, this is in accordance with the sayings of the philosopher Chu - While there is no great contradiction in this, it is perhaps not fully in accord with the original thought of the Great Learning. The saying, "Unless one thus maintains his mind one is not able to extend knowledge to the utmost," is not fully in accord with the meaning of the Great Learning, and perhaps not with the saying of the Doctrine of the Mean, "The superior man honors his virtuous nature and maintains constant inquiry and study." [1] But this class of sayings is so numerous that it is possible to discuss them only when talking face to face Later scholars have agreed with reference to the commentary and have failed to investigate thoroughly the meaning of the classic text. Guided by the meaning of the characters, they fail to search out the real purport in their own persons and minds. Thus they constantly deviate from the right path and to the end fail to get what they desire. Perhaps this is not the mistake of holding to the classics and failing to study the commentaries

Wang Discusses Sincerity of Purpose and the Investigation of Things

Your letter also says: "If the individual does not start from an investigation of fundamental principles but immediately adds his own effort to be sincere in person, his sincerity is perhaps false rather than genuine."

This is very well said. But I do not know how you proceed in making the person sincere. How fortunate it would be, if you would investigate and appreciate this further!

You say. "The expression, 'Rest in the highest excellence,' may be compared to a traveler who is going to a large city as a place of rest. He does not excuse himself because of danger, hindrances, hardship, and difficulty, but goes forward with a fixed determination. This may be

---

[1] Doctrine of the Mean, Ch. 27, ¶ 6.

compared to maintaining one's mind. If this man does not know where the city is, but recklessly desires to advance, he may go south to Chekiang or north to Kiangsu." (4)

Your comparison is essentially correct. But if you use the traveler's not excusing himself because of danger, hindrances, hardship, and difficulty, and his fixed determination to go forward, as representing a maintaining of the mind, you will not avoid difficulties and will fail to get an understanding of the important thing. This "not excusing himself because of danger, hindrances, hardship, and difficulty," and "having a fixed determination to go forward," really signify that he is sincere in purpose. That this is actually so is shown by the fact that he makes inquiry regarding the road. Preparing money for his expenses and making provision for boat and cart, are things which are indispensable. If not, how could he without them have the fixed determination to go forward, or how could he advance? The person who does not know where the large city is, but recklessly desires to go, really only desires to go, and has not actually gone anywhere. Because he merely desires to go but has not gone, he makes no inquiry regarding the way, prepares no money for his expenses, and makes no provision for boat or cart. If he definitely determines to proceed, he will really go. Can he who actually goes be of such a type? This is the most indispensable element of the task. For an individual of your high intelligence and real genuineness, the situation is clear before mention is made.

Your letter says: "The people of the past used the investigating of things with the object in view of protecting themselves against external things. Having fended off external things, the mind itself was cherished. The mind was cherished that they might extend knowledge to the utmost. All this was for themselves."

In speaking thus you imply that fending off external things and the extension of knowledge are two separate

affairs The saying, "To fend off external things," does
no great harm; but to carry on the resistance with reference only to the things outside the mind does not carry
with it the idea of eradicating the disease, nor is it in accordance with the saying, "Subdue yourself and seek virtue." What is more, my own teaching regarding the investigation of things is not in harmony with this. The
saying, "To be sincere in purpose," taken from the
Great Learning, is to be identified with the saying, "To be
sincere in person," taken from the Doctrine of the Mean.[2]
The saying, "Investigation of things to extend knowledge
to the utmost," taken from the Great Learning, carries
with it the same idea as the saying, "Understand what is
good "[3] The extensive study (of what is good), accurate
inquiry (about it), careful reflection (on it), clear discrimination (of it), and the earnest practice (of it), may
all be identified with the task of understanding the good
and being sincere in person[4] (5) This does not mean that
beyond understanding what is good there is the additional
task of attaining sincerity in person. Is there, in addition
to the investigation of things in order to extend knowledge
to the utmost, the further task of becoming sincere in purpose? The saying, "Be discriminating," from the Book
of History, as the saying of the Analects, "The superior
man extensively studies all learning and keeps himself under the restraint of the rules of propriety," and the saying
of the Doctrine of the Mean, "The superior man honors
his virtuous nature, and maintains constant inquiry and
study," have this meaning.[5] These are important principles of the task of learning. It is said that a little difference at this point may result in great mistakes. Since

---

[2] Doctrine of the Mean, Ch 20, ¶ 17; Great Learning, Introduction,
¶ 4 and 5; Ch. 6, ¶ 1 and 6
[3] Ibid.
[4] Vide Doctrine of the Mean, Ch. XX, ¶ 19.
[5] The Shooking, Pt. II, Books of Yu, Book II, ¶ 15; Analects,
Book VI, Ch. 25; Doctrine of the Mean, Ch 27, ¶ 6

the exquisite and minute manifestations of mind cannot be described in words, how can they be fully expressed with the pen?

I am delighted that you have been advanced in official position, and that a day has been appointed for your departure to Peking. If you can take a round-about route and come to the river bank, I will consult with you for a night. Perhaps there are points which I am able to explain. Just now I am in the midst of business affairs, and thus cannot take up all the points fully.

Comment — If the individual views the idea expressed in "investigating things" too superficially, he will branch off and thus fail to understand that there is only this one path on earth. When referred to things, it is principle; and when referred to the mind, it is virtue (excellence). The investigation of things is to be identified with understanding the good. That it should be said in one word is appropriate. It implies that a house which has been dark for a thousand years has been lighted by a single light. It does not permit of being expounded in words.

First Letter to Lu Yüan-ching

Written in the sixteenth year of Emperor Cheng Te

Lu Proposes to Devote Himself to Cultivating His Health

I sent a memorial to the emperor and received an auspicious reply when the courier returned, bringing your letter. I am much comforted. I note that because of protracted illness, you are going to devote yourself to cultivating your health. Formerly because of frequent illness, I also devoted myself to the same task. Later I understood that the matter of nourishing one's life is really another affair. At that time I redirected my entire purpose to the learning of the sages and virtuous men. The nourishing of virtue and the nourishing of one's body are essentially the same thing.

Lu Refers to the Physical Immortality of the Taoist

You, Yuan-ching, said. "If in my effort to cultivate myself I really am cautious with respect to that which I do not see, and apprehensive of that which I do not hear, and devote my purpose to this task, my mental energy, my passions, and the very essence of my being endure and are stable What the Taoists call living eternally and seeing always (physical immortality) are included."

Wang Discusses Taoist Immortality

The learning of the Taoists is different from that of the sages, and yet the help they gave in the beginning was given with the desire to lead men to the truth. (6) In the appendix of the Wu Chen P'ien we have the statement: "Huang Lao being grieved because of the desire of other men, used the magic of Taoism and gradually and systematically led them."[6] If you take the Wu Chen P'ien and look it over, you will readily comprehend its purpose. From the time of Yao, Shun, Yü, T'ang, Wen and Wu, up to Chou Kung and Confucius, all virtuous men had a mind which had regard and love for things. Since there was nothing of virtue which they did not attain, it is unfortunate that they did not use the fact, if there really is such a thing as immortality. Take the cases of Lao-tzu, P'en Ch'ien, and others.[7] Their long life was due to native endowment, and not to ability in learning to reach it After that there is a class of men to whom Pai Yü-ch'en and Ch'iu Chang-ch'un belong, all of whom, as far as learning is concerned, are designated patriarchs of the sect, yet they did not reach an age of over fifty or sixty years Thus there are things about the expositions of immortality which need to be elucidated. Yuan-ching, since you have a low degree of vital energy and are often ill, you

---

[6] Wu Chen P'ien is a Taoist book, "Aid to Comprehending the Truth."

[7] P'en Ch'ien is said to have lived 767 years

should put aside mere reputation, purify your mind, bring your desires down to few, and fix your mind on the accomplishments of holy men and sages.

Lu is Admonished Not to Believe Heterodox Doctrines

Referring to what you have said about cultivating yourself, you should not over-readily believe heterodox doctrines and thereby needlessly confuse your own intelligence. In corrupting and enervating your mental and physical energies, you waste months and years. If for a long time you do not return to the path of sages and virtuous men, you will easily, because of your delay, become a person whose frenzy has injured his mind. Formerly it was said that he who has three times set a broken upper arm is a good physician. Though I am not a good physician, I have three times set a broken arm.[8] Yüan-ching, you should carefully listen and heed.

I have heard that the Board has consented to answer my request to visit my father. Having received permission from the emperor, I should withdraw into the mountains. It will not be long before the emperor will bestow a reward on you, and the day will come when you will be promoted. If you are in a position to consult with me at the Yang-ming Grotto at the foot of the mountain, I ought to be able to dispel the doubt which you express.

Comment — The nourishing of virtue is nourishing one's self. This is an admonition to him who seeks to nourish his life. That neither a premature death nor long life cause any doublemindedness, but one uses the cultivation of the person in waiting, is the truly correct learning of sages and virtuous men.[9] If a person deludes himself in the matter of physical immortality, it is evident that he is a mass of desire, sufficient in itself to injure the nourishing of virtue. (7)

---

[8] By this he means that he has had much experience in the matter under consideration.

[9] Mencius, Book VII, Pt. I, Ch. 1, ¶ 3.

Second Letter to Lu Yüan-ching [10]

Written in the first year of Emperor Chia Ching

Wang and His Disciples Are Accused of Heterodoxy

I am lacking both in filial piety and in faithfulness to my prince. I have brought this calamity upon my parent The extreme punishment (of Heaven) is not sufficient. That I have reached the point where I am judged by many, is quite as it should be. I have troubled you — the virtuous one — to the extent of wilfully offending you and of causing you to be disliked by others because of having contended for my innocence I have been the object of your love of reason and right For all this I am profoundly grateful to you. Verily this is not what I, a stupid orphan, dared to hope. Do not contend for my innocence, and their vilifying will cease Since I have already heard the instruction of former scholars, I should the more rest in this

Because of the differences in the discussions of heroes and leaders everywhere regarding learning, deliberations on, and discussions of, learning arose Can we fully analyze and discuss these things? We ought to change our method and seek within ourselves, whether perhaps what they say may be true, or may contain some things which we have not accepted Under such circumstances, we ought to seek for the actual facts and not get into the habit of considering ourselves right and others wrong. Should their words be wrong and we already have believed our own point of view, we should the more reach the place where we take a firm stand on that which is genuine. We should use this to seek humility within ourselves. This is in accordance with the saying, "Think it over and you will attain it, do not speak and you will believe it" Since there is so much talking about us, why are we not influenced to be patient, and why do we not mutually admonish

---

[10] Written after the death of Wang's father

and refine one another? Moreover, that we are criticised is certainly not because others privately harbor ill will against us, but because they guard the doctrine. Their sayings have originally come from the connected discourses of former scholars. Certainly each one of them has his evidence. Moreover, our words often differ from those of past scholars and appear to be empty and original. They do not know that the learning of the sages is from the beginning of that type, but drifting into tradition lose the truth itself.

Wang Lays Bare the Mistakes of Later Scholars, Admitting that He, too, Has Fallen Short of the Ideal

The discussions of earlier scholars have daily branched off more and more from the true learning, and later scholars have followed in the course of these practices and have multiplied their errors until they are very numerous. Since they have been perverse and have been harboring the thought of not believing, they are unwilling to make investigation with a receptive mind. Moreover, during discussion and criticism, perhaps having been overwhelmed by a desire to excel and by giddiness, we will not be able to avoid excess in our opposition and excitement. (8) Thus it is natural that they will either ridicule our views, or fear them and be suspicious of them. This reproof we cannot attribute wholly to their wrong doing. Alas! When we expound learning shall we strive to make our views either different from those of others or similar to them? Or shall we strive to use the good in overcoming others and in educating them? We have proclaimed with our lips only, the learning which exhibits the fact that knowledge and practice should be unified. Where have we really united knowledge and action? If we push the investigation in order to find out why, then a man like me must have heavy transgressions. Ordinarily we merely use words to explain the situation, but have never made an investigation of our own person. Prior to having extended his knowledge to the utmost, the individual says that the saying of former men, that knowledge should be extended to the utmost, cannot be exhausted. This may be compared to a poverty-stricken man who speaks about gold, but cannot resist following others and begging. Sir, our fault lies in mutually believing and loving one another to excess We love, but do not know the evils that are inherent therein. Consequently we have all brought about the present disorderly discussion. All this is due to my transgression.

Those Who at First Criticise May Later Believe

Although the superior men of the past were exhibited to the world as wrong, they paid no attention to the fact. Even though many generations considered them wrong, they did not heed it, for they sought only their own integrity. Could then the temporary slander of their name move their minds? But this point of view has not yet been fully established within us. How, then, can we consider what others say to be completely wrong? If I-ch'uan and Hui-an, in their time, were unable to avoid calumniation and abuse, what can we expect?[11] In our actions we often fall short, so that it is right that we bear calumniation and abuse. Scholars that wrangle and dispute about learning and its method in this day, certainly also have their purpose set on study. They cannot be said to be heterodox and consequently more than ordinarily remiss. All men have a mind which is able to discriminate between right and wrong.[12] But they are hindered through long-standing practices, and in consequence cannot easily analyze my learning. When first you, Sirs, heard me speak, did not some of you ridicule and slander my exposition? After a while you became enlightened through reflection, until you were influenced beyond what you should have been (9) How can I know that those who now

[11] Hui-an refers to the philosopher Chu *Vide* footnote 28, p 100.
[12] *Vide* Mencius Book VI, Pt. 1, Ch. 6, ¶ 7.

mutually criticise and oppose me will not later believe in me profoundly?

I am in the midst of mourning and weeping, so that this is not the time to discuss learning. However, the welfare of the truth does not permit me to cease thinking. Unconsciously, I have talked to this extent though my words have not developed the thought consecutively. Fortunately, you will make allowances for my intention. In Kiangsi I formerly fully discussed the saying, "extending knowledge to the utmost," with Wei-chün, Ch'ung-i, and my many friends. Recently Yang Ssu-ming visited me and I again discussed it very minutely. Now Yüan-ch'ung and Tsung-hsien are returning to you. Sirs, you should still mutually investigate this matter. There should be nothing abstruse left. Mencius says: "The mind which is able to discriminate between right and wrong has knowledge." [13] This is characteristic of all men and is what I call intuitive knowledge of good. Who lacks this intuitive knowledge? But the individual is unable to extend it to the utmost. The Book of Changes says: "If one knows the utmost one should attain it." He who knows the utmost really knows, and he who attains what he thus knows extends knowledge to the utmost. Thus knowledge and practice are a unity. Recently in speaking of investigating things in order to extend knowledge to the utmost, the matter of knowing is not emphasized and thus the task has not even been slightly touched. Thus knowledge and practice become two different things.

Comment — Not to grumble against men, is learning which sages and virtuous men naturally acquire. If the individual discusses right and wrong with others, it appears as though he were trying to influence all the world to consider his learning perfectly good. This implies that he does not fully understand the truth.

---

13 *Ibid.*

Third Letter to Lu Yüan-ching

Written in the third year of Emperor Chia Ching

Lu Complains that His Mind is Never Quiet and Tranquil

Your letter, which has come to hand, says "When I begin to work (study), I realize that my mind is not for a moment quiet and tranquil, but that the unmannerly, disorderly mind of a certainty begins to stir, and the mind which has regard for this condition also bestirs itself. Since the mind is constantly stirring in this way, it does not cease even temporarily." (10)

You are dominated by the purpose to seek tranquility, and for that reason the mind is the more unquiet The disorderly, unmannerly mind thus bestirs itself, but the mind which has regard for this does not really begin to be exercised If it constantly has regard for its condition, it will always be stirring and always be tranquil. Heaven and earth endure, and yet are always in motion and always tranquil The mind which has regard for its own condition surely cares for itself; and the disorderly, unmannerly mind also has regard for itself. They are not two things, and thus they do not rest. If it temporarily stops, it has stopped permanently, and has not reached the condition expressed in the words, "To entire sincerity there belongs ceaselessness." [14]

Intuitive Knowledge of Good Has No Beginning

Your letter further says, "Does intuitive knowledge of good also have a beginning?"

Perhaps you have heard this and have not yet investigated it. Intuitive knowledge of good is native to the mind and is to be identified with what I have above called the characteristic of having constant regard for itself. The original nature of the mind has no beginning, and yet it does not lack a beginning. Although disorderly thoughts

---

[14] Doctrine of the Mean, Ch. 26, ¶ 1.

are manifested, the intuitive knowledge of good has been present; but the individual does not know how to cherish and evaluate it, and thus there are times when it may be rejected. Though the mind is darkened and obstructed, the intuitive knowledge of good is clear. But the individual does not know how to observe it closely, and thus there may be times when it is concealed. Though there may be times when it is rejected, it has in reality not been absent. It should be cherished. Though there may be times when it is obscured, it really has not been unclear. It should be carefully scrutinized. If you say that the intuitive knowledge of good has a point at which it begins, that would imply that there are times when it is absent. This does not convey the idea of its being the mind's original nature.

Your letter makes the following inquiry: "Is the former discourse upon being discriminating (devoted to the essence) and undivided to be identified with doing the task of the sage?" [15]

The Task of the Sage Does Not Go Beyond Being Discriminating and Undivided

The character *ching* (精, meaning "unmixed" or "essence") of "devotion to the essence" (being discriminating), should be construed as referring to moral principles. The same word *ching* (meaning "essence"), of "mental essence" (energy), is to be construed as referring to the vital force. Heaven-given principles are the principles of the vital force. The vital force represents the functioning of the heaven-given principles. Without these principles there could be no functioning of the vital force, and without this functioning those things that are called principles could not be seen. Devotion to the essence (discrimination) implies mental energy and includes the manifesting of virtue. It signifies being undivided. It is mental energy and sincerity of purpose. Being undivided

---

[15] English and Chinese Shooking, Books of Yü, Book II, ¶ 15.

is devotion to the essence. It implies manifesting illustrious virtue. It is what is called being transformed.[16] It is being sincere in purpose. They are not originally two things. (11) But the sayings of the later scholars and of the Taoists are prejudiced in this one aspect, that they do not use them interchangeably. Though my former discussion of devotion to the essence and being undivided was occasioned by your desire to nourish your mental energy and animal spirits, the task of the sage does not go beyond this.

Your letter says that the original energy (spirit), the original temper (feeling), and the essence (germinating principle) have a place where they are stored up and from which they come forth. You further say that there is an essence (germinating principle) characteristic of the inferior (receptive) power, called Yin, and a temper (feeling) characteristic of the directing (forming) power of the universe, called Yang.

Wang Asserts the Unity of Yin and Yang

There is but one intuitive faculty. When reference is made to its wonderful use, it is called energy (spirit); when reference is made to its natural manifestations, it is called temper (feeling); when reference is made to its aggregated fulfillment, it is called essence (germinating principle). How can it be sought for in any form or image? The essence of the true Yin is the matrix of the temper of the Yang.[17] The temper of the Yang is the father of the essence of the true Yin. The Yin is the cause of the Yang, and the Yang is the cause of the Yin. They are really not two. In case my sayings regarding intuitive knowledge of good are understood, then such things as these are all explained without speaking about them. If

---

[16] Doctrine of the Mean, Ch. 23.

[17] The Yin is the inferior or receptive power of the dual powers of Chinese philosophy. The Yang is the superior or forming, directing power.

this is not understood, then, as your letter says, though the three organs of sense (ear, eye, voice) return to it seven times and again nine times, there still remain an infinite number of things that can be doubted.

Does Intuitive Knowledge of Good Exceed the Natural Functioning of the Mind?

Your letter says: "Intuitive knowledge of good is *ab initio* characteristic of the mind and is to be identified with the following: the virtuous disposition, the equilibrium of having no stirrings of feelings, the state of perfect tranquility, and the state of perfect fairness and impartiality. Why is it, then, that ordinary men are all unable to carry it out, but are obliged to wait until they have learned it? If the equilibrium, complete tranquility, and perfect fairness already belong to the mind, they may be identified with intuitive knowledge of good. As I today investigate these things in my own mind, I find that my intuitive knowledge at no point lacks goodness, but my mind lacks the equilibrium, the stillness, and the fairness. Does this imply that the intuitive faculty exceeds the natural functioning of the mind?" (12)

Wang Answers in the Negative

Since nature at no point lacks excellence, the intuitive faculty at no point lacks goodness. The intuitive knowledge of good is the state of equilibrium in which there are no stirrings of feelings, and this is the original nature of perfect fairness and tranquility. It has been prepared and provided for in the case of all men, but will under circumstances be darkened and obscured by desire. For this reason it is necessary to learn how to dispel any darkening or obscuring that has taken place. However, the original nature of the intuitive faculty from the very beginning cannot have the least added or taken away. Intuitive knowledge at no point lacks goodness. That the equilibrium, the tranquility, and the perfect fairness cannot be complete, implies that the darkness and dullness have not been entirely cleared away, and that what the mind has preserved is not pure. The original nature of the mind is the original nature of the intuitive faculty, and the functioning of this nature is the functioning of the intuitive faculty. How can there be any functioning beyond that of nature?

Can there be Activity and Tranquility of the Mind at the Same Time?

Your letter says: "The philosopher Chou said, 'Let tranquility and stillness be in control.' The philosopher Ch'eng said, 'Whether active or quiet, the mind should be fixed.' You say, 'The mind is *ab initio* fixed.' This implies that when the mind is at rest it is fixed; but it is not to be identified with the saying, 'Do not see, nor hear, nor think, nor act,' but with the saying, 'It always knows heaven-given principles, always cherishes them, and is always controlled by them.' This always knowing, always cherishing, and always being controlled by principles clearly implies that there is activity and that this is being manifested. How can this be called tranquility, or be spoken of as the original nature of the mind? Does this tranquility and fixedness also penetrate into and link up with the activity and tranquility of the mind?"

Principles are not subject to being affected or moved. He who always knows them, always cherishes them, and is always controlled by them, is said not to hear, see, think, or act. But this does not mean that he is dead and lifeless. If he sees, hears, thinks, and acts entirely in accordance with principles, but has had nothing with reference to which he sees, hears, thinks, or acts, there is activity present, but without excitement. In that state both the activity and the tranquility of the mind are fixed. Both are a source of its natural functioning.

Your letter says: "Is the condition of the mind, in

which it has no stirrings of the feelings, present prior to the condition in which stirrings of feeling have manifested themselves, or is it present in the condition in which the stirrings have been manifested but are controlled?[18] (13) Is the mind subject to the categories of time and space? Is it all one structure and substance? In speaking of the activity and the tranquility of the mind, are these in control both when one is occupied with affairs and when one is unoccupied? Does it mean that they are in control when the mind is at rest as well as when it is excited and stirred, when it obeys heaven-given principles as well as when it follows desire? If it is tranquil when it is in accord with principles, and active when it follows desire, it is at variance with the saying, 'In the midst of activity there is tranquility, and in the midst of tranquility there is activity. Though active in the highest degree, it is tranquil; though tranquil in the highest degree, it is active.' If it is considered as active when it is occupied and in a state of excitement, and as tranquil when it is unoccupied and at rest, it is then at variance with the saying, 'It is active and yet not stirred, tranquil and yet not at rest.' If one says that the state in which there are no stirrings of feeling precedes the state in which there have been stirrings of feeling, then tranquility begets activity; and this implies that to entire sincerity there belong times of resting (ceasing), and that the doctrine of the sages vacillates. This, of course, will not do. If one says that the state of no stirrings is in the midst of the state of having had stirrings of feeling, then I do not know whether both of these states are pervaded with tranquility or not. Is the state in which there are no stirrings of feeling to be considered as tranquility, and the state in which there are stirrings of feeling as activity of the mind? Are both to be considered as active and tranquil? I am under obligation to you for instruction.''

---

[18] Yang-ming considered the condition when there are no stirrings of feelings the natural condition of the mind.

The Intuitive Faculty is Not Subject to the Categories of Time and Space

The equilibrium in which there is no stirring of feeling is the intuitive faculty.[19] It is not subject to the categories of time and space, but is all one structure and substance. One may say that activity and tranquility refer to the times when the mind is occupied and unoccupied; but when reference is made to the intuitive faculty, no distinction is made between the mind's being occupied or unoccupied. The states in which the mind is at rest or is excited may be said to represent activity and tranquility; but when reference is made to the intuitive faculty, no distinction is made between the mind's being at rest and its being active. When the original nature of the mind experiences activity and tranquility, it really makes no distinction between them. Principles are not subject to being affected or moved, for those conditions indicate the presence of desire. If the mind acts according to principles, though amidst ten thousand changes of pledging between host and guest, yet it has not been affected; if it follows desire, though it appears to be free from it, yet whenever it has thought there has been no tranquility. Why should there be any doubt that the mind may be tranquil while it is active, and active while it is tranquil? It may be said that the mind is thoroughly moved (influenced) when it is occupied, yet its tranquility has not been decreased. One may really say that the mind is tranquil when it is at rest, yet its activity has not been decreased. Why should you doubt that the mind may be active and yet not excited, at rest and yet not tranquil? (14) It is a consecutive whole having no such attributes as the earlier and the later, the inner and the outer.

It is not necessary to explain your question regarding the saying, 'To entire sincerity there belongs stillness.' That the state in which there is no stirring of passion

---

[19] This faculty mediates intuitive knowledge of good.

should be included in the state in which there already has been stirring of passion, does not imply that in addition to this latter state there has been another condition, in which there has been no stirring of passion. Again, that the state of having had stirrings of feelings is included in the state of having no stirrings of feelings, does not imply that, in addition to this latter state, there is a state in which there has already been a stirring of the feelings. If there has been no condition in which activity and tranquility were absent, it is not possible to distinguish between activity and tranquility.

Tranquility from the Standpoint of the Yin and the Yang

Whoever reads the sayings of the ancients will get their meaning, if thought is used to meet the scope thereof. If the person adheres obstinately to the meaning of terms, then the sentence from the ode called ''The Milky Way''—
    ''Of the black-haired people of the remnant of Chou,
        There is not half a one left''— [20]
would imply that not one of the people of Chou was left. The saying of Chou, ''Extreme tranquility is activity,'' if not carefully considered, is mistaken. This idea has been expressed from the point of view that when the Great Monad moves, it brings forth Yang; and when it is quiet, it brings forth Yin. The principle of the continual begetting of the Great Monad is that its wonderful influences and activity do not cease and its substance does not change. The continual begetting of the Great Monad is the continual begetting of Yin and Yang. Thus in the continual begetting it shows that its wonderful influences and utility do not cease. This is called its activity — the begetting of the Yang. It does not mean that it was moved and thereafter brought forth Yang. In the continual begetting it shows that its substance does not change. This is called its state of tranquility — the begetting of the Yin. It does

---

[20] Mencius, Book V, Pt. I, Ch. 4, ¶ 3.

not mean that, having been tranquil, it thereafter brought forth Yin. If after being quiet it brings forth Yin, and after having been moved it brings forth Yang, then Yin and Yang, activity and tranquility, are separated and each represents a distinct thing. Yin and Yang are one vital force — the primordial aura. When this one vital force contracts and expands, it produces Yin and Yang respectively. Activity and tranquility are one principle. When this one principle is hidden and manifested, it results in activity and tranquility. Spring and summer may be considered as representing Yang and activity, but this does not mean that Yin and tranquility are lacking. Autumn and winter represent Yin and tranquility (rest), but not in the sense that Yang and activity are not present. Insofar as spring and summer, autumn and winter are unceasing, they are called Yang and active. When reference is made to their continued respective identity, they are called Yin and are said to be at rest. This is true of them all from the time of the first revolution (successive change) of the world — the seasons, the month, and the day, up to the quarters of hours, seconds, and tenths of seconds. (15) He who knows need only think, to realize what is meant by saying that motion and rest have no origin, and Yin and Yang no beginning. This cannot be exhausted by speaking. If one adheres closely to terms and sentences, and compares and imitates, then the mind follows in its motion the lead of modes and forms instead of itself creating.

Has the Intuitive Faculty a Vital Relation to the Feelings?

Your letter says: ''I continually test my own mind to find out the way in which I am affected by joy, anger, sorrow, and fear. Though I am exceedingly under their influence, nevertheless when my intuitive faculty once realizes it, these passions are stopped and forthwith cease. They may be checked at the beginning, or controlled while they are in progress, or changed at the end. However, it is as though the intuitive knowledge of good were present at the time when I am tranquil, at leisure, and unoccupied, and were in control then; but had no real, vital relation to joy, anger, sorrow, and fear.''

If you know this, you know that the equilibrium in which there is no stirring of feelings is the original form of tranquility. Moreover, you then have acquired the condition in which the feelings have been stirred, the harmony in which they act in their due degree, and the mystery of having them influenced and immediately perceived. However, there is still an error in your saying that it is as though the intuitive knowledge of good were present at the time when you are at leisure and unoccupied. Though the intuitive knowledge of good is not present in the state of joy, anger, sorrow, or fear, these are not outside the influence of the intuitive faculty.

The Relation of Intuitive Knowledge of Good to Caution and Apprehensiveness

Your letter says, ''The Master (referring to Wang) yesterday referred to the intuitive faculty as the thing that oversees the mind. I say that the intuitive knowledge of good is the original character of the mind, and that overseeing the mind is the task of the individual, consisting of being cautious and apprehensive. The overseeing of the mind is identical with thought. Is it permissible to identify this being cautious and apprehensive with the intuitive knowledge of good?''

It is permissible to identify the state of being cautious and apprehensive with intuitive knowledge of good.

The Disorderly Mind is Conscious of Its Condition

Your letter says: ''The Teacher further says that the overseeing mind is not moved. Is this tranquility due to the fact that it acts in accord with nature? The disorderly, unmannerly mind also oversees its condition. Is it because intuitive knowledge has been present within it and elucidated the situation, and because what at the time is seen, heard, said, and done, does not exceed rule or pattern, that all this is considered as being in accordance with natural law? (16) Having discussed the disorderly, unmannerly mind, you say that it has regard for its condition, and that from the point of view of the overseeing mind it is considered disorderly and unmannerly. What difference, then, is there between the disorderly mind and the mind at rest? Thus to connect the overseeing of the disorderly mind with the saying, 'To entire sincerity there belongs ceaselessness,' is something I do not understand. May you again instruct me in my ignorance!"

The mind which has regard for itself is not aroused, because it has a natural, clear realization of its original nature, and therefore has had no stirring of the feelings. As soon as stirring and excitement are present, it is disorderly and unmannerly. The disorderly mind also has regard for itself, because the natural clear realization of the original nature has been present. Whether it is stirred up and excited or tranquil, it has regard for itself. Lacking the disorderly element, it lacks also regard for it. But this does not imply that disorder is to be construed as carefulness, nor carefulness as disorder. The careful mind has regard for itself, and the disorderly mind is disorderly and unmannerly. It appears as though there were disorder and regard, but if both a disorderly and a circumspect mind were present, they would seem to be two different things. If they are two different things, then there must be periods of rest and cessation. If the mind cannot be disorderly without having regard for itself, there is but one; and if there is but one process, then it is unceasing.

The Pure Heart Guards Against Passion and Subdues It When It Appears

Your letter says: "In nourishing life, it is important to have a pure heart and few desires. A pure heart and few desires are the final accomplishment in becoming a sage.

However, if there are but few desires, the mind is naturally pure. By a pure mind is not meant that one casts aside business and, living secluded, seeks tranquility. If the individual desires to have his mind completely dominated by heaven-given principles, it cannot be encumbered with the least selfishness. If he desires to do this while he allows passion to come up, then, though he subdues it (passion), the root of the defect will be there continually, and he cannot prevent its cropping out in the west while it is being eradicated in the east. If he wishes to cut out, peel off, wash out, and dissipate all desires before they have sprouted, he has no point at which he can apply his strength, and will needlessly cause the mind to be unclear and unclean. Moreover, if he seeks for it in a vexatious, minute way, in order to banish it, the situation is similar to that in which one leads a dog into the guest hall and then drives it out again. This is even more unfeasible."

To desire to have the mind completely dominated by heaven-given principles and to be entirely free from the selfishness of passion, is doing the task of the sage. (17) But this is not possible, unless one guards against passion before it has sprouted, and subdues it at the time when it appears. To guard against it before it has sprouted, and subdue it at the time when it appears is what is meant by the "being cautious and apprehensive" of the Doctrine of the Mean and the "extending of knowledge to the utmost through investigation of things" of the Great Learning. There is no task beyond this. What you say regarding its cropping out in the west while it is being eradicated in the east, and regarding one who leads a dog into the guest hall and then drives it out again, shows that you have private motives and that you seek your own advantage. You welcome the perplexity of foregone conclusions and arbitrary pre-determinations, rather than the difficulty of controlling and cleaning out the passions. Now, as to what you have said regarding the necessity of purifying the mind and lessening the desires in order to nourish life, these two words, *yang seng* (養生, meaning "to nourish and foster life"), imply that private motive and the seeking of your own advantage are the source of your foregone conclusions and your arbitrary predeterminations. With this root of evil hidden in your mind, you should have the misfortune that when passion is eradicated in the east it crops out in the west, or that you drive the dog out after having brought it into the guest hall.

The Buddhists Do Not Understand the Original Nature of the Mind

Your letter says: "The position of the Buddhists, that the individual recognizes his original nature at the time when he reflects neither on good nor on evil, is at variance with our Confucian position, that one should investigate carefully all the things which one meets. We Confucianists devote ourselves to the task of extending knowledge to the utmost at the time when we think neither of good nor evil, and this has a real relation to the thinking of good. It is only at the time when one just awakens from sleep that one does not have any desire for good or evil, and the intuitive faculty is perfectly quiet and at ease (at rest). This is in accord with what Mencius says regarding the restorative influence of the night. But one is not long in that condition. Suddenly one realizes that solicitous thoughts have already arisen. I do not know whether he who has worked long at this task is continually in the condition of one who has just awakened from sleep and has desire neither for good nor for evil. The more I desire to seek tranquility, the less tranquil I am; and the more I desire to keep selfish thoughts from sprouting, the more they sprout. How can I cause the earlier thoughts to be obliterated, the later thought not to crop out, and intuitive knowledge of good alone to be manifested? How can I take pleasure in creating things?"

The position of the Buddhists, that they recognize the original nature at the time when they think neither of good nor of evil, shows that they do not understand the original nature. They may conveniently be viewed in this way. (18) The original nature is what we Confucianists call the intuitive faculty. Since you understand fully what the intuitive faculty is, I need not have spoken thus. To investigate whatever thing one happens upon is the task of extending knowledge to the utmost, and is identical with the constant realization of the Buddhists. It implies the constant cherishing of the original nature. The serially arranged tasks of both conceptions of nature are essentially alike, but the Buddhists have a mind which is dominated by private motives and seeks the advantages of the individual. Therefore there is some difference. Their desire to think of neither good nor evil and to make the mind pure, tranquil, and at ease, implies that they have selfish motives and seek their own advantage. They have a mind which welcomes foregone conclusions and arbitrary pre-determinations, and for this reason they emphasize the time when they think of neither good nor evil. Application to the task of extending knowledge to the utmost thus already has a real relation to being distressed with thinking about the good.

Since the Intuitive Faculty is by Nature Tranquil, It is Not Necessary to Seek Tranquility

What Mencius says about the restorative influence of the night, also has reference to the individual who has lost his intuitive knowledge of good; for he (Mencius) exhibits the point at which the intuitive faculty has its origin that, following this, it may be nourished and cultivated, and passion be expelled. Inasmuch as you understand the intuitive faculty and constantly devote yourself to extending knowledge, it should not be necessary for me to speak of the restorative influence of the night. However, after having taken the hare, you do not know how to keep it, but instead keep vigil over the stump, and in so doing again lose the hare. Your search for tranquility and your desire to keep disorderly thoughts from arising, show that private motives and desire for advantage are opening the way for foregone conclusions and arbitrary pre-determinations. Under such circumstances the more you think, the less tranquil you will be. There is but one intuitive faculty, which by its own nature discriminates between good and evil. What good and evil are there to think about? The intuitive faculty is by nature tranquil, but you have added the idea of seeking tranquility. The intuitive faculty naturally brings forth thoughts constantly, while you wish that it might not bring them forth. Not only is the task of extending knowledge as practiced by the Confucianists different from this, but the Buddhists themselves do not thus welcome foregone conclusions and arbitrary pre-determinations. Reflection regarding the intuitive faculty reveals the fact that its details are infinite. This implies that the earlier thoughts do not die, and that the later disorderly thoughts do not arise. You, however, desire that the earlier thoughts should die and that the later thoughts should not arise. This is what the Buddhists designate as destroying the germ (essence) of nature, and becoming lifeless and dead. (19)

Lu's Questions Show that He Does Not Fully Understand the Intuitive Faculty

Your letter says: "Is the saying of the Buddhists, constantly to bring one's thoughts to one's notice, to be identified with the saying of Mencius, 'There must be (constant) practice (of righteousness),' and with your saying, 'Extend the knowledge of good to the utmost'?[21] Is it to be considered as meaning constantly realizing, constantly remembering, constantly knowing, constantly cherishing the original nature of the mind? If I meet with affairs

---

[21] Mencius, Book II, Pt. I, Ch. 2, ¶ 16.

and things while a thought is kept before me, there must be some proper method of response. But perhaps these ideas are not often brought to notice and are frequently dissipated. Thereby true effort is interrupted. That these ideas are dropped is largely due to the influence of selfish desire and ceremoniousness. When I suddenly come to a full realization of this state, I later observe that they have been dropped. At the time that I do not bring them to my notice I am usually not conscious of the confused, disorderly condition of my mind. Since I desire to become daily purer and more intelligent, what method should I pursue in constantly keeping these thoughts before my notice? Would you consider the fact that they are constantly kept in view and not dropped as representing a task perfectly carried out? Or is it necessary, in the midst of cherishing and not dropping these, to add devotion to examining and controlling myself? I fear that I shall not be able to cleanse my mind from selfish desire, even though I constantly keep the thoughts before my mind, if, while doing so, I fail to be cautious and apprehensive and to control myself. If I am cautious and apprehensive and control myself, this should be construed as being solicitous about good affairs and thus lacking thorough acquaintance in one respect with the original nature. How can I find a way through this?"

This matter of being cautious and apprehensive and of controlling one's self is just what is meant by bringing one's thoughts to one's notice and not scattering them. It certainly means that one is occupied with affairs. Are there two separate things to be discriminated in this? The first portion of what you have asked about in this section you have yourself clearly explained; but with regard to the latter part, you have confused yourself. You have branched off until you have no doubt as to your thorough acquaintance with one aspect of your nature. This, however, is the defect of allowing private desire and private advantage to open the way for foregone conclusions and arbitrary predeterminations. If you will get rid of the root of this evil, you will get rid of the doubt.

Your letter says: "He whose natural ability is excellent may understand the intuitive faculty completely, and his disposition for evil will then be totally transformed and changed. Why should he be said to understand completely? In what way is his disposition for evil totally changed?"

The Intuitive Faculty Clears Away All Feculence

The intuitive faculty is by nature clear. He whose natural ability is not excellent cannot easily understand because of much feculence and heavy obscuration. He whose native disposition is excellent has originally little feculence and slight obscuration. (20) In case he devotes himself to extending knowledge to the utmost, his intuitive faculty will naturally clearly apprehend. As light snow cannot remain in hot water, so the little feculence that may be present cannot obscure the mind. This is not very difficult to understand. That you, Yüan-ching, should have doubts regarding this, I judge to be due to the fact that you do not fully comprehend, and perhaps desire to advance too rapidly. On a previous occasion I have discussed the matter of understanding virtue with you, saying that if you understand you will be sincere. This is not in accordance with what later scholars have said — that knowledge of good is not profound.

The Chief Characteristics of Nature

In your letter you make the following inquiry: "Are quick apprehension, clear discernment, far-reaching intelligence, and all-embracing knowledge, really native ability? Are benevolence, righteousness, propriety, and wisdom really native disposition? Are pleasure, anger, sorrow, and joy really passions? Are selfish desires and ceremoniousness really to be identified or not? In the instance of

the following and other talented men among the ancients —
(Chang) Tzu-fang. (Tung) Chung-shu, (Huang) Shu-tu
(Chu-ko) K'ung-ming, Wen Chung, Han (Ch'i), and Fang
(Chung-yen) — whatever virtuous instruction they gave,
all came from the intuitive faculty; and yet they were not
designated as having heard and perceived the truth. How
can this be? Supposing one says that they had exceptionally excellent native ability, would they not belong to those
who are born with knowledge and carry it out in practice
with natural ease, and thus do not need to learn by study
after a painful feeling of their ignorance and by strenuous
effort? According to my stupid idea, one may say that
these scholars merely emphasized one aspect, but to say
that none had heard would probably imply that later scholars had fallen into the excess of reverencing and emphasizing the matters of recording, recitation, instruction, and
comments. Am I correct in my judgment or not?''

There is one nature, and that is all. Charity, righteousness, propriety, and wisdom are by nature characteristic
of it; quick apprehension, clear discrimination, far-reaching intelligence, and all-embracing knowledge are native to
it. Pleasure, anger, sorrow, and joy are the passions (feelings) of this nature; selfish desire and ceremoniousness are
things that obscure it. The native ability may be either
clear or turbid. The passions may be manifested unduly
or insufficiently. Obscuration may be slight or profound.
Selfish desire and ceremoniousness are one disease with two
different types of pain, and should not be considered two
different things. Chang (Tzu-fang), Huang (Shu-tu),
Chu-ko (K'ung-ming), Han (Ch'i), and Fang (Chung-
yen) were all men of excellent native ability who naturally
acted in accordance with the mystery of the doctrine.
Though one cannot assert positively that they were born
with a knowledge of learning or that they perceived the
truth, they naturally had their degree of learning and
did not depart far from the truth. In case they heard the

learning and thus knew the doctrine, they belong to the class of I (Ying), Fu (Yueh), Chou (Kung), and Shao (Kung) [22] Of Wen Chung-tzu one also cannot say that he did not know learning. His books were written mostly by his own disciple, and contain many things that are not correct; but his general trend of thought can be understood from them. (21) However, since we have long passed his time, we lack substantial evidence and cannot definitely decide just what he had attained

All Men Have Intuitive Knowledge of Good, but It May Be Obscured

The intuitive knowledge of good is to be identified with the path of duty (truth), and this knowledge is in the minds of men   Not only the sages and virtuous men, but also ordinary men are thus gifted   If selfish desire of things has not arisen to obscure the mind, and it (the mind) manifests itself and acts in accordance with intui-tive knowledge, everything that transpires will be in accordance with the path of duty.   In the case of the common people, the mind is often obscured by a desire for things, so that it cannot act in accordance with the dictates of the intuitive faculty.   Since the native ability of the men mentioned above was pure and clear, and had not been much obscured by the desire for things, they naturally had real knowledge and did not depart from the truth, in so far as their intuitive faculty manifested itself and came to fruition   If the student learns only that which is in accord with the intuitive faculty, he is said to have learned through study, but he knows only that which is in accord with the intuitive faculty   If the men mentioned above did not know how to devote themselves to the intuitive knowledge of good alone, but drifted beyond the bounds of the intuitive faculty into divergent views and

[22] Sages of the Shan and the Chou dynasties, who lived about 1154-1122 B.C

were confused and befooled by shadows and echoes, they either departed from the doctrine, or at any rate were not completely in accordance with it. At the time that they had intuitive knowledge of good they were sages. Later scholars held that these philosophers all acted in accordance with their natural ability, and that they could not do otherwise than manifest and investigate the truth. This also should not be considered as putting it too strongly. However, concerning those who they say manifested and investigated the truth, later scholars were inclined to be narrow in what they heard and saw. They were obscured by habitual practices, and in accordance with their determination resembled each other in the matter of confining themselves to shadows and forms. This is not what the sages mean by manifesting and investigating. Could they use their own ignorance in examining the intelligence of others? The two characters, *chi* (知, meaning ''knowledge'') and *hsing* (行, meaning ''practice''), of ''being born with knowledge and practicing them with ease,''[23] are said with reference to using one's faculties. If the original character of knowledge and practice has reference to intuitive knowledge and practice of good, then, though it be an individual who acquires the knowledge after painful feeling of ignorance and practices by strenuous effort,[24] he may still be said to have been born with knowledge and practice with ease. The two characters, *chi* and *hsing*, should be more carefully investigated.

Did the Joy of Confucius Have Its Roots in the Seven Passions?

Your letter says: ''Formerly Chou Mou-shu frequently ordered Po-shun to find the places where Chung-ni and Yen-tzu were pleased.[25] I venture to ask whether this

---

[23] Doctrine of the Mean, Ch. 20, ¶ 9.

[24] *Ibid.*

[25] Chou Mou-shu was the teacher of the philosopher Chen (Po-shun); Chung-ni is a name given to Confucius.

pleasure is to be considered as the pleasure of the seven passions.[26] (22) If they are the same, then ordinary individuals by giving rein to their desires can all have pleasure. Why should it take a sage or a virtuous man? If, in addition to this, there is a genuine joy, then is that joy present when the sage and virtuous man meet with great sorrow, great anger, great terror, and great fear? Moreover, since the mind of the superior man is continually cautious and apprehensive and is continually in sorrow, how does he get joy? I am nearly always depressed in spirit; I have not yet acquired the experience of true joy. I wish I might experience it."

Joy is an original characteristic of the mind. Though this joy is not to be identified with the pleasure of the seven passions, it is not a joy over and beyond the joy of the seven passions. Though sages and virtuous men may have another true joy, ordinary people have it in common with them, but are not conscious of it. They bring upon themselves a great deal of sorrow and affliction, and increase their confusion and their self-abandonment. Even in the midst of sorrow, affliction, confusion, and self-abandonment, this joy is harbored in the heart. As soon as their thoughts have been cleared so that the person is sincere, this joy is at once apparent. In discussing this matter with you, Yüan-ching, I have had no other idea. That you still have things to inquire about, is as though you were not able to get rid of the defect of seeking the donkey while riding it.

Your letter says: "According to the Great Learning, the mind cannot be rectified if it is under the influence of fond regard, of passion, of sorrow and distress, of terror.[27] The philosopher Ch'eng said: 'Since the sage's feelings are easy and rhythmical in all things, he has no passion.' As concerns him who has the passions, in 'The Instruc-

---

[26] Joy, anger, sorrow, fear, love, hatred, desire.
[27] Great Learning, Ch. 7, ¶ 1.

tions for Practical Life' (Ch'uan Hsi Lu) the figure of one stricken with malaria is used to explain this minutely and exactly. If the philosopher Ch'eng's saying is accurate, then the passion (feeling) of the sages is not begotten in the mind but has reference to things. How is this to be construed? Moreover, when things influence the mind and the passion responds thereupon, right and wrong can be investigated. In case one says that the passions are present before the mind has been influenced by things, they have no real form; and if one says they are not there, then the root of evil is present in their absence. How can I extend my knowledge to the utmost under such circumstances? If study lacks the seven passions (feelings), though the embarrassment be light, one has nevertheless left the class of scholars and entered that of the Buddhists. What do you think of this?'' (23)

The Intuitive Faculty Gives Accurate Information on Matters of Truth

The sage's effort at extending his knowledge to the utmost is characterized by entire sincerity and ceaselessness. His intuitive faculty is as bright as a clear mirror and is not dimmed in the least. Whether a handsome or an ugly woman comes, in accordance with the object presented the image will be manifested, but no taint is left on the clear mirror after she has gone. This signifies that the feelings are easy and rhythmical in all things, and that there is no passion. That the passions have no place of abode but are begotten in the mind, has been said by the Buddhists, and this should not be considered wrong. The clear mirror responds to the object. If handsome, the reflection is handsome; if ugly, it is ugly. That every reflection is true to the object shows that the feelings are begotten in the mind. That the handsome reflection of the handsome woman and the ugly reflection of the ugly woman pass away and do not remain shows that they have no abiding place. If you have clearly grasped the simile of the man stricken with malarial fever, you will be able to understand what you have asked in this section. In the case of the man who has malaria, the root of the disease is present though the fever has not appeared. Shall the patient neglect to take the medicine which has been prescribed? If he does not take the prescribed medicine until after the fever has appeared, it will be too late. No discrimination should be made between a time of leisure and one of affairs in the matter of extending knowledge. Why should one discuss whether or not the disease has appeared? In general, the things that you, Yüan-ching, are in doubt about, though there may be differences, all spring from the fact that your private purposes and your striving for personal advantages arise from foregone conclusions and arbitrary predeterminations. When this has been eradicated, what you are first and last in doubt about will melt as ice and disappear as a fog, and will not wait until you have made inquiry and discussed it.

Comment — The condition in which one's own private motives and gain open the way for foregone conclusions and arbitrary predeterminations shows that there is anxious excessive thinking present in the matter of seeking virtue. Those below the very virtuous are of necessity like this. Yüan Hsien was suffering from this embarrassment when he asked Confucius the question: "When love of superiority, boasting, resentments, and covetousness are repressed, may this be deemed perfect virtue?"[28] Confucius answered him saying: "(This may be regarded as the achievement of what is difficult.) But I do not know that it is to be deemed perfect virtue."[29] This implies that he instructed him to devote his energies to that which is difficult. Why point out that this is virtue? If the individual desires to get rid of this embarrassment, it will dis-

[28] Analects, Book XIV, Ch. 2, ¶ 1.
[29] *Ibid.*, ¶ 2.

appear, if, as in the case of Yen Tzu, he subdues himself and returns to propriety.[30]   (24)

Letter to Lu Yüan-ching

Written in the eleventh year of Emperor Cheng Te

Wang Advises Lu to be More Careful and Systematic in His Study

I have received your letter.   I know that your disease is cured again, and am exceedingly glad.   In your letter you make diligent inquiry about learning because you fear that you may lose it or allow it to crumble into ruins.   This is sufficient to make me know that your determination to advance in virtue and to cultivate it is not lax.   Because of this I am also very much pleased.   Toward whom except you shall I look to exhibit this doctrine in the future, so that later generations may arise and prosper because of it? I had already prepared a rough copy of the notes on the Great Learning and the Doctrine of the Mean; but since what I had produced was not perfectly good, I was not able to avoid the defect of devoting myself to external things and of desiring that it be done quickly.   Thereupon I burned it.   Recently, though I realize that I have some idea of advancing in virtue, I cannot venture to say that I have attained the highest excellence.   To reach that goal I shall wait until some future time.

Of my discussions with my disciples concerning the means of attaining the highest excellence, no record has been kept.   The general purpose of it I surely have already expressed on ordinary occasions for the sake of Ch'ing Po.   Therefore you should the more investigate, for you ought to see it yourself.   If you seek this too eagerly, you may not be able to avoid your former disease. The saying regarding extensive study I have formerly carefully explained.   How am I to interpret it, that you now

---

[30] *Ibid.*, Book XII, Ch. 1, ¶ 1.

seem to bring it forward again? This also would seem to show that your purpose is not firmly fixed and that you are embarrassed by ordinary habits. In case I truly have a mind that does not covet honor and gain, then, though I devote myself to the making of money, or the raising of rice, to military equipments, or to carrying wood and water, what is there that does not involve genuine learning, and what affair is there that does not imply heaven-given principles? How much more is this true if I devote myself to the books of the sages and virtuous men, or to history, or to poetry, or to essay-writing, or to similar things! If I still cherish a mind that covets honor and gain, then, though I daily speak of virtue, benevolence, and righteousness, it is all a thing of merit and gain. How much more is this true in the case of the books of the philosophers, history, poetry, essay-writing, and similar things! All sorts of sayings regarding the necessity of expelling the desire for merit and gain are firmly embedded in old habits. Because in expending your efforts you do not appear to develop strength and power, I say to you: Rid yourself of your vulgar, plebeian ideas and return to your former purpose. If you think of the comparison of daily drinking, eating, and cultivating the person, and of the comparison I made regarding the planting, cultivating, and watering of the tree, you will understand the saying, "Things have their root and branches; affairs have their end and their beginning. To know what is first and what is last will lead near to what is taught." [31] You speak as though you did not understand the real object of the end and the beginning, the root and the branches. This means that you do not follow the natural order of root and branches, the beginning and the end, and that you wish to use your private purpose in order to complete the task.

---

[31] Great Learning, Introduction, ¶ 3.

Answer to a Letter from Shu Kuo-yung (25)

Written in the second year of Emperor Chia Ching

Shu Makes Satisfactory Progress in Study and is Urged Not to Assist the Growth

Your letter, which I have received, is sufficient to show that you have an earnest purpose in your study. The ordinary student is distressed because he does not know the underlying principles of study, or if he knows these principles he is distressed because he lacks real earnestness of purpose. Since you, Kuo-yung, know the underlying principles of learning and are also able to fix your purpose thus earnestly, who can hinder your advance? What few things there are in regard to which you are in doubt, all arise from the fact that you are not perfectly familiar with the task, and that you desire to hasten the growth. If you use your purpose to get rid of this desire to assist the growth, and daily advance in an orderly, methodical way, you ought to reach the goal. The things regarding which you formerly had doubt will be dissipated as the melting of ice. Why wait for my remarks? The pleasant or disagreeable taste of food should be recognized by him who eats, for another person cannot accurately inform him.

The few things regarding which you are in doubt have of late been continually doubted by those of your companions who have a common purpose with you. I have not yet told them, but today I speak for your sake. You say that an increase of self-poise and carefulness entails the embarrassment of losing freedom, and that one is self-poised and careful because of the application of his purpose. You ask how anyone can be self-poised and careful without being aware of it. How can these qualities come of themselves, so that a person does not have any doubt regarding his actions? All of these involve what I call the defect of desiring to assist the growth.

What the Self-poise and Carefulness of the Superior Man Signify

What the superior man means by being self-poised and careful is not what is meant by being under the influence of terror, sorrow, and distress, but by being cautious with reference to that which is not seen, and apprehensive with reference to that which is not heard.[32] The saying of the superior man regarding freedom does not carry with it the connotation of the swaggering and dissipation implied in giving rein to the seven passions and in acting unscrupulously. It means that the mind is not embarrassed by desire and that the individual can find himself in no situation in which he is not himself.[33] The mind is by very nature the embodiment of heaven-given principles; and the clear, intelligent realization of these principles is what is meant by intuitive knowledge. The cautiousness and apprehensiveness of the superior man is probably due to his clear, intelligent preception. If there is anything that obscures or tends toward dissipation, it degenerates into self-abandonment, moral deflection, depravity, and recklessness, so that the correctness of the original nature is lost. If the cautiousness and apprehensiveness of the superior man is never interrupted, heaven-given principles will be constantly cherished. (26) Moreover, in him who clearly and intelligently perceives and realizes heaven-given principles, the original nature is free from defect or obscuration. No selfish desire intervenes to annoy and give trouble. There is nothing present because of which the mind is either in dread, or in sorrow and distress, or because of which it is under the influence of fond regard or of passion, or with reference to which it has foregone conclusions and arbitrary predeterminations, obstinacy and egoism, or because of which it is discontented or ashamed. But it (the original nature) is clear and bright. Filled and satiated, it mani-

---

[32] Great Learning, Ch. 7, ¶ 1; Doctrine of the Mean, Ch. 1, ¶ 3.
[33] *Vide* Doctrine of the Mean, Ch. 14, ¶ 2.

fests itself in such a way that all the movements, of the countenance and of every turn of the body, are exactly adjusted. They carry out the desires of the mind, but not to excess. This is what is meant by truly dropping one's dignity and being untrammelled and self-contained.

Such a condition is begotten out of a constant cherishing of heaven-given principles, and the constant cherishing of heaven-given principles is begotten when cautiousness and apprehension are uninterrupted. Who would say that an increase of self-poise and carefulness involves the embarrassment of losing one's freedom? Such an individual fails to know that freedom is original to the mind, and that self-poise and carefulness are manifestations of freedom. To distinguish them as two things, and thus divided to use the mind, causes mutual opposition. As soon as there is much opposition, one drifts into a desire to assist the growth materially. Thus, what you designate as self-poise and carefulness is what the Great Learning means by terror, sorrow and distress, and not what the Doctrine of the Mean describes as being cautious and apprehensive. The philosopher Ch'eng always said that what people thought of as lacking purpose really could be said to connote the absence of a selfish mind and not the loss of mind. To be cautious regarding that which one has not seen, and apprehensive regarding that which one has not heard, shows that there must be purpose present. To be under the influence of dread, sorrow and distress implies that there must be selfish purpose present. The cautiousness and fearfulness of Yao and Shun, and the carefulness and respectfulness of Wen Wang signify self-poise and carefulness. They spontaneously arise out of the original nature of the mind, and are not manifested because of any special reason. Self-poise and carefulness make no distinction between activity (excitement) and rest (tranquility). Self-poise is for the purpose of rectifying the mind, and righteousness for the purpose of correcting the conduct. When both self-poise and righteousness have been fixed, the heaven-appointed way will be open, and there will be no doubt concerning the individual's conduct. In all that you have written, the underlying idea is correct. You may use this to encourage yourself, but certainly not to reprove others. The superior man does not seek the confidence of others; for if he has confidence in himself, that is enough. He does not seek notoriety or popularity: if he knows himself, that is enough. Because I have not completed my father's grave and am exceedingly occupied with affairs, and your messenger waits for the reply, I have written in a careless, incoherent manner. (27)

Comments — The character *ching* (敬, meaning "self-poised, respectful, reverent") signifies that the sages and virtuous men understand thoroughly from first to last. The caution and fear of Yao and Shun; the reverence for his resting-places of Wen Wang; the learning without satiety and instructing others without being wearied, of Confucius; the accumulation of righteous deeds, of Mencius; all are connoted by this one character *ching*.[34] They naturally emerge out of the original nature of the mind and are not a forced growth. This is what is meant by self-poise and carefulness, by dropping one's dignity and being self-contained. It does not mean that one becomes self-contained by being cautious and apprehensive. The respectfulness and ease of the Master (Confucius) was of that type.[35]

Second Letter to Huang Mien-chih

Written in the third year of Emperor Chia Ching

After you left me, my wife became more ill, while I myself continued to be afflicted with a cough and with diarrhoea. I have not been free from them for a day. Moreover, I was so engrossed in business that I could not reply. Referring to the use of the original text of the

---

[34] Great Learning, Ch. 3, ¶ 3; Analects, Book VII, Ch. 2; Mencius, Book II, Part I, Ch. 2, ¶ 15.

[35] *Vide* Analects, Book VII, Ch. 37.

Great Learning, I have had no opportunity to express myself in writing, and thereby I have done an injustice to your exceedingly diligent purpose. However, I will gradually exhibit this. The difficulty is that I have only the text itself in mind and am not always able to explain it adequately. Because of this I am troubled. I really have no time to answer the questions you ask. However, when I see the exceeding sincerity you display at the close of your letter, I can but speak.

Huang Gives a Clear Statement of the Chief Characteristics of the Intuitive Faculty

Your letter says: "He who allows the instruction of the intuitive faculty to nourish the mind will realize that he is fully acquainted with activity and tranquility, with day and night, with the ancient past and the present, with life and death. There is nothing with which the intuitive faculty does not make one acquainted. It is not necessary to deliberate in the least, nor is it necessary to assist its development in any way, for it is very trustworthy and perfectly clear. When it is stimulated it responds, and when it is influenced it perceives clearly. There is nothing that it does not make clear, nothing that it does not realize, nothing that it does not apprehend. All the sages have traversed this road, all the virtuous men have followed this track. There is nothing else that is like a spirit, for it is the spirit; nothing else emulates Heaven, for it is Heaven; nothing else is more in accordance with the Supreme Ruler, for it is the Supreme Ruler. (28) It is by nature in a state of equilibrium and always perfectly just; is always characterized by reciprocity and is never excited; is always unoccupied and yet one never sees it at rest; is truly the spiritual, intelligent substance of Heaven and earth, and the mysterious, wonderful manifestation of man. I consider that the intelligence of the sincere man of the Doctrine of the Mean is to be interpreted as the intelligence of the intuitive faculty, and that the cautiousness and apprehensiveness of the sincere man implies that the intuitive faculty is cautious and apprehensive.[36] They should be considered as belonging to the intuitive faculty as well as the feeling of commiseration (at seeing a child fall into a well) and the feeling of shame and dislike [37] It is the intuitive faculty that experiences and knows caution, apprehension, commiseration, shame, and dislike, and that is intelligent ''

In this section you have discussed the matter clearly and in detail If you know this, you know that there is no further task before you than that of extending intuitive knowledge to the utmost Knowing this, you understand the saying, ''He sets them (his institutions as ruler) up before Heaven and earth and finds nothing in them contrary to their mode of operation He presents them before spiritual beings, and no doubts about them arise He is prepared to wait for the rise of a sage a hundred years after, and he has no misgivings.''[38] You will understand that this is not mere talk Intelligence is the product of sincerity, and cautiousness and apprehensiveness are the products of the intuitive faculty They do not connote two different things Having become thoroughly acquainted with the fact that activity and tranquility, death and life, all connote this one thing, how can any other thing take the place of developing intelligence from sincerity, and effecting cautiousness and apprehension, and the feelings of commiseration, shame, and dislike?

Are Joy and Delight Native to the Mind?

Your letter says   ''When the powers of the Yin and Yang move back and forth rhythmically and are spread harmoniously, they bring forth all things (the universe). The begetting and growing of things all emanate from this

---

[36] *Vide* Doctrine of the Mean, Ch. 21

[37] *Vide* Mencius, Book II, Pt. I, Ch. 6, ¶ 4.

[38] Doctrine of the Mean, Ch. 29, ¶ 4.

harmonious spreading of the vital force. Therefore, the principle of the development of the human being naturally spreads itself harmoniously, and there is nothing with reference to which it does not manifest joy. When a man sees the hawk fly, the fish leap, the bird call, the animal play, the plants joyously reviving, he is joyous with them all. But because of ceremoniousness and desire for things, this harmonious spreading of the vital force is influenced, and having been interrupted is no longer joyous. In saying, 'Is it not pleasant to learn with a constant perseverance and application!' Confucius laid the foundation of an uninterrupted task.[39] Pleasure is the first rising (sprouting) of joy. When friends come (to learn of me) learning is completed, and the joy of one's original nature has been reinstated. It is for this reason that he says, 'Does it not make me joyful to have friends come from a distant place?'[40] Though others do not know me, I do not permit the least irritation to intercept the joy and delight of my nature. (29) The sage (Confucius) feared that the delight of the students might be interrupted, and therefore said this. There are the sayings: 'I do not murmur against Heaven; I do not grumble against men'; 'With coarse rice to eat, with water to drink, and my bended arm for a pillow, I have still joy in the midst of these things'; and 'He did not allow his joy to be affected by it.'[41] Do not all these imply uninterrupted joy and delight?''

Joy and delight are native to the mind. The mind of the man of the highest virtue considers heaven, earth, and all things as one; and the rhythmical moving back and forth,

---

[39] Analects, Book I, Ch. 1, ¶ 1.

[40] *Ibid.*, ¶ 2.

[41] *Ibid.*, Book XIV, Ch. 37, ¶ 2; Book VII, Ch. 15; Book VI, Ch. 9. The complete saying is: ''Admirable indeed was the virtue of Hui! With a single bamboo dish of rice, a small gourd dish of drink, and living in his mean narrow lane, while others could not have endured the distress, he did not allow his joy to be affected by it.''

and the harmonious spreading (of the Yin and Yang) continue without interruption.

Your letter says: "The principle of the development of the human being naturally manifests itself harmoniously and engenders delight in all things. But because of ceremoniousness and desire for things, the harmonious spreading of the vital force is interfered with, and having been interrupted fails to bring joy."

This is correct He who studies with a constant perseverance seeks to reinstate the original nature of the mind. In delight, this is gradually restored When friends come (to learn), the rhythmical moving back and forth and the regular harmonious spreading of nature are complete and uninterrupted — its original condition. From the beginning nothing has been added to it, and thus it follows that if no friends come and nobody knows me, nothing will have been subtracted. What your letter says regarding its being uninterrupted is correct Even being a sage implies no more than uninterrupted sincerity with concomitant constant application The important thing about constant application is watchfulness over one's self when alone Such watchfulness over one's self when alone implies extending intuitive knowledge to the utmost, which is the real nature of delight. This, in general, is also correct, but the individual should not be obstinate with reference to anything

Does Love Include Perfect Virtue?

Your letter says: "In general, I consider Han Ch'ang-li correct when he said: 'Universal love is the perfect virtue ' I do not know why the scholars of the Sung Dynasty said that he was wrong, and considered love as related to passion, and perfect virtue as related to nature.[42] How can love be considered as the highest virtue? My idea is that nature is to be identified with the condition in which the

---

[42] Referring to the teaching of the philosopher Chu.

seven passions have not been manifested, and the seven passions with the condition in which nature has manifested itself. Perfect virtue is love not manifested; love is perfect virtue manifested. Why should not love be used for perfect virtue? In saying love, perfect virtue is included. Mencius said: 'The feeling of commiseration is perfect virtue.'[43] The philosopher Chou said: 'Love is perfect virtue.' The words of Ch'ang-li are not very different from the ideas involved in Mencius and Chou. (30) One must not neglect him because he is a literatus.''

Wang Says that Love of Right is the Perfect Virtue

The saying regarding universal love is originally not very different from the idea of Mencius and the philosopher Chou. Fan Ch'ih made inquiry regarding the perfect virtue, benevolence. The Master said: "It is to love all men."[44] Why should not the word *ai* (愛, meaning "love") be considered as having the same meaning as *jen* (仁, meaning "perfect virtue" or "benevolence"). The former scholars in estimating the words of the ancients often manifested prejudice against various kinds of persons.[45] This is one such instance. Moreover, the original nature of love may surely be said to be perfect virtue. But there is a love of the evil as well as of the right. If the original nature of love is that of love of right, love can be called the perfect virtue (benevolence). If one knows only universal love, but does not say whether it is love of good or evil, a mistake is involved. I have said that the character *po* (博, meaning "universal, general") is not as exhaustive as the character *kung* (公, meaning "just, equitable"). In general, the explanation of the meaning of a character is only approximate. The detailed, wonderful ideas conveyed are reached through

[43] *Vide* Mencius, Book II, Pt. I, Ch. 6, ¶ 5.
[44] Analects, Book XII, Ch. 22, ¶ 1.
[45] "Former scholars" refers particularly to the philosopher Chu.

reflection. They cannot be explained by talking. Later scholars adhere obstinately to the style and emphasize the form and appearance. Seeking to find the meaning only from the characters themselves, their mind follows in its motion the lead of modes and forms.

Huang Asks for Further Information Regarding Love

Your letter says: "The Great Learning says: 'As when one loves what is beautiful and hates whatever has a bad smell.' [46] Referring to the hating, one can say that whenever an evil is perceived, one always despises it. Surely this offers no difficulty. When we come to the matter of always loving what is beautiful, then the question arises as to whether we should love every beautiful thing that passes our eyes. The instruction of the Great Learning makes use of man's constant inclination to drift into the habit of loving and despising, in order to make clear the sincerity of the sages' love of the good and their hatred of evil. Perhaps it implies that sages and virtuous men also love what is beautiful. Does it imply that when beauty passes their eyes, though they know its winsome, captivating nature, their thoughts are free from any obliquity, and the original nature of the mind is not in the least embarrassed? The Book of Poetry says that if a man says that a woman is as the cloud, he knows her beauty, but does not cherish that thought. To say that he does not cherish that thought implies that his thoughts are sincere and do not embarrass the original nature of his mind. Or it is as though one sees a chariot, a crown, gold, and precious stones, and knows what they are, yet has neither desire nor longing for them. (31) I do not know whether I understand this clearly or not."

---

[46] Great Learning, Ch. 6, ¶ 1. The complete quotation is: "What is meant by making the thoughts sincere is the allowing of no self-deception, as when we hate a bad smell and as when we love what is beautiful."

Wang Says that True Love Involves Sincerity

In ordinary loving and hating there is perhaps at times lack of real genuineness. But loving what is beautiful and hating evil odors, are in every instance manifestations of the real mind. When one seeks rapid fulfilment of one's desires, there is not the least hypocrisy. The Great Learning makes use of an easily comprehended illustration of genuine love and hate, in order to show what the sincerity of loving good and hating evil should be like. It is done merely for the sake of expressing the meaning of sincerity. If to the love of the beautiful you add a great many of your own ideas, you will not be able to avoid the defect of mistaking the fingers for the moon. Many former scholars were influenced and their minds obscured by a single word or sentence, and reached the point where they gave wrong expositions of the holy classics. This is the same sort of defect and must be investigated. When you say that we always despise an evil odor and that this point surely offers no difficulty, you are subject to error. You should investigate this more thoroughly.

Did Confucius Carry on Reflection to Excess?

Your letter says: "There are those that desire to cease all reflection because it is said that Pi Wen-ch'ing's excessive reflection did violence to his passion nature. Shall I also hold that Confucius carried on reflection to excess and did violence to his passion nature, when he says, 'I have been the whole day without eating, and the whole night without sleeping in order that I might think'? [47] As I apprehended it, reflection beyond one's intuitive knowledge of good is called reflection to excess. If one very thoughtfully seeks for explanation within the realm of the intuitive faculty — just as Confucius reflected all day and all night — he is not carrying on reflection to excess. If one

---

[47] Analects, Book XV, Ch. 30.

does not exceed the bounds of the intuitive faculty, how can there be excess of reflection or anxiety?''

To say that excessive reflection implies doing violence to one's passion nature is correct. But if, prompted thereby, one desires to cease reflection altogether, it is as though one put aside food because of a stoppage in the throat. You have laid hold completely of my idea when you write, ''Reflection beyond one's intuitive knowledge of good is called reflecting to excess. If one very thoughtfully seeks for explanation within the realm of the intuitive faculty — just as Confucius reflected all day and all night — this is not carrying on reflection to excess. If one does not exceed the bounds of the intuitive faculty, what is there to reflect upon or be anxious about?'' (32) As regards the saying of Confucius: ''I have been the whole day without eating, and the whole night without sleeping: occupied with thinking. It was of no use. The better plan is to learn,'' it is not likely that the sage himself really did this. He said this to show the defect of merely thinking without learning. He did it to instruct others. If he only reflected and did not learn, why not say that he carried on reflection to excess?

Comment — The man (Pi Wen-ch'ing) knew that his nature was being obscured by something — that he was striving for things and that his nature was changed thereby. When his learning had reached the point where he had extended his intuitive knowledge to the utmost, all his actions were in harmony with the path of duty. He then constantly practiced this doctrine, and friends came because of it. That he felt no discomposure when men did not know him, is due to this. Perfect virtue and love of nature, love of the good and hatred of evil, reflection and anxiety are all due to this. If one really knows how to attain to a condition in which intuitive knowledge is extended to the utmost, all other things will be arranged in a satisfactory manner.

Letter Answering Chou Tao-t'ung

(First Letter)

Written in the third year of Emperor Chia Ching

Two of Chou Tao-t'ung's Students Deliver a Letter to Wang and Confer With Him

Your two students, Wu and Tseng, have arrived and have spoken about your (Tao-t'ung's) earnest purpose in studying the doctrine. I am much comforted in thought. A man like you can be said to be sincerely faithful and to love learning. I regret that because of illness I have not been able to discuss matters in greater detail with the two students, but they also continue to purpose devoting themselves to learning. Whenever I see them, I at once realize that they have made progress. I cannot disregard the fact that they have come a great distance, and that they, too, perhaps remember their purpose in coming so far. As they were about to depart, they made use of your letter in informing me of your wishes, and asked me to write to you. But I am in such a mental confusion that I cannot express myself. Because of the inquiries you make in your letter, I will undertake to write a short reply. This is but a very rough sketch, which gives nothing in detail. Your two students will be able to give you details.

Chou Asserts that Discussion is Essential to Progress in Learning

Your letter says: "As I have daily applied myself only to fixing my determination, I have recently become more and more certain regarding your admonitions and instructions. However, it is necessary that I discuss it with friends, for thus my purpose becomes firm, capacious, and active. In case from three to five days elapse without the opportunity of mutually discussing it with friends, my purpose becomes small and weak. (33) If I meet any affairs under such circumstances, I am apt to be in difficulty or even to forget my purpose entirely. However, if I meet with these on a day when there are no friends to discuss it with me, and I sit quiet and read or move about, knowing that when I look at anything or use my body I use this to cultivate my purpose (will), then I realize fully that my purpose has reached a condition of harmony. But it does not compare with the time in which I discuss learning as related to the actual purpose of making progress and of developing. Since I have left my many friends and live isolated, what better method is there of accomplishing this?''

Wang Advises Chou to Continue Fixing His Determination and to Adjust Himself to Circumstances

This section is sufficient to verify what you get out of your daily work. This, in general, is the way to proceed. However, there should be no interruption. When you have reached a point where this attitude is perfect and habitual, your ideas will be different. Generally speaking, I may say that in application to learning, the necessary point of departure is fixing the determination. What you mention as the defect of being distressed and forgetting, is due to the fact that the purpose lacks genuineness and earnestness. He who loves the beautiful does not experience the embarrassment of being distressed and forgetting, for his love is genuine and earnest. If a person experiences pain or itching, he is able to realize that fact and scratch or rub the distressed member. Since one knows that one has pain or itching, one can but scratch and rub it. The Buddhists say, ''For good works there is always a way of doing.'' This implies that the individual adjusts himself to circumstances. It is difficult for any other person to expend energy for you in this matter. There is but one way.

Your letter says: ''Shang Ts'ai often asked, 'Why is it

necessary to reflect or be anxious?' [48] I-ch'uan [49] answered, 'This attitude is reasonable, but it is manifested too soon in the work of the student.' There certainly are things that should not be forgotten, but it is also necessary to understand the proper way in which one may reflect and be anxious. It is correct that they should be viewed together. If one does not know the exact method, one will really have what is called the defect of assisting the growth. If one knows how to think and how to be anxious, but forgets that there are things concerning which he may think and be anxious, he will probably reach the state in which he is free from thought and anxiety. It is necessary that one should not be precipitated into them nor be free from them. Is this correct?'' (34)

Thought and Deliberation are Permissible Only When They Deal with Heaven-given Principles

What you say is approximately correct. But you have not fully analyzed and realized Shang Ts'ai's question and I-ch'uan's answer. Shang Ts'ai's question and I-ch'uan's answer are slightly at variance with the purpose of Confucius as exhibited in the Hsi Tz'u. [50] The Hsi Tz'u in speaking of the manner of thinking and deliberating asserts that heaven-given principles are the only things concerning which thought and deliberation (anxiety) are permissible, and that they are allowable under no other circumstances. It does not say that there is to be no thought and no anxiety, but that these have reference to heaven-given principles in various ways. There is one effect from many deliberations. Does answering the question, How must the individual think and deliberate? by saying: There are different ways; and, There are a hundred different things to deliberate about, imply that there is to be neither thought

---

[48] Referring to heaven-given principles.
[49] The philosopher Ch'eng I-ch'uan.
[50] A section of the Book of Changes.

nor deliberation? The mind is by nature the embodiment of heaven-given principles. It is this and no more. How can there be anything else to think about or to deliberate on? Heaven-given principles are perfectly calm and quiet, and from the first, when set in operation, have a penetrating effect The student in his efforts — though he thinks a thousand times and deliberates ten thousand times — need only revert to the original function of his mind. This means that he cannot use his personal ideas in this matter. Therefore Ming-tao [51] said, "The learning of the superior man is perfectly fair and without favoritism. He responds to the affairs he meets in an appropriate way." The application of a selfish purpose in arranging one's thoughts implies using wisdom for selfish ends. How to think and deliberate, and with reference to what, is indeed a task. In the instance of the student it is forced I-ch'uan, referring to the result, said, "It comes too soon." A little later he said, "But one must apply one's self." Thus he himself knew that what he had said before was not exhaustive Lien Hsi's discussion on, "Let tranquility be the controlling factor," also has this idea Though what you say gives evidence that you have some knowledge of the facts, you are still unable to avoid making two things out of this one.

Recognizing the Bearing and Manner of a Sage Follows from a Clear Apprehension of the Implications of the Intuitive Faculty

Your letter says "When a student once knows how to apply himself, he should know and recognize the air and bearing of the sage. When he recognizes the bearing of the sage and uses it as his ideal and pattern, he will then really carry out his task without being prone to make mistakes, and will do the work of a sage. I do not know whether this is correct or not." (35)

---

[51] The brother of Ch'eng I-ch'uan.

In the past it has been customary to say that one must first recognize the bearing and air of a sage, but this standpoint also is inadequate. The bearing of a sage naturally belongs to a sage. How can I know it, if I do not genuinely and earnestly recognize it through investigation carried on in accordance with the intuitive faculty? This may be compared to using steelyards without any appropriate marks to weigh with, or to using an unpolished mirror to reflect beauty. This is just what is meant by saying, "He uses the mind of an inferior man to estimate the mind of a superior man." How shall I know the bearing of the sage? My own intuitive faculty is originally like that of the sage. If I realize this clearly through the introspection of my own intuitive knowledge, then the bearing of the sage is not in the sage but within myself. The philosopher Ch'eng often said, "If one watches Emperor Yao in order to learn his way of acting, but lacks his quick apprehension, clear discernment, far-reaching intelligence, and all-embracing knowledge, how can one have every movement of the countenance and every turn of the body exactly as he had?" He also said, "If the mind clearly apprehends the path of duty, it then is able to distinguish clearly between right and wrong." In addition to this I ask: In what way does one clearly apprehend the path of duty? From whence come quick apprehension, clear discernment, far-reaching intelligence, and all-embracing knowledge?

The Individual Should Exhaust His Energy in Cultivating His Nature

Your letter says: "Referring to getting practice in virtue from the affairs of life, I do not ask whether one is or is not occupied with affairs during the day, it is only necessary to devote one's self completely to cultivating the source (*i.e.* nature). Whether one is stimulated by meeting some affair, or is influenced quite by himself, if his mind is present, how can he be said to be unoccupied? But when the mind is occupied, once let it think and it will usually realize that the underlying principle of things is as described. Adjusting one's self as though there were no affairs, one should exhaust his mind in cultivating nature. How is it, however, that at times the person attains the good and at others does not? Moreover, if perchance affairs crowd in upon him, he should use some method in his responses. Whenever native ability and strength are insufficient, distress always follows. Though he uses his greatest effort in supporting his mental and bodily energy, he realizes that they are weak. When he reaches this point he can but desire to retire and think. As this is extremely serious, he can but cultivate his nature. What do you hold of this?"

What you have said about the method of procedure, you should, following your own native ability, actually carry out. It is unavoidable that there should be both an expending and a gathering in. Whoever devotes himself to learning does so for just this one reason (i.e. to cultivate nature). (36) From youth to old age, from morning to evening, the individual, whether occupied or not, is engaged in this task only. This is what is meant by saying that one always is occupied. If you say, "Rather than allow things to come to a bad way, he will cultivate his original nature," you still consider them as two distinct things. There certainly is something which one must neither forget nor assist. When a person meets affairs or things, he should respond to them to the best ability of his intuitive faculty. This is implied in the saying. "When one cultivates to the utmost the principles of his nature and exercises them on the principle of reciprocity, he is not far from the path." [52] The fact that the individual at times attains the good and at others fails to do so, until at last he is precipitated into the misfortune of being distressed and of losing control of the regular order, is all an implication of

---

[52] Doctrine of the Mean, Ch. 13, ¶ 3.

getting or losing the slander or praise of others. It is due directly to failure in extending knowledge to the utmost. If one is really able to extend intuitive knowledge to the utmost, he will understand that what he ordinarily considers virtue (good) is not virtue, and what is called evil is perhaps really connected with getting or losing the slander and praise of others, and that thus he injures his own intuitive faculty.

The Investigation of Things is Included in Extending Knowledge to the Utmost

Your letter says: "Concerning the extending of intuitive knowledge to the utmost, I received the advantage of your instruction in the spring, and am thus thoroughly conversant with the method of applying myself. I also realize that application is easier than heretofore. But when I discuss this matter with those who are beginning to learn, I am under necessity of connecting it with the idea of investigating things, in order that they may know the point of departure. Originally the extending of knowledge and the investigation of things are connected, but the beginner does not know how to begin his task. It is still necessary to explain the investigation of things to him, before he understands what is meant by extending knowledge to the utmost."

The investigation of things is implied in extending knowledge to the utmost. He who knows how to extend knowledge to the utmost also understands how to carry on the investigation of things. He who does not understand the investigation of things does not yet understand how to extend knowledge to the utmost. I have recently written a letter to a friend in which I have very carefully discussed this matter. I now send you a similar letter. If you read it carefully, you should be able to understand.

It is More Important to Discover and Discuss One's Own
Mistakes than Those of the Philosophers Chu and Lu

Your letter says· "The discussions regarding the philosophers Chu and Lu have not ceased. Whenever I speak to my friends, I say that inasmuch as the true learning of the sages has not been understood for a long time, we should not needlessly expend our mental strength in wrangling about the right and wrong of the philosophers Chu and Lu. Following your ideal regarding the fixing of the determination, we should instruct others. If the individual is really able to comprehend this idea and is determined to apprehend this learning, he has a fairly good understanding of the situation (37) Though he does not discuss the philosophy of Chu and Lu, he is really in a position to appreciate the facts   I have often observed that some of my friends criticise your words, frequently becoming excited in doing so   That the transmitted sayings of the two former philosophers Chu and Lu are often criticised in a disorderly way by later generations shows that their work is not perfectly mature   Evidently they stir up the passions   In the case of the philosopher Ch'eng Ming-tao there is nothing of this sort present. See how he discusses the learning of Chieh Pu with Wu She-li, saying: 'If you make known to me the learning of Chieh Pu, though it brings no advantage to you it certainly will help me.' How congenial his bearing was!   I have often seen you quote these words in letters to friends   I heartily wish all my friends acted thus   What do you think of this?"

What you say in this section is exceedingly well said. I wish that you could go around and tell it to all who have this common purpose. Each one should discuss his own mistakes and not those of the philosophers Chu and Lu To use words in criticising others is a shallow criticism, if one merely says what one has heard and is not able to verify the facts in person. He who spends his days in clamorous vociferations and devotes his person to criticism and slandering, criticises deeply. If those who are now criticising me have done so rightfully, they have really refined me (ground, cut, and filed me). Thereby they urge me to reform, and cause me to be diligent in fulfilling my duties, in cultivating my person, and in examining myself that I may make progress in virtue. Formerly people said, "He who attacks my short-comings is my teacher." Why should a teacher be hated?

Nature Includes the Feelings

Your letter says: "There are those who quote the philosopher Ch'eng's saying, 'When a man's passion nature is in a state of tranquility, it is not necessary to speak of that which follows in the text' (according to the Great Learning).[53] To say that this tranquility is one's nature, already implies that it is not the nature of him who speaks. Why is it not necessary to speak of what follows? Why is this not nature? Hui-an said, 'It is not allowable to speak of what follows, because there is no nature to speak of.' If it is not nature, it must be because it is mixed with feeling (passion). (38) I am unable to understand the words of the two teachers. Whenever I reach this point in reading, I am always confused. Will you kindly explain it for me?"

Life is what is understood by nature. The word life here forthwith implies feelings. If one says that these feelings are to be identified with nature, then these feelings forthwith are nature. When the philosopher says, "If man's passion nature is in a state of tranquility, it is not necessary to speak of what follows," he refers to the fact that the feelings are to be identified with nature. Thereby he has already deviated to one side, for feeling is not originally characteristic of nature. Mencius in speaking of nature as "good," does so in accordance with its original characteristics. However, the truth of nature's being good

---

[53] *Vide* Great Learning, Introduction, ¶ 2. This refers to the necessity of knowing rest before the object of pursuit is determined.

must first be seen in the realm of the feelings. If there is no feeling, it cannot be seen. Commiseration, shame, dislike, modesty, complaisance, approval and disapproval, are feelings. The philosopher Ch'eng says, "To speak of nature and not of feeling makes the discussion incomplete; to discuss feeling and not nature makes the discussion unclear." He said this because his students all knew or recognized but one aspect, so that he could not speak otherwise. When one understands one's nature clearly, the feelings are included in nature, and nature is included in the feelings. The two cannot be separated.

Answer to Inquiries Made by a Friend

Written in the fifth year of Emperor Chia Ching

You make inquiry saying, "From the beginning, former scholars all thought that study, inquiry, reflection, and discrimination pertained to knowledge, while earnest practice referred to activity; and that these two (knowledge and practice) were two separate things. Now you say that knowledge and practice are one. I can but doubt."

Wang Discusses the Unitary Character of Knowledge and Practice

I have often spoken about this. By practice is meant that one really and earnestly does a definite thing. (39) If one devotes himself to study, inquiry, reflection, and discrimination, he practices these things. Study implies studying how to do a definite thing, and inquiry implies inquiring how to do a definite thing. Reflection and discrimination imply reflecting and clearly discriminating how to do some definite thing. Thus practice also includes study, inquiry, reflection, and discrimination. If you say, "I first study, inquire, reflect, and discriminate, and thereafter practice," how can you genuinely study, inquire, reflect, and discriminate, so as to get knowledge? Moreover, when you practice, how can you attain what is called

study, inquiry, reflection, and discrimination? Knowledge
is to be defined as the condition in which one clearly recognizes and minutely investigates methods of practice;
while practice is defined as the state in which knowledge is
genuine and true. If one practices, but is unable to investigate minutely and realize clearly (what he is practicing),
his practice is inaccurate and immature. "Learning without thought is labor lost."[54] For this reason knowledge
must be mentioned. If one has knowledge but is unable
genuinely and truly to practice (what he knows), he is disorderly and incoherent in his thoughts. "Thought without
learning is perilous."[54] For this reason practice must be
mentioned. From the beginning they imply but one task.
Whenever the ancients spoke of knowledge and practice,
they referred to correcting or clarifying some one thing.
They did not, as do present-day scholars, separate them into
two distinct functions. Though in my assertion that knowledge and practice are one I follow the present-day emphasis
upon correcting and clarifying defects, knowledge and practice are as a matter of fact fundamentally of this sort. My
friend, you need only appreciate this through introspection
in your own person and mind, in order to be aware of it
the next time. At present you estimate this merely from
the assertions of others and from the meaning of the characters, and for that reason you are influenced to emphasize
that which is inexact. The more you speak, the more confused you become. This is a defect in which you are unable to appreciate the unity of knowledge and practice.

Comparison Between the Teachings of Wang and Lu
Hsiang-shan

Your letter says: "The discussions of learning as represented by the philosophers Lu Hsiang-shan and Chu Hui-an
are in many respects similar and in many respects dis-
similar. You have frequently said that Hsiang-shan was

---

[54] Analects, Book II, Ch. 15.

able to make straight and clear distinctions at the point where learning begins. As I view his discussions, I can say that his learning is clearly expounded and accurate. In his exposition of the meaning of extending knowledge to the utmost and of investigating things, he does not differ from the philosopher Chu Hui-an. But his standpoint is different from yours regarding the oneness of knowledge and practice." (40)

Does the superior man, in his learning, emphasize points of likeness and difference? He seeks correctness. The points of similarity between my learning and that of Hsiang-shan are not superficial, and I do not hide what points of difference there are. My discussions are in some respects different from those of the philosopher Chu Hui-an, but not because I seek to differ from him. The points of likeness do no injury to the places where we are alike. In case the philosophers Po I and Liu Hsia-hui are in the same hall with Confucius and Mencius, what they all see will be partial in one aspect and perfect in another. Their judgment and criticisms also will not be alike in detail. However, they must in this do no injury to their status as sages and virtuous men. The scholars of later generations who discuss learning defend those who have the same opinions, but attack those who differ from them, because their minds are selfish and their convictions (feelings) unsubstantial. They consider the occupation of the sage and virtuous man mere child's play.

Your letter says further: "In your discussion of learning you place special emphasis upon the fact that knowledge and practice are one. Since this is different from the saying of Hsiang-shan, I venture to ask in what respects the two points of view are similar."

Knowledge and practice are originally two different words, but they refer to one and the same task. In this task it is necessary to emphasize these two aspects, for then only can it be explained perfectly and without any abuse.

If one clearly understands their source, one sees that they have the same point of departure. Thus, though they are discussed separately, ultimately they will make one complete whole. At first the individual perhaps does not fully comprehend; finally, however, it will be true as said, "Many deliberations will reach one result." In case the point of departure is not clearly apprehended and knowledge and practice are considered two different things, then, though they are said to be one, they will ultimately not be unified, for the individual will act as though they were still separate. Thus, from the beginning to the end it will be the more impossible to arrive at a result.

You further say: "Your teaching regarding extending intuitive knowledge to the utmost is truly an instance of the saying, 'He is prepared to wait for the rise of a sage a hundred ages after, and has no misgivings.' [55] Hsiang-shan is able to apprehend clearly the point of departure. (41) Why does he differ from you here?"

The extending of knowledge to the utmost and the investigation of things have from the beginning been thus handed down by scholars. Therefore it transpires that Hsiang-shan follows them in this (separates knowledge and practice), and comes upon no doubts. Moreover, in last analysis Hsiang-shan has not been discriminating in this connection. I cannot conceal this.

At the point at which knowledge is truly genuine and sincere, it passes into and includes practice. The clear apprehension and minute investigation of practice includes knowledge. If, at the time of knowing, the mind is not genuine and sincere, knowledge cannot be characterized by clear apprehension and minute investigation. This does not imply that at the time of knowing one needs only clear comprehension and careful investigation, without needing sincerity and minuteness. If the mind does not clearly comprehend and fully grasp the truth when the individual

[55] Doctrine of the Mean, Ch. 29, ¶ 3.

practices (his knowledge), his actions cannot be sincere and genuine. Moreover, it does not mean that at the time when he practices he needs to be genuine and sincere, but need not clearly apprehend and grasp the truth. One should know that the mind is by nature like the transforming, nurturing power of heaven and earth, and like the great beginning thereof.

Comments — The saying that knowledge and practice are one was not first pronounced by the Teacher. The Doctrine of the Mean in quoting the saying of Confucius connects the proposition, "I know how it is that the path is not walked in," with, "The knowing (intelligent) go beyond it and the stupid do not come up to it"; and the proposition, "I know how it is that the path of the mean is not understood," with the further proposition, "The men of talent and virtue go beyond it, and the worthless do not come up to it." [56] This is just the idea of the unity of knowledge and practice. Mencius says, "The path is as a great road. Is it hard to know? Man's defect is that he does not seek it." [57] If he does not seek, how can he be said to know it? This implies that sages and virtuous men have long since passed through and understood, but no attention has been paid to this fact.

Letter Answering Ou-Yang Ch'ung-i

Written in the fifth year of Emperor Chia Ching

Intuitive Knowledge Does Not Have a Sensory Source; the Senses Represent the Functioning of the Intuitive Faculty

Your letter says: "The intuitive knowledge of the virtuous nature does not come from seeing and hearing. (42) If one says, 'I hear much, select what is good and follow it; see much and keep it in memory,' [58] one seeks only the

---

[56] Doctrine of the Mean, Ch. 4, ¶ 1.
[57] Mencius, Book VI, Pt. II, Ch. 2, ¶ 7.
[58] Analects, Book VII, Ch. 27.

result of seeing and hearing, and thereby has fallen in with the second idea that intuitive knowledge comes from experience. Though according to my view intuitive knowledge of the good does not come from experience, the knowledge of the student is nevertheless manifested as a result of experience. To be impeded by that which is seen and heard is, of course, unfortunate. However, seeing and hearing are also functions of the intuitive faculty. Now, the statement that some have fallen into the second idea is perhaps addressed to those who consider seeing and hearing (experience) as constituting learning. If the individual extends his intuitive knowledge to the utmost and in addition seeks experience, this, too, would appear to imply a unification of knowledge and practice. Is this correct?''

The intuitive knowledge of good does not come from seeing and hearing, and on the other hand all hearing and seeing are functions of the intuitive faculty. For this reason, the intuitive faculty does not rest with merely seeing and hearing, nor does it separate itself from them. Confucius said, ''Have I knowledge? I have not.''[59] Apart from the intuitive faculty there is no knowledge. For this reason, extending intuitive knowledge to the utmost is the fundamental principle of learning, and the foremost idea of the instruction of the sages. To say that the individual seeks the result of seeing and hearing, implies that the fundamental principle has been lost and that he has fallen into the second idea (that knowledge comes from experience). Among those who are of like purpose with us, there are none who do not know that it is necessary to develop the intuitive faculty to the utmost, but there are some who are desultory and careless in their efforts. Verily they lack this one thing.

In study it is necessary to pay particular attention to the correctness of the point of departure. In case the individual is firmly determined regarding the point of departure

---

[59] *Vide* Analects, Book IX, Ch. 7.

and makes the developing of the intuitive faculty to the utmost his occupation, then, however much he may hear or see, all will be included in this task of extending intuitive knowledge to the utmost. Though in the experiences of the mutual intercourse of the day there be innumerable beginnings, there is nothing which is not the result of the progressive manifestation of the intuitive faculty. Eliminate the experiences of mutual intercourse, and thereby the development of the intuitive faculty is made impossible. For this reason the task is but one. If anyone says, "I develop my intuitive knowledge to the utmost and seek experience," he makes them two things. Though this is slightly different from devoting one's self to seeking the result of experience, it fails to reach the point at which the purposes of discrimination and undividedness are unified. (You quote:) "Hearing much and selecting what is good and following it; seeing much and keeping it in memory." (43) Since it says selecting and also keeping it in memory, the intuitive faculty already has acted upon this, but in fixing his purpose the individual devotes himself to selecting and remembering what is good out of that which he has often seen and heard. In so doing he has missed the point of departure (lost the fundamental principle). You, Ch'ung-i, should understand these points clearly. Your inquiry truly serves to elucidate this and is of great advantage to your companions. However, the idea is not clear, and therefore may lead to small and great mistakes. You should carefully investigate this.

Thought Must Be Freed from Every Selfish Purpose

Your letter says: "You say that what the Hsi Tz'u [60] says regarding the manner of thinking and deliberating implies that natural law (heaven-given principles) is the only thing concerning which thought and deliberation are permissible, and that there is nothing else regarding which thought and

---

[60] *Vide* footnote 50, p. 273.

deliberation are allowable. But this does not imply that there is to be no thought and deliberation. Since the mind in its original nature embodies heaven-given principles, what else is there to think and deliberate about? Though the student employs innumerable thoughts and deliberations, what is really necessary is that he revert to his nature. This means that he cannot use his personal ideas in arranging his thoughts. If he uses a selfish purpose in arranging his thoughts, he uses his wisdom for selfish ends. The defects of learning consist either in sinking into abstraction, or in remaining secluded, or in making provision for profound meditation. In the sixth and seventh years of Cheng Te, I was in the former condition. Now I am taken with the latter. Deep thinking is a manifestation of the intuitive faculty. How can it be distinguished from the condition in which one prearranges his thinking by selfish purposes? Perhaps I am treating a thief as a son. I am in doubt about it and do not know.''

"Reflection is called far-reaching intelligence and this far-reaching intelligence is called sageness."[61] "Reflection is a function of the mind. Through reflection it gets the right view of things."[62] Can reflection then be dispensed with? To sink one's self into abstraction and keep perfectly motionless, and to prearrange one's thinking, truly imply using wisdom according to one's selfish purposes. These must be considered as dispensing with intuitive knowledge. The intuitive faculty is the point of clearness and consciousness which heaven-given principles attain. For this reason the intuitive knowledge of good is to be identified with natural law. Reflection is the manifestation and use of the intuitive faculty. If reflection has reference to the action of the intuitive faculty, there are no thoughts except such as are in accordance with natural law. (44) The reflection of the intuitive faculty in action

---

[61] Shooking, Books of Shang, Book IV, ¶ 6.

[62] Mencius, Book VI, Pt. I, Ch. 15, ¶ 2.

is naturally clear and simple, for the intuitive faculty is by nature able to know. If selfish ideas prearrange reflection, it naturally is confused, laborious, and annoying; but the intuitive faculty is readily able to distinguish this. Concerning the discrimination between right and wrong, obliquity and genuineness, the intuitive faculty naturally is clear. Therefore "treating a thief as a son" implies that one does not clearly understand what is meant by extending knowledge to the utmost, and that one is not aware that this must be recognized through introspection within the intuitive faculty itself.

The Intuitive Faculty Does Not Need to be Strengthened

Your letter says: "You teach that devotion to learning implies from first to last but a single task; whether one is occupied with affairs or not, there is but this single task. If one says that in the instance of very serious and prolonged affairs the intuitive faculty must be additionally strengthened, two things are distinguished. The apprehension that one's mental energy and strength are insufficient to bring the affair to a successful termination is due to the intuitive faculty. In a serious and prolonged affair the cultivation (strengthening) thereof is just what is meant by extending knowledge. In what does this divide the task into two things? When changes come and some affair must be terminated, then, though my mental energy and strength are weak, if I arouse myself I am able to hold my own. By maintaining firmness of will it is used as the leader of the passion nature. Moreover, if words and action are not supported by the strength of the passion nature, one is exceedingly tired by the time the affair is ended. Is this not approximately what is meant by doing violence to the passion nature? Surely the intuitive faculty knows how light, heavy, slow, or explosive this passion nature is. Nevertheless one may be embarrassed by the influence of affairs. How, then, can one care for one's men-

tal energy and strength? Or one's mental energy and
strength may be tired out. How can one then have regard
for the influence of affairs? How can this be satisfactorily
adjusted?''

The idea of additionally strengthening the intuitive faculty in case of serious, prolonged affairs, or crises, it not
without advantage, when told to those who are just beginning to learn. But if it implies doing two things, there is
trouble inherent in it. Mencius said: ''There must be
constant practice of virtue.''[63] This means that the learning of the superior man consists from first to last in the
accumulation of righteous deeds. Righteousness is the
necessary ideal. When the mind attains what is proper
and right, it is called righteous. He who is able to develop
his intuitive knowledge to the utmost has a mind which attains what is fit and proper. Therefore the accumulation
of righteousness implies extending intuitive knowledge to
the utmost. (45) In the many changing circumstances of
mutual intercourse, the superior man acts when it is fitting
and proper. Whether it be ceasing from activity, living or
dying, everything is done in accordance with the ideal. In
deliberating upon and settling difficulties, he seeks self-
enjoyment in developing his intuitive faculty.

''The superior man does what is proper to the station in
which he is.''[64] His reflection does not go beyond his station. Whosoever schemes to get that which his strength is
unable to attain, or forces his intuitive faculty with reference to that which he is unable to know, cannot be considered as having attained the condition in which he is extending intuitive knowledge. Whosoever exercises his sinews
and bones with toil, exposes his body to hunger, subjects
himself to extreme poverty, acts until he has confused his
own undertakings, stimulates his mind, and hardens his nature in order to supply his incompetencies, is extending his

---

[63] Mencius, Book II, Pt. I, Ch. 2, ¶ 16.

[64] Doctrine of the Mean, Ch. 14, ¶ 1.

intuitive knowledge. If one says that in serious, prolonged affairs the intuitive faculty must be strengthened, it implies that one first seeks merit and gain. If one goes minutely into the matter of succeeding or failing, of being sharp-witted or obtuse, and moreover delights in taking and rejecting, he recognizes an almost terminated affair as one thing, and the strengthening of the intuitive faculty as another thing. This means that one has the idea that what is within the mind is correct and right, while that which is outside the mind is wrong. It also implies that one uses wisdom on one's private purposes and makes righteousness something external — a defect explained by the words, "What produces dissatisfaction in the mind is not to be helped by passion effort." [65] Thus he does not extend his intuitive knowledge to the utmost in order to seek self-enjoyment. You say that when you hold your own by exerting yourself, you are very much tired out by the time the affair is ended. You further say that at times one is embarrassed by the influence of affairs, or finds one's mental energy and strength fatigued. This means that you have made two things of them and therefore have this experience. The task of learning, when there is devotion to the one thing (*i.e.* undividedness), is sincere; and when there is devotion to two things (*i.e.* dividedness), is false, for the purpose of extending the intuitive faculty lacks sincerity. The Great Learning says, "What is meant by 'making the thoughts sincere,' is the allowing of no self-deception, as when one hates an evil odor and loves what is beautiful. This is called enjoying one's self." [66] Have you ever seen that he who hates an evil odor and loves what is beautiful need hold his own in this matter by exerting or arousing himself? Has there been anyone who at the end of such an experience is exhausted or because of its influence is mentally and

[65] Mencius, Book II, Pt. I, Ch. 2, ¶ 9.
[66] Great Learning, Ch. 6, ¶ 1.

physically fatigued? Thus you can know that this has grown out of some defect.

The Intuitive Faculty Has the Ability to Foresee Deception

Your letter says: "The source of the pretense of human passions manifests itself in a hundred ways. He who deals with them (the passions) is constantly deceived by them. As soon as he becomes aware of them, he begins to anticipate and think beforehand. (46) This anticipating of deception is itself deception, and thinking beforehand of not being believed is itself lack of faith. He cannot know that he is going to be deceived by others. Is it to be considered clear apprehension of the intuitive faculty, not to anticipate deception and not to think beforehand of being disbelieved, and yet to realize it beforehand? Moreover, in the mere fraction of a minute, the intuitive faculty secretly realizes that those who act deceitfully are many."

Neither to anticipate deception nor to think beforehand of not being believed, and yet to realize this clearly, was mentioned by Confucius, because the people of his time devoted their minds to anticipating deceit and thinking beforehand of not being believed, and thus precipitated themselves into deceit and lack of faith in others.[67] Moreover, some neither anticipated deception nor thought beforehand of not being believed, but failed to understand the task of developing the intuitive faculty and were constantly deceived by others. He did not teach others to harbor this mind and desire to realize beforehand the deception and unbelief of others. To harbor this mind is the suspecting, disliking, wickedness and meanness of later generations. Moreover, when once this thought has taken possession, the individual is unable to walk in the path of Yao and Shun. He who neither anticipates nor thinks beforehand, but is deceived by others, still cannot be said not to do the good; but this is not to be likened to extending his intuitive

---

[67] Analects, Book XIV, Ch. 33.

knowledge. Moreover, he who under such circumstances realizes beforehand is the more virtuous. Ch'ung-i, you say that he alone has a clear intuitive apprehension, and thus have divined the underlying purpose through your cleverness. I fear that you have not reached the limit (the bottom).

Wang Discusses the Absolute Perfection of the Intuitive Faculty

The intuitive faculty is in man's mind. It has pervaded all generations of the immemorial past, filled heaven and earth, and was in no wise different from what it now is. It knows without any cogitation. Constantly and easily it knows dangerous paths. It is able to act without learning. Constantly and easily it knows what things tend to hinder its progress. It strives first for heaven-given principles and does not trespass them. How much more is this true in the instance of men, of spirits, and of gods! Your saying that it secretly knows those who act in accordance with deceit, means that though the individual does not anticipate deceit he perhaps can not avoid deceiving himself. Though he does not think beforehand that others will not believe him, he perhaps can not really have faith in himself. It implies that perhaps he constantly seeks to realize this beforehand, but may not be able himself to know it. He who constantly seeks to have previous knowledge has already drifted into anticipating and thinking beforehand sufficiently to obscure his intuitive faculty. This secret realization that humanity acts under false pretenses cannot be avoided.

The superior man learns for his own sake. He has not thereby considered or been anxious that others may deceive him, but perseveres rather in not deceiving his own intuitive faculty. (47) He has not been anxious that others may not believe him, but perseveres in believing in his own intuitive faculty. He has not sought a previous realization of the deceit and unbelief of others, but constantly devotes himself to realizing his own intuitive faculty. Not deceiving himself, he keeps his intuitive faculty free from pretense and hypocrisy, and thereby is sincere. Being sincere, he is intelligent. Having faith in himself, his intuitive faculty is in doubt regarding no one and is therefore intelligent. Being intelligent, it is sincere. Intelligence and sincerity develop *pari passu*, and for this reason the intuitive faculty constantly realizes and constantly reflects. Since it constantly realizes and constantly reflects truly, it is like a suspended bright mirror. Whenever a thing appears before it, it cannot conceal beauty or ugliness. How is this? Not deceiving but always sincere, it does not permit anything to deceive it. If it is deceived, it realizes it. Being itself faithful and sincere, it does not permit anything in which it does not believe; and in case it does not believe it, it is conscious thereof. This means that it easily knows the dangerous path and whatsoever hinders its progress. Tzu-ssu says, "He who attains complete sincerity is like a spirit." [68] Such individuals are able to foreknow. However, Tzu-ssu's statement that he who is like a spirit is able to foreknow seems to express two meanings. In the first place, it explains the results of the effort to make the thinking sincere; in the second place, it seems to have reference to those who are not able to foreknow. If it is interpreted as referring to entire sincerity, then the wonderful use of entire sincerity carries with it the meaning of a spirit, and the individual should not be described as being like a spirit. Being completely sincere, there are things which he does not know and others that he does know. It should not be said that he foreknows all things.

Comment — In this letter the first section says that the intuitive faculty does not rest in and depend upon seeing and hearing, and further that it does not disregard seeing

---

[68] Doctrine of the Mean, Ch. 24. Tzu-ssu was the compiler of the Doctrine of the Mean.

and hearing. For this reason extensive study and profound inquiry are necessary. The second section says that the thoughts of the human mind may be right or wrong, oblique or true, and that for this reason it is necessary to employ careful reflection and clear discrimination. The third section says that the learning of the superior man consists from first to last in the accumulation of righteousness and the earnest practice of this. The final section says that intelligence and sincerity are attained by an appreciation of their meaning. (48)

Reply to Letter from Ku Tung-ch'iao

Written in the fourth year of Emperor Chia Ching

Later Scholars Devote Themselves to External Things

Your letter says: ''Recent scholars have devoted themselves to external things and have lost interest in the internal (subjective). They study extensively and get few fundamental principles. For this reason you (the Teacher) especially introduce the idea of making the will sincere. Thus to probe into fundamentals (to use the acupuncture needle in the vitals) is truly a great kindness.''

My disciple, you thoroughly apprehend the defects of the present age. How shall they be removed? Moreover, my mind has been fully expressed by you in a sentence. Why should I elaborate it further? Making the purpose sincere is naturally the first principle which the sages teach others to use, but present-day students view it as being of secondary importance. For this reason I simply select some of the more important things. This does not imply that I am especially able to introduce them.

Ku Thinks that Wang is too Erudite in His Discussion of
Learning

Your letter says: ''But perhaps you have discussed learning too profoundly and have executed the task too cleverly. Later scholars and students, exaggerating the message (tidings), will not be able to avoid coming under the influence of the Buddhist doctrines of seeing one's nature by the light of one's intelligence and of fixing intelligence by sudden inspiration. It is not strange that those who hear your views are in doubt.''

Wang Insists that His Views Are Not Buddhistic

My sayings regarding the investigation of things, the development of the intuitive faculty, the making sincere of the purpose, and the rectifying of the mind, refer to the student's use of his original nature in his various daily tasks in order to investigate and firmly maintain the truth. This implies a great deal of orderly advance and development. Surely it is just the opposite of the empty, meaningless, sudden enlightenment of the Buddhists. My hearers do not purpose being sages, nor have they ever investigated this matter minutely. That they should be in doubt is not enough to disturb me. A man of your high intelligence naturally should understand it in a moment. Why should you, too, say that I discuss learning too profoundly and execute my task too cleverly?

Knowledge and Practice Should Advance Pari Passu

Your letter says: ''You give instruction that knowledge and practice advance *pari passu*, that no distinction should be made as to the precedence of the one or the other, and that this is what is meant in the Doctrine of the Mean by saying, 'The superior man honors his virtuous nature, and maintains constant inquiry and study.'[69] It implies mutually cultivating and conjointly manifesting the internal and the external, the source and the result. We have here the doctrine of an all-pervading unity. But in the progress of the task there must be a distinction between that which is first and that which follows. If one knows what food is, one may eat; if one knows what soup is, one may drink; if

---

[69] Doctrine of the Mean, Ch. 27, ¶ 6.

one knows what clothes are, one may wear them; if one knows the road, one may traverse it. (49) There is no case in which one performs the act before one has a realization of the thing in question. This all happens in a moment. It does not mean that I wait until I know it today and act tomorrow.''

Since you have said that the cultivation and mutual manifestation of the internal (referring to knowledge) and the external (referring to practice), of the source and the result — once having been considered as a unity — are to be identified with the mutual advance of knowledge and practice, there should be no further doubt arising in your mind. You further say that in the progress of the task there must be a distinction between that which is first and that which follows. Is not this a case in which the spear and shield oppose each other (self-contradiction)? Your sayings — that knowledge of food, for example, precedes eating it — are easily comprehended. But you, my disciple, are obscured in mind as a result of what you have recently heard, so that you do not examine yourself. The individual must first have a desire for food, and after that he knows what it means to eat. Having this desire for food, he immediately gets the purpose to acquire it; and this is the beginning of the act. The good or evil taste of the food must first enter his mouth, and after that he knows it. Is there anyone who does not need to wait until he has experienced the taste, before he knows whether the food is good or bad? One must first have the desire to traverse the road, and after that he may learn to know it. Having the desire to traverse it, he forthwith determines to do so; and this is the beginning of the act. He knows the dangers and advantages of the forks of the road after he himself has traversed them. Is there anyone who does not need to wait until he himself has traversed the forks in the road, before he knows their disadvantages and advantages? That one drinks after one knows the soup, and wears the clothes after one knows them, all these usages cannot be doubted. As for your comparisons, they mean that before one sees the thing, the act is already present. You say that this all occurs in an instant and does not mean that today's knowledge is followed by tomorrow's act. This also shows that your investigation has not reached fundamentals. However, in accordance with your discussion, knowledge and practice are united and advance together. That, of course, cannot be questioned.

Real Knowledge Includes Practice

Your letter says: "If one truly has knowledge, he practices it; if he does not practice it, he cannot be said to know it. This is the most important instruction for the student in causing him to devote himself to practicing his learning. (50) If he says that genuine practice is to be identified with knowledge, he may merely seek to attain his original nature and thus lose the principle of things. There will thus be points at which he is confused and not intelligent. Or is this, also, a method by means of which the sages advance knowledge and practice together?"

When knowledge is genuine and sincere, practice is included; when practice is clear and minutely adjusted, knowledge is present. The two cannot be separated. Unfortunately, later scholars have separated them and thereby have lost the original character of knowledge and practice. It is for this reason that I say that they are united and advance together. Genuine knowledge is practice. Where practice is absent there is no real knowledge. This is in accordance with the illustrations your letter gives regarding knowing food and then eating, etc. You will observe that I have already discussed that in a general way. Though this was really said in order to remove a defect, knowledge and practice are by nature like this. It is not a case of using one's own purpose to assist or repress. Merely to carry out this saying implies following the impulse of the moment; merely to seek the original nature of the mind and thus to lose sight of the principles of things is an instance of losing sight of the original nature of the mind.

The Principles of Things Are Not External to the Mind

The principles of things are not to be found external to the mind. To seek the principles of things outside the mind results in there being no principles of things. If I neglect the principles of things, but seek to attain the original nature of my mind, what things are there then in my mind? The mind in its original character is nature (disposition), and nature is principles. Since the mind has the experience of being filial, there is a principle of filial piety. If the mind lacks filial piety, there is no principle of filial piety. Since the mind has the experience of being loyal to the prince, there is a principle of loyalty. Without a mind that is loyal to the prince there can be no principle of loyalty. Are these principles external to the mind? Hui-an said: "He who devotes himself to study should devote himself to a study of the mind and of principles." Though the mind in one aspect controls merely the body, it really exercises control over all the principles under the heavens. Though these principles are distributed in ten thousand affairs, they do not exceed the mind of any man. Because one (the philosopher Chu) separates them and another (Wang) unites them, it is inevitable that students should enter into the mistake of making them (mind and principles) separate things. The later scholar's misfortune of merely seeking to attain to the nature of his mind, while losing the principles of things, arises out of his ignorance that mind is the embodiment of principles. (51) He who seeks the principles of things outside the mind will inevitably become confused and unintelligent. The philosopher Kao spoke of the external character of righteousness, and for that reason Mencius said that he did not know what righteousness is. The mind is a unit. The feeling of commiseration of the entire mind is called benevolence (the highest virtue). If one refers to the mind's getting what rightfully belongs to it, one speaks of righteousness. When one refers to its order, one speaks of principles. One should not seek either for the highest virtue or for righteousness outside the mind. Is the search for principles an exception to this? To seek for principles in external things implies separating knowledge and practice. The instruction of the sages, that knowledge and practice are united, implies seeking for principles within the mind. What doubt can you, my disciple, have regarding this?

He Who is Able to Exhaust His Mental Constitution is Able to Exhaust His Nature

Your letter says: "In your explanation of the original edition of the Great Learning, you say that the extension of intuitive knowledge to the utmost has really the same purport as the exhausting of the mental constitution as given by Mencius. The philosopher Chu also held that abstract realization is a capacity of the mind. However, the exhausting of one's mental constitution follows from knowing one's nature, whereas the extension of knowledge to the utmost consists in the investigation of things."

You say, "The exhausting of one's mental constitution follows from knowing one's nature, whereas the extension of knowledge consists in the investigation of things." This is correct. But as I investigate the source of your ideas, I find that you say this because you still do not fully understand the situation. The philosopher Chu considered that things had been investigated and knowledge completed, when one had exhausted his mental constitution, knew his nature, and knew Heaven.[70] He held that preserving one's mental constitution, nourishing one's nature, and serving Heaven, were to be identified with making the purpose sincere, rectifying the mind, and cultivating the person.[71]

---

[70] Great Learning, Introduction, ¶ 4; Mencius, Book VII, Pt. I, Ch. 1, ¶ 1.

[71] *Vide* Mencius, Book VII, Pt. I, Ch. 1, ¶ 2.

He held that the saying, "Neither premature death nor long life causes a man any doublemindedness, but he waits while he cultivates his person," implied the most complete knowledge and the utmost virtue, and was applicable to the sages.[72] My own point of view is exactly the reverse of that of the philosopher Chu. Exhausting one's mental constitution, knowing one's nature, understanding Heaven, being born with knowledge (of duties) and practicing them with a natural ease, refer to the sages; while preserving one's mental constitution, nourishing one's nature and serving Heaven, knowing (duties) through study and practicing them with a desire for advantage, refer to the virtuous man. The sayings that "neither a premature death nor long life causes a man any doublemindedness," that knowledge of duties is acquired after a painful feeling of ignorance, and they are practiced by strenuous effort, refer to the learner (student). Is it correct to regard the exhausting of one's mental constitution in order to know one's nature as knowledge, and to hold that preserving one's mental constitution, nourishing one's nature and serving Heaven are to be identified with practice? You, my disciple, upon first hearing this will certainly be alarmed. (52) However, there is nothing in it that really is to be doubted. I say this especially to you. The mind in its original character is called nature (disposition); the source of nature is Heaven. He who is able to exhaust his mental constitution is able to exhaust his nature. The Doctrine of the Mean says, "It is only he who is possessed of the most complete sincerity that can exist under Heaven, who can give full development to his nature."[73] It also says: "(He) knows the transforming and nurturing operations of Heaven and earth."[74] "That he presents himself before spiritual beings, without any doubts arising, shows that he knows

[72] Mencius, Book VII, Pt. I, Ch. 1, ¶ 3.
[73] Doctrine of the Mean, Ch. 22.
[74] Ibid., Ch. 32.

Heaven.'' [75] The sage alone is able to do these things, and
it is for this reason that I say that he is born with knowledge (of duties) and practices them with natural ease. He
who preserves his mental constitution is unable to exhaust
it, and therefore he needs to add this effort of preserving
his mental constitution. Having thus preserved his mind
for sometime, he should not rest in this state. When there
are no circumstances in which he does not preserve his
mental constitution, he is able to advance and to speak of
exhausting it.

Heaven's Decrees are Embodied in Mind and Nature

Knowledge of Heaven is like the knowledge of the officials
who know the *chou* and the *hsien*.[76] The *Chih-chou* has for
his work the affairs of the *chou*, and the *Chih-hsien* the
affairs of a *hsien* (district). This implies that they are
united with Heaven. That serving Heaven is like a son's
serving his parents, or a minister's serving his prince,
means that Heaven is considered as a second separate thing.
Heaven's decrees for me are my mind and my nature. I
preserve these and dare not lose them; I nourish them and
dare not injure them. As father and mother, it begets
them perfect, and as son I return them. For this reason
I say that it is the business of the virtuous man to learn
(the duties) by study, and to practice them from a desire
for advantage.

Regarding the saying, ''Neither a premature death nor
long life causes any doublemindedness,'' I wish to say that
this is different from preserving one's mental constitution.
Though he who devotes himself to preserving his mental
constitution is not able to exhaust it, he surely is devoting
himself completely to doing good. If at times he does not
preserve (maintain) his mental constitution, all is well as

---

[75] *Ibid.*, Ch. 29, ¶ 4.

[76] The Chinese name of the mayor or magistrate is *Chih-chou* or
Chih-hsien, meaning to know the *chou* or the *hsien*, which is a district.

soon as he does. But if one says that neither a premature death nor long' life causes doublemindedness, it seems as though the fact that they might cause doublemindedness implies that the portion of his mental constitution which does virtue is unable to be unified. If the individual is not able to maintain his mental constitution in every regard, how can he be said to exhaust it? Now you say that the individual is in a condition in which premature death and long life do not cause doublemindedness. The individual may say: "Death and life — be it premature death or long life — are determined by Heaven. I will devote myself to acting according to virtue and will cultivate my person, while I await the decree of Heaven." But this implies that he has not yet learned the decree of Heaven. (53) Though the idea of serving Heaven makes the individual a separate being from Heaven, he nevertheless knows where the decrees of Heaven are to be found. He merely is respectful and receives the decree without a murmur. If you say that he is waiting (for Heaven's decree), then he does not really know in what the decrees of Heaven consist and therefore appears to be waiting. For this reason we say "determine" (establish) the decrees of Heaven. The character *li* (立 , meaning "to fix, to determine") is the same as the *li* of *chuan li* (創立, meaning "to found, to begin"). It is like establishing one's virtue, establishing truths, establishing one's merit, or one's reputation. Whenever one says "fix" (establish), it means that the thing was formerly not there but is now being established (fixed). Confucius said: "Without recognizing the ordinances of Heaven, it is impossible to be a superior man." Therefore I say that knowing them after a painful feeling of ignorance and practicing them by strenuous effort refers to the student.[77]

The Beginner Should Not Be Confused by Others

To consider "exhausting one's mental powers in order to

---

[77] *Vide* Doctrine of the Mean, Ch. 20, ¶ 9.

know one's nature and Heaven" the same as "investigating things in order to extend intuitive knowledge," makes it impossible for the beginning student to avoid considering his mind as a separate thing. Moreover, it demands that he forthwith utilize the condition of a sage, and be born with knowledge of duties and practice them with natural ease. Confused, as one who seizes the wind and grasps the shadows, he will not know what to do. How can his mind fail to reach the condition described by the words, "The whole Empire is kept running about upon the roads"? [78] Thus you can easily see the defect of present-day instruction regarding the extension of knowledge and the investigation of things. Does your suggestion concerning devotion to the external and neglect of extensive internal study with accompanying meagre results, perhaps refer to my mistake? Failure at this important point of learning will result in failure in all. This is where I risk the reproach and ridicule of the people. Forgetting that I have fallen into wrong-doing, I can but clamor.

Wang Points Out One of Chu's Mistakes

Your letter says: "I have heard you say to students that the investigation of the principles of all things with which we come into contact also means finding one's amusement in things and thereby ruining one's aims. You take the philosopher Chu's sayings, such as disliking disorder and controlling it, and preserving and nourishing the source, and exhibit them to students, explaining that they are principles of his old age. May not this also be wrong?"

The saying of the philosopher Chu regarding investigation of things is to be found in the expression, "We must investigate the principles of all things with which we come into contact." [79] (54) This means that in all affairs and things the individual should seek for fundamental princi-

---

[78] Mencius, Book III, Pt. I, Ch. 4, ¶ 6.

[79] Great Learning, Ch. 5. These words are taken from the philosopher Chu's comments on the Great Learning.

ples, and should use his mind in seeking these principles in affairs and things. Thereby mind and principles are separated. This seeking for fundamental principles in things and affairs is exemplified in seeking the principle of filial piety in one's parents. If a man seeks the principle of filial piety in the parents, is it, then, really in his own mind or is it in the person of his parents? If it is in the person of the parents, is it true that after the parents are dead the mind in consequence lacks the principle of filial piety? If one sees a child fall into a well, there must be commiseration. Is this principle of commiseration present in the child or is it to be found in the intuitive faculty of the mind? Whether the individual is unable to follow the child and rescue it from the well, or seizes it with his hand and thus rescues it, this principle is involved. Is it, then, in the person of the child, or is it rather in the intuitive faculty of the mind? What holds here is true with reference to the principles of all affairs and all things. Thus you may know the mistake of severing mind and principles — a severing which is in accordance with the philosopher Kao's sayings that righteousness is external. This mistake Mencius fully exposed. You are familiar with the matter of devoting one's self to external things and thereby losing sight of the internal, as well as that of studying extensively but with meagre results. In what sense is this true? Would it seem improper to say that it implies finding amusement in things and thereby ruining one's aims? What I say about extending knowledge to the utmost through investigation of things means extending and developing my intuitive knowledge of good to the utmost on all affairs and things. The intuitive faculty and its knowledge of good are heaven-given principles. If I extend and develop the heaven-given principles of my intuitive faculty on affairs and things, then all affairs and things partake of heaven-given principles. That extending the intuitive faculty of the mind to the utmost is extending knowledge to the utmost, and that the condition in which all things and affairs partake of these principles is to be identified with the investigation of things, means that mind and principles are one. And if this is true, then what I have formerly said, and what the philosopher Chu formerly discussed, will be understood without further discussion. (55)

Your letter says: "In its original nature the mind is clear with reference to all things, but the passion-nature restrains it (changes it) and things obscure it, so that it inevitably becomes one-sided. Without study, inquiry, deliberation, and discrimination, one cannot understand the principles of things, nor can the influences of good and evil, and the discrimination between the true and the false be known of themselves. The evil inherent in following passions and fancies cannot be fully expressed in words."

Wang Again Discourses on Knowledge and Practice

What you have said in this section appears to be true, but is really not. I must refute this defect of supporting and following the traditional sayings. Inquiry, deliberation, discrimination, and practice are all to be considered as learning. Learning and practice always go together. For instance, if the individual says that he is learning filial piety, he will certainly bear the toil of his parents, take care of them, and himself walk in the path of filial piety. After that he may speak of learning filial piety. Can he who merely says that he is learning filial piety, therefore be said to be learning? He who learns archery must certainly take the bow and fit the arrow to the string, draw the bow and shoot. He who learns writing must certainly straighten the paper and take the pen, grasp the paper and dip the pen into the ink. In all learning of the Empire, there is nothing that can be called learning unless it is carried out in practice. Thus the beginning of learning is surely practice. The earnest one, being sincere and honest, has already practiced his learning. Making his practice sincere and earnest, he does not cease from his work.

Doubt Precedes Inquiry.

Since doubt must arise in connection with learning, inquiry is necessarily present. Making inquiry, the individual forthwith learns and practices. Since doubt arises there is deliberation. Deliberating, the individual learns and again practices. Being in doubt, he also begins to discriminate, and thus both learns and practices. When discrimination is clear, deliberation careful and sincere, inquiry discerning, learning competent and skillful, and application constant, practice is earnest. It does not mean that after study, inquiry, deliberation, and discrimination, one first is ready to practice.

Mind and Principles Are One

For this reason I hold and say that seeking to be able to do anything is learning; seeking to dissipate any doubt connected therewith is inquiry; seeking to understand the underlying principles is deliberation; seeking to get at the essence is discrimination; seeking to carry out its genuineness in action is practice. (56) Any discussion of the situation that splits the task gives us these five stage. If the whole affair is united, it is one. This is the substance of my saying that mind and principles are one; it is the task of mutually developing knowledge and practice. This is the real point at which my sayings are different from those of later scholars.

The Importance of Practice

You have especially selected study, inquiry, deliberation, and discrimination as the method whereby the principles of all things are to be thoroughly investigated, but you fail to reach the point of earnest practice. This means that you consider study, inquiry, deliberation, and discrimination as knowledge, but in this investigation of principles do not include practice. Is there a single instance in the Empire in which a person has learned without practice? Is there an instance in which there has been an actual investigation of principles without practice? Ming-tao says: "It is only by investigating principles most thoroughly that one exhausts his nature in attaining the decrees of Heaven."[80] After virtue has reached its highest development, the individual may be said to be able to exhaust the principles of virtue in his investigation. After righteousness has reached its highest form, it may be said that he is able to exhaust in his investigation the principles of righteousness. When he has acquired the greatest development of virtue, he has exhausted that part of his nature which refers to virtue. Of righteousness the same holds true. Is there such a thing as that the individual has reached the point where he is able to investigate exhaustively the principles of things and yet does not practice them? For this reason, if knowledge of principles without practice cannot be considered learning, knowledge without practice cannot be considered an exhaustive investigation of principles. If knowledge without practice cannot be considered exhaustive investigation, then you may know that in the unity and mutual development of knowledge and practice no distinction can be made. The principles of things and affairs are not to be found external to the mind. If anyone says that it is insufficient to use the intuitive faculty in making an exhaustive investigation of the principles of things, and that it is necessary to seek externally in the Empire so as to supplement and strengthen this, he thereby splits mind and principles into two things. As for study, inquiry, deliberation, discrimination, and earnest practice, it is true that, though the individual in his stupidity and in his expenditure of effort uses a hundred efforts where another man succeeds by one, but nevertheless advances until he exhausts his nature in knowing Heaven, he is in reality doing nothing more than develop the intuitive faculty of his mind. Can anything further

---

[80] *Vide* footnote 18 on p. 130.

be added to the intuitive faculty? If he says that he is trying to investigate exhaustively the principles of things, and yet does not know that he must seek within his own mind, the influence of good and evil and the discrimination of the true and the false set aside the intuitive faculty. How, then, will he advance in his introspection? (57)

Passion Obscures the Mind

When you, my disciple, say that the passion-nature restrains the mind and things obscure it, you speak truly. If you wish to get rid of this obscuration and do not know how to use your strength to the utmost in this matter, but seek for relief in external things, your vision is not clear. Instead of assisting with medicine and nursing your eyes in order to cure them, bewildered and undecided you seek for relief in external things. Can you really effect the cure in this way? The injury resulting from following one's passions and one's fancies, also is due to the inability discriminately to investigate heaven-given principles within the realm of the intuitive faculty. This error, both small and great, I can clearly discriminate. Do not say that I have been too harsh in my discussion.

Wang is Charged with Being too Abstract

Your letter says: "You instruct the individual to extend his intuitive knowledge to the utmost in order to understand virtue, and warn him not to adhere to external things in making an exhaustive investigation of principles. This really causes the unenlightened scholar to live isolated and sit in abstraction. Can he who does not hear instruction attain complete knowledge and illustrious virtue? Or perhaps it causes him to sit in a state of realization in which he partly understands his original nature. Even then he has fixed his wisdom on a matter that is useless. Will he really be able to know past and present, to understand the changes of events, and to use the results for the Empire? He says that knowledge is the substance of the idea, while things are the manifestation thereof, and that 'investigation of things' should read 'rectify things' and thus is like the 'rectify' of 'rectifying what is wrong in the sovereign's mind.' Though this is excellently realized and specific, it does not follow in the wake of former points of view. Moreover, it is perhaps not harmoniously blended with the doctrine.''

My discussion of extending intuitive knowledge to the utmost, and of the investigation of things, truly is for the purpose of exhaustively investigating principles. I have not warned others not to carry on such investigation, causing them to live isolated in abstraction without any occupation. If you mean that the student is to investigate the principles of all things he comes into contact with, and be one, as you formerly said, who devotes himself to external things, then there are things that should be altered. If the unenlightened scholar really is able to investigate carefully the fundamental principles of the mind as experiences come and go, and does this in order to develop the original intuitive faculty, then, though dull he surely will become intelligent, and though weak he surely will become strong. He will be established in the great fundamental virtues of humanity and will practice the duties of universal obligation.[81] (58) He will unite the nine standard rules into an all-pervading unity without a loss of any one of them.[82] Why still be solicitous that he will not attain to a genuine use of them?

---

[81] These duties are five: viz., the duties between sovereign and minister, between father and son, between husband and wife, between elder brother and younger, and those belonging to the intercourse of friends. (Doctrine of the Mean, Ch. 20, ¶ 8.)

[82] The nine standard rules are ''the cultivation of their own characters; the honoring of men of virtue and talents; affection towards their relatives; respect towards the great ministers; kind and considerate treatment of the whole body of officers; dealing with the mass of the people as children; encouraging the resort of all classes of artisans; indulgent treatment of men from a distance; and the kindly cherishing of the princes of the States.'' (Doctrine of the Mean, Ch. 20, ¶ 12.)

Wang Objects to Mere Abstractness as Such

The devotees of stupid abstraction and empty tranquility are unable to investigate the fundamental principles of the mind, as things and affairs are experienced. Thus what they attain is not the original intuitive knowledge of good. They lose or set aside their five human relationships. That they continually make use of vacuity and tranquility, shows that because they desire these, they cannot govern home, state, or Empire. Does anyone say that the learning of the sages, which inculcates thorough investigation of principles and the exhausting of one's mental constitution, also has this defect? The mind is lord of the person (body). Moreover, the abstract and pure intelligence and clear realization of the mind are the original intuitive knowledge of good. When this intuitive faculty with its abstract and pure intelligence and clear realization is influenced and active, it is called purpose (idea).

A Thing is to be Identified with the Functioning of the Purpose

The intuitive faculty comes before the purpose, and without it there would be no purpose. Is not, thus, the intuitive faculty the body of the purpose? When purpose is manifested it is of necessity with reference to some thing, and that thing is an affair. When the purpose is used in study, then study must be considered a thing; and when the purpose is used in hearing litigation, then that is a thing. Wherever the purpose is applied, there some thing is present. If there is a particular purpose, there is a particular thing present corresponding to it; and without this particular purpose the particular thing is lacking. Is not, then, a thing identical with the functioning of purpose?

The Investigation of Things Elucidated

The character *ko* (格 , meaning "investigate, rectify") also contains the instruction of the character *chih* (至, meaning "to attain, to go to"). For instance, the Book of History says, "Shun went to the temple of the accomplished ancestor."[83] Then we have the saying, "The prince of Miao came to make his submission."[84] These both convey the instruction of attaining (coming to). However, in going to the temple of the accomplished ancestor he certainly was completely filial and reverent. If there was anything regarding which he was unenlightened, there was nothing the principles of which he did not reach. Not until then could he be said to have gone to the temple. In what the natives of Miao were obstinate, Shun diffused his accomplishments and virtue among them, and thus could reach them. Thus, it also has the meaning of rectifying. The idea of attaining does not exhaust it. The idea of investigating the evil of the mind, and the idea of investigating the evil of the prince's mind, both imply rectifying that which is not true in order to revert to the right condition. They do not convey the instruction of merely reaching (locating). As for the instruction to investigate things, which is contained in the saying of the Great Learning, how does anyone know that it does not contain the instruction of rectifying, instead of merely that of attaining? (59) If the idea of attaining were to be conveyed, it would be necessary to say "investigate until you reach the principles of affairs and things," in order to make the saying explicit. This implies that the important thing in the task rests entirely in the investigating, and that the point of application is principles. If the idea of investigating at the beginning and the idea of principles at the end are taken away, and one says directly that the extension of knowledge to the utmost consists in reaching things, can this be clear?

[83] Shooking, Pt. II, Book I, ¶ 14.

[84] *Ibid.*, Books of Yü, Book II, ¶ 21.

This matter of investigating principles to the utmost and of exhausting one's mental constitution, which is the complete finished instruction of the sage, is to be seen in the Hsi Tz'u.[85] If the investigation of things has really the same connotation as investigating principles to the utmost, why did not the sage in a straightforward way say that the extension of knowledge to the utmost consists in investigating principles to the utmost? Did he at this point change and not finish his saying, in order to start the confusion and errors of later scholars? Though the investigation of things as given by the Great Learning has the same general purport as the investigation of principles to the utmost as given in the Hsi Tz'u, still there are some slight differences. Exhaustively examining principles includes attending to and devoting one's self to the investigation of things, the extension of knowledge, the making sincere of the purpose, and the rectifying of the mind. For this reason it is said that the investigation of principles to the utmost includes the investigation of things, the extension of knowledge, the making sincere of the will, and the rectifying of the mind. If I say investigating things, I certainly equally mean that after extending knowledge, making the purpose sincere, and rectifying the mind, the task is first perfect and thorough. You, in a one-sided way, brought forward the investigation of things and forthwith said that it meant investigating principles to the utmost. This would convey the meaning that the investigation of principles relates only to knowledge and that the investigation of things does not include practice. This not only fails to reach the purport of the investigation of things, but also loses the idea of investigating principles. The learning of later scholars distinguishes an earlier and a later in knowledge and practice. They are constantly getting farther away from the truth, and because of this the learning of the sage becomes more and more injurious to

---

[85] *Vide* footnote 50, p. 273.

the unenlightened. This error really has its source here. My disciple, you have not been able to avoid receiving and following these long-standing abuses. That you consider my point of view out of harmony with the doctrine is not your mistake.

The Extension of Knowledge in Its Relation to Practical Affairs of Filial Piety

Your letter says: "How can that which you call the task of extending knowledge to the utmost have reference to caring for the comfort of parents in winter and summer and respectfully nourishing them? This implies making the purpose sincere. Not to include the investigation of things, is perhaps also a mistake." (60)

You speak thus because you estimate my view in accordance with your own ideas. This is not what I told you. If the situation is really as you say, can it be cleared up again? My view is that the purpose (will) must desire to make the parents comfortable in winter and summer; that it must desire respectfully to nourish them. What I mean by purpose does not necessarily mean a sincere purpose. It is necessary really to carry out in practice the desired purpose of making the parents comfortable in winter and summer, of nourishing them, of seeking self-enjoyment but without allowing self-deception, before the purpose can be called sincere. He who knows how to carry out in practice this caring for the comfort of the parents in winter and summer, and this respectful nourishing of the parents, may be said to know, but he cannot be said to have extended his knowledge to the utmost. He needs to extend to the utmost his knowledge of how the parents are to be made comfortable in winter and summer, and truly to carry this out in practice; he needs to extend to the utmost his knowledge of the essentials of nourishing the parents, and to carry it out in practice, before he can be said to have extended his knowledge to the utmost. Caring for the comfort of the parents in summer and winter and nourishing them are things; but this cannot be said to be a case of investigating things. He must minutely exhaust in knowledge and practice what his intuitive faculty knows about carrying out these things for his parents, before he can be said to have investigated this thing. When the thing which is called providing for the comfort of the parents in winter and summer has been investigated, after that, first, will the intuitive faculty which knows this be developed to the utmost. The same holds true with regard to nourishing parents. For this reason it is said that, when things have been investigated, knowledge will have been extended to the utmost. When the intuitive knowledge which knows how to care for the comfort of parents in winter and summer has been extended to the utmost, the purpose of thus providing for parents will be sincere. The same holds true with regard to nourishing parents. These are my sayings regarding making the purpose sincere, completing knowledge, and investigating things. If you become familiar in thought with this point, you will no longer be in doubt. (61)

Wang is Questioned About the Intuitive Faculty and Explains Its Function Minutely

Your letter says: "The main divisions of the doctrine are readily understood. Common, simple men and women can understand what is meant by intuitive knowledge of good and native capacity of doing good. But concerning the details of the rites and of the change of circumstances, where a small error involves a great one, it certainly is necessary to wait until one has learned before he can know. Is there anyone who does not know what is meant by the filial piety involved in providing for the comforts of parents in winter and summer and in inquiring regarding their health both morning and evening? But when one reaches the facts that Shun married without informing his parents; that Wu put troops into the field before having buried his father; that the philosopher Tseng nourished the will of his father, whereas Tseng Yüan nourished the mouth and body of his father (the philosopher Tseng); that the son endures a small stick but evades the large one; that he cuts flesh from his thigh to feed his ill parent; that he erects a straw hut beside the grave of his parent, or any similar thing, then it is necessary to seek earnestly for what is right and wrong in these things, and to do this in prosperity or adversity, in excess or neglect and short-coming, in order that one may carry out in practice the fundamental principles of regulating affairs.[86] After that the original nature of the mind will not be obscured, nor will it be lost when affairs arise."

It is perfectly true that the main divisions of the doctrine are readily understood. Notice how later scholars neglect this fact, taking no advantage of it, but think that learning consists in seeking that which is difficult to understand! This is what is meant by saying, "The path of duty lies in what is near, and men seek for it in what is remote. The work of duty lies in what is easy, and men seek for it in what is difficult."[87] Mencius says: "The way of truth is like a great road. Is it difficult to know it? The evil is only that men will not seek to do it."[88] In the matter of intuitive knowledge of good and native ability to execute the good, common simple men and women are like the sage. But the sage is able to extend his intuitive knowledge to the utmost, while common folks are not able to do so. It is from this point on that they differ. It is not that the sage knows the rites and the changes of circumstances, but he does not consider merely these as learning. What he means by learning consists simply in

---

[86] *Vide* Mencius, Book V, Pt. I, Ch. 2, ¶ 1; Book IV, Pt. I, Ch. 19, ¶ 3.

[87] *Ibid.*, Book IV, Pt. I, Ch. 11.

[88] *Ibid.*, Book VI, Pt. II, Ch. 2, ¶ 7.

developing his intuitive knowledge in order to investigate minutely the natural laws of the mind. In this he differs from the learning of later scholars.

My disciple, you have no leisure for the development of your intuitive faculty, but with unremitting effort you are solicitous in caring for that which is correct. This is the evil of considering that learning consists in seeking that which is difficult to understand. The intuitive faculty is to changing circumstances as compasses and squares are to squares and circles, and measures are to length and shortness. The changes in circumstances relative to paragraphs and sections (of the doctrine) cannot be determined beforehand, just as the size of the square or circle and the length or shortness cannot be perfectly estimated. (62) But when the compasses and squares have been set there can be no deception regarding the size of the square and the circle. However, the squares and circles of the universe cannot all be used. When the rule and measure have been fixed, there can be no deception as to the length or shortness, but the lengths and shortnesses under heaven cannot be exhausted. When the intuitive faculty has been completely developed, there can be no deception regarding its application to changing details. However, the changing details under heaven cannot all be complied with. If both small and great errors cannot be investigated in the recondite, abstruse thoughts of the intuitive faculty, how shall its learning be applied? If the individual does not use compasses and squares, and yet desires to determine squares and circle; if he does not use the measure, and yet desires to measure length, he in my estimation is unreasonable and perverse; he is daily laboring without completing his task.

You say, "Who does not understand the filial piety involved in caring for the comfort of parents in winter and summer and in inquiring about their health both morning and evening?" And yet but few are able to extend their knowledge to the utmost at this point. If you mean that the individual roughly knows the ceremonial usages of caring for the comfort of parents both in winter and summer, and of inquiring about their health both morning and evening, and say that he is thus able to complete his intuitive knowledge, then whosoever knows what is meant by saying that the prince ought to be benevolent is able to extend his knowledge of benevolence, and whosoever knows what is meant by saying that the minister ought to be loyal is able to extend his knowledge of loyalty. Thus considered, who in the entire Empire does not extend his intuitive knowledge? This will serve to make clear that the extending of knowledge depends upon practicing, and that without the act there clearly can be no extending of knowledge. In the matter of unity of knowledge and practice, is it necessary to add more comparisons?

As for Shun's marrying without telling his parents, was there anyone previous to that time who served as an example of such a practice? In what historical and mythological documents did he find a precedent? Of what individual did he make inquiry before he acted? Or did he rather make use of his intuitive knowledge to estimate what should be done, and there being no other way, act as he did? As for Wu's putting troops into the field before burying his father, was there anyone previous to his time who had put troops into the field before burying his father? In what historical and mythological document did he find a precedent? Of what individual did he make inquiry before he acted? Or did he also utilize intuitive knowledge to estimate what was proper, and there being no other way, act as he did? (63) If Shun's mind was not sincere in the matter of having no posterity, and Wu's in the matter of saving the people, and the former married without telling his parents and the latter put an army into the field before burying his father, then their lack of filial piety and loyalty was great. Later scholars do not earnestly develop their intuitive faculty in order minutely to investigate righteousness and principles in the experiences of the mind influenced by mutual intercourse. On the contrary, they desire vainly to examine and discuss these out-of-the-ordinary questions, and think that when they have apprehended these, they are able to control the root of the matter. It is also far from correct to seek to preserve the root of the matter when affairs arise. The rest of the sections of your letter can be explained in a similar way. In this way the ancient philosophy of extending knowledge to the utmost can be understood.

Does the Original Nature of the Mind Make Provision for All Phases of Life?

Your letter says: ''It would seem that the saying of the Great Learning regarding the investigation of things is probably in harmony with seeking the original character of the mind. But the following things from the Six Classics and Four Books should all be clearly sought within the limits of the books, to-wit: hear much and see much; what former sages have said, should be carried out in practice; 'I am one who is fond of antiquity, and earnest in seeking knowledge there'; 'extensive study of what is good and accurate inquiry about it'; 'he cherishes his old knowledge and is continually acquiring new'; 'in learning extensively and discussing minutely what is learned, the object of the superior man is that he may be able to go back and set forth in brief what is essential'; 'Shun loved to question others and to study their words.'[89] Certainly confusion

---

[89] Analects, Book II, Ch. 18, ¶ 2. The complete quotation is: ''Hear much and put aside the points of which you stand in doubt, while you speak cautiously at the same time of others — then you will afford few occasions for blame. See much and put aside the things which are perilous, while you are cautious at the same time in carrying the others into practice — then you will have few occasions for repentance.'' Confucian Analects, Book VII, Ch. 19, ¶ 1; Doctrine of the Mean, Ch. 20, ¶ 19; Ch. 27, ¶ 6; Mencius, Book IV, Pt. II, Ch. 15; Doctrine of the Mean, Ch. 6.

cannot be permitted in discussing the details of the rites and the order of the task.''

The idea involved in the investigation of things I have already thoroughly discussed. As for your doubt concerning the connection between this and devoting one's self to seeking the original nature of the mind, I judge that you will not need to wait until I have again explained it. Hearing much and seeing much was said by Confucius because Tzu-chang devoted himself to external things, loved superior position, and vainly considered learning to consist in hearing and seeing much. He was unable to seek within his own mind in order to put aside the things regarding which he stood in doubt and which seemed perilous. Thus, both in his words and in his deeds, he was unable to avoid being blamable and having occasions for repentance. Moreover, the meaning of seeing and hearing much amounts to a dependence upon devotion to external things, and to love of lofty position. For that reason Confucius said this to rescue him from the error of depending upon hearing and seeing much, and not for the reason that he wished him to consider this as learning. The Master has said: ''There may be those who act without knowing why. I do not do so.'' [90] This has the same idea as the saying of Mencius, that all men have the mental capacity to distinguish between right and wrong.

Knowledge Does Not Depend upon Learning Much and Remembering It

These sayings really have reference to understanding the intuitive knowledge of one's virtuous nature, and not to hearing and seeing much. (64) If anyone should refer to ''hearing much and selecting what is good and following it; seeing much and keeping it in memory,'' this would imply a mere seeking for the result of seeing and hearing. It carries with it the second idea, and therefore

---

[90] Analects, Book VII, Ch. 27.

the Master said that "this is the second style of knowledge." He thus considers the knowledge from seeing and hearing as the second type. What, then, is above this knowledge? Here you can have a peep at the place where the sage uses his effort in extending his knowledge. The Master said to Tzu-kung, "Ts'ze (sic), you think, I suppose, that I am one who learns many things and keeps them in memory? . . . No, I seek a unity all-pervading." [91] If knowledge really depends upon learning much and remembering it, why did the Master mistakenly speak as he did? Was it in order to deceive Tzu-kung? If his seeking a unity all-pervading does not refer to extending his intuitive knowledge of good, to what does it refer? The Book of Changes says: "The superior man remembers former sayings and virtuous practices in order to cultivate his virtue." Which of these do not contribute to cultivating virtue, if the individual uses them for this purpose? This surely is a task which implies a unification of knowledge and practice. Confucius says, "I am fond of antiquity and earnestly seek (knowledge there)." [92] If he loved the learning of the ancients, he earnestly sought to know the principles of the mind.

Mind is Principles

Mind, I say, is just what is meant by principles. He who studies should study the mind and he who seeks should seek the mind. Mencius said: "The end of learning is nothing else but to seek for the lost mind." [93] This is not the same as when later generations consider fondness of antiquity to consist in extensively remembering and reciting the phrases of the ancients. Moreover, with unremitting effort they seek for renown, gain, and advancement in that which is external. I have previously thoroughly dis-

[91] Op. cit., Book XV, Ch. 2, ¶ 1 and 3.
[92] Ibid., Book VII, Ch. 19.
[93] Mencius, Book VI, Pt. I, Ch. 11, ¶ 4.

cussed the matter of extensive study and careful inquiry.
As regards cherishing old knowledge and yet continually
acquiring new knowledge, the philosopher Chu also held
that the cherishing of the old referred to honoring one's
virtuous nature. Is it possible to search for this virtuous
nature outside the mind? Only if this continual acquiring
of new knowledge proceeds from the cherishing of the old,
can one cherish the old and acquire the new. In this way
you can also verify that knowledge and practice are not
two things.

As regards the saying of Mencius, "In learning extensively and discussing minutely what is learned, the object
is to go back and set forth in brief what is essential," if, as
he said, their value lies in opening the way to go back and
set forth in brief what is essential, for what reason does he
advocate them?[94] Shun in loving to question others and to
study their words used only the mean in governing his people, and extended his devotion to the essence of his mind in
complete loyalty to the path. (65) A mind loyal to the path
of duty is what is meant by the intuitive faculty. When
has the learning of the superior man absented itself from
the affairs of life and discarded discussions? However, he
who devotes himself to the affairs of life and to discussions
should know that the unification of knowledge and practice involves developing the intuitive knowledge of his
mind. He should not be like the world, which considers
vain speaking and hearing as learning, and which, by separating knowledge and practice, is able to discuss an order
of first and last in this.

Miscellaneous Questions

Your letter says: "The following are indefinite (confused) and not accredited: The virtue and righteousness
of Yang and Mo; the good, careful people of the villages in
their confusing of rightheartedness and truth; the abdica-

---

[94] *Ibid.*, Book IV, Pt. II, Ch. 15.

tion of Yao, Shun, and Tzu-chih; the rebellions of T'ang, Wu, and Ch'u Hsiang; the prince regency of Chou Kung, Wang Man, and Tsao Ts'ao.[95] What clue is there regarding these? What about the changes in circumstances (the details), both past and present, as well as the ceremonies, music, names, and things which have not been investigated to the point of knowing them? When the government desired to erect and establish a Brilliant Palace, or an Imperial Pavilion of Examination, or make rules for the calendar, or build an altar to worship a sacred hill, how did it proceed? For this reason the Confucian Analects speak of those who are born with possession of knowledge, referring to righteousness and principles. Regarding ceremonies, music, names of persons and things, and the changes of past and present, it is necessary to wait until they have been learned before one can verify their validity in practice. This can be said to be definitely determined."

What I have to say regarding Yang, Mo, the good, careful people of the villages, Yao, Shun, Tzu-chih, T'ang, Wu, Ch'u Hsiang, Chou Kung, Wang Man, and Tsao Ts'ao, can in general be arranged for explanation as I have formerly done in the discussion of Shun and Wu. Referring to your doubt concerning the changes of past and present, I have previously in the discussion of intuitive knowledge compared these with compasses, squares, and measures. You should in this matter, also, not need to wait until I repeat my explanation.

Wang Discusses the Brilliant Palace

Concerning the Brilliant Palace, the Pavilion for Examinations, and the rest, it seems that I must speak. However, the discussion will be very long. I merely follow your words and rectify them, for in this way your doubt will be dissipated. The rules and plans of the Brilliant

---

[95] Mencius, Book III, Pt. II, Ch. 9, ¶ 9; Book VII, Pt. II, Ch. 37, ¶ 8.

Palace and of the Imperial Pavilion for Examinations are first met with in the Yueh Ling (Book of the Seasons) of Lü Shih, the commentary of the scholars of the Han dynasty.[96] In the Four Books and Six Classics they had not been minutely discussed. Is the virtue of Lü Shih and of the scholars of the Han dynasty as worthy and good as that of the Three Dynasties?[97] (66) At the time of King Hsüan of Ch'i the Brilliant Palace had not yet been destroyed. At the time of the emperors Yu and Li the Brilliant Palace of the Chou dynasty had not yet come to grief.[98] Yao and Shun lived in thatched houses with earth steps, and thus the rules and plans of the Brilliant Palace were not ready at that time. But this did no injury to their government of the people. The Brilliant Palace of Yu and Li surely dates back as far as the time of Wen, Wu, Ch'eng, and K'ang. Why were they not able to save themselves from rebellion and confusion? Was it due to the fact that Yao and Shun with a commiserating mind practiced a commiserating government? Though their place of residence was a thatched house with a front step made of earth, it certainly was a Brilliant Palace. On the other hand, the application of the mind of Yu and Li to the administration of government eventuated in oppression and tyranny even though the ruler lived in the Brilliant Palace. The emperor Wu of the Han dynasty first began to discuss the Brilliant Palace. By the time of Empress Wu Hou of the T'ang dynasty it was completely finished.[99] What was the condition of the government, unquiet or peaceful? The college of the emperor was called the Imperial Pavilion for Examinations and that of the feudal princes was called the College of the Feudal State. They were both

---

[96] The Han dynasty ruled 206 B.C. to 220 A.D.

[97] *Vide* footnote 28, p. 69.

[98] The emperors, Yu and Li of the Chou dynasty, reigned at 878 and 781 B.C.

[99] Empress Wu ruled 684 A.D.

named from the topography of the place where they were situated.

Ancient Rulers of China and Their Work

During the Three Dynasties, learning was directed toward illustrating the five human relationships; at that time they did not estimate it by its having proceeded out of the Imperial or the State colleges. Confucius said: "If a man be without the virtues proper to humanity, what has he to do with the rites of propriety or with music?"[100] In the regulation of the rites of propriety and the playing of music it is necessary to have entered the state of equilibrium and harmony. He whose words may serve as a law and whose person as a measure (ideal), may be spoken of in this way, especially with reference to the number of utensils used in sacrificing, the kind of music, and the supervision of the master of ceremony. It is for this reason that the philosopher Tseng said: "There are three principles of conduct which the man of high rank should consider especially important. . . As to such matters as attending to the sacrificing vessels, there are the proper officials for them."[101] Yao instructed Hsi and Ho that in reverent accord with the great luminous heaven they should calculate and delineate the movements of the sun, moon, and stars.[102] He considered it important to give the people the times (*i.e.* definitely to determine the seasons). Shun depended on the Hsüan-chi with gem-inlaid transverse attached.[103] He considered it important to use the seven regulators — sun, moon, and five planets. This means that

---

[100] Analects, Book III, Ch. 3.

[101] *Ibid.*, Book VIII, Ch. 4, ¶ 3.

[102] Shooking, Part I, Book of T'ang, ¶ 3.

[103] An astronomical instrument of some kind, said to have been used by this legendary emperor, probably with tube attached. It is thought to have been a kind of armillary sphere made to represent the revolutions of the heavens, the transverse being a tube of precious stone placed athwart the sphere for the purpose of celestial observation. (Giles, op. cit., p. 491.)

he devoted himself with unremitting effort to having a mind which loved the people and to having a government which nourished the people. The regulating of the calendar and the understanding of the seasons really emerged out of this. The calculations of Hsi and Ho could not be carried out by Kao and Ch'i. King Yü and his minister Chi of the Hsia dynasty also could not have done so. "The wisdom of Yao and Shun did not extend to everything." [104] Thus Yao and Shun also could not do this (what Hsi and Ho had done). However, up to the present, generations have practiced the ideas of Hsi and Ho. (67) Even though a man with false knowledge and small wisdom, or an astrologer of mean ability is now able to foretell the weather without error, does this mean that the present-day man with his false knowledge and small wisdom is superior to those of the time of Yü, Chi, Yao, and Shun?

Sychophantic Scholars Sought Flattery and Departed from the Good Tried Way

In the matter of worshiping the sacred mountain, there has been even greater departure from the standard. This is due to the fact that later eloquent, artful men and sycophantic scholars sought the flattery of others. They took the initiative in boasting and lavish expenditures, in order to agitate and unsettle the mind of the prince, thereby wasting the money provided for the expenses of the government. They were shameless men of talent who deceived Heaven and wronged the people. A superior man does not even mention them. It is for this reason that Ssu-ma Hsiang-ju is ridiculed by later generations in the Empire. That you, my disciple, consider this something that a student should study is perhaps due to the fact that you have not seriously thought about it. The sage is a sage just because he is born with knowledge.

---

[104] Mencius, Book VI, Pt. II, Ch. 46, ¶ 1.

The Knowledge of the Sage

Moreover, in explaining the Analects, you say that being born with knowledge includes both righteousness and natural law, but that with regard to the constant changing of the rites of propriety, music, renowned men, and things, one must wait until one has learned before one can get at the truth connected therewith. These things certainly have a relation to carrying out the tasks of the sage. If the sage is not able to know these before he has learned them, then it cannot be said of him that he is born with knowledge (of them). To say that the sage is born with knowledge refers to righteousness and knowledge, but it does not refer to ceremonies, music, renowned names, and things, for these things have no vital relation to the task of the sage. If the saying that the sage is born with knowledge refers only to righteousness and natural law, and not to ceremonies, music, renowned names, and things, then, he who knows after study need only learn to know righteousness and natural law; and he who knows after a painful feeling of ignorance also need know only righteousness and natural law.

Present-day Students Are Mistaken

At present students who are trying to learn to become sages are not able to learn to know that which the sage is able to know, and yet with unremitting energy they devote themselves to seeking that which the sage is unable to know, as though it were learning. Has the student not thereby lost the means by which he hopes to become a sage? All that I have said corresponds to the points regarding which you are in doubt, and to a small extent explains them; (68) but it does not constitute an exhaustive discussion, and without this there is no clear understanding in the Empire. The more there are who are learning in this way to become sages, the more difficult they are to manage. They enter the class of animals and barbarians, and yet seem to think that they have the learning of the sage. Though my sayings may be temporarily understood, the situation will ultimately be like the ice which while melting in the west freezes in the east, or the fog which is dissipated in front but rises in clouds in the rear. Though I discuss vociferously until I am distressed unto death, I shall eventually not be able to save anything at all in the Empire.

The Mind of the Sage Described

The mind of the sage considers heaven, earth, and all things as one substance. He makes no distinctions between the people of the Empire. Whosoever has blood and life is his brother and child. There is no one whom he does not wish to see perfectly at peace, and whom he does not wish to nourish. This is in accordance with his idea that all things are one substance. The mind of everybody is at first not different from that of the sage. If there is any selfishness in it, which divides it through the obscuration of passion and covetousness, then that which is great is considered small and that which is clear and open as unintelligible and closed. Whoever has this mind gets to the place where he views his father or son or elder and younger brothers as enemies. The sage, distressed because of this, uses the occasion to extend his virtuous attitude, which considers heaven, earth, and all things as one substance, by instructing the people and causing them to subdue their selfishness, remove the obscuration, and revert to the original nature of their minds.

The People and Officials of the State under Yao, Shun, and Yü Were Simple and Virtuous

The main divisions of this instruction Yao, Shun, and Yü have mutually received and transmitted in the saying, "The mind which cherishes the path of duty is small. Devote yourself to the best, be undivided, sincerely hold fast the due Mean.''[105] The details of the task were given to Hsieh by Shun.[106] He said, ''Between father and son there should be affection; between sovereign and minister, righteousness; between husband and wife, attention to their separate functions; between young and old, a proper order; between friends, fidelity.''[107] At the time of Yao, Shun, and the Three Dynasties, only this was considered instruction by the teachers and by the students. All that time men did not differ in their opinions, nor homes in their practices. He who adjusted himself to this was called a sage; he who was diligent in carrying it out was called virtuous; he who disregarded it was considered degenerate, even though it was the intelligent Tan Chu.[108] The man at the village well or in the rural district, the farmer, the artisan, the merchant, everybody had this learning (of the human relationships) and looked only to the perfecting of character as important. (69) How is this to be accounted for? They were not subject to the confusion inherent in much hearing and seeing, nor to the annoyance of remembering and reciting, nor to the extravagance of speech and composition, nor to the striving and gaining of honor and advantage. The result was that they were filial toward their parents, respectful to their elders, and faithful toward their friends. They considered this as reverting to the original nature of the mind. This means that they certainly had these things by nature and did not need to acquire them from without. Thus, who was there that could not do them?

The government schools were devoted to perfecting virtue. In accordance with differences of capacity the students were to complete their virtue — whether they excelled in the rites of propriety and music, in capacity for ruling, or in ability

---

[105] Shooking, Pt. II, Book II, ¶ 15.

[106] Hsieh was one of the five celebrated ministers of Emperor Shun.

[107] Mencius, Book III, Pt. I, Ch. 4, ¶ 8.

[108] The son of Emperor Yao, whom Yao did not make his successor because of his lack of virtue.

to carry on agriculture. And this was done in order the more to refine their ability in the school, that when their virtue came into evidence and they were given employment, it would cause them from first to last to remain in their calling without change.

Those who employed others devoted themselves mutually to virtue alone, that they might give peace to the people of the Empire. Judging whether the individual's ability was suitable, they did not consider those of higher position and those of lower social standing as more or less worthy of consideration, nor labor and leisure as honorable or dishonorable.

Those who were employed also knew only this one thing, mutually to devote themselves to virtue for the purpose of giving peace to the people of the Empire. If they were able to carry this out in practice, then, though they were continually in the midst of increasing perplexities, they did not consider them laborious, and though they were placed in the midst of trifling, vulgar things, they did not consider them low and ignoble. At that time the people of the Empire, with clear, resplendent virtue, all viewed one another as relatives of one home. Those whose ability was lowly, engaged in agriculture, labor, or commerce. All were diligent in their various occupations for the purpose of nourishing one another. Moreover, they did not strive for exalted position and desire external things.

As for the varying degrees of natural ability, there were Kao, K'uei, Chi, and Hsieh. When they took up official position they did their best. They represented the occupations of a single home, attending to and managing the matters of clothes and food, having dealings with those that have and those that lack, and providing the utensils of the home. They brought together their plans and united their efforts, in order that in accordance therewith they might devise means whereby above they might serve their parents and below they might support their wives and children.

They were solicitous only lest perhaps in carrying this responsibility some might be indolent or selfish. For this reason Chi was a diligent farmer and not ashamed that he did not understand official admonitions. He viewed the excellent official admonitions of Hsieh as his own. K'uei was in charge of the music and was not ashamed because he did not understand the rites of propriety. (70) He considered I's clear understanding of ceremonies as though it were his own. The learning of their minds was pure and clear.

They had the virtue of perfecting their original nature, and therefore their mental energy and their purpose were penetrating and unifying. They did not distinguish between themselves and others, nor between things and themselves. They can be compared with the body of a single person. Eyes, ears, hands, and feet all assist in the functions of the body. The eyes are not ashamed because they are not intelligent. If anything of importance occurs to the ears, they certainly attend to it. The feet are not ashamed because they cannot grasp things. If there is anything that the hands feel for, the feet certainly move forward. The original vital fluids pervade, and the blood vessels branch out and penetrate the entire body. It is self-evident that itches and pains, expiration and inspiration cause excitement and exhilaration, and the spirit responds. The learning of the sages is extremely simple; it is readily understood and easily followed. Their learning was easily acquired and their ability readily gained, because the main divisions of their learning consisted in reverting to the original nature of the mind. They did not discuss understanding and talent.

Later Decay of State Was Due to Heterodoxy and Sham

The decay of the Three Dynasties was due to the extinction of rule by right, and increase of rule by might. After Confucius and Mencius had died, the learning of the sages became obscure and strange, and heterodox teachings unreasonable. The teachers did not consider the learning of the sages as instruction, nor did the students consider it as learning. The followers of those that ruled by might secretly appropriated things that seemed to be like those of the first king. Externally they made use of his doctrines, but it was done in order to assist their own selfish desires. There was no one in the Empire who did not respect and cherish this point of view. The doctrine of the sages was obstructed with a luxuriant growth of weeds. The people imitated one another and daily sought knowledge through which they might become wealthy and powerful — plans directed toward deception, and schemes for rebellion, things that impose upon heaven and injure mankind. Temporary success was utilized in the earnest pursuit of honor and gain. Of men such as Kuan, Shang, Su, Chang, and their class, there were an indefinite number.

The Learning of the Sages Was Entirely Neglected

After a long time of quarreling, plundering, sorrow, and affliction without ceasing, these men sank into the condition of animals and savages, and even their violent schemes could not all be carried out. All scholars were extremely distressed in their noblemindedness. They sought to find the sage emperor's laws and regulations, and arrange and renovate what was distressing them. Their purpose was to restore the path of the former kings. (71) As the learning of the sages was left in the distance, the transmitted precepts of violent practices became more numerous, intense, and pervasive. Even those who had the knowledge of the virtuous man could not avoid being tainted by the practices then prevalent. That they explained and renovated their doctrines in order to spread enlightenment over the world, only extended the boundary of force. The gate and wall of the learning of the sage could not be seen. Under such circumstances expository learning prevailed and was transmitted for the sake of making reputation. Learning that consisted in remembering and reciting was considered extensive; and formal learning was viewed as elegant. Men of this type confusedly and noisily came up in great numbers and disputed among themselves in order to establish their point of view in the Empire. I do not know how many groups there were. They came from ten thousand by-paths and a thousand different ways, but I do not know what they attained.

Wang Describes the Worldly Students

The students of the world may be compared to a theatre where a hundred different acts are presented. The players cheer, jest, hop, and skip. They emulate one another in cleverness and ingenuity; they laugh in the play and strive for the palm of beauty. On all sides the people emulate one another in striving to see. They look toward the front and gaze toward the rear, but cannot see it all. Their ears and their eyes are confused; their mental and physical energy is disturbed and confounded. Day and night they spend in amusement until they are steeped in it and rest in it, as though they were insane. They do not know what has become of their family property. Under the influence of the sayings of such scholars, princes and kings are confused and devote their lives to vain, useless literary style. They do not themselves know what they say. Some among them realize the empty distance between their doctrines and those of the sages, and their errors and perversity. They realize that they have branched off and have impeded the doctrine of the sages, and even rouse themselves to extraordinary effort, because they desire to see the truth and reality underlying all action. But the highest standpoint these views may in time reach, pertains merely to getting wealth, honor, or gain — the occupation of the five tyrants (of the sixth century B. C.). The learning of the sages is left farther and farther in the distance and is more and more obscured, while practices are directed toward acquiring honor and gain. The farther they go, the more they fall into error. Though some among them have been deceived by Buddhism and Taoism, yet even the sayings of Buddha and Lao-tzu, in last analysis, are unable to overcome the mind that is devoted to honor and gain. Though they have weighed the opinions of the mass of scholars, the discussions of these also are unable to break into their point of view — that of devoting themselves to honor and gain. When we consider present conditions, we find that the poison of honor and gain has penetrated the innermost recesses of the mind, and the practice thereof has become second nature.

For several thousand years people have mutually boasted of their knowledge; they have crushed one another because of power, and wrangled with one another for gain. They have mutually sought for superiority in cleverness, and each has sought for reputation. (72) When they come into prominence and are appointed to official position, those who should be in control of the taxes also desire to serve as military officials, and those who are in charge of the laws, ceremonies, and music, also wish positions on the Board of Civil Office. He who holds the position of a prefect or a magistrate thinks of being the treasurer of a province or a provincial judge; he who is censor hopes to become a prime minister. As a matter of fact, he who is unable to carry out the particular task of his position cannot hold other official positions at the same time, and he who does not understand these sayings (of the sages) cannot expect the praise that attaches to them. Where memory and ability to recite are extensive, they tend to increase pride; and extensive knowledge tends toward doing evil. Much hearing and seeing tends toward disorderly behavior in discussion, and wealth in literary style tends to patch up and brighten one's hypocrisy. It was because of this that Kao, K'uei, Chi, and Hsieh were unable to unite two things in one office. But present-day young students who are just beginning to learn, all desire to understand their sayings and investigate their methods and mysteries. Under false pretenses, they have said that they wish to reform the affairs of the Empire, but this is not the real idea of their minds. They are looking for something to help their selfishness and fulfill their desires.

Alas! because of these abuses, and because of this purpose and these devices of study, they naturally should hear the instruction of the sages. But they view it as an excrescence, a tumor, a handle-hole, and thus they consider their intuitive faculty as insufficient. They are certain to reach the point where they say that the learning of the sages is of no value. Alas! how can the scholars living on earth still seek the learning of the sages, or how can they still discuss it? Who is there among the scholars of this generation who, desiring to devote himself to study, is not in toilsome labor and great difficulty, is not also bigoted, does not stick to literary style, and is not in great danger? Alas, one can but feel sympathy for them! It is fortunate that heaven-given principles are in the mind of man; that in last analysis there is something which cannot be destroyed; and that the clearness of the intuitive faculty is the same as in the most ancient times. Thus, when they hear my exhaustive discussion they must surely commiserate their own condition and be in distress because of it. They must be sorry to a degree that is painful. They must rise up with renewed effort, as water flows into a river in spite of every hindrance. Only the superior scholar can promote this. To whom shall I look for it? (73)

Comment — This letter at first thoroughly investigates the unity of knowledge and practice, widely illustrating and extensively discussing it. Alongside, it makes historical allusions and gives various illustrations. It does no less than dispel the clouds so that the sun can be seen. The later discussion of pulling up the roots and stopping up the source makes clear the reason of the rise and fall of ancient and present-day methods of learning. It truly exhibits the five vital things and the eight precious things which the eight genii carry in their hands, in order to display its meaning. In studying this, unenlightened and simple-minded individuals suddenly come to a realization. This is an instance in which the mind of the Teacher, which considers all things as one, is not afraid to speak in detail in order to instruct later scholars. It should be examined in detail and not neglected.

BOOK IV

LETTERS WRITTEN BY WANG YANG MING
(Continued)

Letter Written to the Students at Ch'engchung
Written in the fourth year of Emperor Cheng Te

Wang's Appreciation of the Friendship of His Students

For two years I was in disgrace, and at that time had nobody with whom I could confer. When I returned I acquired you. How very fortunate this was! Then first did I rejoice, and when I was suddenly obliged to leave you I was very much discontented. Those who hinder true learning are many; those who seek the path of duty are few. One man from the state of Ch'i, among a multitude from the state of Ts'u, is readily disturbed and overinfluenced.[1] Excepting men of heroic virtue, few are firm and unchangeable. You, my friends, mutually refining and helping one another to be firm, should certainly strive that your learning be made complete.

He Advises His Students to Discard Renown and Glory and
Use Genuine Effort on the Self

Among scholars and officials there have recently been some who in a measure seek the path of duty, but they are slandered by the common people, because genuine virtue has not been completed in them and because they mutually advertise one another. Constantly cast down and unable to stand, they hinder the doctrine. You, my friends, should consider this as an admonition; discarding renown and glory, you should in your innermost selves genuinely use effort. What I formerly said in the temple with refer-

---
[1] *Vide* Mencius, Book III, Pt. II, Ch. 6, ¶ 1.

ence to sitting tranquilly, did not imply that I advise sitting like a priest and falling into abstraction. Because we are at ordinary times confused by affairs, we do not devote ourselves to the self. What I advocate is the use of quiet meditation as an aid to the beginning student, in regaining the intuitive knowledge which he has lost. The philosopher Ch'eng Ming-tao said: "At the time when a person learns, he should know where to apply his energies. Having learned he should know at what point he has acquired strength." If you, my friends, use your energies in this direction, you will make progress and later you will have points of strength.

Learning must strike into the inner nature. "It is the way of the superior man to prefer the concealment of his virtue, while it daily becomes more illustrious."[2] Though of devotion to fame and gain, the former is clear and pure and the latter impure and degenerate, nevertheless in the desire for advantage they are alike. "The humble man reaps advantage." "Do not seek to be different from others, but seek to live in accord with the principles of Heaven." (2) These sayings should be written on the wall where the eyes constantly rest upon them. Application to writing the Chüjen's essay need not hinder anyone from acquiring the truth, but he may be fearful lest it deprive him of his higher purpose in life. You should systematically carry out what we formerly agreed upon; then the two will not interfere with one another. Knowledge and attainment, even though they refer to sprinkling and sweeping the ground and to answering and replying, are minute and mysterious.

Comments — The true learning of the sages and virtuous men consists not in seeking to be different from others but in seeking to live in accordance with principles. Perhaps the philosophers Chu, Ch'eng, Chou, and Su did not clearly discriminate this.

---

[2] Doctrine of the Mean, Ch. 33, ¶ 1.

In general, he who seeks to be different from others has many of his ideas arising out of his desire to be like others. If persons are really unable to stand by themselves and seek that they be blameless, they become dependent upon the mutual publishing of one another. Establishing schools of their own, they boast that they differ from others of their time. They do not know that "the superior man stands erect in the middle, without inclining to either side," and that they ought not to be as they are.[3] This defect has been transmitted down to the present, until finally it has become habitual. In the case of learning and any merit accruing thereto, all is ruined when any part is ruined. Those who have the purpose to learn the truth should frequently repeat this.

Reply to Wang Shih-t'ang

Written in the sixth year of Emperor Cheng Te

Wang Discusses the Nature of the Passions, Showing that They are Functions of the Mind

I have received the instruction contained in your letter. For a number of days I have been much afflicted with boils and therefore was unable to write. I lack the time to ask for more instruction. Your letter says that what we formerly discussed is both mysterious and difficult, and that since great importance attaches to it, you feel that you must speak about it. I agree with you and for that reason cannot forthwith cease discussing it. Pleasure, anger, sorrow, and joy are feelings (passions). You have said that they cannot be considered as not having been manifested by the mind. The condition in which pleasure, anger, sorrow, and joy have not been stirred has reference to the character of the original nature. This saying comes from Tzu-ssu and was not first spoken by the philosopher Ch'eng.[4] Since you do not consider it correct, you should

---

[3] *Ibid.*, Ch. 10, ¶ 5.
[4] *Vide* footnote 68, p. 293.

date it from the time of Tzu-ssu's Doctrine of the Mean. Pleasure, anger, sorrow, and joy, together with deliberation and consciousness, are all manifestations of the mind. (3) Nature and feeling are included in mind. Nature is the structure, and the feelings are the functioning of the mind. The philosopher Ch'eng says that the mind is a unity. Its structure is perfectly tranquil, and in functioning it responds immediately when it is stimulated. Since this saying cannot be improved, you should investigate this matter of the structure and the function.

Structure and function have a common origin. If you know that the structure is for the sake of the function, you know that the function is for the sake of the structure. However, the structure is minute and difficult to understand, and its function is manifest and readily seen. What you have said is correct. Your saying that from morning till evening you do not have a moment in which there is tranquility and no stirring, shows that you refer to the functioning and not to the structure of the mind.

The Student Should Try to Understand the Structure of the Mind by Means of Its Functioning

When the superior man devotes himself to learning, he utilizes its functioning in studying the structure. Whenever the philosopher Ch'eng speaks of having deliberated, stirrings of the feelings are implied; and when he speaks of having become conscious, he refers to the mind's having been stimulated. He refers to seeking the state of equilibrium at the time when pleasure, anger, sorrow, and joy are not being manifested, but does not mean to say that they are never manifested. The philosopher Chu also at first frequently had doubts regarding the matter of there not having been any stirrings of passion. In his writings, his discussion of difficulties with (Chen) Nan-hsien includes some tens of letters back and forth, and then first did he fix his saying — to-wit, the present commentary of the Doctrine of the Mean. He was not careless in this matter. Only in his exposition of being cautious and apprehensive, until it reaches the very heart of utmost tranquility, and in his exposition of being watchful over one's self when alone, up to the highest point where one preserves this watchfulness in response to the stimulation of things, does he proceed too far in his differentiation. Since then, those who read his exposition separate them into two different things, and are doubtful lest there are perhaps other times when there is tranquility and the restfulness of nourishing the intuitive faculty. They do not realize that in the continual cherishing of cautiousness and apprehension the task does not have a moment's interruption, and that it does not necessarily follow that their cherishing takes its departure from not seeing and hearing.

You, my brother, should apply further energy at the point where there is stirring. Do not allow any interruption to occur. If there is harmony in the stirrings of the feelings, there is equilibrium in tranquility. You should yourself apprehend what is designated as the tranquil, unmoved structure. (4) If you estimate before you have reached the object, you cannot, in last analysis, avoid speaking to a pagoda about transmigration. Moreover, the philosopher Chu had the idea of realization though his sayings do not explicitly contain it, and thus this matter is not perfectly clear. You, my brother, since you doubt, must have some idea, but in your doubt you have gone to the excess of one who discards food because it happens to choke him. You need to investigate further. If the discussions of superior men differ from those of the ancients, you must not immediately come to a decision. You should rather, following the exposition, investigate the situation; and if the expositions contain portions that are not perspicuous, you should later estimate and judge them. This shows that in clear discrimination and explanation there is an inherent ability to get at fundamental principles. How is it that a man of your learning, your exceptional intelligence, and your sagacity and integrity, is unable to comprehend this? Your mind, my brother, is not like that of the man who, deeming himself superior, stands apart from others; but you seek for the truth only. Therefore I venture to speak thus without concealing anything. If I have not exhausted the situation, do not hesitate to instruct me. Though no advantage comes from it to you, it certainly will be advantageous to me.

Comment — The defect of customary learning consists in emphasizing function and forgetting structure. But, in casting aside function and seeking structure, there is the inevitable danger of reverting to the tranquility of the Buddhists, and of not getting a glimpse of the wonderfulness of the common source of both structure and function. In separating motion from rest and the feelings from mind and nature, vagueness and obstructions arise, and there is lack of a definite plan. Only in understanding that the structure and function have a common source does the idea contained in tranquility and lack of stirring convey the subtle idea of being influenced and understanding. The time of being influenced and of understanding, is the condition of tranquility and lack of stirring. Feelings, mind, and nature are an all-pervading unity.

Reply to Huang Tsung-hsien and Ying Yüan-chung
Written in the sixth year of Emperor Cheng Te

The Student Should Continue to Think about Perplexing Problems, for He May Receive Sudden Enlightenment

Last night I fear I spoke too much; but in meeting you both I was unable to do otherwise. Because my attainment was not perfect (mature), some of the things I said were not clear. (5) However, they had reference to a portion of our real task. When you cannot think coherently do not immediately cease thinking, for there should be points at which you suddenly understand. The mind of the sage naturally cannot allow the least obscuration, nor does it need to be polished and refined. The mind of the ordinary man is as a mirror which is exceedingly spotted and dirty, and which must be scraped and polished until its many spots have been completely removed. After that the least dust will at once be seen. The mirror need then only be brushed to be clear, and there is no need of expending any great energy. When the individual has reached that point, he recognizes and knows the real structure of the highest virtue. Though the many spots have not been cleared away, there are quite naturally some bright spots left, and if a little dust falls upon them, it may readily be seen and needs only be brushed off. But when the dust heaps on the portion that is darkened, it cannot be seen. Thus there is a difference between the matter of knowing the duties of the path and practicing them from a desire for advantage, and that of acquiring knowledge of them after a painful feeling of ignorance and practicing them by strenuous effort. I trust that you will not consider this as perplexing, and therefore be in doubt.

The feelings and passions of men invariably favor ease and hate difficulty. In this, of course, selfishness and habits of the passion-nature intervene and obscure. After you have clearly distinguished this, you will see no difficulty in it. The ancients who reached the point where they took delight in this task, though they passed through many extreme difficulties, also realized this; but you, having seen the idea involved, naturally are unable to explain the task. Now that you have perceived this part, there is the danger of your loving ease and hating difficulty, and of therefore drifting into Buddhism. Yesterday we discussed the difference between Confucianism and Buddhism. What the philosopher Ch'eng Ming-tao designated as being reverent in order to rectify the mind, they (the Buddhists) have; but they lack the external acts of righteousness. In last analysis, it is approximately correct to say that they also lack the reverence that rectifies the mind.

Comments — In all the world there is no real learning of the sage and virtuous men. There is only fear of difficulty and illicit desire for peace. This letter gives advice to up-root this evil.

Letter to Huang Tsung-hsien

Written in the eighth year of Emperor Cheng Te

Wang Commends Tsung-hsien for His Loyalty

Your letter in which you mention the affair of Shun-pu has reached me. The way in which you wrote shows your earnestness to the fullest extent. From this I know that your loyalty to a friend is a love of the highest order. As the world decays and customs degenerate, even among friends who commonly love and respect one another exceedingly, there are many who change completely. (6) They maintain two types of speech (are insincere), because they emulate that which is customary and strive to keep up external appearance. This is an exceedingly decadent and lamentable state. You, my brother, truly can be said to be earnest in your loyalty to right principles and to give full development to your maintenance of virtue. How fortunate this is!

Wang and Shun-pu are Estranged but Wang Continues to be His Friend

When I was at Nanchang, I lived very near Shun-pu, seeing him every month or two. Whenever I had occasion to admonish him, I always did it with an attitude of esteem and sympathy. Though I never found the least fault with him, he may have been somewhat offended. My own frame of mind I am willing to divulge to all the spirits and gods. Later, he went north in another official capacity, and at that time I first realized his indifference. Soon thereafter he was exceedingly repentant. "For should it be," he held, "that when we were thus together, I should be so indifferent and sink into the worldly danger of finding fault with you and thereby becoming so very unconcerned?" Thereupon all misunderstanding was cleared away (the ice was melted and the fog disappeared).

Later, word from others frequently reached me. There were some who were zealous in their speech and grave on my behalf, but I continued to treat him as I had previously done. I truly did not give way one day and forget Shun-pu. I did this naturally because of my extreme esteem and warm affection. Within ten months another mutual friend came from Peking and transmitted fully what Shun-pu had said, but I privately feared that fickle, narrow-minded, untrustworthy men found delight in our estrangement, and mutually arousing and exciting us thereby increased it. I felt certain that these things did not all come from the mouth of Shun-pu. I do not simulate these words. In fact, our friendship was so deep that I would not doubt him. I have a genuine love for Shun-pu, which is not actuated by any deep-seated selfishness, so that if he treats me shabbily it should not be from selfish reasons. I have not been intimate with Shun-pu in selfish purposes, nor he cold toward me. Why should I allow my mind to find fault with our mutual relationship?

Formerly, when I saw that commonplace friends readily begot a feeling of mutual dislike and disagreement, it had this significance for me, that they were merely externally brought together and lacked natural bonds. The result was that I privately commiserated them. I said to myself that if we all should be suddenly separated so that we lived in the enemies' country and home, we would still not come to that. (7) It is entirely unforeseen that we have this present discussion, and this alone should cause us to reprove ourselves. Mencius said: "If a man love others and no responsive attachment is shown to him, let him turn inward and examine his own benevolence." He also said: "When we do not, by what we do, realize what we desire, we must turn inward, and examine ourselves in every point.''[5] Therefore, unless one has experienced this himself, he does not know the lasting interest that attaches to these words and the earnestness of this idea.

In Study Emphasis Should Be Placed on Essentials

Recently, in discussing learning with my friends I have spoken only of establishing one's sincerity. As in killing a man, it is necessary to place the knife to the throat, so in our devotion to study we should expend the energy of mind and marrow in penetrating into the essentials, for then it will be trustworthy and clear. Though selfish desire happen to sprout, it is like dropping a little snow upon a large stove; for the great fundamental virtue of humanity has been established. If the individual devotes his attention to the topmost branch (instead of to the great root), in order to come to a decision, then that which is ordinarily designated as study, inquiry, reflection, and discrimination is just sufficient to increase his arrogance and his disposition to evil. Believing himself to have become superior, intelligent, clear, and magnanimous, he does not realize that he has sunken into great calamity and dangerous jealousy and dislike. Truly he is to be pitied! Judging from recent events, you are in a position the more to see that our former discussions were directed at the very heart of the matter. This is a genuine transmissal of the learning of the sage. How unfortunate that it has so long been buried and concealed! In the past my view was confused, and even recently I have made no progress, except that at this point I am able to distinguish very clearly. I am really much elated and can not again doubt. However, I have been separated from you a long time and have nothing to report to you.

Does Yüan-chung often discuss learning with you? Not

---

[5] Mencius, Book IV, Pt. I, Ch. 4, ¶ 1 and 2.

long ago I received a letter from him and observed that his outlook is very different from what it formerly was — a fact very comforting to me. I have also sent a letter to him, but have not been able to enter into detail. I hope that when you see him you will allow him to peruse yours. My plan to return home has not been definitely settled, but after ten months I propose to mention it again to the emperor. It is not possible to determine the day when I shall meet you, and in consequence I am very sad as I write this.

Comments — The expression, "In killing a man, it is necessary to place the knife at the throat," should bring the student to prompt self-realization. It may be compared to being suddenly frightened while sleeping and dreaming.

Letter to Huang Tsung-hsien

Written in the sixth year of Emperor Chia Ching

The Value of Friendship

When one bears the responsibility of official position, his work is ten times as difficult as when he retires into the mountain forest. (8) Unless he gains a good friend who constantly admonishes and refines him, that upon which his determination is ordinarily fixed will be secretly removed and silently taken away, and it will inadvertently sink into deterioration and ruin. Not long ago I said to Ch'eng-fu that at Peking one meets few friends. You two should come to an understanding in advance, that whenever either sees the least striving of passion, he will forthwith remind the other of the saying regarding developing the intuitive faculty, and thus you will mutually rectify one another.

Of What the Modern Scholar Is Not but Should Be Ashamed

The man who resolutely ceases and remains silent when in his speech he is just about to reach rapid satisfaction; who controls his ideas just when they are about to be displayed in force; who is able to dissipate anger and licentiousness when they are just about to overflow, is the most courageous man in all the world. However, when a man intimately comprehends the intuitive faculty, this task is not difficult. These several defects, which the intuitive faculty by nature lacks, are later present because it has been obscured and obstructed. As the coming forth of the sun makes the shadows (spirits) disappear, so is the intuitive faculty, when it has once come to realization. The Doctrine of the Mean says: "To possess the feeling of shame is to be near to energy."[6] The feeling of shame here refers to shame as a result of inability to extend one's intuitive knowledge of good to the utmost. At present, men consider it something to be ashamed of, if they are unable to use their words in forcing others to follow them, or if the force of their ideas is unable to crush others, or if their anger and passion are not able to attain what they purpose and desire. They do not know that these several defects are all the agents for obscuring and obstructing the intuitive faculty. This is exactly what the superior man should be extremely ashamed of. Today the situation is reversed, and men are ashamed because of inability to obscure and obstruct their intuitive faculty. Is it not exceedingly to be deplored, that men are ashamed of that concerning which they should not be ashamed, and fail to be ashamed of that concerning which they should be ashamed?

Wang's Ambition for His Friends

You, Sirs, are my everyday, intimate friends; I esteem you highly, but am unable to help you. I am willing that each of you may be like a great minister of ancient times. Those who were called great ministers in ancient times were not noted because of deep wisdom and ability, but because they were plain and sincere without pretending to additional abilities, and because they were men of a simple, upright mind and possessed of generosity. (9) Your

---

[6] Doctrine of the Mean, Ch. 20, ¶ 10.

intelligence and ability naturally surpass that of the multitude. Insofar as you lack faith in yourselves you are unable to develop to the utmost your own intuitive faculty, and consequently fail to attain plainness, sincerity, simplicity, and uprightness of mind.

The present condition of the Empire is like that of a man stricken with a severe, chronic illness. Any hope that he who is at death's door may live, rests in you, Sirs. If you are unable to get rid of your own defects, how can you cure the defects of the Empire? This is my sincere thought, and for that reason I am compelled to tell it completely and exhaustively to you. Whenever you meet, I wish you would use this idea in rectifying one another. Only in subduing your own private and selfish motives, in considering heaven, earth, and all things as one structure, in helping to secure the repose and prosperity of the Empire, and in reëstablishing the rule of the Three Dynasties, will you keep from disregarding and becoming unmindful of our virtuous, intelligent prince. Only then will you requite his kindness and have been born to some purpose in this great enterprise. Stricken with disease, I am lying in the mountain forest and can at best only alleviate the illness with medicines, in order to prolong my life. However, your going out to be officials and your returning, after having served, arouse my sympathy. Without realizing it, I have written thus in detail. I hope that you will make allowances for my feelings.

Comment — Both learning and exhortations to officials are contained in this letter.

Letter to Chu Yung-ming

Written in the sixth year of Emperor Cheng Te

The Matter of Getting a Degree Early in Life is Not the Essential Thing

I have received your letter, and am delighted at the advance you have recently made in your application to study.

The superior man fears lest the profession of study be not regulated and cultivated, but he does not discuss the matter of getting the second and third degrees early or late in life. Moreover, I always hope for something truly greater than this for you, but I do not know whether you have your purpose fixed on study or not. When convenient let me know about this.

I heard that the nephews of Chieh Yang all took the A. B. examinations last year. It is not that I do not take delight that they should have a determination so early in life, but I personally consider their selfish ambition wrong. (10) If, unfortunately, they should at once attain the object of their ambition, will not their lives be hindered and obstructed? The excellent abilities of a youth should be nourished and cultivated. If the doctrines of Heaven are not harmoniously brought together, they cannot be manifested. How much more is this true in the case of man! A flower that has a superabundance of petals does not bear fruit, because its luxuriance is manifested to excess. If these nephews do not consider my admonition as distorted, they should make some progress.

Your letter exhorts me to take up official position. I am not a single-minded, unsullied man; but the reason why I should remain in obscurity is not because this is the time to remain obscure, but because my learning itself is not perfect. Years and months do not wait. After several years my mental and physical energies will be more decrepit. Although I then desire to enter forcefully into learning, I shall not be able and must thus to the last leave it incomplete. This is due to the fact that strength and dignity do not permit me to cease. But from my grandfather down none are pleased that I should enter official service. Can I today determine to do this and vainly deliver myself into so lamentable a condition?

Comments — Of late, fathers and brothers in the instruction of their sons and younger brothers are vexed, that the child is not able to write essays and take the first examinations as soon as it is able to distinguish sentences. They think that the early acquiring of the degrees of Chüjen and Chinshih is excellent in the extreme. Everybody feels only a heart-longing for gain, honor, advantage, and official promotion. How can learning and real merit fail to be completely ruined?

First Letter to Wang Shun-pu

Written in the seventh year of Emperor Cheng Te

The Superior Man Does What is Proper to the Station in Which He is

After you had left a man came from Wuch'eng and said that, when you first reached home, your father was very much displeased, and that your plan to return had been met with still greater opposition.[7] When I first heard of it I was surprised and annoyed, but later I was glad. Then another man came from Nanking and said that you had already taken up official position and that neither higher nor lower officials were coöperating with you. When first I heard of this I was startled, but later I was delighted. What alarmed me was ordinary selfish feeling; what made me glad you yourself should know. How could I but bear somewhat patiently with you, and stimulate your mind, and harden your nature, that you might enlarge your undertakings? For instance, when the gold is tried in the furnace, passes through the roaring blaze, and is handled with the nippers and hammers, that is the time when it suffers. (11) But others are glad that the gold is being more refined until perfect purity is obtained, and fear only lest the strength of the fire and the power of the hammer are insufficient. When it has been taken out of the furnace, the gold is also glad that the rough treatment and refining have been completed. Whenever I looked with disdain upon my

---

[7] Wuch'eng is in the province of Shantung.

companions, esteeming lightly the ways of the world, though I later condemned myself, I was only able to control myself and to perform my duties perfunctorily with regard to outward appearance. But when I had been in disgrace in Kweichow for three years and had suffered a hundred difficulties, then for the first time did I have wisdom and believe that the words of Mencius, ''We see how life springs from sorrow and calamity, and death from ease and pleasure,'' are not deceptive.[8] I grasped the truth of the saying: ''The superior man does what is proper to the station in which he is; he does not desire to go beyond this. In a position of wealth and honor, he does what is proper to a position of wealth and honor. In a poor and low position he does what is proper to a poor and low position. In a position of sorrow and difficulty, he does what is proper to a position of sorrow and difficulty. The superior man can find himself in no situation in which he is not himself.''[9] The superior man of later times should also do what is proper to his station and learn not to desire to go beyond this. In wealth and honor he should learn to live in wealth and honor; and in poverty and lowliness, in sorrow and difficulty, he should learn to occupy these positions. Then, he, too, can find himself in no position in which he is not himself. I have previously said this for your benefit, and you heartly agreed. I do not know, however, how you have recently applied yourself.

The Superior Man Manifests Strength of Character

Of late, whenever I have discussed matters with the students, all except Huang Tsung-hsien and a few others have at every meeting praised your high intelligence. Now that you have again thus met with this temporary affliction, your progress can not be measured. You should earnestly forge ahead. Wang Ching-yen has recently become magistrate

[8] Mencius, Book VI, Pt. II, Ch. 15, ¶ 5.
[9] Doctrine of the Mean, Ch. 14, ¶ 1 and 2.

at Taming. As he was about to leave, he requested further instruction. I spoke to him with reference to changing one's mental and moral character — a thing which is ordinarily not seen — saying that it implies that at the time of meeting injury, or passing through changing circumstances, or encountering injustice and disgrace, he who ordinarily becomes angry does not lose his temper, and he who ordinarily is distressed, afraid, and at a loss what to do, is not distressed, afraid, or bewildered. This implies that where he is able to acquire strength, he is also able to use it. Though the affairs of earth change indefinitely, he will make appropriate response to them within the realms of pleasure, anger, sorrow, and joy. This is the important thing in learning, and serving in official capacity is included. (12) When Ching-yen heard this he understood it plainly. Recently I received a letter from Kan-ch'üan. He has chosen a place called Lake Hsiang near Hsiaoshan, some tens of li east of the Yang-ming Grotto. His library is nearly completed. When I heard this I was greatly delighted. To be able to meet with friends and together to make progress on the path of duty, is there anything more pleasing? Is what I have experienced of glory or disgrace, of attainment or loss, worth mentioning?

Comments — The superior man attains within himself. In consequence he should always adjust himself to circumstances and not forget thoughts of distress, diligence, caution, and encouragement. In a position of distress and opposition, he will not lose sight of the necessity of introspection and of maintaining his ordinary self-control. Thus, whether under ordinary circumstances or amidst change, he is always the same and is not influenced by circumstances. If he considers himself remarkable and strange because of disappointment, poverty, and lowliness, he has fallen into the habit of esteeming the world lightly and of being proud and arrogant.

Second Letter to Wang Shun-pu

Written in the eighth year of Emperor Cheng Te

Self-Righteousness Hinders Progress in Learning

The words in which you have couched your inquiry are very humble, but among them are some that really give the impression that you feel certain that you are correct. Generally speaking, it is true that the individual who considers himself correct does not have the desire to receive further instruction. At first I did not desire to answer your letter, for I feared that it would fail to penetrate your mind. As I had made a beginning in a former letter, I held that next spring, when I cross the river, you would learn fully; but having thought the matter over, I realize that the coming together and separation of friends cannot be definitely determined. You consider yourself correct because you are still blinded. You do not realize your error, but claiming to be correct seek me. Can I cease instructing you? For this reason I have fully prepared these words for you.

Shun-pu Makes Inquiry about Understanding the Good and Attaining Sincerity

Your letter says: "Study is surely for the purpose of understanding the good and attaining sincerity, but I do not know what is meant by the good, nor whence it comes, and where it is to be found at this time. I do not know what is the means of understanding it, nor how to make a start. Nor do I know whether in it, and in attaining sincerity, there is a regular, systematic order. In what is sincerity to be attained? (13) These details are minute and complicated. I earnestly desire to ask you to explain them, and for that reason manifest my doubts in this way. I commit myself to you, that you may help me."

Wang Calls Shun-pu's Attention to the Necessity of Exercising Self-control

I have read and re-read it and find that it is at this point that you have attained strength, and that it is also at this point that you are defective. You ordinarily simply know the saying about cherishing the mind, but have not really added self-control to this. For this reason you are not able to bring together activity and tranquility, and whenever you meet affairs you always fall into confusion. Now that you are able to push your inquiries to this point, you certainly are gradually realizing that you formerly fell into vanity. Because of this, I say that you have attained strength at this point. However, you have, without knowing it, acquired the error of branching off and going to external things. The mind is master of the body; nature (disposition) is completely included in mind; and virtue is originally to be found in nature.

The Concept "Good" is Not Subject to the Category of Space

In Mencius' saying, "Nature is good," the word good refers to my nature.[10] Since it has no form which can be pointed out, and no place at which it can be located, can it be considered a thing which has come from somewhere? For this reason I say that you are also mistaken at this point. You have not thoroughly inquired into the true learning of the Confucianists, but are still accustomed to the comments of later generations. You hold that every affair and every thing has its highest virtue, that it is necessary to seek this in affairs and things, and that having accomplished this, you will understand the good. Therefore you ask where it originally comes from and where it now is. Perhaps you fear lest I may have fallen into vanity, and

---

[10] *Vide* Mencius, Book III, Pt. I, Ch. 1, ¶ 2; Book VI, Pt. I, Ch. 2. The expression "my nature" seems to refer to the higher rational nature of man.

therefore use this to make my obscuration manifest. It is not that I do not know how to be grateful to you for this purpose, but as a matter of fact I have not fallen into vanity. The principles of things, righteousness in adapting one's self to them, and good in nature, are thus differently designated because of the things to which they refer, but in reality they are all manifestations of the mind. Outside of and apart from the mind, there are neither things, affairs, principles, righteousness, nor goodness. When the mind is engaged with affairs and things, and is at the same time characterized by unmixed principles and devoid of falseness, we have the good (virtue). There is no definite place nor way of seeking it in things and affairs. That righteousness consists in adapting one's self to things, means that the mind has attained what is proper in some particular affair. Righteousness cannot be externally seized and taken. (14) Investigation refers to investigating the good and extending it to the utmost.

The Good Should Not Be Sought for in Things and Affairs

To insist that the highest good (excellence) is to be sought in affairs and things implies leaving it and separating it into two things. The saying of the philosopher Ch'eng I-ch'uan, "If you are clear with reference to that, you know this," appears to speak of it as two things. That and this are not to be distinguished in nature, nor in principles and excellence.

Attaining Sincerity Means Understanding the Good

You say, "I do not know what is the means of understanding the good, nor how to make a start. Nor do I know whether in understanding the good and in attaining sincerity there is a regular systematic order. To what does attaining sincerity refer?" You think that understanding the good has a definite way of procedure all its own, and that attaining sincerity in person also has its own method.

According to my idea, the process of understanding the good is the same as that of attaining sincerity in person. Sincerity means being free from error and guile. To attain sincerity in person means striving to be free from error and guile. The task of attaining sincerity means understanding the good. Therefore, he who studies extensively studies this; he who makes careful inquiry, does so with reference to this; he who reflects carefully, reflects carefully regarding this; he who clearly discriminates, does so with reference to this; and he who earnestly practices, practices this. These all, therefore, imply using one's energy in understanding the good and attaining sincerity. For this reason "there is a way to the attainment of sincerity in one's self."[11] To understand virtue is the way to attain sincerity in one's self. "If a man does not understand what is good he will not attain sincerity in himself." There is no other way of attaining sincerity than that of understanding the good. When one sets out to attain sincerity in the person, the person is not sincere, and for that reason we have the saying, "understand the good." When goodness is thoroughly understood, the person is sincere. If one says that there is the task of understanding virtue and the further task of attaining sincerity in the person, a division is made between the two. Thus it is difficult to avoid mistakes, both small and great. In this letter I would tell you still more, but paper and pen do not suffice for me to enter into the minutiæ. Should this be inadequate, it will do no harm for us to write to and fro.

Comments — That understanding the good is truly attaining sincerity in one's self is what the Great Learning means by saying that when the purpose is sincere knowledge is complete.[12] Sincerity and goodness are not two different things. As man's nature is originally good, and goodness is the principle of genuineness and freedom from

[11] Doctrine of the Mean, Ch. 20, ¶ 17.
[12] *Vide* Great Learning, Introduction, ¶ 5.

error and guile, it is said to be sincere. When man confuses it with error and deception, goodness is obscured and sincerity lost. How can sincerity of person be attained apart from understanding the good? (15)

First Letter to Hsi-yüan

Written in the seventh year of Emperor Cheng Te

In a Decadent Age the Sage May Meet Problems in an Indirect Way

Having encountered such conditions your plan to return home is good, but you are rather precipitate.[13] If you will leave two or three months later under the guise of illness, every trace will be destroyed. Since you will not have aroused the indignation of others, you will also not have lost your uprightness. When a sage or virtuous man is placed in a decadent age, his treatment of men and his response to things is at times indirect, but his method of procedure has never been other than correct. To make one's self superior, while one causes others to be small and inferior, is not the manifestation of the mind of the benevolent man who is true to the principles of his nature, practices reciprocity, and has a sympathetic mind. You will surely consider my saying too inclusive, but the principles of the path are of this sort. I myself am receiving a liberal salary and bear the responsibility of position. That I should desire to throw this off and secretly leave is certainly difficult. In your position there is ample opportunity to advance or recede. Now that you have become thus involved, you will appreciate that the occasion when the ancients hung up the official cap and loosed the string of the seal was also not easily met.[14]

Comment — The benevolent and superior man surely responds in this way.

---

[13] Returning home here signifies leaving official position.

[14] To hang up the official cap is to retire from official position.

Second Letter to Hsi-yüan

Written in the seventh year of Emperor Cheng Te

The Practice of Virtue is a Personal Obligation

Having received a letter from Ling of Soochow, I knew that you were there. At that time Shou-chung was at Shanyin.[15] Recently Chang Shan-yin came from Shanyin and I know that you have returned to that place. Moreover, Shou-chung has gone to Chinghua. Formerly you lived at home and Shou-chung was a guest at Ch'i. This is now re-occurring. Does the fact that you two friends are constantly separated perhaps contain elements of fate? To practice the highest virtue depends upon the individual himself and cannot be committed or transferred to some one else. Again, friends truly cannot afford to go without the advantage of mutual watchfulness and refinement for a single day. (16) In addition, the groups of Tzu-yung and Ming-te are separated from one another some tens of li and cannot see one another morning and evening.[16] Are you not perhaps also sighing because you are alone and cannot be with friends? Your former discussion of Pan Kuei is perfectly correct. Scholars who live in the mountain forests devoid of all desire to enter into life's opportunities are rare. They differ greatly from those who run about in confusion wherever honor and gain can be attained. The characters of men are not uniform. Sages and virtuous men perfect others according to the ability which these possess. Regarding the methods of teaching Confucianism, men have different opinions. It was not until recent times that scholars began to discuss the matter of uniformity. However, few of them perfected their virtue and enlarged their capacities. Why was this? You should reflect about this, and determine how the situation is.

Comments — Later scholars really discuss superficially

---

[15] Shou-chung was Wang Yang-ming's brother.

[16] *Cf.* Biography, footnote 11, p. 12.

when they speak of uniformity in the instruction of others. The farther they proceed, the farther away they get; to the last they do not arrive at reality. Sages and virtuous men speak of uniformity only with reference to the source, and thus perfect others in accordance with the ability which these possess. All can enter the path of duty. This is in accordance with the saying that all reach the same place (the path) by different roads. The methods of later scholars appear to be uniform, but in reality are not; while the methods of the sages seem to differ but are really uniform. The difference between the learning of the sages and that of the present day is subtle.

Letter in Reply to an Inquiry Regarding Immortals (Genii)

Written in the third year of Emperor Cheng Te

Wang Discusses Immortality

You ask whether there are immortals or not, and also inquire for further information. Thrice you have written and I have not replied, not because I did not wish to answer, but because I had nothing to say. Yesterday your younger brother arrived and hoped surely to get an answer. When I was eight years old, I loved to hear about this. Now I am more than thirty years old, my teeth are gradually loosening in their sockets, a few of my hair have become white, my eyes are becoming dimmed, and my ears are dull. Also, I frequently am stricken to my couch with disease for a month, and my ability to take medicine rapidly increases. Such is the outcome. But my intimate friends erroneously say that I am able to understand immortality, and you, having erroneously heard this, use it to make inquiries of me. There is no way out for me: I must reply. (17) Under the circumstances, I discuss it in an incoherent manner.

Immortality is Not an Accomplishment of Man's Effort

In ancient times there were some most excellent men, who, characterized by pure genuine virtue, made the perfect path a fact. They harmoniously blended the Yin and the Yang and adjusted themselves to the four seasons; they left the world and its customs; they stored up and perfected their mental and physical energies; they wandered about everywhere and experienced things beyond the realm of ordinary experience. Referring to Kuang Ch'eng-tzu, who did not lose his vigor though he reached an age of one thousand five hundred years, and Li Po-yang, who lived through the Shang and Chou Dynasties and, going west, went through the Hanku pass in Honan, it is a fact that these things have actually transpired.[17] If true, and I should say that they are not, you would fear that I was deceiving you. But in their expiration and inspiration (breathing), in their activity and their rest, they considered the doctrine of immortality as fundamental. That their mental energies and their lives were preserved perfectly for a long period was a natural endowment from the time before they breathed. Immortality is perhaps an accomplishment of Heaven and not the result of any strenuous effort on man's part.

The Taoists Employ Secret Devices

Later generations say that Taoists pick up their houses and go up to heaven, that they transform things and have the ability magically to present and take things; but these delusive, eccentric, marvelous things are but secret devices and deceitful ingenuity. They are what Yin Wen-tzu calls magic, and the Buddhists designate as heterodoxy. If I say that these things actually occur, you will also fear that I am deceiving you. Whether there are or are not such

---

17 Li Po-yang — or, as he is better known, Lao-tzu — the founder of Taoism, is said to have written the Tao-Teh-King there and never to have returned.

immortals, words cannot tell. After long reflection it will be understood. If you will cultivate it profoundly, you will attain it. If you have not reached this point, and I forcibly reveal it to you, you will not attain it, though you believe.

The Immortality of the Confucianists

We scholars also have the doctrine of immortality. The philosopher Yen died at the age of thirty-two, but up to the present he has not perished. Are you able to believe this? The later group which imitated Shang Yang-tzu and others, consisted of exceptionally skillful, cunning Taoist priests who did not act in accordance with the doctrine. The followers of Ta Mo and Hui Neng nearly reached immortality, though this is not an easy matter to discuss. If you wish to hear about immortality, you must live in the mountain forest for thirty years. When you have perfected ears and eyes and unified mind and purpose, when your mind is clear, clean, and free from all vice, you will be in a position to speak about this. At present you are still far from the path of immortality. I have spoken incoherently. Do not be offended.

Comments — It is not possible to discuss the doctrine of immortality with anyone whose worldly mind is not clean. He must go into seclusion for thirty years. The Teacher has pointed out these things in detail. The great path is not far distant. The shore is just back of the man of strength and courage. For this reason, Confucius spoke to Yen Yüan about subduing himself in a single day; for after having done so for a single day, he would have subdued himself. Why use thirty years? (18) These words of the Teacher constitute an admonition for those who have sunken deeply into a desire for advantage and official salary.

Letter to Huang Ch'eng-fu

Written in the eighth year of Emperor Cheng Te

A Man's Determination is an Index of His Character and His Actions

I have recently discussed the fixing of the determination, to the point where it becomes annoying. But in writing to you, my intimate friend, I cannot put it aside. When the determination is fixed upon truth and virtue, no literary degree is sufficient to embarrass the mind; when it is fixed upon acquiring literary degrees, wealth and honor are insufficient to perplex the mind. But at the present time truth and virtue are identified with literary degrees, and literary degrees are identified with wealth and honor. The man of the highest virtue confines himself to what is right and proper, and does not plan for his own advantage; he exhibits the truth of the doctrine, and does not devise schemes for acquiring fame and merit. He who has a mind devoted to plotting and scheming, acts for the sake of fame and gain, though he confines himself to what is right and in addition exemplifies the truth of the doctrine. We now live separated and Yüeh-jen is also about to depart for a distant place; but when we meet we should, while mutually urging one another to reform, manifest a determination fixed upon virtue. Thus perhaps it will not be relaxed. Your feet, Ch'eng-fu, should traverse a thousand li in a day, for the burden is heavy and the distance great. To whom shall I look, if not to you? The words spoken at the time of parting, while we are gloomy, cannot be forgotten, but are profoundly cherished.

Comments — I hold that wealth and honor are not the things that embarrass men, but that men allow themselves to be embarrassed by them. If the determination is fixed upon truth and virtue, wealth and rank afford an opportunity for practicing virtue and becoming established in it. From most ancient times on, it has not been heard that virtue was granted to Ch'ao and Yu and disputed in the instance of I and Lü. Even though a person is willing to be poverty-stricken all his life, if the determination is not fixed on truth and virtue, he is but a miserable creature. The student should earnestly devote himself to distinguishing the nature of his purpose.

Letter Addressed to Li Tao-fu

Written in the tenth year of Emperor Cheng Te

Wang Praises Li Tao-fu Because of His Loyalty to True Learning

A long time has passed since the learning of the sages was discussed. I consider that my own point of view exhibits this learning exceedingly well, but those that hear me constantly slander me as being heterodox. You alone have full confidence in me. (19) You do not entertain any doubt, and this is a source of joy and comfort to me. How like hearing a footstep in a deserted valley! After our separation I heard scholars and officials speak of this. And when Ts'ü Yüeh-jen returned from Kiangsi, I heard more fully of your courage and fearlessness in executing virtue, and of the firmness with which you grasp it. It is enough to cause one to leap nimbly for joy. "The scholar must have breadth of mind and vigorous endurance. His burden is heavy and his course is long." [18] Two or three men of your breadth of mind and vigorous endurance would be sufficient to serve as an example and guide for all men. Though they be many in number, what do those amount to who trust to following others and being humbled before them? How very fortunate! How very fortunate! Not long ago I heard that when you reached your position as prefect, you desired to use this learning immediately as instruction. To the mind of the man of the highest virtue this is natural. I rejoice because of you, and on the other hand I am also distressed.

---

[18] Analects, Book VIII, Ch. 7, ¶ 1.

Wang Compares His Generation to a Man in the Midst of Great Sea Waves

Learning is interrupted and the truth is forgotten. The overwhelmed, sunken condition of the manners and customs of our times may be compared to a man in the midst of great sea waves. He must first be assisted to the shore before clothes and food can be given to him. If clothes and food are thrown to him while he is struggling with the waves, they will merely add weight and increase his danger. He will not consider this as treating him according to virtue, but as a token of your disliking him or having a grudge against him. Whosoever lives in this generation must influence and lead others according to the opportunities presented. Utilizing some definite affair he may exhibit the necessity for reform. Magnanimously and pleasantly, he may gradually but thoroughly influence others. When they have been influenced, he may unfold the true learning. In this way strength will be readily applied and returns will be large. If this plan is not pursued, he will not only be unable to overcome the difficulties, but will complicate the responsibilities of the superior man's love for others. I do not know what your idea is. I have sent in a second memorial regarding my illness, but have not yet received a reply. If things turn out as I wish, we may some day converse together when the ship passes Chiaho.

Comments — If the superior man in instructing the people is hasty and impatient in his desire to see the work accomplished, we have an instance of embarrassment from a desire for speed. This must be criticised. (20)

Letter to His Younger Brothers [19]

Written in the thirteenth year of Emperor Cheng Te

Not Absence of Transgression but Reform is Essential to Character and Sageness

I have frequently received letters from you, and all mani-

---

[19] The term ''younger brother'' is here used in a general sense.

fest reform, awakening, and enthusiasm. These things are a source of infinite joy and comfort to me; but I do not know whether they are really the result of a sincere mind, or are simply replies for the time being. The clearness of the original mind is as that of the sun in the daytime. There is no one who has made mistakes or transgressed that does not know it, but the unfortunate thing is that he is not able to reform. Once determine to reform, and forthwith the original nature of the mind is reinstated.

Who among men is without transgressions? Reform is the dignified, honorable thing. Chʻü Po-yü, a man of staunch virtue, said that he wished to make his faults few but was not able to do so.[20] Chʻeng Tʻang and Confucius, two great sages, alone said that he who is not sparing in his reform is able to get along without any great transgressions. Everybody says, "How can anybody but Yao and Shun be without transgression?" This is also handed down through long familiarity and is not adequate for use in understanding the mind of Yao and Shun. If such a mind as that of Yao and Shun considers itself as having no transgression, it thereby loses its sageness. At the time that they (Yao and Shun) exchanged advices Yao said, "The mind of man is restless and prone to err; its affinity for the right way is small. Be discriminating, be undivided, that you may sincerely hold fast the Mean."[21] As they themselves held that the mind of man is restless, their mind is like that of men generally. This unsteadiness and restlessness implies transgression. Only because they were fearful and cautious, and continually added discrimination and undividedness, were they able to hold fast the mean and avoid transgression.

The sages and virtuous men of the past continually realized their own transgressions and corrected them. Because of this they were able to avoid transgression, and not be-

---

[20] Analects, Book XIV, Ch. 26, ¶ 2.
[21] Shooking, Books of Yü, Pt. 2, ¶ 15.

cause their mind was really different from that of others. He who is cautious with reference to that which he does not see, and apprehensive with reference to that which he does not hear, constantly sees the results of his transgressions.

The Effect of Habit upon Action and Character

Recently I have really apprehended that this learning has application to daily life, but I am chronically affected by the blemishes of habit. Though I subdue myself, I still lack the requisite energy. For this reason I earnestly tell you this in advance, lest you also be profoundly influenced by evil habit and thereafter find it difficult to subdue and control yourselves. In youth the physical and mental energy has been sufficiently aroused and exerted, and the perplexities and embarrassment of the body and home life have not borne down on the mind. Therefore, it is very easy to use one's strength at that time. This continues until one gradually grows up and the perplexities and embarrassments of the world daily increase, and physical and mental energies gradually decrease. However, if the individual is able to keep his determination unremittingly upon learning, he still has the wherewithal to act. (21) When he reaches forty or fifty, his condition is as that of the setting sun, which, gradually becoming smaller, finally disappears and cannot be recalled. It was for this reason that Confucius said, "If he reach the age of forty or fifty and has not made himself heard of, then indeed he will not be worth being regarded with respect," and on another occasion said, "When he is old, and the animal powers are decayed, he guards against covetousness."[22] Recently I have comprehended this defect, and therefore earnestly tell you in advance. You should at the appropriate time use your energies, lest after the time has passed you repent in vain.

Comments — The individual who realizes his own trans-

---

[22] Analects, Book IX, Ch. 22, ¶ 1; Book XVI, Ch. 7.

gressions must really be able to control himself, for then he begins to become conscious of them. Of those who superficially and vainly discuss nature and fate, and proclaim sacrificial things and principles, there is not one but considers himself correct. Therefore Confucius said, "I have not seen one who could perceive his faults, and inwardly accuse himself." [23] Such a one is hard to find. As an explanation of genuine application to subduing and controlling one's self, nothing surpasses this letter.

Answer to an Official Named Lo Cheng-an

Written in the fifteenth year of Emperor Cheng Te

I beg respectfully to make the following statement: Yesterday I received your letter regarding the Great Learning, but as I was hurried because of dispatching the ship, I was not able to respond. This morning, as the ship proceeds, I have a little leisure and so have taken your letter and reread it. Fearing that after I reach Kanchou affairs will again be endless, I have prepared a sketch, which you will please read.

Wang Expresses Delight in Having the Opportunity to Discuss True Learning

Your letter says: "To see the truth is surely difficult; fully to appreciate it is still more difficult. Truly it is not easy to apprehend, but the learning thereof cannot but be discussed. I fear that I cannot rest merely in what I see and thereupon consider myself as having realized the utmost."

This is well expressed. How is it that I should hear this? How can I venture to consider myself as having realized the utmost and as resting therein? I really think that I should improve this time, when the Empire is in possession of the truth, plainly to discuss it. For a number of years those who have heard my discussion of the truth have ridi-

---

[23] Op. cit., Book V, Ch. 26.

culed it, or taunted and slandered it, or put it aside as inadequate to test and discuss. Under such circumstances, who would be willing to instruct me? If anyone had been willing to instruct me, would he not again and again have proclaimed it to me sympathetically, only fearing lest he be unable to rescue the truth? (22) However, among those who hold me in high esteem, there surely is none that does so as profoundly as you. How grateful I should be!

The Doctrine of the Sages Can Be Apprehended Only After It Has Been Investigated

The matters of leaving virtue without proper cultivation, and of not thoroughly discussing what is learned, occasioned solicitude in the mind of Confucius, but the students of the present generation consider themselves as understanding learning, as soon as they are able to give some instruction regarding the commentaries.[24] They do not again manifest what is called a striving for the exposition of learning. How pitiable! This doctrine of the sages must first be investigated and after that it will be apprehended: it is not a case of first apprehending and after that adding investigation. The truth must first be learned and after that it will be understood: it is not a case of investigating learning externally, and then having an understanding of the truth of the sage. There are two types among those who investigate learning. Some use personality and mind; others merely mouth and ears. The latter, thinking to fathom it, seek only shadow and echo, while those who use their person and mind act with understanding, and do so habitually in investigation. They really have possession of themselves at every point. He who knows this understands the learning of the Confucianists.

---

[24] *Vide ibid.*, Book VII, Ch. 3.

Wang Justifies His Use of the Old Edition of the Great Learning

Your letter says that the Great Learning which I use is a revival of the old (original) copy; that in matters of learning which others are trying to acquire, I hold that learning must be sought within, while according to the expositions of the investigation of things given by the philosophers Ch'eng and Chu, it is not possible to avoid seeking it in external things. It is not because I am voluntarily venturesome that I reject the division into chapters and undertake the excision of the commentaries which he has added. Is learning subject to the category of space? The original Great Learning is the old edition which Confucianists have transmitted. The philosopher Chu feared that parts had been lost and that errors had crept in, and thus corrected it and added to it. According to my view, the old edition had not been lost even in part, nor had errors crept in. He who would thoroughly comprehend it, must follow the old edition. My mistake lies in believing Confucius too much. It is not without reason that I reject the philosopher Chu's division into chapters and undertake an excision of his commentaries. It is good that learning is acquired in the mind. If it is sought in the mind and there is something wrong, though the words are those of Confucius, the mind will not accept it as correct. How much more is this true in the instance of anyone who is not equal to Confucius! If the learning is sought in the mind and the thing is right, then, though it be in the words of an ordinary man, the mind will not venture to consider it wrong. How much more is this true, if the words are those of Confucius!

Moreover, the old edition of the Great Learning has been transmitted for a number of thousands of years. Those who study its literary composition in this day and generation already understand it thoroughly. (23) The task involved in understanding it is simple and easily comprehensible. In accordance with what evidence does Chu undertake to determine that this section belongs in the place of that section and that in the place of this? How does he determine that this is incomplete and that incorrect? On what authority does he correct it and add to it? Is it not unavoidable that I should transgress heavily against Chu and at the same time lightly against Confucius?

Introspective Investigation is More Important than External Investigation of Things, for Nature, as Such, is Not Subject to the Category of Space

Your letter says: "If it really is necessary in the interest of learning not to trust to external investigation but to depend upon careful internal investigation, why are rectifying the mind and making the purpose sincere not exhaustive? Why is it necessary, when entering the door, laboriously to use the investigation of things?"

Certainly! Certainly! If you speak of underlying principles, then the matter of cultivating the person is also sufficient. Why speak in addition of rectifying the mind? To rectify the mind is also adequate. Why speak in addition of making the purpose sincere? To make the purpose sincere also is sufficient. Why speak in addition of extending knowledge to the utmost and of investigating things? It is only for the sake of details and profundity; the underlying principle is one and the same. For this reason I consider this as the learning which implies discrimination and undividedness. Really you cannot but deliberate upon this. Principles are not subject to the category of space; nature has no internal and external; and therefore learning also has no within and without. Explaining, practicing, investigating, and discussing do not imply the denial of the internal; introspection and internal investigation are not relegated to the external. To say that in the interest of learning it is necessary to rely on the external investigation, implies that one's nature has external aspects, and that righteousness, too, is external. Such an exposition shows small wisdom. To say that introspection and internal investigation imply seeking learning internally, implies that the individual considers his nature as having an internal. This is selfishness. All of this indicates a lack of knowledge of the fact that nature is devoid of internal and external.

Therefore, I say that the essence of learning enters the soul in order that it may be fully developed in practice, and that well utilized, it gives tranquility to the person in the esteem and practice of virtue. These are virtues belonging to nature, and constitute a method of uniting the external and the internal. Thus one may understand what is meant by the "investigation of things," which constitutes the real starting-point of understanding the Great Learning and runs through the whole process from beginning to end. From this point on, until the individual must learn to become a sage, there is but this one way. It is not only present at the beginning. The rectifying of the mind, the making sincere of the thoughts, the developing of knowledge to the utmost, and the investigating of things, all imply cultivating the person. (24)

He who engages in the investigation of things can there see where he must apply his strength. He who investigates things carries on this investigation with reference to the things of his mind, purpose, and knowledge; he who rectifies his mind rectifies the mind manifested in his things; he who makes his purpose sincere does so with reference to the purpose of his things; and he who develops his knowledge to the utmost does so with reference to the knowledge of his things. Are there, then, such distinctions as internal and external, as this and that? The underlying principle is one only. Referring to the accumulating of the principles in the individual, it is called nature; referring to the controlling factor in this accumulating of principles, it is called mind; referring to the manifested activity of the controlling power, it is called purpose; referring to the intelligence and clear realization of the manifested activity, it is called knowledge; referring to the stimulation and response to this knowledge, it is called things. Thus, as pertaining to things, it is called investigation; as pertaining to knowledge, one speaks of developing it to the utmost; as pertaining to purpose, of making it sincere; as pertaining to mind, of rectifying. He who rectifies, does so with reference to this; he who is engaged in making it sincere, does so with reference to this; and in the highest development and investigation he does the same. They include all that is involved in thoroughly investigating principles for the sake of completely developing one's nature. Under heaven there are no principles or things to be found outside of or apart from nature.

Learning is not revealed, for the reason that worldly scholars understand principles to be external and do not understand the saying regarding external righteousness.[25] Mencius has therefore already criticised this. But the individual thus unconsciously reaches a condition where he falls into incidental deeds of righteousness. Is not this a condition in which he appears to be right, and yet has difficulty in understanding? You surely must examine this. In whatever respect you have begun to doubt regarding the investigation of things, you will say that it defends the internal and denies the external, that it pertains to introspection and internal investigation and sets aside explanation, practice, search, and discussion; you will say that it consists in having the purpose fixed upon the limits of underlying principles and the original source, but neglects the minutiæ of the branches and verses; you will say that it sinks the individual into the error of a lifeless contemplation, but does not completely exhaust the changes in the principles of things and the affairs of men. In investigation such as this, has not the individual sinned against the philosopher Chu as well as against the sages? (25) Any-

---

25 *Vide* Mencius, Book II, Pt. I, Ch. 2, ¶ 15.

one who embraces this heterodoxy which deceives the people, transgresses the doctrine, and confuses the truth, should eradicate it. How much more should this be true of a man of your integrity! Whoever partly understands the commentaries of the classics and hears the connected discourses of former wise men, knows that such investigation is incorrect. How much more is this true of a man of your intelligence!

Moreover, what I mean by investigation of things is all included in the nine sections of the philosopher Chu. But in carrying these out there is an indispensable element: in the practical application we are not alike. Truly this is what is called a very small difference, but out of it there arises a tremendous mistake. I cannot but criticise it.

The Mistakes of the Philosophers Yang and Mo

Mencius showed that the philosophers Yang and Mo reached a state where they did not recognize father or prince. The two philosophers were virtuous men of their times. Inasmuch as they were contemporary with Mencius, they surely would be considered virtuous. Mo's principle of loving all equally is a case of excess in the practice of benevolence; and Yang's principle, "Each one for himself," is a case of excess in the practice of righteousness. Do not these sayings destroy principles and confuse long-established usage? Are they not sufficient to deceive the Empire? Moreover, with reference to their defects Mencius fully compares them with beasts and barbarians. This is what is called the destruction of later generations of the Empire by means of learning.

Does not the defect of present-day learning mean that benevolence and righteousness are learned to excess, or that, on the other hand, there is an excess of learning which lacks benevolence and righteousness? I do not know what it would accomplish in case a great inundation or ferocious animals threatened. Mencius said: "Am I fond of disputing? I am compelled to do it."[26] The doctrines of Mo and Yang pervaded the Empire; and those who, in Mencius' time, honored and believed Yang and Mo should be compared with those who now reverence the sayings of the philosopher Chu. And Mencius alone protested in their midst. Alas, how pitiable! Han said that the injurious effects of Buddhism and Taoism surpass those of Yang and Mo. The virtue of Han Yü was not equal to that of Mencius. Mencius was not able to rescue his age before it had been injured, but Han Yü desired to restore his age after it had been injured. He did not estimate his own strength, and in consequence found his own person in danger without the opportunity of rescuing himself from death. (26) Alas! if I fail to estimate my strength, I also will experience danger in person and be unable to save myself from death. In the midst of merriment, I alone weep and lament. If the entire world contentedly hastened after these erroneous doctrines, I alone with aching head and knit brow would be distressed thereby. If this is not due to the fact that I am insane and have lost my mind, it must be due to a genuinely great grief hidden away in my mind. If the most virtuous man in the Empire can not thoroughly investigate this, who can?

The Philosopher Chu's Discussions of Later Life Agree in All Essentials with Wang's Standpoint

I maintain my contention regarding the philosopher Chu's Discussions of Later Life, because I can not do otherwise. As to which of these was announced earlier or later in his life, I really have not carried on an investigation. Though not everything contained therein comes from his later years, surely most of it does. The underlying idea consists in considering an understanding of true learning as important, and in adjusting and harmonizing the tortuous sayings. Ordinarily, I have considered the sayings

---

[26] Mencius, Book III, Pt. II, Ch. 9, ¶ 1. See also ¶ 9.

of the philosopher Chu as clarifying and exhibiting the obscure and mysterious. If I transgress the truth and seek in external things with him for a single day, my mind is unable to endure it. Thus I cannot change in this. Those who know me say that my mind is solicitous, and those who do not know me ask what I am really seeking. That I cannot bear to strive against Chu, is due to the original nature of my mind; that I cannot but strive against him, is due to the fact that in behalf of truth I surely must do it, for if I am not frank truth will not be manifested. Can I venture to deceive my own mind with reference to that in which you insist that I am different from the philosopher Chu? This truth and this learning are for everybody in the Empire. They are not the property of the philosopher Chu only, nor even of Confucius only. They are open to all under heaven, and should be openly and generally discussed. Therefore, when what is said is correct, it is of advantage to me, though it differs from my point of view; and when what is said is wrong, it injures me, though it be in accordance with my own views. What is of advantage to the self, the self rejoices in; and what injures the personality, the self will despise and reject.

The Philosopher Chu Would Be Glad to Correct His Faults

Thus, though what I say today differs from Chu's point of view, he surely would rejoice in it. "The faults of the superior man are like the eclipses of the sun and moon. When he changes them, all men look up to him." [27] But "the mean man is sure to gloss his faults." [28] Though I am not equal to the superior man, I cannot venture to treat Chu as a mean man would. (27)

Lo Cheng-an Fails to Understand Wang Fully

That you instruct me, back and forth with several hun-

[27] Analects, Book XIX, Ch. 21.
[28] *Ibid.*, Book XIX, Ch. 8.

dred propositions, is due to the fact that you do not comprehend my dicta regarding the investigation of things. If my dicta are once understood, these several hundred propositions need not first be refuted until they present no hindrance. Therefore I do not venture to enter into a detailed discussion, lest I annoy you with a multitude of trifles. However, unless my dicta are elucidated face to face, the writing of letters cannot suffice. Insofar as you have instructed and informed me, I can say that you have been in earnest, even to details. Can there be anyone else who holds me in such high esteem as you do? Though I am very simpleminded, can I fail to appreciate the things for which I am profoundly thankful to you and respect you? But I cannot disregard the sincerity of my own mind. Meanwhile I hear and receive what you say, because I cannot disregard your high esteem for me. I wish to requite it. When the autumn is past and winter comes, we will seek to meet in conference, that we may finish the discussion of the things regarding which you make inquiry. I sincerely hope that this may transpire.

Comments — This letter discusses the philosopher Chu. That in evidence he mentions the philosophers Yang and Mo, as well as Buddhism and Taoism, makes it inevitable that his words should be over-zealous. The philosopher Chu naturally has points in his discussion where he is strong, and surely should not be forced to be just like others. The dispositions of men are not uniform. Even in the disciples of Confucius — Yen, Tseng, Yu, Hsia, Jan, and Min — the points of strength varied with the men, but the direction of their progress was correct. One must remember that the Teacher earnestly discussed this, not stopping with these arguments, not because he accused Chu of shortcomings, but because later scholars dote on the commentaries and make a pretext of considering Chu a criterion. Therefore the Teacher used the decisions of Chu's later life as a standard for understanding his real attitude, and as making good the defects of his learning. No doubt the philosopher Chu would thus become installed in the side gallery of the Confucian temple. Scholars should not forget this.

Letter Written to Yang Shih-ming
Written in the sixteenth year of Emperor Cheng Te

Wang Asks to be Excused for Not Undertaking to Write an Inscription for a Tombstone

Your messenger has come, and I know that your elder brother was buried last winter and that the grass is growing on the grave. As I did not have the opportunity to weep, I am exceedingly grieved. Referring to the inscription which you request me to make for the tombstone, I am not well and am, in addition, very much occupied, and would suggest that you select one of your most intimate friends for this purpose, for then it can be properly done. (28)

The Intuitive Faculty as a Guide in Learning

With reference to the individual's daily effort at examining and investigating learning, your letter says that each one should follow his own intuitive faculty, clear away all hindrances, and extend his original nature in order that he may exhaust it. Moreover, he should not allow his determination to be moved and follow customary procedure merely in order to follow the fashion of the times. You have expressed this very well. If really carried out, it is an instance of extending knowledge to the utmost through the investigation of things, of understanding virtue, and of making the person sincere. If actually carried into practice, what can prevent virtue from being daily renewed and those that occupy themselves in studying this learning from increasing the stock of knowledge?

The True Methods of Confucianism Involve the Extension of Knowledge to the Utmost

What you say about daily arranging and examining learning without being able to do so completely, implies that the task of extending knowledge to the utmost is interrupted. The highest virtue also depends upon being familiar with it. You also say that for this reason it is necessary to examine critically the meaning of the words of former scholars in order to detect similarities and differences; and that, if thereby the task is shown to lack unity, doubt and embarrassment are continually begotten. Why should this be? The "extension of knowledge to the utmost," which I discuss, conveys the true methods of Confucianism. If you see this truly and correctly, you are in the condition which the Doctrine of the Mean describes in the words: "The doctrines of the superior man are rooted in his own person, and sufficient attestation of them is given by the masses of the people. He sets them up before heaven and earth, and finds nothing in them in which he transgresses. He presents himself with them before spiritual beings, and no doubt about them arises. He examines them by comparison with those of the three Kings, and finds them without mistakes. He is prepared to wait for the rise of a sage a hundred ages after, and has no misgivings."[29] Only he who understands this, understands the truths of the sages; only he who attains this in his own person, is in possession of virtue. Learning that is different from this is heterodox, and sayings that depart from this are heretical. Practices that confuse and becloud this are dismal and obscure. Though a thousand demons and ten thousand monsters confuse and blind and delude, it is only necessary to run against them in order to dispel them, and to meet them in order to dissipate them. When the sun comes out, spirits, demons, and sprites of mountains and streams have no way of hiding themselves. Why, then, have any further

---

[29] Doctrine of the Mean, Ch. 29, ¶ 3.

doubts or embarrassment? What differences or agreements are adequate to cause confusion? This is what I mean by saying that this learning is established in space (is perfectly free) and that it nowhere needs supports. None of life's affairs are allowed to vitiate it. In every particular the individual should have confidence in its original form, and not permit anything to be added or subtracted. If he places his own arrangements and ideas into it, its unity is destroyed.

The fact that you say there are at times passages that are not perspicuous, shows your ability to perceive these and understand them in part. This is sufficient cause for rejoicing. But you must of necessity apply yourself earnestly, for then your efforts will be of use. (29) If you merely talk, you will not be able to avoid judging and estimating according to appearances. Thereupon you will belong to the class of those who merely use their bodily vigor. Though this is somewhat different from the malady which those have, who in this age investigate things, it is nevertheless the same defect. The scholar does not cast aside constant study of and practice in the writing of odes and essays. This is in accordance with Confucius' saying that "the virtuous man will be sure to speak." [30] If he adds his own purposes, schemes, and plans, he is certain to act from a mind that strives to excel. Former generations of scholars are said to have had desires. That their doctrines are of this kind is due to the fact that they did not overcome their habits. Since you understand what is meant by completing knowledge, such a condition should be obviated by a simple personal examination. It will not do to hide it.

Comments — Judging and estimating according to appearances is a general defect among students. Earnestly and sincerely to apply one's self is of first importance.

---

[30] Analects, Book XIV, Ch. 5.

Reply to Fang Shu-hsien

Written in the fourteenth year of Emperor Cheng Te

Earnestness in the Development of Self is of the First Importance

I have recently received your letter, as well as your letter to and reply from Kan-ch'üan. Immediately upon having read them, I was delighted, as is a man suffering from excessive heat, when a cool wind strikes him. How superior and penetrating your apprehension is! Truly it is like traveling a thousand li in a day. That the original edition of the Great Learning should thus return to popularity is a task of no small dimensions. I rejoice exceedingly in this. In his discussion of Hsiang-shan, Kan-ch'üan mentions what Mencius says about losing the benevolent mind; but he considers it inadequate, and says that sages arise in all quarters, that mind and principles are alike, and that everything in the universe comes within the scope of the individual's duty.[31] What he says has emphasized the important points. But I hold in esteem the intimacy and earnestness of Hsi Ch'iao, for if a man's view emphasizes the great essentials, his efforts must be intimate and earnest. Unless one really is intimate and earnest in the performance of one's task, the view, which is said to attain to essentials, is empty and vain. Ever since Mencius said that nature is good, ordinary scholars have been able to talk back and forth, but their learning, after all, branches off into external striving without their being conscious thereof. (30) This is due to a lack of earnestness in the performance of the task. Thus I take delight in what Hsi Ch'iao says about truly applying one's self with extreme earnestness, for this is surely a remedy for present-day defects. The learning of the ancients teaches real earnestness in the development of self, and not vain devotion to exposition and discussion.

By sending letters back and forth, one is after all not able

---

[31] *Vide* Mencius, Book VI, Pt. I, Ch. 11.

to discuss matters as exhaustively as face to face. Moreover, letters are apt to cause the individual to sink his feelings into what is written, to overemphasize mere formalities, and to cultivate a mind which strives to excel. In writing the letter he seeks to have his exposition free from defects, and thus does not realize the many defects of his mind. This is a common mistake of this age. Even the virtuous and wise do not avoid it. You should carefully look into this. As Yang Shih-te is leaving, I reply without special effort.

Comments — The Doctrine of the Mean discusses the path of the sage up to the point where he nourishes all things and rises to the height of heaven, including three hundred rules of ceremony and three thousand rules of demeanor.[32] This may be said to be great and inclusive. But it is necessary to start from constant inquiry and study, and use the honoring of one's virtuous nature, before the doctrine can be made a fact. How very familiar and intimate this is! If not, you may also consider it as great and fundamental; but this means that you have acquired only the outer shell, while the truth is lost. How can one then say that the truth is a real fact? The Teacher's additional word about earnestness and intimacy is the great learning according to which the superior man renovates his virtue and makes the doctrine a fact.

Reply to Fang Shu-hsien

Written in the sixteenth year of Emperor Cheng Te

Truth is a Unified System or Whole

I have received your letter regarding the Great Learning. From the first I knew that you were applying yourself to the profound and thorough study of this. The path of duty (truth) is one only. Referring to its great root and source, the Six Classics and Four Books give expression to it and

---

[32] *Vide* Doctrine of the Mean, Ch. 27.

are in full harmony with it. The relation is not merely that of the Great Plan to the Great Learning.[33] This thought I have frequently expressed to my friends. The point of similarity between grass and trees is in their growth, but you also wish to carry this similarity to the quantity and quality of flowers and fruit, and to the height of the branches. I fear that the operations of nature are not like the carving and engraving of man. My brother, you rejoice within yourself, because you consider that you alone have perceived it and have been the first one to apprehend it; and what is more, you resolutely try to maintain this attitude. (31) Though I hold your confidence and esteem, one exposition is inadequate to introduce you fully to my point of view. I hope that you, my brother, using your own point of view, will really investigate your own person. You surely will have doubts; but even if you should have none, you will gain some advantage. Should you also lack this, you surely will have private opinions. After that my sayings will penetrate your mind.

For several hundred years true learning has not been understood. Fortunately, certain ones who have a common purpose with me — such as Kan-ch'üan and you — desire to carry on an exhaustive investigation and really have a clue. But if you, too, are suddenly over-influenced by the literal meaning of the characters, to whom shall I turn? In his discussion of learning, the superior man surely follows the lead of the truth only, and considers harmony and agreement noble and dignified. Concerning the actual beginning of the task of comprehending the Great Learning, there are instances in which discussion cannot be obviated, but in this a very small mistake may eventuate in a very great error. Kan-ch'üan's explanation of extending knowledge to the utmost through the investigation of things, is slightly different from mine, but does no injury to the general fundamental agreement that exists between us. Your

---

[33] The Great Plan is a book in the Canon of History.

sayings appear to be different from his. We are so far from one another that I fear my exposition in this letter will be inadequate to convey my idea. For this reason my straight-forward words will offend you, for I have not again yielded to you. That I recently wrote to him about this, should not be considered an offense on my part.

Comments — This being influenced by the literal mean-ing of the characters is a defect that lies in carrying on the investigation in the realm of words instead of in the mind itself. This comparing and contrasting, however accurate, is in last analysis like scratching through the clothes and not really getting at the pain and itching. For such a de-fect no medicine can be prescribed. Therefore the Teacher ordered Fang Shu-hsien to investigate and examine this matter in order to dispel the doubts of his own mind.

Reply to Lun Yen-shih

Written in the sixteenth year of Emperor Cheng Te

Wang Praises Yen-shih as Being an Earnest Student

Last year when your boat passed Kanchou, you were not self-sufficient and self-satisfied. Though you were in a higher official position, you humbled yourself and made earnest inquiry concerning the truth. Truly this is what in ancient times was called being of an active nature, and yet fond of learning![34] After I had left you I was con-tinually occupied with affairs, and thus did not get time to write you a letter of inquiry, though I thought of you most earnestly. Recently your brother passed by the capital, and I again received a letter from you. How can any per-son whose learning is shallow and superficial reach the point which you have reached — the point where the deter-mination is energetically fixed upon the truth, the direction of advance correct, and diligence and attentiveness on the increase? (32) I am in fear and trembling.

---

[34] Analects, Book V, Ch. 14, ¶ 1.

*The Learning of the Superior Man Makes no Distinction
Between the Activity and the Tranquility of the Mind,
for the One Involves the Other*

Your letter says that your study lacks the foundation of
tranquility, that under the stimulation of things you are
easily influenced, and that you often repent because of
things done. These three things show the more clearly
that you have recently given genuine application to the
task. I lack the ability to impart the desired information.
How can I venture to answer the question of a virtuous
man? In general, these three things are a disease with a
common reason for their existence. Since in your devotion
to study you seek in addition a foundation of tranquility,
you naturally are afraid that under the stimulation of
things you are easily influenced. Since under the stimulation of things you fear that they may easily influence you,
you have many occasions for repentance because of what
you have done. The mind is by nature characterized neither by activity nor by tranquility. Tranquility has reference to its original structure, and activity to its functioning. For this reason the learning of the superior man
makes no distinction between activity and tranquility. He
is constantly aware of the tranquility, and thus, as it is
always present, it constantly responds. He constantly fixes
and controls the functioning, and thus lacks real excitement.
Therefore he is always quiet. Constantly responding and
constantly quiet, he will have both activity and tranquility
present.

This is what is meant by saying that the individual is accumulating righteousness. Since he accumulates righteousness, he is free from any repentance. Both activity and
tranquility include having the mind fixed. The mind is one
and undivided. Since its structure is by nature tranquil,
he who seeks to restore the root of tranquility thereby dis-
turbs the original nature. Since activity is mind functioning, he who is fearful lest it be active, sets aside its func-

tioning. The very seeking for tranquility implies activity, while an aversion to activity does not mean tranquility. The mind is active when in a state of tranquility, as well as when engaged in some activity. This movement back and forth is endless. As a result we say that obedience to principles is tranquility, and assent to desire is activity. This assent to desire does not refer only to the allurements of things heard, or of colors seen, or even of possessions and wealth, but to whatever personal, private things the mind harbors. Therefore, where there is obedience to principles, tranquility is present, even amidst the changing vicissitudes of life. Chou Lien-hsi's idea that where tranquility is in control there is no desire, implies that the accumulating of righteousness prevails. Wherever there is compliance with desire activity is present, even though the mind is dignified and the individual sits in abstraction. The philosopher Kao's teaching regarding forced restraint, nourishing the passion nature, and assisting the growth, implies that righteousness is external.[35] Though in my application to this problem I realize my insufficiency, I now offer you what I apprehend to be true. At a time convenient to you let me know what you think about it. (33)

Comments — The equilibrium in which there are no stirrings of feelings, and the harmony resulting after they have been stirred, refer to the principles of nature and the decrees of Heaven. Activity and tranquility are like a circle in that they have no beginning. The learning of the superior man makes no distinction between activity and tranquility. Therefore he is able to exhaust his nature and carry out the decrees of Heaven. This is a point of view according to which structure and its function are one

---

[35] "Let us not be like the man of Sung. There was a man of Sung, who was grieved that his growing corn was not longer, and so he pulled it up. Having done this, he returned home, looking very stupid, and said to his people, 'I am tired today. I have been helping the corn to grow long.' His son ran to look at it, and found the corn all withered." — Mencius, Book II, Pt. I, Ch. 2, ¶ 16.

source. It combines the internal sage with the external king. To put aside activity and seek the root of tranquility results in landing nowhere.

The learning of the superior man must distinguish clearly between principles and desire. It is not necessary that it distinguish to excess between activity and tranquility. The learning of the philosopher Yen exhausts the matter of subduing the self, and the learning of the philosopher Tseng exhausts the examining of the person. When the private desires of the mind are all cleansed, then, though there are an indefinite number of responses to stimulation, these will all be in harmony with heaven-given principles. This implies resting in the highest excellence and consists in having one's determination fixed and the mind tranquil. Why, then, seek for additional tranquility? If the individual does not inquire whether or not his own selfishness has been completely cleansed, he will not acquire tranquility, though he speak of tranquility and activity all day long.

Answer to Ts'ü Ch'eng-chih
(First Letter)
Written in the first year of Emperor Chia Ching

Wang's Comments on Yü-an and Ch'eng-chih's Discussion of Lu Hsiang-shan and Chu Hui-an

I have received your letter in which you make inquiry regarding points of similarity and difference between the philosophers Lu and Chu. The art of study has not been understood for a long period. This really is a thing which we should now explain and discuss clearly. From a careful reading of your letter I see that if Yü-an is mistaken in his dependence upon Hsiang-shan, you in your dependence upon Hui-an also fail to attain the truth. The scholars of the Empire have long since determined that Chu is correct and Lu mistaken, and thus it is difficult to bring about a change. Though he overcome your arguments, can Yü-an on his part carry out in practice what he says? For this reason I hold that you should both not insist on excelling. If you devote yourself to showing that Hsiang-shan is wrong and Hui-an correct, and do this to the point of exhausting the very sources, you are able in the smallest things to see whether or not the details are correct. If an official of ability sits in judgment in a law-suit, he must clearly distinguish in what respect the particular affair is perverse; and in the interpretation of what is said or written, he must also point out what things are not satisfactory and on a secure basis. (34) He does this that the real condition of the culprit may be made manifest, and that he who receives redress may likewise be unable to shirk his responsibility. In so doing, he has exhausted the equitable principles of that affair. Forthwith his mind is at ease, and he is able to wait a hundred generations for a sage. The discussion between you men appears to be actuated by a desire and striving to excel, and this shows that the passion nature is stirred. If there is a stirring of the passion nature, then you are far (a thousand li) from the truth which you are discussing. What sort of a discussion of right and wrong can there be under such circumstances? Whenever there is a discussion regarding the attainments of the ancients, the individual is not allowed to use his own estimation in summarily judging them.

Yü-an's discussion of Hsiang-shan is to the effect that in so far as Hsiang-shan considers the honoring of one's virtuous nature of first importance, he is unable to keep from falling into the abstraction of the Buddhists. However that may be, what he maintains is correct and real, so that he does not lose the place of disciple of the sage (Confucius). In exclusively maintaining a constant inquiry and study, Hui-an has departed from the path and does not revive the learning of the Confucianists, which inculcates making one's purpose sincere and rectifying one's mind.

Your discussion of Hui-an is to the effect, that, though he

considers the maintaining of constant inquiry and study of
first importance, he is unable to avoid being lost in customary learning. However that may be, still, following
the prescribed order of study, he gradually advances and in
last analysis does not transgress the teaching of the Great
Learning. If Hsiang-shan is exclusive in his devotion to
man's virtuous nature, he sinks into abstract contemplation
and does not revive the teaching of the Great Learning,
which inculcates investigation of things for the sake of extending knowledge to the utmost. But since he speaks of
honoring man's virtuous nature, he can not be said to have
fallen into the emptiness of the Buddhist learning. If he
had fallen into this, he could not speak of honoring man's
virtuous nature. Since he spoke of maintaining constant
inquiry and study, he cannot be said to have lost himself in
the digression of worldly learning. Had he lost himself in
this, he could not have spoken of maintaining constant inquiry and study. The explanations of the two philosophers
are so near alike that not even a hair can be placed between
them.

But both of your discussions cannot fail to include your
private estimates. Formerly Tzu-ssu in his discussion of
learning left not less than a thousand and several hundred
sentences; but he included the honoring of one's virtuous
nature, and the maintaining of constant inquiry and study
in one sentence.[36] According to the explanations which
you both advance, the one considers the honoring of the
virtuous nature as of first importance, and the other the
maintaining of constant inquiry and study, and thereby you
make them into two different things. (35) Surely you cannot avoid being partial. Moreover, neither the correctness
of Lu nor that of Chu has as yet been determined. How
can each of you take one as correct and fundamental, and
forthwith consider the other one mistaken? For this reason,
I wish that you would both be just and magnanimous, and

---

[36] *Vide* Doctrine of the Mean, Ch. 27, ¶ 6.

not strive to excel. Striving to excel while in the discussion of learning, is not what is meant by honoring one's virtuous nature or by maintaining constant inquiry and study. As I see it, not only do you wrong Hsiang-shan, while Yü-an wrongs Hui-an, both of you missing the real mistakes, but insofar as you consider Hui-an correct and Yü-an considers Hsiang-shan correct, you have not reached the facts of the case. When later I have time, I will discuss it clearly with you. Meanwhile, devote yourself to nourishing your mind and quieting your dispute.

Comments — The common defect of scholars is to estimate in accordance with their own ideas the correctness of what they hear and make inquiry about. This discussion of the Teacher frankly penetrates to the bottom of this.

Reply to Ts'ü Ch'eng-chih

(Second Letter)

Written in the first year of Emperor Chia Ching

A Second Letter Regarding the Standpoints of the Philosophers Lu and Chu

Yesterday as I sent my reply, a guest from a distant place was here, and as we had much to confer about, I did not have time to go into detail. Meanwhile I wish that you would both desist in your wrangling about this matter which has not been settled, and that each would in introspection carefully examine what he considers correct. If in what each believes to be correct there is not the least particle of disappointment and dissatisfaction, then you are in a position to approach the mistakes of others. Your letter says that my sayings are indefinite and vague, but that when the purpose of the sentences is completely unravelled they surreptitiously support Yü-an. When I read this, I involuntarily laughed. Would I have anticipated that you, my brother, would speak thus? I have always thought that when a superior man discussed any matter he should first discard any selfish ideas; for when self is stirred, the mind falls into meanness and depravity. Though what is said under such circumstances is completely in accordance with principles, the essential thing has been lost. I have frequently said this among my friends, but you yourself are now falling into that mistake. Can anyone afford not to examine himself carefully as to whether he is unconsciously beginning to fall into meanness and depravity? Should you not do this again and again? (36) What you said yesterday gave no indication of this. May not your own words show your mistake? Though you do not have that purpose, what you say is not completely in accordance with right, and therefore you cannot be free from error. Dare I say that what I have said is completely in accord with principles? Kindly suggest that in which each of you considers himself right so that we may get at the facts.

Yü-an considers Hsiang-shan correct and says that he (Hsiang-shan) considers the honoring of one's virtuous nature as of first importance. In examining the contents of his works, he frequently instructs his disciples that in studying they should exhaustively investigate principles. He himself says that it is necessary to pay attention to style and characters. That in which he was very different from others was that he really desired to investigate and verify these things in his own person. For the sake of admonishing others, he talked about and used the following: In retirement be sedately grave; in the management of business be reverently attentive; in intercourse with others be strictly sincere; subdue yourself and return to propriety; all things are already complete in us; there is no greater delight than to be conscious of sincerity on self-examination; the great end of learning is nothing else but to seek for the lost mind; let a man first stand in the supremacy of the nobler part of his constitution and the inferior part will not be able to take it (the mind) from him.[37] Can the

---

[37] *Vide* Analects, Book XIII, Ch. 19; Book XII, Ch. 1, ¶ 1; Men-

words of Confucius and Mencius be considered empty and meaningless? Only the sayings about its being easy and simple and about being conscious of an awakening (realization) are most doubted at the present time. However, the saying that it is easy and simple is taken from Hsi Tz'u.[38] Even if the saying about being conscious of an awakening (realization) is similar to the saying of the Buddhists, it is nevertheless true that this similarity does not mitigate the fact that the points of difference between the Buddhists and the Confucianists are just in the details and minutiæ. Why should anyone conceal this similarity and not venture to speak of it? Why should he seize upon their differences and hesitate to investigate them? That Yü-an considers Hsiang-shan correct surely does not exhaust his correctness.

You consider Hui-an correct and say that he emphasizes as important the maintaining of constant study and inquiry. Yet Hui-an's words are: "Cultivate reverence and carry on an exhaustive investigation of principles"; "Unless the individual cherishes his mind he cannot be said to be extending his knowledge to the utmost."[39] He also said: "The mind of the superior man constantly cherishes reverence. Though he is able neither to see nor hear the particular thing he yet dare not disregard it. Thus he cherishes the very source of heaven-given principles and does not allow them to depart from him for a moment."[40] (37) Though this is not all perfectly clear, in what way does he fail to consider the honoring of one's virtuous nature as important? Or in what way does he depart from the truth? Ordinarily he is concerned with making comments. Whether

cius, Book VII, Pt. I, Ch. 4, ¶ 1 and 2; Book VI, Pt. I, Ch. 11, ¶ 4; Book VI, Pt. I, Ch. 15, ¶ 2.

[38] *Vide* footnote 50, p. 273.

[39] The philosopher Chu's comments on the Doctrine of the Mean, Ch. 27, ¶ 6.

[40] *Ibid.*, Ch. 1, ¶ 2.

it be the writings of Han, the Ch'u Tz'u, or the Ying Fu, he explained and investigated them all with his commentaries.[41] But those that discuss them forthwith suspect that they are mere playthings. Fearing lest students would acquire learning without following definite steps, or fall into the error of initiating false activity, Hui-an caused them first to devote themselves to the investigation of things for the purpose of extending knowledge to the utmost, as including an understanding of all things, and then to apply themselves to making their purpose sincere and rectifying their minds, that they might avoid mistakes.

Wang Thinks that the Desire to Excel is the Basis of the Discussions Between Yü-an and Ch'eng-chih, and that for This Reason no Real Advantage Accrues to Them

Ordinary students are anxious about one thing, and thereby lose sight of ten thousand. The more they seek it the further they lose it, so that they are in life-long distress. Embarrassed to the end by the difficulties, they ultimately fail to make an entrance. In accordance therewith people judge that this is a defect of later scholars. Did Hui-an arrive at this in his own actions? You consider Hui-an correct, but fail to exhaust that in which he is right. Since that which you both consider correct is not all correct, is it, then, true that that which you fear to be incorrect is necessarily all incorrect? Engrossed by your discussions back and forth, you cannot examine yourselves. For this reason I fear that perhaps the discussion emanates from a desire to excel. When this desire for victory appears, the real root of learning has been lost. Why then discuss learning? I wish that you would carry on an introspective examination of yourselves. Why should it be said that my sayings are indefinite and vague, and that I surreptitiously take sides with Yü-an? The discussion of the superior man is

---

41 The Ch'u Tz'u is the record of the state of Ch'u; Ying Fu is a Taoist sutra.

directed toward appreciating the thing discussed in the mind. What the mass considers correct, he does not venture to consider right, if in seeking it in his own mind he is not able to verify it. What the mass considers wrong, he does not venture to consider wrong, if in seeking it in his own mind he is able to verify it.

What is the mind? It is what I have received of natural law. It does not distinguish between heaven and men, or between past and present. If I exhaust my mind in seeking the truth, though I may not hit the mark, I will not fail far. What is learning? It is seeking to exhaust the possibilities of the mind. (38) For this reason it implies honoring one's virtuous nature and maintaining constant study and inquiry. He who honors, honors this; he who maintains, maintains this. Can he be considered as devoting himself to study who, unable to acquire it in his own mind, merely considers what others say as learning?

Hsiang-shan is Just as Much a Disciple of the Sage as Hui-an

As for Hui-an and Hsiang-shan, I hold that though they appear to have points of difference in their learning, both are disciples of the sage. The people of the Empire at present learn and practice the learning of the philosopher Chu from youth. Since it has penetrated deep into the minds of the people, it is not permissible to discuss it and dispute regarding it. People reject Hsiang-shan owing to the fact that he engaged in a discussion with Hui-an. It is permissible that they should make the difference between them like unto that between Yu and Tzu.[42] But may it not be too extreme when they liken them to an inferior agate and a beautiful gem, and thus discard the learning of Hsiang-shan? Hui-an discriminates between and modifies the sayings of a large number of scholars in order to make clear

---

[42] Yu (Tzu-lu) and Tzu (Tzu-kung) were two disciples of Confucius.

and plain the purport of the Six Classics, the Analects, and Mencius. That he encourages the mind of the later scholars, truly cannot be criticised. Hsiang-shan explains the difference between righteousness and gain; he establishes the great root of learning, and seeks for the lost mind, in order to show later scholars how earnestly and genuinely to apply themselves to and for themselves.

Wang Declares that He Has Received Benefit from Hsiang-shan and Hui-an

How can anyone accuse and malign his achievements? However, the worldly scholars are unanimous in their accusations and do not investigate what is really true. They sum up their views by holding that his learning coincides with that of Buddhism, and thus actually wrong him. Therefore I have desired to brave the ridicule of the Empire, that I may exhibit and proclaim the sayings of Hsiang-shan. Though I thereby offend others, there is no anger on my part. From Hui-an, also, I have received unlimited benefit. Can I, then, desire to seize the lance (fly to arms) and enter his house? I hold that Hui-an's learning has been manifested in the Empire like unto the sun and stars, but that Hsiang-shan has been subject to slander and calumny without the least foundation of truth. For four hundred years no one has taken his part. Should Hui-an get knowledge of this, he would not be able to enjoy himself in peace for a single day in the annex of the Confucian temple. This, my utmost feeling on the subject, I surely must disclose to you. How can I recklessly use two kinds of exposition in order surreptitiously to help Yü-an? (39) I dislike the incompleteness of what he says.

Hsiang-shan and Hui-an Have Both Made Mistakes

The art of study is the art of learning from sages and virtuous men of the present and the past, and is common to everyone in the Empire. It is not a thing that belongs to us three men privately. This universal art of learning should be expounded to everybody. Is it then only for Yü-an?

You also mention the explanation of the "Absolute." You hold that Hsiang-shan is not able to understand clearly the meaning of words and literature, and that Yü-an only with forced explanation believes it himself. "Where," you say, "is there anything to cultivate?" Your saying that the idea conveyed by Hsiang-shan does not go into details, does no injury to the fact that he has not gone into detail. Your saying that what he cultivates is not exhaustive, does no harm to that which he has not reached in his discussion. When the learning has not reached that of the sage, how can it fail to make the mistake of exceeding or not realizing what is correct? If those engaged in the discussion wish to consider themselves correct and set out to generalize, I fear that Hui-an's ridicule of Hsiang-shan's learning as belonging to the Buddhists can but eventuate in unfairness. That the one did not manifest discernment concerning the meaning of the literary style and the other influenced others to be unfair, shows that both manifested inadequacy in the task of cultivation.

Later Scholars Should Appreciate What Hsiang-shan and Hui-an Have Accomplished

Confucius was a great sage, and yet he said, "If some years were added to my life, I would give fifty to the study of Yi and then I might come to be without great faults." [43] When Chung Hui praised Ch'eng T'ang he also merely said, "He was not slow to change his errors." [44] What harm can it do to the fact that the two teachers are virtuous men, if what they cherish and cultivate falls short of being perfect? These things truly are accounted for in the bearing and environment of Hui-an and Hsiang-shan. That they did

---

[43] Analects, Book VII, Ch. 16. "Yi" refers to the Book of Changes.

[44] The Shooking, The Books of Shang, Book II, ¶ 5.

not reach the clear perception and understanding of the truth, which Yen had, is manifest. We should look up with respect to that in which they cannot be equaled, and privately appreciate that which they did not acquire, so that it may serve as a model to be realized in our task of cultivating and disciplining ourselves. We should not add our private motives to it and unite in adding to, or subtracting from it. "The faults of the superior man are like the eclipses of the sun and moon. He has his faults and all men see them; he changes again and all men look up to him."[45] "The mean man is sure to gloss his faults."[46]

The scholars of this age consider Hui-an a great scholar and philosopher, and hold that no faults should be ascribed to him. They spare no effort in concealing and adorning his defects, and in enhancing his strong points. They wrongfully accuse Hsiang-shan of advocating Buddhist doctrines, and do this in order that they may exhibit their sayings. (40) They hold that they are thereby helping Hui-an, and thus more and more mutually influence one another by saying that they support true and real discussion. They do not know that Hui-an has the fault of a superior man, while they themselves, on the other hand, use the views of a mean man and gloss it over. They do not know that, when Hui-an was told of his faults, he rejoiced. Yet you do not only vainly follow him, but engage in apologizing discussions in his behalf. Hui-an's purpose was that later generations might aim at the learning of sages, virtuous men, and superior men; but present-day scholars serve him as they would the person of a mean man. How much they thereby wrong Hsiang-shan, and how coldly they treat Hui-an!

My discussion of today has regret not only for Hsiang-shan, but for Hui-an also. Since you, my brother, know my every-day attitude toward Hui-an, though you have

---

[45] Analects, Book XIX, Ch. 21.

[46] *Ibid.*, Book XIX, Ch. 8.

waged such a discussion, you will also believe that this is my purpose. You should cast aside worldly customary wisdom, and with empty, receptive mind acquire sincerity. Do not seek to make them alike, but investigate that in which they are different. Do not hold that lack of faults is characteristic of the elevated station of sages and virtuous men, but consider the correcting of error as typical of their learning. Do not consider their failure to attain completely, as a thing to be concealed, but hold that the constant harboring of the attitude of not being complete and entire is typical of the mind of sages and virtuous men. Then your discussions with Yü-an will not need to wait for an explanation, but will be self-evident. Mencius said: "Superior men strive to be perfectly virtuous. Why should they be alike in everything?"[47] I trust that you will with discrimination select and rectify that which you two have discussed.

Comments — The philosophers Chu and Lu are both disciples of the sage (Confucius) and have their points of difference. It is not necessary to go to great effort to conceal this. This fact merely determines the limits of their learning. Not only is it true in this case, but the same method can be used in discussing the ancient past.

Hsiang-shan completed his own learning, as did also Hui-an. They did not actually borrow from one another. When the superior man devotes himself to study, he introspects and views his own nature and in contemplation distinguishes between his own right and wrong. Having determined his own right and wrong, the right and wrong of Chu and Lu is naturally clear. If he does not proceed in this way, and succeeds in explaining the situation perfectly, what relation has it to his own nature? (41) What is described as depending upon Buddhist methods is, in last analysis, a result of not viewing one's nature. Thus in the Teacher's records there is no discussion of the correctness and mistakes of Chu and Lu, as the student well knows.

---

[47] Mencius, Book VI, Pt. II, Ch. 6, ¶ 2.

Reply to Ts'ü Ch'eng-chih

Written in the sixth year of Emperor Cheng Te

Wang Commends Ch'eng-chih for Genuine Devotion to Learning and Warns Him to Beware of Selfishness

Ju Hua and I met as guests and I heard in detail of your every-day life, but I have never had occasion to meet you. Vainly I increase my grief because of this. Of the scholars from my native village is there another who, like you, with earnest perseverance loves to devote himself to study? Can one find another who rejoices when he hears of his own faults and who "faithfully admonishes his friends and skillfully leads them on"?[48] Unless you think of it and tell me when I have faults or help me in my task of learning, who is there that thinks about it? My friend Ch'eng-chih, how fortunate it is that you esteem yourself thus profoundly. From the point at which the individual puts aside the object he loves, perfect virtue (benevolence) has long been difficult to complete. Formerly when you were indefatigable in your effort to establish yourself in your native village, everybody ridiculed you as stupid, but you did not alter your course in the least. Though at the time I partly realized the necessity of esteeming and reverencing you, and did not follow the crowd in their ridicule, I did not realize how difficult it is to get a man such as you are. Is it not greatly to be regretted that, now that I know the difficulty of finding one like you, I do not find the opportunity both morning and evening of meeting you?

The matter of cultivating the self and of governing others is by nature the result of a single method. Though official business increase and become annoying, it is all within the precincts of study and inquiry. I believe that you are under all circumstances acquiring learning, but how shall I hear your most excellent discussions, that they may relieve my near-sight? Thus your love for me cannot

---

[48] *Vide* Analects, Book XII, Ch. 23.

be of any assistance to me. Recently as I have thought about the advance you have made in learning, I have partially realized the extreme care you have manifested.

The saying of former scholars that determination should be earnestly directed toward the truth, surely implies making the purpose sincere. However, if one strives for this too insistently, it eventuates in selfishness. This, too, must be examined. In the occupations of the day what is there that is not the progressive manifestation of natural law? If in this the mind is constantly cherished and not lost, righteousness and principles will naturally be familiar material. Mencius' saying, "Let not the mind forget its work, but let there be no assisting the growth," is a profoundly constructed saying, the advantages of which he had himself gained.[49] (42) How can study and inquiry be slow and lax in their advance? But the danger is that in adding one's own ideas to control and encourage this advance, contrary to expectation, one is not able to be at rest, even when one attains it. Surely your learning is not of this type, but I seem to see a recent tendency that way. Thus I dare not venture to speak otherwise than exhaustively. I also am aware that ordinarily you are glad to hear of your faults and that you seek instruction in accordance with the right.

Reply to Lu Nei-chung

Written in the fourth year of Emperor Chia Ching

Wang Writes of the Advantages of High Ideals and a Broad Outlook

Your recent letter has stimulated me very much. I am aware of a feeling of gratitude; but acute dyspepsia interfered so that I had no inclination to reply. However, I would like to consult with you about the things which you say concerning study. I cannot bring upon myself the re-

---

[49] Mencius, Book II, Part I, Ch. 2, ¶ 16.

proach of neglecting your purpose, and therefore write this. The philosopher Ch'eng said, "What the individual perceives and hopes for should be far away and of large proportion." But in carrying out this idea one must measure his strength and proceed gradually. If the purpose is far-reaching but the heart distressed; if the strength is limited and the burden heavy, there is danger that the affair will end in a catastrophe. Having determined surely to carry into practice the determination of becoming a sage, the scholar need only comply with the points which his intuitive faculty clearly realizes and sincerely extend them to the utmost. He will then daily acquire something new in the regular order. From the beginning there will be very much doubling together and piling up.

If there is outside slandering or praise about one's being right or wrong, it is well to use this for the purpose of warning and refining one's self. However, the individual should not allow this to stir his mind, for otherwise he will drift into a condition in which his mind is distressed, and he unwittingly becomes daily more unsuccessful and unskillful. You, Nei-chung, are firm and resolute in purpose and thus naturally are a man who takes upon himself the responsibility of sustaining the truth. But in these matters you will need to consult with Ch'ien-chih in a forbearing way and should thus get additional understanding. The road before one's eyes should be clear and open, for then it will permit one to go back and forth. If it is too narrow and confined, there is danger that one will find no place to advance.

Confucius Participated in the Activities of the Common People

The conduct of the sage is at the beginning not very different from the disposition and feeling of the ordinary man. When the men of Lu had a shooting match, Confucius also took part. "When the villagers were going through their ceremonies to drive away pestilential influences, he put on his court robes and stood on the eastern steps."[50] Even in the case of the people of Huhsiang, with whom it was difficult for him to converse, he allowed a lad of that place to enter for an interview with him.[51] (43) At that time some people doubted the wisdom of this procedure and questioned it. "The Master having visited Nan Tsze (*sic*), Tsze-lu (*sic*) was displeased." Having reached this point, in what way did the Master discuss right and wrong with Tzu-lu? The best he could do was to take an oath. Why? Had he desired to expound the correctness of his conduct, how much passion-strength it would have taken. Had he followed the idea of Tzu-lu and acknowledged it as a mistake, Tzu-lu would never have understood his real motive. In last analysis, this learning will never be clear. This kind of mental distress Yen-tzu alone was able to understand. It was for this reason that the Master said, "In what I say there is nothing in which he does not take delight."[52] Truly this is the great point of departure.

Wang Advises Nei-chung to be Lowly and in a Receptive Frame of Mind

I venture to suggest that you should be similar to this, and wish that you would make your mind lowly and receptive, enlarge your capacity, and put aside the distinction between self and others, as well as foregone conclusions and arbitrary predeterminations. Thus you naturally will have profound apprehension at the great point of departure. You ought to sigh, saying, "Though I wish to follow it, I find no way to do it."[53] In general, this strange, extraordinary, antithetical method of acting in which later scholars rejoice, who hope for superiority and covet great-

---

[50] *Vide* Analects, Book X, Ch. 10, ¶ 2.

[51] *Ibid.*, Book VII, Ch. 28.

[52] *Ibid.*, Book XI, Ch. 3.

[53] *Ibid.*, Book IX, Ch. 10, ¶ 3.

ness, is not considered excellent and honorable by sages and virtuous men. For this reason, if one lives in obscurity and acts strangely, later generations mention him with honor; and if he lives in accord with the course of the mean, he will surely pass into obscurity and be unknown. If after learning has perished and truth has suffered injury someone arises to discuss learning, it is as the sound of a footstep in an empty valley. If such footsteps resemble that of a man, all is well. If the situation is as you say, then among those who discuss learning there would be only two or three like you, but that would be sufficient. However, men like you cannot continually come and discuss learning, and thus the grass is ten feet high in front of the hall of precepts. You have the disposition to make advance in the truth, but have partly lost it in narrow conceptions. I dare not conceal my aversion to glossing over wrong and to self-righteousness, and therefore have talked excessively. You should apprehend this idea. Do not merely seek within the words and sentences themselves.

Comments — When the view is too narrow, it is not adjustable to things, and implies a mere seeking to excel. Thus there arises a fondness for mutual glorification in order to exalt one's self. As a result one views one's self as alone correct and others as wrong, and perfect fairness and selflessness are far off. (44) This letter contains ideas similar to those in the letter to Tsou Ch'ien-chih.

Answer to Kan-ch'üan

Written in the fourteenth year of Emperor Cheng Te

Wang and Kan-ch'üan Have a Common Purpose but Do Not Agree in Every Detail

Ten days ago when the messenger from Yangshihte reached me, I received your letter and also your reply to Tzu-hsin. I am now thoroughly acquainted with the progress you have made in your learning, as well as the point you have reached in the task. In general, from this time the learning of our groups is becoming unified. This is fortunate for me, as well as for later scholars. Your most earnest instruction is a reproof to me that for a long time I have not requested further instruction. This shows that you hold me in high esteem, and it also manifests my shortcoming. If our purposes correspond and the principles on which we act are alike, and if we know how to apply ourselves to these, the outcome will be the same, though there be a hundred things to be solicitous about and many different methods of approach. If this is not the policy, though every word gives evidence and every sentence seeks for the truth, there will at first be slight, but at the end great (a thousand li) differences. How may I venture to hope for such profound advance in learning and such prolonged cultivation of the self as you have carried out? If by well-directed attention and straightforward advance we, by striving, get this purpose, there will be points of unity without previous arrangement and of agreement without aiming for them. At times it is not possible to obviate small differences, but as you do not regard me lightly, I also do not with unremitting effort try to influence you.

Having a common purpose we are like two men who both go to the capital. Whether the road which is traversed be circuitous or direct, we know that at a future day we shall arrive at the same place. Formerly when you and I were together in a ship at Lungchiang, I frequently promoted the use of the old edition of the Great Learning. My exposition of the investigation of things you did not consider correct at that time, and I, thereupon, put it aside and did not again force a discussion, for I realized that it would not be long before you would spontaneously be liberated at this point. Now I have really obtained what I hoped for, and I rejoice beyond expression. The spring in K'unlun at times flows silently underground, but it nevertheless finally reaches the sea.[54] I am an unceremonious, rustic man. Though I have obtained the princely gem, others do not believe it, thinking that it certainly is an imitation. Now that the gem has reached the home of one who is prepared, it will of course be shown to the Empire and I shall avoid the transgression of neglecting and forgetting it. (45) However, this comparison has an ambiguous meaning; for priceless gems are acquired by seeking in external things, while the thing to which I refer is something that I myself have and do not need to acquire as something external. But I may suddenly and unexpectedly neglect or forget it. Or in case I have not neglected or forgotten it, it may be unexpectedly or suddenly screened from sight.

Though I am not yet fifty, I am decrepit and diseased as a man of sixty or seventy, and daily contemplate returning to the Yang-ming Grotto. I believe it is true that "if a man in the morning hear the right way, he may die in the evening without regret."[55] Thrice I have sent in a memorial about my return, but without receiving the consent of the emperor. I desire to lay aside my official duties and depart on a long journey, following the example of the great masters, but I fear that the result would be startling and thus must deliberately wait until I have a favorable reply. Winter will be past and spring begun before my wish is complied with. Affairs are in confusion as in a great rain storm and the sudden falling of leaves. How can they be adjusted?

Comments — Of Kan-ch'üan it can be said that he and the Teacher held to the same truths and were united in their determination. But it was impossible for them not to have differences in their viewpoints. From this it is manifest that in application to true learning the only thing

---

[54] A famous mountain in Tibet said by the Chinese to be the source of the rivers and the sea.

[55] Analects, Book IV, Ch. 8.

sought is agreement of purpose. At the point of entering there may be many changing circumstances, and it is not necessary insistently to hold to one road. Why enter into a profound explanation of the points of likeness and difference between the Teacher and the philosophers Chu and Lu?

Letter to Hsi Yüan-shan

Written in the sixteenth year of Emperor Cheng Te

Wang Praises Hsi Yüan-shan for Having Assumed the Burden of True Learning and Expresses a Desire to Meet Him

I have received your letter and the Ming Yuan Lu.[56] Having read it, I could realize what strength you have acquired in your study since leaving me. You have most thoroughly assumed the burden of sustaining the true learning. It would seem as though the people all consider what you say incorrect, but you pay no attention to it. You are not like those who, blindly agreeing with one another, reiterate the same things and imitate the grief and joys of others. I am exceedingly glad for this.

There are some things which I really should discuss with you personally, but I regret that there has been no occasion for my meeting you. I have recently heard that you have been advanced to the position of Nei-tai,[57] and thus know that you must pass by Ch'ienshan. It is convenient for me to return home to see my parents at this time. Thus we can stop our boats somewhere along the road that for a night we may converse together. The man whom I sent to await you at Fenshu did not get an answer for me. I waited five days for you at Hsinch'eng and left disappointed. (46) How unfortunate it is that Heaven did not ordain a meeting!

---

[56] A book, probably revised by Hsi Yüan-shan.
[57] The Nei-tai was an official of high rank.

Sincerity of Person Holds the First Place in True Learning

In general, the reason why this learning is not clear is because we have not been able to make ourselves sincere by what we heard and expounded. It may be compared to merely speaking about drinking and eating. How can such men really experience the pleasure of drinking and eating to satiety? It is only a few years since I first fully comprehended this learning and actually reached the state of one who is prepared to wait for the rise of a sage a hundred ages hence and has no misgivings. Among my friends there also have gradually arisen three who really believe it, and do not retract. Those that half believe and half doubt, and whose views are not fixed, have for the most part the serious defect which arises out of holding to old interpretations. Moreover, they are concerned about acquiring and losing, criticism or praise, and are unable to devote their minds and fix their entire determination on hearing the true learning. What is more, this also is due to the fact that we have not been together for so long a time, or, having met, we forthwith are separated. Thus I have had no opportunity to give a detailed exposition.

The learning of Lu Hsiang-shan is simple, definite, and discriminating. After Mencius, he is the first man. Though his exposition of study, inquiry, reflection, discrimination, extending knowledge to the utmost, and the investigation of things does not escape the embarrassment of conforming to tradition, other philosophers have not attained his clear understanding of fundamentals. Usually one is able to have profound confidence in his learning. This also should be investigated. It may be compared to seeking the finest gold. This must be purified until it has reached an adequate color. Not the least dross should be allowed to remain, for after this has been removed it is perfect and changeless. In manifesting or destroying learning, the bone of contention is insignificant.

I have recently heard that Yung-hsi has gone to the capital. Since our friendship has long been very profound, I wish that you would admonish him to engage in study and inquiry, if he has not left home. There is no other learning than that of cherishing the mind and cultivating one's nature. When you meet him, I trust that you will use this to influence him.

Comments — The path of study and inquiry consists in making the entire person sincere. The farther this task proceeds the finer it becomes. If a superficial learning which trusts alone to speech and hearing is the ideal, one gets farther from the truth the more it is discussed. The one expression, "make the person sincere," contains the epitome of study and inquiry.

First Letter to Tsou Ch'ien-chih

Written in the fifth year of Emperor Chia Ching

The Discussions of Learning Center About the Intuitive Faculty

We have recently surely had much sorrow in our home. (47) In my work I have used great effort, and as a result view the intuitive faculty as more personal and important than I formerly did. It really is the great root from which grow all human actions, and the universal path which all should follow. Put it aside, and there is no learning to discuss. The exposition to seek and appreciate the heaven-given principles everywhere, has been in the main correct; but if it is necessary to advance in the investigation from the very foundation, it is not possible to avoid the mistake of chasing the wind and grasping shadows. If the individual forcibly turns within, he has thereby been separated somewhat from the task implied in developing the intuitive faculty, as outlined by the sages. If one loses sight of this in the least, it involves a tremendous error. Whenever any of common purpose with me come here, I need only suggest this idea and all are forthwith alert. However, it is not easy to get one who in reality clearly understands it.

Various Reasons Cited Why Men Do Not Cherish Higher Learning

Among those that lack a fixed determination some have been driven into habits of emphasizing honor, gain, and literary style; some realize what they ought to seek in accordance with nature, but are fettered and restrained by a learning that appears to be right, while it is really wrong, and thus they never become autonomous. Since men lack the true determination of becoming sages, they cannot avoid cherishing the desire for small advantages and quick results. It is quite enough for me to have this type of learning pass by my eyes in a perfunctory manner. Even a hero with a heavy burden and a distant road to travel will rest quietly in the midst of his task, if his purpose is the least irresolute. Since you have in your learning reached the root of the matter, I have of late thought that you have had long experience and thus should be exceptionally discriminating and clear in your task. We have had no opportunity to discuss matters at the same table, and mutually to improve one another with our attainments.

The building of the ancestral hall of the Fans certainly is also a real benefit to the manners and instruction of the people. I myself have no special ability in writing large characters, and, what is more, I have not written for a long time. Concerning the tablet which you need for the ancestral hall, you ought to take a large brush pen and write it yourself, for then it will be well executed. I am sending your messenger back, as the year is about to come to an end, but am leaving unsaid some of the things I would like to mention.

Comments — The desire of gaining small advantages and of having things done quickly is due to an over-anxiety for having things completed. It also is a result of the fact that at the time one fixes his determination, he estimates the importance of his ability too lightly. (48) If a man knows that the learning of the sages and virtuous men is by nature one with all things and far-reaching as heaven and earth, he, of course, will be free from such a defect. He who fixes his determination should first determine within himself what he is able to do.

Second Letter to Tsou Ch'ien-chih

Wang Discusses Propriety

I have received your letter regarding important principles of customary propriety. In general, it can be said that if one follows the domestic propriety of Han Wenkung and simplifies it, he is not far from human nature and feelings.[58] This is very well said. If you, Ch'ienchih, did not have your purpose fixed on transforming the people and perfecting the manners and customs, you would not be willing to apply yourself to this with unremitting effort. Learned ancient scholars were not able in their day to give an exhaustive exposition of the existence of ancient propriety, while the ordinary people, considering it troublesome and difficult, put it aside entirely and did not carry it out. When officials of the present day desire to instruct and exhort the people in propriety, it is not difficult to instruct them in detail and with the idea of perfection, but it is desirable that the instruction should be simple, readily understood, and easily carried out in practice by the people.

The Arrangement of the Ancestral Tablets Was Determined by Former Kings in Harmony with the Feelings of Men

As for the arrangement of the ancestral tablets of great-great-grandfather, great-grandfather, grandfather, and father, as well as matters concerning sacrifice to ancestors, I myself formerly wanted to change these things so that they would be more in conformity with customary pro-

---

[58] Han Wen-kung was a scholar of the T'ang dynasty.

cedure. Now I plan to carry them out in agreement and harmony with the nature and feelings of mankind. The nature and feelings of men both past and present are the same. Former kings determined the rules of propriety and divided them into sections according to the feelings and passions of men. This implies that they are a universal pattern for all times. If, perchance, my own mind is not in harmony with the principles of propriety and custom, it is either because there has been some error in transmission, or else because this is justified by the difference between the manners and customs of past and present. Though former kings did not mention this, the idea is included. The Three Kings did not repeat and imitate these rules completely. If the people merely adhered to the past and carried out the rules ignorantly, when they did not harmonize with their mind, they would not be exercising propriety, but would act without exactitude and practice without investigation. Later generations do not discuss that learning which considers the mind as the point of departure. The people have lost their own nature. How difficult it is to discuss propriety with them! However, if the intuitive knowledge of good is in the mind of man, the ancient past seems but as a day. If a man renders obedience to his intuitive faculty in order to develop it to the utmost, he is in harmony with the saying, "Though one makes sandals without having previous knowledge of the foot, I know he will not make them as big as baskets." [59] (49) "The emperor alone orders ceremonies and fixes measures." [60] That I do this, does not mean that I try to order and fix ceremonies. I merely, because in these later days propriety has been set aside completely, point this out in order to introduce and advance it. I make special effort to use simple language, because I want it to be easily understood and followed.

[59] Mencius, Book VI, Pt. I, Ch. 7, ¶ 4.
[60] Doctrine of the Mean, Ch. 28, ¶ 2.

In addition to the ceremonies of capping the youth, marriage, burial, and sacrifice, agreement with the regulations of the Hsiang also has a helpful influence upon the customs of the people.[61] Concerning the rules of propriety in archery, it seems as though another book should be made to instruct the learner, but not for the sake of seeking to give instruction in customs. If I were to include the customs in this book, I fear some of the people would not appreciate archery as something to be constantly practiced or as of any importance whatsoever. Moreover, I fear that, thinking the exposition difficult to understand, they would cast it aside, together with the donning of the cap, marriage, burial, and sacrifice — things easily understood. Is it not perhaps the same underlying idea which comes out in the fact that the rules of domestic propriety of the scholar (Han) did not include archery? How fortunate it would be if you would plan further about this! My own idea with reference to the arrangement of the ancestral tablets in the ancestral hall, as well as with reference to sacrifice, I have some time ago discussed in detail with Ts'ü Yüeh-jen, and he has made record of the main points. I will ask him to make another copy for your inspection that it may be ready for you to select from.

The Domestic Propriety of Han Wen-kung and of Wang's Time

Some one has made inquiry regarding the rules of domestic propriety of Han Wen-kung, thinking that the ancestral tablets of his great-great-grandfather, great-grandfather, grandfather, and father, which at first faced the west, were later placed so that they faced the east, because his mind was ill at ease.

To this I, Yang-ming, replied, "The ancient temples all

---

[61] The Hsiang is a part of a city or community associated under an eldership.

faced toward the south and the ancestral tablets all faced the east. At the time of general sacrifice the row of tablets on the right was moved to the north window and the row on the left was moved to the south window. All, like the tablet of the 'T'ai-tsu' (first ancestor), faced the east. Therefore after facing west they later faced east. Now the system in the ancestral hall has changed from what it formerly was, and there is no common facing of the tablets toward the east as in the case of that of the first ancestor. Thus arose the reference to their facing toward the west. Truly there was reason for not being completely at rest.''

He (anonymous) said: ''How should this be arranged in this generation?''

I replied: ''Propriety is adjustable to circumstances. In the instance of death or birth, the tablet of the great-great-grandfather should face south and the tablets of the great-grandfather, grandfather, and father should face east and west according to rank, and should be given a little lower position. Moreover, they should not be placed exactly opposite. Thus it would seem as though the mind could be at rest. I have seen the sacrifice at the Chengs at P'uchiang. The four generations of male and female ancestors all had a different position. The great-great-grandfather's and the great-great-grandmother's tablets faced the south; the tablets of the great-grandfather, the grandfather, and the father all faced west, while those of the corresponding women faced the east, each according to the order of the generation. Moreover, there was a slight descent in their position (referring to rank). (50) Thus the distinction between men and women, and the differences in rank, have received what is due them. In my own home we carry this out, but I fear that the halls of some of the people are small and narrow, and that some of the required utensils and other things have not been prepared. Thus it could not be universally practiced.''

Perplexing Problems in Propriety

He (anonymous) made further inquiry saying, "In the case of one who has no descendants, the sacrificing devolves upon his nephews. Surely he can be given a lower rank in the ancestral hall. What shall then be done about his ancestors?"

To this I (Yang-ming) replied: "In the ancient past a great officer had three temples, but he did not sacrifice to his great-great-grandparent. A fine scholar had two temples, but he did not sacrifice to his great-grandfather. Now it has come to pass that the people sacrifice both to the great-great-grandparents and to the great-grandparents, and this is doubtless a result of following sympathy to the extreme. If, when classified according to ancient regulations, this is artful, how much more is this true in the instance of one who has no progeny. In ancient times, if a great official had no son, descendants were fixed for him. Thus there were very few who did not have descendants. In later generations the feelings and emotions were remiss. Then the poverty-stricken began to be set aside and neglected and were left without heirs. Those who in ancient times were spoken of as being left without descendants all belonged to the class of those 'who died before puberty.'

Concerning the method, five classes of children were the objects of sacrifice in the rank of king. These were his own son, his grandson, his great-grandson, and so on down to the fifth generation. In the rank of the second order (marquis), three generations were the objects of sacrifice; in that of a great officer, two generations. In the case of an eminent scholar up to that of the mass of the people, sacrifice stopped at the son. Thus there is no sacrifice to later descendants on his behalf, but his grandsons may do so. Since the people make sacrifices to four generations, and as a result of this idea sacrifice may be offered, it may pertain to younger brothers and sons.

Some time ago a literary family in Hunan had a great-granduncle (elder brother of the great-grandfather) and a granduncle (younger cousin of the grandfather), both of whom were virtuous but without descendants. Some wished to fix descendants for them, but this could not be done within the family group of the same name because they did not wish sacrifice to be offered to them. When they thought of the virtue of their two relatives, they could not acquiesce, and asked another man about it. This man said, 'No sacrifice has been offered to them for twenty or thirty years, and yet you insist on fixing a line of descendants for them. This cannot be carried out. Were they great officials, you could, utilizing the idea of following the family, offer a special sacrifice at the spring and autumn festivals.' Whosoever of the family group is without descendants, in accordance with the degree of consanguinity, may according to the position on the right or the left (referring to the tablet) be the object of sacrifice. (51)

Comments — If propriety consists in introspectively seeking that which gives rest to the mind, it is possible to get at the source of renovating the people and perfecting the manners and customs, and there is then very little to dispute about, as far as points of correctness and incorrectness are concerned. If the individual does not understand the learning of the mind, but talks excessively about the feelings, he provides a byway to those who fear nothing. This really is not easy to discuss.

Third Letter to Tsou Ch'ien-chih

The Work Done in Tsou Ch'ien-chih's College Pleases Wang

Your letter has come to hand. It is sufficient to comfort my disquietude because of your absence, and instructs me regarding the commentary on the Analects of Confucius. It is executed in so clear and definite a style, and is so very keen, that it is quite adequate to clear up points which the philosopher Chu did not reach. When the students hear it, some should make progress like plants after a rain. The mind of the people of later generations is reprobate. Misery and confusion succeed one another in quick succession; and this is all because they do not understand the learning which gathers about the mind. It is only necessary to point this out clearly, to arrange the point of departure of this learning, and to cause the individual clearly to apprehend that it is the very source of his own life and fate. It is not necessary to seek it in external things. For instance, it is natural that the tree which has roots should have a luxuriant growth and wide-spreading branches. It is not necessary specially to discuss the fact that it is the source of pleasure, delight, and lack of discomposure.[62] The essays written in your college are well organized, dignified, discriminating, and exact. They are splendid, covering many different topics, and all incorporate directly what is really apprehended by the mind. When once the emptiness and superficiality of the habits of recent scholars have been disposed of, one does not write in vain.

The Meaning of the Intuitive Knowledge of Good is Both Simple and Profound

Of late I have come to realize that though the meaning of the intuitive knowledge of good is daily more profound, it is withal more simple. Both morning and evening I discuss and practice it with my friends, but am nevertheless unable to explain what it really means. Since everyone by nature has the intuitive faculty, it is merely necessary to mention it, and even the most simpleminded and the most depraved will realize what it is. But in the matter of determining its meaning in the fullest sense, even the sage, with his extended knowledge, is certain to be disappointed. For this reason I say that the intuitive faculty cannot be fully exhausted though it be investigated to the point of violence. The scholars of this age still have doubts and perplexities about this. To say that one is not able to ex-

---

[62] *Vide* Analects, Book I, Ch. 1.

haust the truth completely, implies that he has not really perceived the true learning. Recently a high official from my neighborhood, ridiculing someone's exposition of learning, said, "If the intuitive faculty is taken out of his discussion, what can he talk about?" That man answered him, saying, "Take away the intuitive faculty and what is there to talk about?" (52) I do not know how your present view of the intuitive faculty compares with your former view, and I lack the opportunity personally to make inquiry in order to satiate my desire. When Cheng-chih goes, he ought to be able to give you a general idea of my desire, but without going into detail.

Wang Exposes the Error of Later Generations

The great error of later generations lies entirely in the fact that they deceive one another with empty literary productions, and do not know anything about sincerity of mind and genuineness of purpose. As these errors have been progressively promulgated, they have crystallized into custom. Even men of a loyal, faithful disposition have been inadvertently deceived, and have sunk into this condition without being conscious of it. For this reason the son is no longer filial and the minister no longer loyal. The evil of the error brought forth misery and suffering, and produced confusion and disorder among the people to an incalculable degree. If relief is to come, return to sincerity and genuineness is the appropriate remedy. Thus our task consists in forcing them into the right way. Advance can only begin when the excess of characters has been reduced. However, in hoping to force them into the right way and in reducing the number of excessive characters, one cannot proceed carelessly or superficially. It is necessary clearly to expound the learning which emphasizes extending intuitive knowledge to the utmost. When I discuss this with those who have a common purpose, I do not know what you think of it. After having discussed learning (with your students), I hope you may often touch upon this.

Comments — The people as a whole have not clearly apprehended whether learning is for themselves or for others. They all seek display and increased advantage. In last analysis, they themselves and others are thereby injured. Return to genuineness and sincerity is the great learning which will save the times.

Fifth Letter to Tsou Ch'ien-chih

Written in the fifth year of Emperor Chia Ching

Wang Explains What the Classics Mean, When They Speak of Being Cautious and Apprehensive

At the time when the two students Chang and Ch'en came, I happened to be returning to Yüyao to sacrifice to my ancestors. Thus I did not see them. I have seriously slighted your profound feeling for me. To investigate and become acquainted with the principles of Heaven in all matters, in following the lead of circumstances, is what is implied by being cautious and apprehensive. If you hold that this is still separate from that (does not include it), you hold to what the multitude says, when it considers that everything has a definite, fixed principle, and seeks it in external things. If you understand what is meant by developing the intuitive faculty, that method of exposition does no harm. But if you do not, it would seem that you cannot avoid being subject to the danger of having a slight error become a very great one. (53) According to your letter, you hold that he who has a feeling of apprehension about doing a certain thing, thoroughly understands its defects.

Further Comments on the Errors of His Generation with Special Reference to the Ambition to Gain Preëminence

Kan-ch'üan's record of the Tsun Ching College, which you sent, is very good. The general idea therein conveyed is similar to the record which I wrote of my own Chi Shan

College, and which I sent some time ago to Kan-ch'üan. I thought I had thereby given a comprehensive exposition of our type of learning. Kan-ch'üan says that wisdom and realization are not of necessity to be sought externally in the classics, nor can one apprehend them by any such thing as simply invoking them. Thus it would seem that he is over-anxious to arrive at a dictum and has not taken time carefully to investigate my idea. That the art of learning is not clearly understood by later generations is not due to the fact that their wisdom and understanding are inferior to those of the ancients; it emanates largely from a disposition to excel others and the inability to lay hold of the good and be mutually humble. Knowing well that what the ancients say is correct, they devote themselves to devising a different exposition in order to excel. This means that the more they expound, the more profoundly they confuse others. That the art of learning is not clearly understood results in later scholars' not knowing what to follow. Vain indulgence in excessive talking is an error that arises out of our mutually striving to excel.

The exposition of the intuitive faculty has definitely set forth the very essence of learning. The matter of everyone's getting rid of this desire to excel rests in all clearly understanding this learning. If in accordance with his capacity each one is by this method skilfully led on, he should naturally arrive somewhere. If he merely wishes to establish his own standpoint, he externally makes use of his name as the defender of the doctrine, while internally he seeks to excel, and pays no attention to the fact that thereby true learning is more and more neglected, and the mind of others more and more confused. Defending those whose ideas are similar to his own, he attacks those whose ideas differ from his. They conceal their shortcomings and wrangle about their advantages. All this they do in order to carry out their private selfish schemes. The benevolent person cannot suffer this patiently. Kan-ch'üan's purpose surely does not emanate from any such motives, but because of the influence of affairs I have abruptly touched upon this topic. Most of those who are now discussing learning have this defect. Perhaps I myself have not been able to avoid it, but I must of necessity energetically control and subdue myself. What do you hold of this? (54)

Comments — The mind which strives to excel is exceedingly difficult to subdue (get rid of), and the injury which it inflicts is very great. For this reason Yüan Hsien held that benevolence consists in keeping from doing four things, and that the foremost requirement is controlling one's self.[63] If the student is able to get rid of the attitude of mind which strives to excel, he has reached a state of perfect fairness and openmindedness. Then he has neither foregone conclusions nor arbitrary predeterminations, nor is he obstinate or egotistic. If he desires to excel, he will consider himself correct and others wrong, he will wrangle and dispute and, in fact, will be equal to anything. The virtuous men of the "Tang Hu"[64] have mostly fallen into this grief. The bearing this has upon the art of study and upon the mind is not small. How careful we should be at this point!

Letter to Chi Ming-te

Written in the fifth year of Emperor Chia Ching

A Letter Discussing the Importance of a Constant Purpose and Its Relation to Sageness

Your comforting letter from the distance has arrived. Because you thought that my cough had not quieted, your anxiety was extreme. I am exceedingly grateful for your

---

[63] Yüan Hsien was a disciple of Confucius. See Confucian Analects, Book XIV, Ch. 2.

[64] The "Tang Hu" was a party of patriotic scholars of the Ming dynasty, organized for the object of discussing and criticising current politics. It was severely dealt with by the government. (Liu Ching-pan).

sympathy. It is true that in the southwest one should not eat too much ginger. I have been eating it temporarily as an astringent medicine. Recently a friend had me change from that to Pei-mu[65] pills. Though this had very good results, it is not equal to the hygienic method you give in your letter — a method which will serve as a means of extirpating the root of the disease. The idea is of fundamental importance, for it applies not only to curing disease, but to study itself.

Your instruction with reference to establishing the purpose more firmly, implies that sageness may be attained through study. You say that by testing your efforts on affairs among your friends, dislike for study is less than it used to be. I am exceedingly glad of this. You also say that the learning of the sage must necessarily be brought about by gradual accumulation. This idea also is correct and exact. Your use of the sayings of Yao, Shun, Wen Wang, Confucius, and Lao-tzu, sufficiently explains the idea of the chapter which treats of fixing the determination, to show me that you have been energetic of late in your advance in cultivating the mind. That, in the midst of the disturbing influences of your magistracy, you are able to be thus discriminating in your thoughts and energetic in your investigation, is a thing which our group of friends has not attained. It is justifiable, if you yourself use this idea to arouse and stimulate your mental energies and to level your purpose and determination. (55)

But if you should desire according to the evidence to distinguish each verse, considering that to be the regular method of ascent into the path of the sage, and if you systematically arrange the old sayings of the sages and include them in your letter, that in this way you may reach the heart of this matter, your case may be compared with that of Yao when he tried Kun because he could not help having doubts; or of Tzu-hsia when he sought to bring out

---

[65] A species of the Fritillaria Thunbergii.

the meaning of Confucius, because his ear was not a receptive organ for the entrance of truth.[66] The perplexity and embarrassment of comparison, calculation, induction, and obstruction of thought are still present. The use of this method of discussion shows that the sage is such through study. Though it clears up the situation somewhat, the stages of advance are very difficult. Thus viewed, one realizes the height and profundity of the sage, but does not realize that being a sage can be learned by all. It does not compare with the last verse, which means that the highest stage has actually been attained.[67]

The matter of not transgressing the right, also is merely the result of this constant purpose. The matter of not transgressing may be attained through study. Is the sage radically different from other men? You further say, "Virtue (excellence) is the fundamental character of the sage, which selfishness alone injures." Man originally had no selfishness. When it is expelled, excellence becomes characteristic, and sageness is complete. Sageness has no excess and lacks nothing. This shows that it is possible to learn to become a sage. But unless the individual has the determination to become a sage, he will not be able to attain that state. To discuss it in this way naturally makes it simple and warm with intimacy. The use of this method in instructing future scholars will be enough to stir them. If the former exposition is used, it is not possible to avoid making the meek and timid afraid and confused so that they fear to try, while the clever man of high aspirations, who devotes his energies to external things, will surely be defeated in his attempt.

---

[66] Kun was the father of King Yü. See also Analects, Book III, Ch. 8.

[67] Analects, Book II, Ch. 4, ¶ 6.

The Constant Purpose is Greatly Helped by Intuitive Knowledge of Good

The transmitted instructions and admonitions of sages and virtuous men are not completely given in the books, and what is given does not exhaust their meaning. Whenever one reads the classics, the point of emphasis is in extending intuitive knowledge to the utmost. Holding to this gives advantage in study. Thus, in whatsoever inverted and transposed order the many allusions from the classics may appear, all are for the use of the individual. If one submerges himself in fixed comparisons, one is fettered thereby. Though the individual may attain special excellence and the advantage of instant illumination, preconceived ideas and arbitrary predeterminations continue and are hidden away within, which in turn serve to obscure the intuitive faculty, though the individual is himself not aware of it. (56) The saying, "Excellence is the fundamental character of the sage," surely conveys the idea of esteeming virtue (excellence); and the intuitive knowledge should thus be designated as the intuitive knowledge of good, for in this way others will more readily apprehend the meaning. I have recently said that the mind's intuitive knowledge of good is what is implied by sageness.

The Importance of Exhausting All the Powers of the Mind

Your letter also says that the individual who devotes himself to educating himself should seek to exhaust heaven (nature).[68] Your idea shows that you desire to unite heaven and men into one all-pervading unity, yet are not able to avoid separating them into two distinct things. Man is the mind of heaven and earth; mind is the lord and master of heaven, earth, and all things; mind is heaven. In saying "mind," you have thereby suggested heaven, earth, and all things, and have done it in an intimate,

---

[68] This is what is meant by illustrating illustrious virtue.

simple way. Thus you might better have said that, when a man devotes himself to educating himself, he must seek to exhaust his mind. Your reply about knowledge and practice is, as to fundamentals, really clear, and your method of exposition is so quiet and harmonious that it is enlightening. Your letter displays penetrating intelligence, but there are some defects, which you have described as a continuing and concealing of foregone conclusions and arbitrary predeterminations. Since these have now been displayed you should in time naturally come to a complete understanding.

In carrying out the sayings of didactic learning, it is best to explain any word which is hard to understand by means of a similar, easily comprehended word. But if the idea conveyed by learning (self-culture) is at the start readily understood, it is not necessary to give instruction in its interpretation. Thus, either the method of carrying out in practice what has been learned, or that of learning to give instruction in carrying out learning may be used. It is not necessary to be obstinate with reference to either. However, the meaning conveyed by carrying out (imitating) instruction is not as perfect as that of learning, (self-culture). When the individual acts in accordance with his nature, nature means the path of duty. When he learns to regulate the path, the path becomes instruction. To say that the regulating of the path is instruction, is permissible; to say that the regulating of the path is learning, is also permissible. When the path is viewed as showing that there must be nothing secret, it is instruction; when viewed as a task that includes the cultivation of self, practice of duty, and complete conformity to principles, it implies learning (self-cultivation). Instruction and self-culture are both included in the path of duty. This is not a thing that man (generic sense) can do. If one knows this, what instruction in interpretation is there to be added? Because of disease I cannot write, but will later make a record of the essentials of this learning. (57)

Comments — The expression: "In devoting one's self to learning one should seek to exhaust the mind," has hit upon the great fundamental fact. Having firmly grasped this fundamental fact, one forthwith in his daily experience of seeing and hearing perceives the progressive movement of heaven-given principles in whatever one meets. No matter how it is expounded, thus it is. For instance, in crossing great waves it is only necessary to grasp the helm firmly, for then the ship will be steady whether on the crest or in the hollow of the waves. If the individual considers comparisons of verses and sentences as displaying the highest type of effort, he will to the end imitate and strive for things.

Reply to Nieh Wen-wei

(First Letter)

Written in the fifth year of Emperor Chia Ching

Wang Feels that Nieh Wen-wei Estimates Him too Highly, but is Inspired by His Attitude

In the midst of summer you have, without getting any advantage, suffered the inconvenience and distress of coming a circuitous route in order to see me. How can I requite such friendship? I would very much have liked to entertain you ten days, that I might use earnest effort on my own ideas, for the sake of the advantage of having them critically examined; but at that time I was engaged in public and private affairs so that I was unable to do so. After you left, I was discontented and uneasy, as though I had lost something. Unexpectedly I received your letter and was comforted. In it you have lauded me too much, showing that you purpose to encourage and support my point of view, but your admonitions are true and exact. Your thought and desire are to place me within the group of sages and virtuous men. That you charge me to honor and follow one thing is done with the most sincere and earnest affection. If this were not profound friendship and earnest affection, how could it have reached this point? I am conscious of a feeling of gratefulness on the one hand, and on the other I am conscience-stricken, for I fear that I am not worthy of this. And yet, how can I venture to do otherwise than urge myself on? Can I merely give place to a feeling of gratitude and complaisance expressed in words?

Your letter says that the philosophers Tzu-ssu, Mencius, Chou, and Ch'eng had no idea that they would mutually encounter one another a thousand years later. It further says that complete acceptance of their philosophies by the entire world is not equal to a real confidence in them on the part of a single man. Surely the learning of these men is to be found where their truths are expounded. That all the world should believe in them is not too much, nor is it too little if a single man believes in them. This is the mind of the superior man, that he is not solicitous when viewed as incorrect. Can it be that the superficial and trifling know enough to reach this? That I cannot remain silent within myself is not because I am concerned with having others believe or disbelieve me. Man is the mind of heaven and earth. Heaven, earth, and all things are one structure with me. (58) Who does not have compassion with the distress and sorrow of the people as though they were his own?

The Socializing Effect of the Development of the Intuitive Faculty

Man does not know that his bodily disease and pain make it impossible for him to distinguish between right and wrong. The mind that distinguishes between right and wrong knows without anxious thought and reflection, and acts without having learned. This is what is meant by the intuitive faculty. It is present in the mind of man without distinction between sage and simple-minded, for all men both past and present have it. If the superior men of this world devote themselves to developing their intuitive knowledge of good, they will be able to be equitable in judging right and wrong, and will have common likes and dislikes; they will view others as themselves and the state as their home; they will consider themselves as one structure with heaven, earth, and all things. Then it will be impossible to see the Empire governed unwisely. Thus men of the past were able not only to view virtue as though it had come from themselves, but to consider the evil they saw as though they had entered it. They viewed the calamities of the people as their own. Moreover, if they failed with reference to a single individual, they viewed it as though they themselves had pushed him into the ditch. But the reason for this was not that they sought to have the people of the Empire believe in them, but rather to develop their intuitive faculty to the utmost and to seek self-enjoyment.

Of the sageness of Yao, Shun, and the Three Kings, it is said that when they spoke all the people believed in them, because they spoke in accordance with developing the intuitive faculty.[69] Further, it is said that when they acted all the people were pleased with them, because they acted in accordance with the developing of their intuitive faculty. Therefore their people were prosperous and happy; they might be killed without murmuring; they might be benefited without thinking of their merit. Their benefits (Yao, Shun, and the Three Kings',) reached to the barbarous tribes of the south and the north, and whosoever had blood and breath honored and loved them; for the intuitive faculty is common to all men. How simple and easy was the method whereby the sages governed the Empire!

In later generations the learning based upon the intuitive faculty was obscured. The people of the Empire used their

---

[69] Doctrine of the Mean, Ch. 31, ¶ 3.

own selfish wisdom in order to crush one another; for, while everybody had a mind, prejudiced, petty, depraved, and vulgar views and crafty, hypocritical, obscure, wicked practices beyond description prevailed. Externally they made use of benevolence and righteousness, while internally they sought self and selfish advantage. They used deceitful phrases in order to flatter the vulgar, and simulated in order to seek praise and popularity. They covered the virtue of others and utilized it to their own advantage. They blazoned other people's selfishness and offered it as their own frankness. They were irritable because they strove to excel one another, but said that they complied with and strove for righteousness; they used violent, dangerous methods for the sake of testing one another, but said that they despised evil; (59) they were envious of the virtue and capacity of others, but considered themselves equitable in judging right and wrong; they gave rein to their passions and followed their desires, but considered themselves as having the same likes and dislikes. They insulted and oppressed one another. Since they have not been able to get rid of the purpose of excelling and defeating the near and dear ones, and have mutually been separated by a bamboo fence, how much less will they be able to view the multitude of people and things in the great Empire as a unity with themselves! Thus it is not strange that, in this confusion, the mutual striving for calamity and disorder has become endless.

Wang Makes a Personal Confession Concerning the Influence of the Intuitive Knowledge of Good Upon His Own Conduct

I myself relied sincerely upon the influences of heaven, when suddenly I realized that the intuitive knowledge of good must be used, that thereby the Empire might be controlled. Whenever I think of the fallen, miserable condition of the people, I am distressed and sore at heart. Forgetting my own depravity I think of using my own person in serving them, even though I do not know its strength. When the people of the Empire see that I am about to act, they ridicule and slander me, considering me insane and out of my mind. Why should I care for this? Have I who feel sore and distressed in person time to consider the ridicule of others? Surely when a man sees his parent, son, or brother fall into a deep hole, he will cry out, crawl on his hands and knees, bare his feet, walk about wildly, drag himself down to the bank, and save the lost one. A scholar near by seeing it will, on the contrary, bow and smile and think that the other man has cast aside his politeness, and that he cries out and stumbles about thus because he is insane and out of his mind. The man who bows and smiles near the man in the pit and does not realize that he should rescue him, must be a traveler who lacks the feelings of genuine blood-relationship. Thus it has been said that he who lacks the feeling of commiseration is not a man.[70] Whosoever loves his parent, son, or brothers, must surely be sore at heart and distressed. He cannot help running about wildly and exhausting himself, nor do otherwise than crawl on his hands and knees, and rescue the one in sore distress. He does not regard the danger of falling into the pit. How much less will he pay attention to anyone's ridicule that he is insane and has lost his mind! How much less will he ask whether others believe in him or not! (60) Alas! It is not impossible that the people of the present generation should say that I am insane and have lost my mind. The mind of the people of the Empire is my own mind. If the people of the Empire seem to be insane, how can I be anything but insane? If they seem to have lost their minds, how can I be otherwise than distressed?

---

[70] *Vide* Mencius, Book II, Pt. I, Ch. 6, ¶ 4.

Confucius Was Misunderstood in His Day

At the time of Confucius some judged him to be syco-phantic, others thought him artful. Some slandered him as not being virtuous and accused him of not observing the principles of propriety, insulting him as Ch'iu from the eastern home. Some were envious of him and threatened him; others hated him and desired to kill him. The gate-keeper (of Shih-man) and the man carrying the straw basket in Wei were virtuous scholars of that day, yet the one said, "It is he (Confucius) — is it not? — who knows the impracticable nature of the times and yet will be doing in them?" and the other said, "How contemptible is the one-ideaed obstinacy those sounds display! When one is taken no notice of, he has simply at once to give over his wish for public employment."[71] Though Tzu-lu be-longed to those who had ascended to the hall, he questioned what he saw and did not like to go with Confucius where he wished to go.[72] Moreover, he considered him as having perverted ideas. Of those who did not believe in the Mas-ter in his own time were there only one or two out of ten? However, the Master was so much pressed with affairs that he acted as if he were seeking a lost son on the road, and

---

[71] "'Tsze-lu happening to pass the night in Shih-man, the gate-keeper said to him, 'Whom do you come from?' Tsze-lu said, 'From Mr. K'ung.' 'It is he, — is it not?' — said the other, 'who knows the impracticable nature of the times, and yet will be doing in them.'

"'The Master was playing, one day, on a musical stone in Wei, when a man, carrying a straw basket, passed the door of the house where Confucius was, and said, 'His heart is full who so beats the musical stone.'

"'A little while after, he added, 'How contemptible is the one-ideaed obstinacy those sounds display! When one is taken no notice of, he has simply at once to give over his wish for public employ-ment. "Deep water must be crossed with the clothes on; shallow water may be crossed with the clothes held up." ' ' '' — Analects, Book XIV, Ch. 41 and Ch. 42, ¶ 1 and 2.

[72] "Ascended to the hall" refers to the substantial progress he had made in his learning.

did not warm his sleeping-mat. How could he merely strive for popularity and for a following of those who believed in him? This would seem to show that his benevolence — a benevolence which he had in common with heaven, earth, and all things — was sore distressed and provoked to the extreme, so that though he might wish to be indifferent he could not give complete consent to such indifference. For this reason he said, "If I do not associate with these people, with whom shall I associate?"[73] This wishing to maintain personal purity and thereby allowing the great human relationships to come to confusion is truly not difficult. If this does not mean sincerity in the matter of the unity of heaven, earth, and all things, who can understand the mind of the Master? Had he concealed himself from the world, he would have been free from grief. Finding joy in a contemplation of heaven and knowing its mandates, he surely would have found himself in no situation in which he would not have been himself, and he would have pursued his path without coming into conflict with them.[74]

Wang Expresses a Desire for Help in the Great Task Which He Has Undertaken

How can I in my depravity venture to appropriate the doctrines of Confucius as my own? On the other hand, I do feel sore distressed, and for this reason I look in four directions full of fear, seeking someone who will assist me and discuss the removal of this defect. (61) If I really find a brave, resolute scholar who has a common purpose with me and who will support and assist me, we will together illustrate and explain the learning which makes the intuitive knowledge of good its basis in the Empire, so that everybody may understand how to develop the intuitive faculty to the utmost, in order that, pacifying and culti-

[73] Analects, Book XVIII, Ch. 6, ¶ 4.
[74] Refers probably to the mandates of Heaven.

vating one another, they may put aside the obscuration of selfish advantage. After they have washed away slander, envy, desire to excel, and resentment, and have brought about a universal brotherhood, my insanity will surely be put off and cured, and I will have completely obviated the calamity of losing my mind. Should I not then be happy! Now that I really seek a brave, resolute scholar who has a common purpose with me, to whom shall I turn, if not to you? Such ability and purpose as you have are really enough to rescue the sunken world. Since we know that this is all present within ourselves and that we do not need to seek without, carrying this out wherever we go, even as a river which has broken its bank flows into the sea, who can resist us? You say that if a single man should believe in my learning it would not be too few. To whom can I depute it?

Hui-chi is commonly spoken of as a place with mountains, running water, great forests, and long valleys, which are found wherever one wishes to go. Whether in winter or in summer, whether cloudy or clear, the climate is always congenial. There one can dwell in peace and plenty, and dust and noise do not annoy. Friends assemble there from the four quarters, and the ideas of the truth are daily renewed. How tranquil and pleasant this is! Where in heaven or on earth can such joy be reproduced? Confucius said, "I do not murmur against Heaven. I do not grumble against men. My studies lie low and my penetration rises high."[75] If I and two or three others of like purposes are about to carry out this saying, why should we turn to external desires? But I cannot remain heartless and indifferent to the distress of my skin (that is, the distress of the people). I have therefore again and again told you this.

I am afflicted with a cough and am under the noxious influence of the summer air, and am thus very remiss in let-

---

[75] Analects, Book XIV, Ch. 37, ¶ 2.

ter-writing. Your esteemed servant has come a great distance, and I have detained him a day. When I took up the pen to write, I could not help writing too much, because of our profound friendship. Though I have thus arranged the foregoing facts, I have not done full justice to the occasion.

Comments — The sage considers everything under heaven as his body. He views the dumbness, deafness or blindness of others as defects of his own body. For this reason it is said that Yao and Shun were distressed. (62) Were it not for the great benevolence of Yao and Shun, it would not have been possible for them to have been thus distressed. Their great benevolence was at the root of their distress. That Confucius wandered about from place to place and Mencius took delight in arguing, was due to the fact that they viewed the defects of the Empire as their own defects. They were not able to sit quiet a single day, and could not get along a single day without speaking. There really was something present that would not allow them to rest. The Teacher (Wang Yang-ming) lived in a dumb, deaf, blind world, devoid of benevolence as a man who talks and ridicules beside the pit into which someone has fallen. He was willing to submit to the ridicule of being insane, that he might exhibit the ideas with reference to which he could not rest. Really this implies having the mind of a sage.

This letter shows that the Teacher himself directly assumed responsibility for this doctrine.

Third Letter to Nieh Wen-wei
Written in the seventh year of Emperor Chia Ching

Familiarity With the Task of the Development of the Intuitive Faculty Clears Up the Details of Learning

Having received your letter, I know of the very rapid advance you have recently made. This is a source of rejoicing and comfort beyond expression. I have critically examined the letter a number of times. That there are a number of places that are not perfectly clear is due to the fact that you are not completely familiar with the task of developing the intuitive faculty to the utmost. When you have fully mastered it, this lack of clearness will vanish of itself. It may be compared to driving a wagon. At times, though one is on the great highway, the carriage is not level and goes diagonally back and forth across the road, because the disposition of the horse is not well regulated and the bit and bridle not well adjusted. However, since the cart is on the great highway, one must not mistakenly enter an adjoining footpath or a winding, roundabout road. Even of those who have a common purpose with me I have not seen many who have reached this stage. Yet even for the few I am gladly comforted, for this is the good fortune of the truth I proclaim.

Though in Very Poor Health, Wang Dares Not Resign Official Position

My body has long been subject to a cough and is in constant dread of heat. Since I have recently come to a very warm climate, these have suddenly appeared again in a violent form. The emperor knows me well, having given me great responsibility. I dare not venture to resign at this time, for military affairs are confused. In all this I carry on my daily affairs, though I am not well. Now, however, matters have fortunately quieted down and I have prepared a memorial in which I ask permission to return and treat my disease. If I can go home and receive the benefits of the clear cool climatic conditions there, perhaps I may recover. After your messenger returned, I wrote resting on my pillow, but I did not do full justice to my regard for you. (63) In addition I send a letter to Wei-chün, which you will please deliver to him.

A Perplexing Problem in Wang's Standpoint

With reference to the questions you ask in your letter, I have hastily answered a few things. During recent years those who have come into the mountains have frequently said that the matters of the mind's not forgetting and of its not assisting the growth of nature are exceedingly hard to carry out. In making inquiry about it they said, "As soon as one places his purpose, he assists the growth; and as soon as he does not place his purpose, he forgets. Therefore it is an exceedingly difficult task." In reply I asked, "To what do the forgetting and assisting have reference?" They were quiet and had no answer, but began to make inquiry. Then I gave them my exposition of it. I did not say that the sayings: "Let not the mind forget; let there be no assisting the growth of nature; there must be constant practice," imply a continual accumulation of righteous deeds.[76] If the individual devotes himself to constant practice, he will have forgotten, if at any time there is an interruption in this practice. Thus, it is forthwith necessary not to forget. If the individual devotes himself to constant practice (of righteousness), he is assisting the growth, if at any time he desires rapid development and seeks results. Thus, it is forthwith necessary not to assist. The entire task centers about the necessity of constant practice. The use of "not forgetting" and of "not assisting" is that of advancing the individual and of bringing him to a state of realization. If the task is not interrupted at all, it is not necessary to speak of not forgetting. If there is no desire for rapid advance, if there is no seeking for results, it is superfluous to speak of not assisting the growth. How clear and simple, how lofty and easy this task is!

The Importance of Practicing Righteousness

Today, however, men do not apply themselves to the constant practice of righteousness, but vainly emphasize

---

[76] Mencius, Book II, Pt. I, Ch. 2, ¶ 16.

the matter of not forgetting and not assisting the growth.
This truly may be compared to heating the skillet without
having put water and rice into it, and then adding firewood
and starting the fire. I do not know what, in last analysis,
one can boil under such circumstances. I fear that if the
fire is started before things have been arranged, the skillet
will first be cracked. Those who expend their efforts on
the matters of not forgetting and not assisting are subject
to this sort of a defect. Continually to carry out the matters of not forgetting and not assisting the growth, and to
urge on and waste one's energies on this, leaves one entirely without a real point of departure. (64) In last analysis
the task will eventuate merely in one's falling into abstraction and quietness, and in learning to become a simple-
ton or an idiot. As soon as such a one meets the affairs
of life, he is hindered and perplexed and is not able to
adjust and control himself. This causes those scholars, who
purpose to apply themselves, to be in distress, to be bound,
and to waste their lives. All this takes its origin from
wrong methods of learning. How pitiful it is!

In All This the Development of the Intuitive Faculty Comes First

Constant necessity of practice implies accumulating righteous deeds, and the accumulation of righteousness implies
developing the intuitive knowledge of good to the utmost.
If one gives an exposition of the accumulation of righteous
deeds, one does not at once get a view of the fundamental
fact. But if the exposition starts with the developing of
the intuitive faculty, one is in a position really to apply
one's self correctly. Thus it comes that I expound only the
matter of developing the intuitive faculty to the utmost.
Whatever affair comes up one should, in accordance therewith and following it, develop the intuitive knowledge of
good. This is what is meant by investigating things.
Really and earnestly to extend the intuitive knowledge of

good to the utmost implies making the purpose sincere. Really and earnestly to extend the intuitive faculty and to be without foregone conclusions, arbitrary predeterminations, obstinacy, and egoism implies rectifying the mind. Genuinely to develop the intuitive faculty insures freedom from the defect of forgetting. Moreover, he who is completely free from foregone conclusions, arbitrary predeterminations, obstinacy, and egoism is also free from the defect of assisting the growth. Thus, if one speaks of investigating things, extending knowledge, making the purpose sincere, and rectifying the mind, he need not in addition speak of forgetting and assisting.

Mencius Criticises the Philosopher Kao in His Exposition of Forgetting and Not Assisting the Growth

Mencius' exposition of forgetting and assisting represents a prescription for the defects of the philosopher Kao. Kao's forced control of his mind was the disease of assisting. For this reason Mencius spoke only of the injury emanating from assisting the growth. Kao's assisting the growth was due to the fact that he considered righteousness external and did not comprehend that he should accumulate righteous deeds in and through his own mind. To apply one's self to the necessity of constant practice is of this sort. If one constantly accumulates righteousness in his own mind, the intuitive faculty will be clear and bright, and, of course, right and wrong cannot then be hidden away. How, then, can there be the obscuration described in the words, "What is not attained in words is not to be sought for in the mind; what produces dissatisfaction in the mind is not to be helped by passion effort"?[77] Mencius' exposition of accumulating righteousness and cultivating the passion nature is surely of great value to later scholars. Since it is a prescription for a defect, and for the most is explanatory, its value is not equal to the investigation of things, the

[77] Mencius, Book II, Pt. I, Ch. 2, ¶ 9.

making sincere of the purpose, and the rectifying of the mind, as quoted by the Great Learning. The latter is more discriminating, undivided, and simple. For discerning heaven and earth, past and present, it never has had and never will have any defects.

The Sages of Different Generations Agree Approximately in Their Discussions of Learning

For the most part, sages and virtuous men discussed learning in accordance with the affairs of the times. (65) Though there were differences of exposition according to the men, they were in harmony regarding the essentials of the task. This was because, in heaven and on earth, there is but this one nature, this one principle, this one intuitive faculty, this one task. Therefore, whenever the task is expounded in accordance with the discussion of the ancients, one most surely should not mix up this one important thing with others, or connect it with others. Then there will quite naturally be no places that are not harmoniously blended and really clear. If the discussion is mixed up with other things, one's own task will not be clearly understood.

It is said that the accumulating of righteous deeds must be connected up with the development of the intuitive faculty in order that the situation may be perfect. This implies that the accumulating of righteous deeds is not yet clearly comprehended and, not being understood, it naturally results in the embarrassment of the intuitive faculty. To say that the development of the intuitive faculty must be connected with not forgetting and not assisting the growth in order to be clear, shows that the matter of developing the intuitive faculty is not yet fully comprehended. That extending the intuitive knowledge of good is not thoroughly understood under such circumstances is quite sufficient to entail the embarrassment referred to in not forgetting and not assisting the growth. All this is due to an explanation of deductions from the meaning of the characters, for the purpose of understanding and gaining assurance. But as the individual has not appreciated this through his own personal efforts, he gets farther from the facts the more minutely he discusses them.

Wang Corrects a Misapprehension on the Part of Nieh Wen-wei Regarding the Intuitive Faculty, Giving a Detailed Statement of Its Functioning

Your discussion is perfectly free from doubt as far as the great root and the universal path are concerned, but you mix up the developing of the intuitive faculty, the investigation of principles, as well as sayings regarding not forgetting and not assisting, or you connect them with other things. You will naturally understand when you have become thoroughly familiar with the task, that this is what I described as going criss-cross on the great highway. From your saying that the development of the intuitive faculty is to be sought in serving one's parents and respecting one's elder brother — which actions serve as something that may be grasped — I realize that this section exhibits clearly your genuine and earnest efforts. But, though I consider this no disadvantage to you, and though you may gather strength from it, the use of this as a definite way of instructing others must eventuate in distributing disease for the sake of the medicine. I am under obligation to explain to you. (66)

The intuitive faculty is the embodiment of natural law. It is quite naturally the point of clear realization. The place of manifestation is to be found in true sincerity and commiseration. This is its original character. Thus, the development of the sincerity and sympathetic feeling of the intuitive faculty when applied to serving one's parents is filial piety; when applied to respecting and obeying the elder brother, denotes acting as a young brother should; and when applied to serving the prince, is loyalty.

There is only one intuitive faculty and only one true sincerity and feeling of sympathetic relation. If the intuitive faculty which is used by the younger brother in obeying his elder brother, does not include the development of his sincerity and sympathy, the intuitive faculty which is used by the son in serving his parents, does not include the development of his sincerity and sympathy. Likewise, if the intuitive knowledge of good which is used in serving one's prince, does not include sincerity and sympathetic feeling, the intuitive knowledge of good which is used in obeying the elder brother, also does not include this sincerity and sympathetic feeling.

Thus it follows that the development of the intuitive faculty which has reference to serving one's prince implies the development of the intuitive faculty which manifests itself in obeying one's elder brother, and the development of the intuitive faculty involved in obeying one's elder brother implies its development in relation to serving one's parents. This does not mean that if the intuitive faculty of serving one's prince cannot be developed to the utmost, one must develop the intuitive faculty of serving one's parents. To proceed in this way again implies departing from the original source and seeking in matters of secondary importance. There is but one intuitive faculty. Compliance with its progressive manifestations is at the time perfectly complete. It cannot be given out or acquired, nor can it be borrowed or loaned. However, in its progressive manifestations there are degrees of emphasis and negligence, but it will not permit of having the least bit added or subtracted. It is the natural state of equilibrium. Though there are degrees of emphasis and negligence, not the least bit may be added or subtracted, for it is a unity. Thus, though it is one only, the degrees of emphasis and negligence also cannot be added to or subtracted from. If it reaches the point where it can be increased or decreased, if it is necessary to increase its capacity by external acquisition, it is not the original true sincerity and native sympathy of the intuitive faculty.

The wonderful and mysterious functioning of the intuitive faculty takes no hard and fast form, and is unlimited. If one speaks of its greatness, nothing in the world can embrace it; if one discusses its minuteness, nothing in the world is able to analyze it.[78] Mencius' saying that the truths proclaimed by Yao and Shun are all included in filial piety and fraternal submission, is in accordance with the saying that if one follows the dictates of the intuitive faculty one's efforts become genuinely earnest and generous.[79] (67) It is not necessary to enlighten anyone with reference to the points where nature has been obscured and is not clear. That which regulates man in serving his prince, selecting his friends, loving the people, and regarding things highly; that which regulates him whether acting or resting, whether speaking or quiet, is just the development of the intuitive faculty, which bears in mind filial and fraternal relations, and which is truly sincere and sympathetic. Under such circumstances, nothing arises that is not in harmony with the path of duty. Though affairs under heaven are continually changing and developing, until it is impossible to investigate them completely, it is only necessary in responding to them to develop the intuitive faculty of serving one's parents and of manifesting fraternal submission which is both sincere and sympathetic in thought. Thus there will be neither deficiency nor loss.

The Intuitive Faculty is All-comprehensive

This is equal to saying that there is but this one intuitive faculty. Apart from the intuitive faculty of serving one's parents and obeying one's elder brother, there is no other intuitive faculty which can be developed to the utmost. Thus it is said that the truths proclaimed

---

[78] Doctrine of the Mean, Ch. 12, ¶ 2.

[79] *Vide* Mencius, Book VI, Pt. II, Ch. 2, ¶ 4.

by Yao and Shun are all included in filial piety and fraternal submission. This, therefore, I consider the learning that emphasizes the importance of being discriminating and undivided. If it is published and extended, within the four seas it will be obeyed and heeded. If bestowed upon and diffused among later generations, there will be none who hear it in the morning, who would not die in the evening without regret.[80] You say that you desire to seek the learning of the intuitive faculty in the practice of filial piety and fraternal submission. If you yourself are able to get advantage for your task in this way of putting it, there is nothing to prevent you. If you say that you develop the sincerity and sympathetic feeling of the intuitive faculty for the sake of carrying out to completion this filial piety and fraternal submission, that, too, is allowable.

The philosopher Ch'eng Ming-tao said: "The practice of benevolence takes its departure from filial piety and fraternal submission. Filial piety and fraternal submission are included in benevolence. To say that they imply practicing the root of benevolence is permissible, but to say that they are the root of benevolence is not permissible." This is correct and similar to the sayings of a prognosticator.

Preconceived Ideas Interfere with True Knowledge

Your statement that sincerity, in whatever way it is applied, is a function of the intuitive faculty, is very excellent. I have already mentioned whatever places of intermixture there are in your expositions. Wei-chün's exposition also is correct. In what you have said, a little should be appropriated from Wei-chün, and then your exposition would be exhaustive; and in what Wei-chün has said, a little should be appropriated from yours, and then it would be clear. Otherwise, it will not be possible for either of you to be complete and independent. Shun closely examined the words of others and questioned the grass and reed cutters

---

[80] *Vide* Analects, Book IV, Ch. 8.

(the people).[81] (68) He did this not because it was necessary for him thus closely to examine the words of others or to question the people: it was simply the result of the natural progressive manifestation of the intuitive faculty. When the light is clear, complete, and bright (referring to the intuitive faculty), nothing hinders or obstructs it. This is great understanding (knowledge). As soon as the individual holds fast to preconceived ideas and foregone conclusions, knowledge becomes small. In the discussion of learning, distinctions naturally are made regarding that which should be put aside and that which should be appropriated. But in really applying one's self in accordance with the mind, one must proceed in this manner, for then only is one able to carry out the three paragraphs of the chapter called "Ching Hsin."[82]

Wang Discusses Other Details of the True Learning

The exposition I have previously given of being born with knowledge, knowing by study, and acquiring knowledge after a painful feeling of ignorance is exceedingly clear and cannot be doubted. After saying, "He who has exhausted his mental constitution knows his nature, and knowing his nature, he knows Heaven," it is not necessary to speak of preserving one's mental constitution and nourishing one's nature in order to serve Heaven, nor is it necessary to say that neither a premature death nor long life can cause any doublemindedness, for one waits in the cultivation of one's

---

[81] Doctrine of the Mean, Ch. 6.

[82] Mencius said, "He who has exhausted all his mental constitution knows his nature. Knowing his nature, he knows Heaven.

"To preserve one's mental constitution, and nourish one's nature, is the way to serve Heaven.

"When neither a premature death nor long life causes a man any double-mindedness, but he waits in the cultivation of his personal character for whatever issues; — this is the way in which he establishes his Heaven-ordained being."—Mencius, Book VII, Part I, Ch. 1.

personal character. Nourishing nature, preserving one's mental constitution, and waiting in the cultivation of the person are already included in these. Though he who preserves his mental constitution and nourishes his nature in order to serve Heaven has not attained to the place where he exhausts his mental constitution and knows Heaven, he has nevertheless sought to attain it. It is not necessary to say that for such an individual neither premature death nor long life causes any doublemindedness, because he waits in the cultivation of his personal character; for this, too, is included.

This may be compared to walking. He who exhausts his mental constitution and knows Heaven may be compared to a mature, strong man who is able to hurry about back and forth for great distances. He who preserves his mental constitution and serves Heaven is as a child which is taught to practice walking in the vestibule. He who knows no doublemindedness because of premature death or long life, but waits in the cultivation of his person, is like an infant supporting himself against the wall and gradually learning to stand and to take a step. Since the individual is already able to hurry back and forth great distances, it is not necessary to have him learn to march in the vestibule, for, of course, he is able to do that. If he is able to walk in the vestibule, it is not necessary to have him support himself against the wall and learn to stand up and take a step, for, of course, he can do that. However, learning to stand up and take a step is the beginning of learning to walk in the vestibule, and learning to walk in the vestibule is the beginning of learning to hurry back and forth great distances. (69) Thus they surely are not separate, distinct things; but the difficulty and simplicity of the task are mutually very different.

The Unity of Mind, Nature, and Heaven

Mind, nature, and heaven are one all-pervading unity. Thus, when it comes to knowing them completely, it all amounts to the same thing. But with regard to these three, the actions of men and their strength have degrees, and the regular order should not be overstepped. A careful perusal of your discussion seems to show that you fear that exhausting the mental constitution in order to know Heaven sets aside the cherishing of the mental constitution and the cultivation of the person, and becomes the defect of exhausting one's mental constitution in order to know Heaven. This implies that you deplore the fact that the work done by the sage (Mencius) should have interruption, but are not conscious of deploring the fact that your own efforts are not genuine and earnest. In our efforts we should devote ourselves exclusively to developing the will. To expend our efforts on the matters of not allowing premature death or long life to cause any doublemindedness and of waiting in the cultivation of the person, implies that we are at the beginning of exhausting the mental constitution and knowing Heaven, just as learning to stand and take a step is the beginning of learning to travel great distances. If I am solicitous now that I cannot rise and take a step, should I forthwith worry that I cannot travel great distances? How much less should I be solicitous, lest he who is able to travel a thousand li should forget how to rise and take a step!

Your penetration by nature surpasses that of others, but your discussion of this shows that you are not able to get rid of former habits of interpreting the meaning of literary compositions. Thus, in analyzing and comparing these three sections so as to make them thoroughly your own, you, on the one hand, naturally add the implications of your own ideas, and, on the other, are not perfectly undivided in your efforts. Of late those who merely carry out the matter of not forgetting and of not assisting have this defect in their views. This is a matter that is exceedingly wasteful of time. No one can afford not to rid himself of it.

The sixth verse of the twenty-seventh chapter of the Doctrine of the Mean says: ''Therefore, the superior man honors his virtuous nature, and maintains constant inquiry and study, seeking to carry it out to its breadth and greatness, so as to omit none of the more exquisite and minute points which it embraces, and to raise it to its greatest height and brilliancy, so as to pursue the course of the Mean. He cherishes his old knowledge, and is continually new. He exerts an honest, generous earnestness, in the esteem and practice of all propriety.'' This, you assert, should be rendered as one and the same thing, and should be even less a matter of doubt. This shows that you have applied yourself correctly, for only then could you speak as you have. Originally this is not a narrow, esoteric truth, which is difficult to comprehend. If individuals should perchance disagree concerning it, a little obscuration (dust) is still concealed within the intuitive faculty. (70) If this is removed, it will be perfectly clear.

After I had finished my letter my bed was moved under the eaves of the house, and as I was not occupied with special affairs I answered it again. Inasmuch as in your learning you have grasped the most important things, these doubts should after some time gradually be dispelled. It would not have been necessary for me to analyze the situation thus minutely, but your regard for me is profound, so that you have sent a man a thousand li to me and have made most careful inquiry. Moreover, since you have humbled yourself completely, I can but speak. However, I have spoken too frankly and with too many implications. Do not count this as a violation of decorum. It would be very good, if Wei-chün could get a copy of this letter for his perusal.

Comments — When the task of learning has reached a resting place, one, of course, cannot stop. How, then, can it be forgotten? It is necessary to think, but it is not necessary to assist the growth. It may be compared to a man who has a definite resting place or home. Thereby he has a permanent place. Though he wishes to forget he cannot, for he has already settled himself permanently and peacefully. Though he should desire to assist himself, what advantage would it be? The Teacher in his instruction made application of strength at filial piety and fraternal submission. How true and genuine this is! If the individual acts thus daily, how can there be either an assisting or a forgetting of the wonderful, mysterious, irrepressive character of growing? Thus you can clearly see the real point of application in investigating things for the purpose of extending knowledge to the utmost.

Reply to Ch'u Ch'ai-hsü

(Second Letter)

Written in the seventh year of Emperor Cheng Te

Wang Evaluates Manhood More Highly than the Outward Demeanor and Bearing of a Master

Yesterday I sent you a hastily written, sketchy letter. My purpose was to seek the truth, and thus I was not aware of detail and confusion. I have received your long letter in reply. You have respected me too much, and have thereby increased my shame. Your letter reproves me as not maintaining the path of a master (sage), and as not devoting myself to sincerity and truth. However, who am I that I should maintain the bearing of a sage? What you say in a former letter about there being differences of rank, also means that I am of superior learning and that others, too, have a desire to find the truth. (71) If the age of the individual is about the same, and if he lacks the purpose of seeking the truth, he should, as customary, be treated as a guest. How can a distinction of rank be made under such circumstances? This would be acting like a madcap.

Moreover, if one should not consider what one's purpose is in coming, is there, then, such a principle as that one should with resisting mien maintain the bearing of a master? The state of master (teacher) cannot be obtained by occupying it personally. If the visitor seeks me, I should respond with the truth. Who in this generation has the appellation of master (teacher)? Those who practice some art or handicraft have teachers; those who practice writing Chüjen compositions and strive for fame and gain have teachers. They believe that handicraft is a means of getting clothes and food, and that writing the master's thesis will bring them fame and gain, and enable them to attain a high degree of nobility. Unless one realizes that making one's nature sincere is of more importance than clothing and food, and official rank and title, who is willing to seek a teacher? If the handicraft is not practiced, the individual merely lacks clothes, and if the writing of the Chüjen's compositions is not practiced he merely loses titles of nobility; but if that which is essential to nature is obscured or transgressed, he cannot be a man. Is it not greatly to be lamented that men clearly perceive the former, but fail to distinguish the latter?

Concrete Example of True Men Cited

When I was formerly with Yang Yin-chih and Liu Ching-su in the T'aihsüeh, Yin-chih at every examination was ahead of Ching-su.[83] But Yin-chih felt that he had not attained the ability of Ching-su in penetrating, connected composition. One day he paid Ching-su the respect of a pupil. I always honored and respected him, believing that a man like Yin-chih truly could be considered an excellent and superior scholar. If he were to change this attitude into one of seeking the truth, what could he not attain of virtue and sageness! However, he was able to devote himself to the former, but not to the latter. When the disease

---

[83] The T'aihsüeh is a place approximating a school.

of the philosopher Tseng was very severe, he changed his mat. When Tzu-lu faced death, he adjusted the tassels on his hat. Heng Ch'ü removed the tiger skin from his seat and had his followers listen to the instruction of the two Ch'engs. Only men of great courage and unselfishness can act in that way.

Suggestions Regarding the Etiquette of Entertaining Inquirers of Different Ages

At this time the waves roll and the winds are high (the people are much disturbed), so that the condition is very little different from that of being severely ill or facing death. However, there are also men who consider their point of view correct and are not willing to seek the truth. (72) In the present generation no one but an heroic, independent scholar, who realizes that the essentials of his nature must be developed and who firmly shoulders the truths of virtuous men and sages, would of himself seek a teacher (master). You also suspect that it is not universally necessary, if their age is greatly different, to treat those as guests who enter the path of duty later, though their natural intelligence and their inclination are inadequate to receive instruction. My former letter amounts to saying that I speak of those who have a purpose to learn the truth regarding something allied. This means that they may or may not be treated as guests. If the age of the inquirer is far different from mine, then the relative position (rank) holds. It is not necessary to wait for this to be said. Confucius caused a youth of the village of Ch'üeh to carry messages between him and his visitors and said about him, "I observe that he is fond of occupying the seat of a full-grown man, that he walks shoulder to shoulder with his elders, that he is not seeking to make progress but wishes quickly to become a man."[84] Though this contains instruction, it has reference to those who are inferior in learning.

[84] Analects, Book XIV, Ch. 47, ¶ 1 and 2.

In the case of an inquirer of carefully perfected virtue and the highest intelligence, his great difference in age makes him my master though he is born twenty or more years after me. If he is slightly inferior to that, he is my friend. Can one discuss them in accordance with their relative age?

Your man hurries away so that I have slighted this letter. Will you not critically analyze what I have written and send me a reply?

Comments — Having read the instructions of the teacher from Ch'ang-li [85] and this letter from the Teacher, I realize that of the three relations the present age has lost one. However, it is not necessary to seek that from other men only. The Master said: "Let every man consider virtue as what devolves on himself. He may not yield the performance of it even to his teacher." [86] Mencius said: "When we get by our seeking and lose by our neglecting, the things sought are those which are in ourselves." [87] If a person is himself able to attain to the position of teacher, everything that is good in all the sages is in the mind. If he insists on setting himself aside and seeking others, it shows that he belongs to the mass of people who wait for King Wen and then have a rousing impulse. [88]

Letter Written to the Two Brothers, Wen-jen Pang-ying and Wen-jen Pang-cheng

Written in the thirteenth year of Emperor Cheng Te

A Scholar May Work for a Literary Degree and at the Same Time Make Progress in True Learning

You are both clever men who take delight in learning. That my two brothers should thus cultivate and refine them-

---

[85] The teacher from Ch'ang-li was Han Wen-kung. The three relations are nobility, age, and virtue. See Mencius, Book II, Pt. II, Ch. 2, ¶ 6.

[86] Analects, Book XV, Ch. 35.

[87] Mencius, Book VII, Pt. I, Ch. 3, ¶ 1.

[88] *Ibid.*, Ch. 10.

selves both morning and evening, is a source of great pleasure to me. When I received your letter, I fully realized the sincerity and earnestness of your progress, and was the more comforted. Since your home is poverty-stricken and your parents are old, what else can you do but seek emolument and official position? If you seek emolument and official position without devoting yourselves to getting the degree of Chüjen, you will not be able to carry out your duties as men, and will find fault with fate to no avail. There is no such principle as that. But if you can firmly fix your determination, in every condition exhaust the truth, and be influenced in thought neither by getting nor by failing to receive the degree, then, though you are obliged to practice for the degree, it will be no real hindrance to the learning of the sage or virtuous man. If at the start you lack the desire and purpose to become sages or virtuous men, you will only complete the defect of devoting yourselves to external things and of loving exalted position, even though you do not strive for the degree of Chüjen and daily converse about the virtue of the path.

In harmony with this the people of the past said that one should neither be perplexed nor hindered by work, but should fear lest one's determination be taken away. This speaking of having the determination taken away (dispelled) implies that there was a will there to be taken away. If the individual has not had a will that can be taken, he should meditate profoundly, investigate, and plan for it at once. Whenever I think of your excellent ability, I estimate it highly. Excellent ability is not easy to get, but it is easily destroyed. The highest truth is difficult to learn, but easily forgotten. Years of prosperity (referring especially to youth) are seldom met with, but pass easily. Habits and customs are hard to change, but readily take a downward course. Continue to apply yourselves.

Comments — The matter of losing the determination does not pertain only to striving for the degree of Chüjen. Even when the individual has fixed his determination on learning, there are both small and great errors in the things of which he is particularly fond. The disturbing, distracting influence of these is extremely subtle. Therefore one should desire to fix the determination upon becoming a sage or virtuous man. It surely takes a man of great knowledge and of great courage to accomplish that.

Reply to Nan Yüan-shan

Written in the fifth year of Emperor Chia Ching

Wang Tenders Words of High Praise to Nan Yüan-shan

Since you left me, three months have passed very quickly, and in that period I have often thought of you. I have privately deplored the fact that you were absent with my followers, and speculated what point you had reached in your journey. By this time, you should long have reached home. Doubtless your mother is well, and there is no sickness in your home. The climate of Weinan should not be different from that of Ch'aisang. Moreover, the advance you have made in your understanding and point of view surpasses that of Yüan-liang. (74) Not long ago I received the letter which you sent while enroute. Reading it affected me as though I saw your very face. You are very diligent and earnest; you find joy only in learning the truth; you occupy yourself in earnest inquiry and study. Perhaps in last analysis you are solicitous about not being able to become a sage. Earnestly and energetically you wrote a very long letter, but there is not a single character in it that makes reference to your acquirements, your losses, your glory, or disgrace. If this is not actually the determination of a man who, having heard the truth in the morning, is prepared to die in the evening, it is at any rate not an easy realm to enter. My former distress has been removed, and I am exceedingly comforted. My students have passed your letter on from hand to hand and have read it;

they have transmitted it by word of mouth and say it over. All look up to you with a sigh, profoundly respecting you, and many have been stimulated to great activity.

Among arrogant and completely dissolute scholars some renounce wealth and honor, esteem pain lightly, cast aside official position and emolument, and paying no attention at all to them go far away; but they follow expositions that delight in external truths, in deceit and heterodoxy, and give themselves over to the pleasures and joys of drinking wine and making poetry, of making pleasure-trips to the mountains, and of displaying their ability; or they are enthusiastic over some of their ideas, or influenced by their desires and anxieties, or implicated in their own indulgences, or emphasize some specific things for the sake of excelling. They are able to put those things aside, but choose these. When they become wearied, when their purpose is unbalanced and their mind careworn, when their feelings and passions are moved by circumstances, then sorrow, distress, and remorse follow in the wake. Since you are actually able to renounce wealth and honor, esteem pain lightly, and cast aside official position and emolument, and be completely happy, will you not be able to control yourself under any circumstances?

The Intrinsic Value of the Intuitive Faculty

The scholar who keeps to the path of duty really has the clear apprehension and realization which come from the intuitive faculty, and is completely in harmony with himself and perfectly intelligent. Magnanimous and spacious, he is one with heaven and earth. What thing is not included in the great vastness of heaven and earth, which, nevertheless, not a single thing can cover or obscure? Now, the intuitive faculty is by nature characterized by quick apprehension, clear discernment, far-reaching intelligence, and all-embracing knowledge. It is magnanimous, generous, benign, and mild; it is impulsive, energetic, firm, and enduring; it is self-adjusted, grave, correct, and true to the mean; it is accomplished, distinctive, concentrative, and searching. All-embracing it is and vast; deep and active as a fountain, sending forth its virtues in due season.[89] The intuitive faculty does not naturally long for wealth and honor, nor is it solicitous because of poverty and humble position. In its natural condition it is not delighted because of attainment, nor distressed because of loss, nor are certain things chosen because of fondness for them and others put aside because they are disliked. Thus the ears could not be used to listen to anything were it not for the intuitive faculty. How could it be apprehended? (75) The eyes could not be used to look at anything were it not for the intuitive faculty. How could it be clearly discerned? The mind could not be used in deliberating on and realizing anything were it not for the intuitive faculty. How could there be any far-reaching intelligence and all-embracing knowledge? Moreover, how could there be any magnanimity, generosity, benignity, and mildness if there were no intuitive faculty? How could there be impulsiveness, energy, firmness, and endurance? How could there be self-control, gravity, maintenance of the mean, correctness, accomplishment, distinction, concentration, and investigation? How could one say of any individual, "All-embracing is he and vast, deep and active as a fountain, sending forth his virtues in their due season"?

The Intuitive Faculty Must Be Kept Unobscured

Thus, whatever belongs to the class of desiring wealth and honor, of being solicitous because of poverty or humble position, of taking delight because of attainment or being distressed because of loss, of choosing certain things because of fondness for them, of casting others aside because of dislike, is sufficient to obscure the natural condition of the intuitive faculty in which it is clear in discernment, far-

---

[89] *Vide* Doctrine of the Mean, Ch. 31, ¶ 1 and 2.

reaching in intelligence, and all-embracing in knowledge. It is sufficient to obstruct my proper functioning as a deep, active fountain which sends forth in due season. It is as though the vision of a clear eye were intercepted by dust and sand; as though an apprehending ear were stopped with a wedge of wood. This disease is grievous and stubborn. That it is about to be extirpated is sufficient cause for rejoicing. How can it be endured a moment? Thus, every scholar who maintains the path (truth) has washed out the dust from his eyes and pulled out the plugs from his ears, in these matters which we have mentioned. He considers his happening upon wealth, honor, poverty, humble position, attainment, loss, love, and aversion, as the passing back and forth of the whirlwind and the floating clouds, which undergo continual changes while the nature of heaven and earth remains constantly great and unlimited.

Yüan-shan, your achievements approximate this, do they not? Does this imply that as with one who tarries with things in order to excel, who casts aside that and chooses this, who is highly excited in purpose and passion-nature, this too can be forcibly made out of the tone of the voice or a smiling manner? You should esteem yourself. From ancient times there have been many heroes from Kuanchung.[90] Many scholars from every quarter, I observe, have loyalty, faithfulness, sincerity, self-forgetfulness of disposition, and commanding talent and strength, but not in so marked a degree as do those from Kuanchung. However, from the time of Chang Heng-ch'ü this learning has not been discussed. Perhaps in this respect it has not been different from the districts surrounding it. That the scholars of Kuanchung will henceforth flourish and prosper in advancing literary ability as far as it pertains to the virtues of the path, and will change from a high-toned, spirited learning to that of the sage and virtuous man, will certainly take a start from you, Yüan-shan, and your

[90] Another name for the province of Shensi.

brother. (76) Does your return at this time mean that Heaven has no purpose? Because of sickness I have not written Yüan-chen a separate letter. Mind, virtue, and learning are the same. Therefore I speak thus to you. I am unable to give any other exposition to make this clear.

Comments — The learning of the superior man consists merely in self-realization. If he pays no attention to a single thing and yet lacks nothing, he is like heaven and the great sea. If one tarries with things, the delight of acquiring, the distress of loss, the choice of that which one loves, the rejection of that which one dislikes, and the multitude and confusion of affairs, will preëmpt one's mind. Arrogance and conceit will never suffice for learning the truth. This is the distinction that should be made between internal and external learning.

Reply to Wei Shih-shuo

Written in the sixth year of Emperor Chia Ching

The Learning of the Intuitive Faculty is Placed into Relationship with the Purpose

Shih-i has reached me and I have heard the details of your renewed devotion to the task of study. I have also received your letter. Your earnestness of purpose has been a source of endless rejoicing and comfort to me. You say that to recognize action according to one's wishes and feelings as the intuitive faculty, amounts to making purpose synonymous with it, and does not conform with the original intuitive faculty. You further say that he who says that he acts according to the intuitive faculty has already investigated and discovered this defect. The purpose should be clearly distinguished from the intuitive faculty. Whenever one deliberates in response to things, it is called purpose. Thus purpose has aspects of right and wrong. The knowledge of the right and wrong of the purpose is the intuitive knowledge of good. He who acts in accordance with the intuitive faculty does nothing except what is right.

The matters concerning which you are in doubt — namely, adhering to superficialities, being under the influence of affairs, and similar difficulties — all imply that the individual is not able sincerely, earnestly, and undividedly to develop his intuitive faculty to the utmost. If he is able to do that, these will be absent. The inability to obtain a starting-point whenever one wishes to act, and negligence and carelessness are caused by not being sincere and undivided in extending knowledge to the utmost, and show that the intuitive faculty is not clearly understood. (77) If it is clearly understood, there will be nothing in external good appearance and the influence of affairs, that will not be recognized as the wonderful function of the intuitive faculty, and apart from these there will be no function of the intuitive faculty. If the individual has become infatuated with external good appearance and influenced by the effect of things, he has already manifested private purpose and has not returned to the real root of intuitive knowledge. Though those of common purpose with us in this task all know that the intuitive knowledge of good is everywhere present, yet, when they enter upon mutual social relationships, they make these and the principles of human relationships and things differ from the intuitive faculty. Truly you must investigate and examine this.

Comments — Good appearance and the influence of things are most thoroughly understood by those who entertain friends and devote themselves to business However, if one's mental and physical energies are all used in bringing these to pass, one is greatly restrained and embarrassed. If one does these things with a true mind and genuine purpose, one does not experience any restraint or embarrassment from them. This gives a realization of the learning which emphasizes making the purpose sincere and developing the intuitive faculty to the utmost.

Letter to Ma Tzu-hsin

Written in the sixth year of Emperor Chia Ching

The Learning of the Intuitive Faculty is the Only True and Orthodox Learning

I have repeatedly received letters from you. These have really assuaged all my thirst. On close examination of your recent letter, I observe that the writing and style are better than formerly. It is right that the roots should be plenteous in number and the branches and leaves luxuriant. However, when the flowers of a plant have a great many petals, they do not bear fruit. Where there are many flowers, there is little fruit. Has your determination not recently been somewhat suffocated? You should carefully inquire into this.

Some time ago I thoroughly discussed the matter of intuitive knowledge of good with you. I am unable to decide whether or not you are able to increase your understanding of it. The philosopher Ch'eng Ming-tao said: "Though I have received some portions of my learning, of heaven-given principles I have gained knowledge through self-investigation." The intuitive knowledge of good is recognized through investigation of the principles of Heaven. This means that it refers to the self and is not made by an exposition of worldly ideas. (78)

Among those of common purpose with me there are none who do not know how to expound the intuitive faculty, but I have not seen any who are really able to recognize and understand it by investigation of their own persons. For this reason they have not been able to avoid doubts. Some say that the intuitive knowledge of good is inadequate to exhaust all the principles under heaven, and that it is necessary to take advantage of thorough investigation to supply the lack. Others hold that a mere development of the intuitive faculty cannot be in conformity with the principles of Heaven. They say one must employ the intuitive faculty as a method for seeking the principles of Heaven. After one can follow it, it will be without defects. Unless the individual really adds this recognition and understanding by investigation on his own person, and is really able to understand the intuitive faculty, it is impossible to distinguish whether his words merely appear correct, or in reality are wrong.

Many virtuous men have come from Fukien. In addition to Kuo-ying and Chih-tao there are several others who engage in mutual culture and refinement. Intuitive knowledge is the only real knowledge, and the extending of this knowledge is the only culture. Knowledge sought elsewhere than in the intuitive faculty is false. All learning apart from developing the intuitive faculty to the utmost is heterodox. For a thousand years the truth has passed into obscurity and the learning which emphasizes the intuitive knowledge of good has been regarded as a tumor. My friends, perhaps, investigate this, as the sound of a footstep in an empty valley. Though I earnestly think of you, I have no opportunity to meet you. I am utterly unable to exhaust this affection in writing this letter.

Letter Written to Mao Ku-an [91]

Written in the sixth year of Emperor Chia Ching

A Letter to a Higher Official, Expounding Wang's Standpoint

I have received your esteemed letter, and am the recipient of your favor in not forgetting me. That you thus humbly make inquiry of one who is your inferior, is the more sufficient to make me look up to and respect your progress in self-culture. You are exceedingly industrious. My joy is beyond words, but I lack opportunity to meet you face to face. That I may carefully state my humble opinion, for the purpose of seeking correction, is what I keenly desire and most earnestly seek.

---

[91] An official of higher rank.

Whenever I speak of extending the intuitive knowledge of good to the utmost, or of developing the intuitive faculty, the idea conveyed is not very different from that which is spoken of as thorough comprehension and appreciation of heaven-given principles. But there is a slight difference in the directness and definiteness. (79) Compared with the cultivation of trees and plants, the developing of the intuitive faculty is like cultivating the growth of the roots and advancing the growth of the branches and leaves. Earnestly seeking to comprehend and appreciate heaven-given principles, is like promoting a luxuriant growth of branches and leaves and later paying attention to the roots. However, the cultivation of the growth of the roots surely and naturally provides for the growth of the branches and leaves. If one desires to promote the luxuriant growth of branches and leaves, how can the roots be neglected? Is there any growth apart from them that can promote luxuriance of branches and leaves? Your natural talent for loyalty, faithfulness, and approximation to the truth surpasses ours.

Not long ago I heard Hu Cheng-jen say that in your daily efforts you are always earnest and thorough, and unlike those of the world who esteem fame and distinction and thus vainly branch off into things external to themselves. If you thus constantly apply yourself, you naturally should gradually, methodically reach your goal. Different roads lead to the same destination. Why change and follow another road or engage in an easier occupation in order to seek learning? You should the more make steady progress by taking advantage of the points where you daily have strength in the task. It may be compared to a traveler on his way to the capital. At first in out-of-the-way districts and secluded regions he must of necessity travel in by-paths and circuitous roads, but if his purpose is not weakened he will surely reach the great highway. I am continually coughing and cannot write much. I am also sending some lectures. The letter at the end which discusses learning clearly exhibits my point of view. When you have time, write to me again.

Comments — These instructions regarding root, branches, and leaves suffice to dispel any doubt regarding the agreement and disagreement of Wang's teaching with the ancient learning.

Instructions for His Disciples at Lungch'ang

Written in the third year of Emperor Cheng Te

You, my disciples, have followed me to this place in great numbers. I fear I am unable to assist you, but will use four different topics to instruct and regulate you, that perhaps I may respond to your idea. I first mention the matter of fixing the determination; then that of studying diligently. (80) The third point is that of reforming (correcting) errors, and the fourth is that of inciting to good by reproofs. Carefully listen to these and do not doubt.

1. ON FIXING THE DETERMINATION

The Determination Must Be Fixed

If the determination is not fixed, nothing under heaven can be completed. Though there are a hundred different professions, there is not a single one but depends upon the determination. The students of the present generation are wasteful and indolent. They trifle with the years and cease from applying themselves for definite periods of time. That nothing reaches completion is all an outcome of the fact that the determination has not been fixed. Thus, if the determination is fixed upon being a sage, one becomes a sage; if it is fixed upon being a virtuous man, one becomes virtuous. He whose determination is not fixed, is like a ship without a rudder, or a horse without a bit. Where will the drifting of the former, and the confused, unrestrained pace of the latter end? It has been said: "If, when a man acts according to virtue, his parents are angry with him, his brother abhors him, his relatives and the village clan under-value him, it is proper not to be virtuous. But if his parents love him, his brothers are pleased with him, and his kindred and village clan respect him and have faith in him because of his virtue, why should he not be virtuous and why not be a superior man? If, when he does evil, his parents love him, his brother is pleased with him, and his relatives and the village clan respect him and have faith in him, it is quite right that he should do evil. On the other hand, if his parents are angry with him, his brother abhors him, and his relatives and clan undervalue and despise him when he does evil, why should he do evil and be a mean man?" If you, my students, think of this, you will understand what is meant by fixing the determination.

2. On Diligent Study

Wang Makes a Statement Regarding the Intrinsic Value of Study

Having fixed your purpose upon being superior men, you should devote yourselves to study. Whosoever lacks diligence in his study, surely lacks a firm purpose. My followers, do not consider wisdom and aroused exertion as superior attainments, but rather look upon diligence, humility, and self-control as virtues of the highest order. (81) My students, carefully examine the members of our group and see whether there is anyone who does not exceedingly despise him who, while empty, affects to be full; while not having, affects having; who hides his own inability and is jealous of the virtue of others; who is self-conceited and self-righteous; who with specious talk deceives others — despise him even if his native ability is of the highest order. Is there anyone who does not consider him low and worthless? If he undertakes to deceive others, would others be actually deceived by him, and not privately laugh at him? Is there anyone among us who does not commend and desire to imitate the one who is humble, thoughtful, self-controlled, and unassuming, who has a firm purpose and virile action, who is diligent in study and takes delight in making inquiry; who commends the virtue of others and blames himself for mistakes; who imitates the strong characteristics of others and realizes his own short-comings, who is loyal, faithful, joyous, and pleased; whose external manifestations correspond to his internal condition — esteem him thus even though he be a man of dull understanding? If he really could not distinguish himself and did not seek to be above others, would others thereupon consider him as without ability? Is there one among us who would not respect him? If you, my students, observe this, you will understand what is meant by devoting one's self to study.

3. ON REFORMING ONE'S ERRORS

The Power to Reform is the Sign of a Strong Character

Errors are unavoidable even in the case of men of great virtue, but this does no serious injury to their being men of great virtue, for they are able to reform them. Thus, the matter of having no errors should not be held in high esteem, but rather the fact that errors can be reformed. Do you, my students, make it a common practice to reflect whether you have shortcomings in humblemindedness, loyalty, and faithfulness; whether you have been neglectful in filial piety and in your intercourse with friends, whether you are sunken in deceitful, remiss practices? My students, I trust that you do not run the risk of reaching this state If, unfortunately, there should be some who do, it is because they have ignorantly and unintentionally trespassed, and because they ordinarily lack the discourse and practice, the planning and instruction of teacher and friend If you will carefully examine yourselves through introspection, you will probably find that some of you are not far from this condition. Surely you cannot but most earnestly reform. However, you should not be dissatisfied with yourselves because of this, thus becoming discouraged in the matter of reforming your errors and becoming virtuous. If in accordance with your defeated condition you reform and practice virtue, you will suddenly be able to liberate yourselves, and to cleanse old infections thoroughly. (82) Though a man was formerly a robber and highwayman, this does not now hinder him from being a superior man. If anyone should say, "I was formerly like this, and though I reform and practice virtue nobody will have faith in me," he would not be saved from his former errors, but would cherish shame, hesitate to stop his evil actions, and voluntarily remain in the depraved, abominable condition to the end. I, too, lose hope for such people.

4. ON INCITING TO GOOD BY MEANS OF REPROOF

The Use and the Misuse of Reproof

To urge to virtuous action by reproof is characteristic of true friendship. However, it must be told in a loyal, devoted, virtuous way. The individual who administers reproof should approach the other man with all his loyalty and love. In a genial, obliging way he should influence him to hear and follow, thereby drawing him out to reform. If he is influenced without being angered, it may be considered well executed. If one begins with a violent statement of his transgression and wickedness and distressingly deprecates his action and blames him exceedingly, so that he cannot bear it, he will manifest shamefacedness and strong hatred. Though he may desire to come down and follow your instruction, the actual condition will not permit him to do so. This is influencing him to act wickedly. Thus, whosoever reveals the shortcomings of others or attempts to exhibit the hidden selfishness of others, in order to trade in his own frankness and uprightness, cannot be spoken of as inciting others to virtuous action through reproof.

Although I cannot use this method in dealing with others, whosoever uses it toward me in reproving my mistakes is my teacher. How can I fail to receive it gladly and gratefully? I have reached no proficiency in the truth; my learning is crude, and I am too much mistaken for you, my students, to follow me to this point. When I think of this during the night, I realize that I cannot avoid evil, and how much less can I hope to avoid transgression! It is said that in following a teacher one should neither offend him nor screen his wrongs. But thereupon to say that the student should not reprove the teacher is wrong. According to the proper way of reproving a teacher or master, frankness should not reach the point where it offends, nor congeniality that of screening the faults. In case I, as teacher, am right, by this means I may come to know it; and in case I am wrong, I may expel it. For teaching and learning grow proportionately. You, my students, should begin with me in your attempt to incite to good through reproof. (83)

Comments — The above may serve not only as rules and regulations for beginners. To fix one's determination and never to change it, not to tire in the love for learning, not to be sparing in reform, to delight in virtue as though one could not be satiated — all these are constant characteristics of the work and efforts of the sage. These facts should be written down and placed to the right and to the left.

Advice and Instruction to Yang Mao of T'aiho [92]

Wang Confers with Yang Mao, a Deaf Man, by Means of Writing, Instructing Him in the Truth

"You are unable to speak or discuss either what is right or what is wrong. You cannot hear what is right or what is wrong. Is your mind still able to distinguish right from wrong?"

Mao replied: "I know right and wrong."

"In that case, though your mouth is inferior to that of

---

[92] This deaf and dumb man, seeking entrance by the back door, visited Wang Yang-ming. They conferred by means of writing.

other men, and your ears are inferior to those of others, your mind is like other men's minds."

Mao replied in the affirmative by nodding his head and thanking with his hands.

"In man, the mind alone is important. If it cherishes the principles of heaven, it is the mind of sages and virtuous men. In that case, though the mouth cannot speak and the ears cannot hear, it is only sageness and virtue that cannot speak or hear. If, on the other hand, the mind cannot cherish the principles of Heaven, it is the mind of birds and animals. Though the individual should have the power of speech and audition, he would be merely a speaking, hearing bird or animal."

Mao struck his breast and pointed toward heaven.

"Toward your parents you should exhaust the filial piety of your mind; toward your elder brother its respectfulness; toward your village clan, your neighbors, your kindred and relatives, its complaisance, harmony, respectfulness, and docility. When you see others disrespectful, you should not become angry. When you see others prosperous, you should not covet their wealth and advantages. Within yourself you should practice what is right and not what is wrong. It is really not necessary that you should hear it, when others say that you are right, nor do you need to hear it, when they speak of your mistakes."

Mao nodded with his head and bowed in thanks.

"Since you are unable to speak, discuss, or hear right or wrong, you are saved the necessity of making distinctions between a great deal of idle, useless right and wrong. The discussion of right and wrong begets truth and error, and brings forth trouble and vexation. By hearing good and evil one increases one's truth and error as well as one's troubles. Since you are unable to speak or hear, you are spared a great deal of useless good and evil, as well as much trouble and vexation. (84) You are much more cheerful, happy, and self-possessed than others."

Mao struck his breast, pointed toward heaven, and replaced his feet on the ground

"My instruction to you today is that it is only necessary to act in accordance with your mind and not necessary to speak; that it is only necessary to listen with your mind and not necessary to hear"

Mao prostrated himself, saluted, and departed.

Comments — When a thought has been revealed to a deaf and dumb man, he is influenced to a realization of the situation. In opposition to this, a wise, intelligent and clever man, who constantly urges on and practices extensively, is eventually dazzled and confused. The truth cannot really be sought with speech. Moreover, whosoever speaks and hears should on reading this be profoundly influenced.

An Exposition on Fixing the Determination Given to His Younger Brother

Written in the tenth year of Emperor Cheng Te

My brother Shou-wen came to me to study, and I instructed him that he should fix his determination. For this reason he asked me to give my exposition in regular order so that he might constantly use it and examine it. He also asked me to make my sentences easily understood and intimate, for thus they could be readily comprehended. For this reason I have written the following for him·

The Importance of Fixing the Determination

In learning (self cultivation) the fixing of the determination is the very first thing. If the determination is not fixed, the cultivation of the roots will be neglected, while vainly banking up the soil and watering. Such labor will end in nothing That some are dilatory and careless, following custom in practicing evil and finally sinking into depravity, is owing to the fact that the determination is not fixed. Therefore the philosopher Ch'eng said: "Those who are determined to become sages may study together."

If a person really has the purpose of becoming a sage, he surely will say and think within himself: "What is the distinguishing mark of a sage, if it is not that his mind is characterized by the pure principles of Heaven and by the lack of selfish desire? If a sage is a sage because his mind is one of unmixed heaven-given principles and free from selfish desire, then my desire to become a sage must be a longing that my own mind be characterized by the pure principles of Heaven and be free from desire and passion." He who wishes his mind to be of that type surely will expel desire and cherish the principles of Heaven. (85) If he devotes himself to this, he must of necessity seek the method whereby it can be accomplished. If he seeks this method, he surely will substantiate and establish all that the sages have said and investigate the lessons of antiquity. Then study and inquiry will be explained, as it were, by necessity.

In correcting all that was perceived before his time by sages and virtuous men, it is true that since he looks upon some particular individual as a prophet and accepts him as his teacher, he should devote his mind to attaining a thorough understanding of his purpose, and should listen to those who have intuitively perceived these things before his time. If what they say does not coincide with his view, he must not cast them aside, but rather meditate upon their words. If he cannot deliberate upon them, he should discriminatingly criticise them. He should earnestly seek for a complete explanation and not immediately begin to doubt. Therefore the Canon of Rites says: "If the teacher is austere and dignified, the truth of the path will be respected and honored; and when the truth of the path is respected and honored, the people will show self-respect and due regard to all position." If culture is not characterized by honor, nobility, earnestness and faithfulness, it is of necessity accompanied by carelessness and indifference. If the teacher speaks and the pupil merely hears the truth but does not use investigation and discrimination, it is as though he had not heard. If he hears but does not ponder it carefully and seriously, it is as though he had not thought at all. Thus, though the pupil claims him as his teacher, he does not use him as a teacher.

The Moral Purpose of the Instructions of Antiquity

In critically studying the instructions of antiquity, we find that all that have been transmitted are methods of instructing men to expel passion and desire and cherish the principles of Heaven. This is true of the Five Classics and the Four Books. If I earnestly seek to expel my selfishness and cherish the principles of Heaven, but do not get the methods of doing so, I am in the very act of seeking as I open the book, like a hungry man in the presence of food — seeking only to satisfy appetite; or like an ill man in the presence of medicine — seeking only to be healed; or like one in darkness in the presence of a lamp — seeking only for light; or like a lame man in the presence of a staff — seeking only to walk. Under such circumstances have there been any who merely remembered, repeated, and discussed, in order to help the defect of mouth and ears?

Confucius Had His Determination Fixed at the Age of Thirty

As regards the difficulty of fixing the determination, the sage Confucius said: "At fifteen I had my mind bent on learning. At thirty I stood firm."[93] This means that his determination was fixed. That he reached the point where he did not transgress the right also shows that his determination did not transgress it. Can the determination then be viewed lightly? "The will is the teacher of the passion nature"; it is the life of man, the root of the tree, the source of the water.[94] (86) If the source is not deep,

[93] *Vide* Analects, Book II, Ch. 4.

[94] *Vide* Mencius, Book II, Pt. I, Ch. 2, ¶ 9.

the flow of the water will cease; if the roots are not cultivated, the tree will dry; if the life is not kept up, the individual will die; if the determination is not fixed, the
passion nature will be confused and disordered.

The Superior Man Keeps His Determination Fixed

The culture of the superior man always includes keeping
the determination fixed. Fixing his eyes and regarding it,
he sees no other things; inclining his ears and listening to it,
he hears nothing else. It may be compared to a cat hunt-
ing a mouse, or a chicken hatching eggs. All the mental
energy and thought are concentrated on this, and there is
no consciousness of self and the object. Then the determination is constantly fixed. When the mental energy is
bright and clear, righteousness and the principles of Heaven
will be evident, and the instant selfishness appears, one will
be conscious thereof. Of course, selfishness cannot be allowed to remain. If a little of it sprouts, the individual
should reprove himself because his determination is not
fixed, and forthwith the selfishness will recede. In case the
least ceremoniousness shows itself, he need only charge himself that his determination is not fixed, and the ceremoniousness will forthwith disappear. If he becomes idle and
self-indulgent, he should reprimand his purpose; or if his
mind begets carelessness and heedlessness, or envy, or resentment, or covetousness, or pride, or parsimoniousness, he
should incite his purpose, and these will disappear. Then
there will not be a moment when his determination will not
be fixed and urge him on to act, and there will not be a
single thing that will not be an occasion for fixing the determination and urging it on.

Desire is the Chief Enemy of the Fixed Determination

Therefore, the task of inciting the determination consists
in expelling desire. It may be compared to the flames of a
fire that singes the hair, or to the sun which, when it appears, drives out spirits and goblins. From ancient times

sages and virtuous men have established instruction in accordance with the times. Though they appear different, the purposes involved may not be so very different. The Canon of History says, ''Be discriminating; be undivided.'' The Canon of Changes says, ''Reverence and respectfulness should be used to direct and strengthen the inner man, or righteousness should be employed as an external method.'' Confucius spoke of investigating things, extending knowledge to the utmost, making the purpose sincere, rectifying the mind, studying extensively and keeping one's self under the restraint of propriety.[95] The philosopher Tseng spoke of loyalty and reciprocity.[96] Tzu-ssu spoke of honoring one's virtuous nature and maintaining constant inquiry and study.[97] Mencius spoke of accumulating deeds of righteousness, of nourishing the passion nature, and of seeking the lost mind.[98] Although according to the opinions of various men they cannot be made to agree, yet when one seeks out the fundamental ideas they harmonize as though they had been matched. (87) How is this? The truth involved is one and the same. Since the truth involved is the same, the mind is also one and the same; since the mind is one and the same, the learning involved is also one and the same. What in last analysis is not alike, is all deflected exposition.

Later Scholars Do Not Have Their Determination Fixed

The great error of later generations consists emphatically in lack of purpose. Thus, in giving you an exposition of the determination, every word and every sentence implies fixing the determination. The life-long task of inquiry and study means simply fixing the determination. If you use this exposition in unifying the injunction to be

---

[95] *Vide* Analects, Book VI, Ch. 25.

[96] *Ibid.*, Book IV, Ch. 15.

[97] *Vide* Doctrine of the Mean, Ch. 27, ¶ 6.

[98] *Vide* Mencius, Book VI, Pt. I, Ch 11, ¶ 3; Book II, Pt. I, Ch. 2, ¶ 15.

discriminating and undivided, every word and every sentence implies discrimination and undividedness; if you use it in matching reverence and righteousness, every letter and every sentence implies reverence and righteousness. Investigation of things, development of knowledge, extensive study, keeping one's self under the restraint of propriety, loyalty, reciprocity, and similar sayings, are all harmoniously blended with this idea of fixing the determination. But this must be really appreciated, before you will believe that my words are not absurd.

Comments — Is not this a sharp, keen exposition for use in interpreting the fourth chapter of the second book of the Analects? [99] Has not the Teacher in this clear and genuine exposition manifested real creative truth?

Monograph on the Fan of a Superior Official

Written in the fourth year of Emperor Chia Ching

Pride and Arrogance Are Two Great Vices

The great disease of the present time is, for the most part, pride and arrogance. Evil and misery of many kinds take their departure from these. Pride and arrogance imply self-exaltation, self-righteousness, and unwillingness to yield to those of humbler circumstances. For this reason a proud, arrogant son cannot be filial; a proud, arrogant younger brother cannot be respectful; a proud, arrogant minister cannot be loyal. Hsiang lacked virtue, and Tan Chu was degenerate, simply because of their pride. [100] Thus they ended their lives. When a man is extremely wicked

---

[99] "The Master said, 'At fifteen, I had my mind bent on learning.

" 'At thirty, I stood firm.

" 'At forty, I had no doubts.

" 'At fifty, I knew the decrees of Heaven.

" 'At sixty, my ear was an obedient organ for the reception of truth.

" 'At seventy, I could follow what my heart desired, without transgressing what was right!' " — Analects, Book II, Ch. 4.

[100] *Vide* Mencius, Book V, Pt. 1, Ch. 2.

and criminal, there is no way of escape   In devoting ourselves to self-cultivation and study, we should first extract this root of disease, and then we can make progress

Humility is the Remedy for Pride

Pride should be superseded by humility, for the opposite of pride is humility. Humility is the appropriate remedy. Not only should the external bearing be lowly and humble, but the mind itself should be reverent, respectful, and obliging   Such individuals continually see their own faults and are able to empty themselves and receive instruction from others (88) Therefore the humble, respectful son is able to be filial; the yielding, retiring younger brother to be respectful, and the unassuming, reverent minister to be loyal. The sagely qualities of Yao and Shun imply humility and respectfulness to the utmost. Therefore they were sincerely courageous and capable of all complaisance. In striving to follow them and in reverencing them, we should avoid the rudeness and negligence of Po and Lu

Comment — Everybody ought to make a copy of this and keep it near him, and consider that it describes the task of controlling one's self.

Instruction Written in the Chung T'ien Ko in Order to Encourage All His Students

Written in the fourth year of Emperor Chia Ching

Wang Urges His Disciples to Meet at the Chung T'ien Ko at Regular Intervals and Discuss Genuine Learning

Things which easily come forth and grow will, after a day in the hot sun and ten days' exposure to cold, be unable to live [101] I am favored with your esteem. Whenever I come back home, you all congregate at this place for the sake of making inquiry regarding study   This is an excellent idea. But I am not able to stay ten days, and

---

[101] *Vide* Mencius, Book VI, Pt. 1, Ch. 9, ¶ 2.

even if I could, I would be able to meet you only three or four times. When I have departed, I immediately realize that I have left the group and live apart. Years pass before we meet again. Is not this like ten days' exposure to the cold? If one seeks for the luxuriant development of buds and sprouts, and the spreading of the branches, it cannot be gained in that way. Therefore I earnestly hope that you, Sirs, will not consider my going or remaining as an occasion for congregating and separating. At intervals of five, six, eight, or nine days, you should cast aside your work and meet at this place, even though the ordinary routine of duties interferes. At that time you should devote yourselves mutually to encouraging and refining one another, so that your exposition of truth, virtue, benevolence, and righteousness may become daily more esteemed and intimate. Thereby the advantages and glory of the world will daily be more discarded. This is the benefit which will result from seeing one another. "Mechanics have their shops to dwell in, in order to accomplish their works." [102]

Whenever you meet you should come in a receptive attitude and with a yielding purpose, mutually esteeming and respecting one another. Friends should consider mutual complaisance and lowliness as of advantage. If, perchance, you are discussing without agreeing, you should patiently practice self-cultivation. In influencing one another you should utilize sincerity, and should not permit the stirring of the passion nature to influence you to strive to excel. (89) Nor should you increase your pride and give way to wrong action. You should devote yourselves to completing and perfecting the thing in hand, while meditating and maintaining trust and sincerity without saying so. If any one among you lauds his own virtues and advantages, and attacks the shortcomings of others, if he is base and treacherous, if he is proud and arrogant in order

---

[102] Analects, Book XIV, Ch. 7.

to gain a reputation and considers the bringing to light of another's misdoings as frankness, if he depends upon a mind that seeks to excel and acts from envy and jealousy, if he has the purpose to ruin and destroy the group, then, though he constantly discusses and practices at this place, it is of no advantage. Think about this, Sirs!

Parting Instructions Given to Kuo Shan-fu upon His Return Home

Given in the tenth year of Emperor Cheng Te

Wang Compares Study with Husbandry

From the time you came from Huang to study, a year has passed, and now you wish to return, saying, "I have learned the Teacher's exposition of fixing the determination and also have an understanding of the method of procedure. Today as I am about to depart I venture to ask for instruction which will urge me on early and late"

The superior man devotes himself to study as the husbandman does to the field. After he has selected good seeds, plowed deeply, cleared the ground of grass and weeds, rid the field of grubs and tares, watered it continually, worked early and thought about it at night, and heavenlike is solicitous for his seeds, he has reason to hope for the harvest in the autumn. The will is the seed. Study, inquiry, deliberation, discrimination, and earnest practice are the plowing, hoeing, and watering that shall bring the harvest. A determination which lacks uprightness may be likened unto tares. If the will is upright but the task is not carried on successively, it may be described in the words of Mencius, "If the grains are not ripe, they are not equal to the tares." [103]

I have seen you seek good seed, but as though you feared it were tares. I have seen you diligently plow and hoe, but as though you felt that the grain were not equal to the

---

[103] Mencius, Book VI, Pt. I, Ch 19.

tares. The husbandman plants the seed in the spring and reaps the harvest in the autumn according to the seasons. From being bent on learning to having fixed the determination is the time from spring to summer; from having fixed the determination to having no doubts is passing from summer to autumn. Is it not also greatly to be feared that, though the time has passed, no effort has been made to plant? If it is true that others succeed by one effort, he who studies, when the time for studying is past, needs to use a hundred efforts. Otherwise, he has no reason to expect anything. Is it not greatly to be deplored, if he works and rests spasmodically? Those who follow me are very many. (90) Though I give them much instruction and guidance, none of this in any way violates the instruction given regarding the fixing of the determination. In my practices I cannot in last analysis set this aside, and give any other type of exposition. You may without any hesitation use this as a method of procedure.

Comments — If the individual has fixed his determination firmly, he will not waste his time. If his efforts lack continuity, it is because the determination is not fixed. The master's (Confucius') saying, "Is it not pleasant to learn with a constant perseverance?" implies nothing more than that the determination is well established.[104] Nothing shows and explains this better than these instructions.

Preface to a Collection of Essays of the Tzu Yang College [105]

Given in the tenth year of Emperor Cheng Te

Hsiung Shih-fang Repaired the White Deer Grotto College and Invited Wang to Speak on That Occasion

Hsiung Shih-fang, a prefect of Hui, having made known his rule within the borders of his district, has greatly renewed and repaired the Tzu Yang College in order to make

---

[104] Analects, Book I, Ch. 1, ¶ 1.

[105] A once famous college at the White Deer Grotto near Kiukiang.

the learning of the philosopher Chu illustrious; and he has
called together the students from the seven schools and instructed them. With this in view, two instructors named
Ch'eng and Tseng gathered together the material having
reference to the prosperity and adversity of the College
into a collection of essays and clothed it in the form of the
customs and regulations of the White Deer, in order to exhibit the government and instruction there. They have
invited me to speak, in order to make my views known
The customs and regulations of the White Deer exhaust the
methods of study and self-culture. Marquis Hsiung's purpose is energetic in admonition and instruction. The reason of the prosperity and decay of the college is completely
given in Mr. Ch'eng's essay. Why, then, should I give an
exposition in this connection?

The Study of the Mind is Most Profound and Inclusive

However, I have heard it said that virtue has its source,
and study its essentials. If one does not start from the
source but proceeds superficially, the exposition, if high
and exalted, is empty, and if lowly and unassuming, de-
viates from the truth. In the end such individuals drift
about, lose the real purpose of virtue and truth, and are
wearied without attaining anything. For this reason the
superior man in his self-culture and study seeks only to
get appreciation and control of his mind. From arranging
heaven and earth to nourishing all things, everything takes
its departure from the mind. The saying of Mencius, "The
great end of learning is nothing else but to seek for the lost
mind," embraces it.[106] Therefore he who studies extensively, studies this; he who makes accurate inquiry, makes
inquiry about this; he who reflects carefully, reflects concerning this; he who clearly discriminates, does so with
reference to this; he who practices earnestly, practices this.
(91) Apart from and outside the mind there are no affairs

---

[106] Mencius, Book VI, Pt. I, Ch. 11, ¶ 4.

nor principles. Thus it follows that there is no learning apart from the mind. With reference to my father and my son, I exhaust the benevolence of my mind; with reference to my prince and my minister, I exhaust the righteousness of my mind. I speak in accordance with the loyalty and sincerity of my mind, and act in accordance with its earnestness and reverence. I restrain the wrath of my mind and obstruct its desires. I promote the excellences of the mind, and correct and reform its mistakes and transgressions. Whatever I do, I always seek to be lowly and modest. Compared with planting and cultivating, the root is the mind; learning and self-culture are the mulching, banking, watering, cultivating, and weeding. The roots are all-important.

The Importance of the Philosopher Chu's Instructions for the White Deer

The philosopher Chu's regulations for the White Deer have the following importance: First, they serve as the chief elements of the five instructions; second, they serve as methods of study; and third, they serve as principles of conduct.[107] That everyone should be informed and circumspect in action, approximates the ordinary purpose of the philosopher Chu. Is it not perhaps an instance of suddenly understanding with a far-reaching penetration the wonders of the saying, "Carry on discriminating examination as matters come, and act with determination"? The students of the present, having lost these things, have continually deviated from the truth and gone into trifling, petty things. Hypocritical and emphasizing external things unduly, they drift into practices that are superficial and directed toward fame and gain. Is the instruction of the philosopher Chu the cause of this? Because of your invi-

---

[107] The five principal elements in the instruction of the philosopher Chu were reverence, magnanimity, sincerity, ingeniousness, and benevolence.

tation, I begin especially with the source in order to encourage you   Thus you have approximately the fundamental principle of exercise, of cherishing the mind, of discussion, and of practice, while I have exhibited the idea which the philosopher Chu has not exhausted

Comments — Hui-an (the philosopher Chu) said: "I am not one who knows external things, but does not know what is within   Can anyone who devotes himself to getting and maintaining his mind, fail to understand and appreciate learning?"   The rules and regulations which he established and used as the established order of study, show that he feared that others might devote themselves to the worthless and empty.   The preface written by the Teacher shows that he feared men might practice the rules and regulations, but forget their source and obscure the purpose of the philosopher Chu.   Therefore he says that he exhibits the idea which the philosopher Chu has not exhausted.   This was a profound purpose

Preface to the Writings of Lu Hsiang-shan

The Philosopher Lu Holds an Honored Place Historically in the Exposition of True Learning

The learning and culture of the sages is the learning and culture of the mind. (92)   When Yao, Shun, and Yü mutually gave and received the throne, this saying was transmitted by them   "The mind of man is restless and unsteady; its affinity for the path of duty is small.   Be discriminating, be undivided, that you may sincerely hold fast the mean." [108]   This is the source of the learning and culture of the mind.   The equilibrium is the mind's affinity for the path of duty [109]   When the mind, in its affinity for the path of duty, is discriminating and undivided, we have benevolence, the highest virtue   This is called the equilibrium.   The learning of Confucius and Mencius empha-

---

[108] The Shooking.   The Books of Yü, Book II, ¶ 15.

[109] *Vide* Doctrine of the Mean, Ch. 1, ¶ 4.

sizes only the seeking of benevolence, and thus we have the transmitted instruction about being discriminating and undivided. However, the defect of that time surely was that some sought learning in external things (instead of within the mind). Therefore, when Tzu-kung began to suspect that Confucius was one who learned many things and kept them in memory, and that a man who extensively confers benefits on the people and assists them all is benevolent, the Master spoke to him of seeking an all-pervading unity and of being able to judge others by what is nigh in ourselves.[110] Thereby he caused him to seek within his own mind. Even at the time of the philosopher Mencius, Mo spoke of the benevolence that made him willing to rub his whole body smooth from his head to his heels. Moreover, the followers of the philosopher Kao also gave expositions regarding the internal character of benevolence, and the external character of righteousness, which greatly injured the learning which emphasizes the mind. Mencius criticised the idea that righteousness is external. In discussing benevolence he said that it has reference to man's mind.[111] ''The great end of learning is nothing else but to seek for the lost mind.''[112] ''Benevolence, righteousness, propriety, and knowledge are not infused into us from without. We are certainly furnished with them, and do not need to deliberate about them,'' he said.[113]

When the public regard for the general welfare ceased, methods of violent control began to be practiced. Those who devoted themselves to fame and gain feigned the appearance of acting according to the principles of Heaven, so that they might assist their selfish desires and deceive others. They said that the principles of Heaven certainly were of that sort, and did not realize that he who does not

---

[110] *Vide* Analects, Book VI, Ch. 28, ¶ 1; Book XV, Ch. 2, ¶ 1, 2, and 3.

[111] *Vide* Mencius, Book VI, Pt. I, Ch. 4, ¶ 1.

[112] *Ibid.*, Ch. 11, ¶ 4.

[113] *Ibid.*, Ch. 6, ¶ 7.

have a mind devoted to principles cannot have the principles of Heaven. From that time mind and principles were
separated into two distinct things, and the learning which
emphasizes discrimination and undividedness was lost. The
mistake of the scholars consists in seeking to understand the
so-called principles of things externally in the dust and
refuse of criminal law, in finished things, and calculations
of various sorts. They do not realize that the mind itself is
the embodiment of the principles of things, and that from
the first it is not necessary to borrow these from external
things. The emptiness of Buddhism and Taoism is shown
in the fact that they cast aside the regular principles of the
five human relationships, as well as those of affairs and
things, in order to seek an understanding of what they
designate as "my mind." They do not realize that the
principles of things are just what is meant by "my mind,"
and that it is not necessary to depart from them. In the
Sung dynasty the two philosophers Chou and Ch'eng again
found the fundamental idea of Confucius and Yen. At
that time the expositions of the *wu-chi* (universal mind
or spirit), and of the *t'ai-chi* (the ultimate immaterial
principles) as the principles of benevolence, righteousness
and integrity had been produced. Moreover, they gave
expositions regarding tranquility, saying, "If the mind is
fixed when it is active, it is fixed when it is at rest. (93)
There is no discussion pertaining to internal and external,
nor to the meeting and receiving of affairs." The purpose
implied was not greatly different from that implied in being
discriminating and undivided.

But His Standpoint is Not Generally Appreciated

After that came Lu Hsiang-shan. Though the unmixed,
perspicuous, harmonious, kindly character of his writings
is not equal to that of those two philosophers, their simplicity and definiteness really agree with the transmitted
sayings of Mencius. If, at times, there are differences in

the development of the discussions, these are due to differences in their bearing and point of view. However, in that they wish those who study them surely to seek the mind, they are in harmony. Therefore I have judged the learning and culture of Lu to be equivalent to that of Mencius, while those who criticise him consider him to have points of similarity and difference with Hui An, and thereupon slander him as a Buddhist priest. The expositions of the Buddhists set aside the five human relationships and completely neglect the principles of things: the Buddhists cannot devote themselves to political affairs. If the learning of Lu really is of that type, he was a Buddhist priest; but the expositions of Buddhism and of Lu have all been preserved. If the student will peruse them, he should detect their truth and error, their agreements and disagreements, without waiting for others to distinguish them. But all flock harmoniously about one leader, they plagiarize and hit upon the same performances. They are like a dwarf viewing a stage, who does not know what is the real occasion for the laughing and weeping. Is not this an instance of unduly honoring the ear and neglecting the eyes? Is it not the error described in the saying, ''What is not attained in words is not to be sought for in the mind?''[114] This talk about the truth and error, the dissimilarity and the agreement, always takes its departure from the individual's desire to excel and put his old habits at ease, and from considering his own point of view correct. Therefore the injury emanating from the desire to excel, and from old practices, cannot be avoided even by virtuous men.

The prefect Li Mao-yüan is about to cut the blocks for Hsiang-shan's essays and asked me to write a preface. What shall I venture to say? On reading the Teacher's (Hsiang-shan's) essays, it is clear that he was fully devoted to seeking the mind, and that he did not utilize the old practice and place his own point of view in the fore-

---

[114] Mencius, Book II, Pt. I, Ch. 2, ¶ 9.

most rank In experiencing it himself, he was able to distinguish between chaff and good, clean rice.

Comments — The distinction between the mind given over to passion and the mind which seeks the path, is the origin of all learning that emphasizes the path of duty. Since the learning and culture of Hsiang-shan are devoted to finding this in the mind, he can be said to have reached an appreciation of the great root and source of learning. (94) .Can it be that Hui-an did not know this? What reason is there for saying that these are Buddhist doctrines? It is perhaps really due to the fact that later scholars do not understand that part of his exposition which is easily realized, but seek to comprehend the points where it is indistinct and unintelligible. This is what the Teacher describes by saying, "A minute error at the start eventuates in a great mistake." This attitude must be criticised. The criticism which Hui-an makes regarding Hsiang-shan resembles that which the Teacher makes regarding Hui-an. The truths of the three teachers mutually complete one another It is not necessary to make inquiry about points of likeness and difference.

Preface to Li Chi Tsuan Yen

Benevolence, Righteousness and Intelligence Are Essentials of Propriety

Ceremonies and propriety are fundamental principles of life; the fundamental principles of life are nature; nature is fate (order of Heaven) "The ordinances of Heaven, how profound they are and unceasing!" [115] Insofar as they refer to man, they are called nature, insofar as they take the form of clear rules, they are called rites, insofar as they are pure, unadulterated virtue, they are called benevolence; insofar as they are definite, clear-cut laws, they are called righteousness, insofar as they are clear and conscious, they are called intelligence, insofar as they are

---

[115] Doctrine of the Mean, Ch. 26, ¶ 10.

blended in nature, the principles involved are the same. Thus, benevolence is the fundamental structure of rites and propriety; righteousness is an essential of propriety; intelligence is the clear perception of propriety.

Propriety Should Serve to Adjust the Great Relations and Virtues of Humanity

Of the three hundred canonical rules of ceremony and the three thousand Chü Li (additional rules of demeanor), there is not a single one that does not have benevolence (virtue) and nature at its base. Since the arrangements and distinctions of Heaven are thus, what a remarkable mind the sage has! As there is nothing in the rules of propriety that is not in accordance with the ordinances of Heaven, "subduing one's self and returning to propriety is perfect virtue."[116] The exhaustive investigation of principles means exhausting nature in order to attain the decrees of Heaven. The exhausting of nature implies that activity, demeanor, and mutual intercourse are in accordance with propriety. I am in doubt about the expositions of propriety given by later generations, for they wrangle confusedly about details and are influenced and regulated by the insignificant things of criminal law. The livelong years they toil hard. Their defect is that they apply their mental energy to the dregs of repeating history. They forget to adjust the great invariable relations of mankind, and to establish the great fundamental virtues of humanity.[117] " 'It is in accordance with the rules of propriety,' they say; 'It is in accordance with the rules of propriety,' they say. Are gems and silks all that is meant by propriety?"[118] (95)

Moreover, "if a man lack the virtues proper to humanity, what has he to do with the rites of propriety?"[119] When

---

[116] Analects, Book XII, Ch. 1, ¶ 1.
[117] Vide Doctrine of the Mean, Ch. 32, ¶ 1.
[118] Analects, Book XVII, Ch. 11.
[119] Ibid., Book III, Ch. 3.

the followers of the philosophers Lao and Chuang left propriety in order to discuss nature, when they said that rites and propriety implied the decline of the virtue of the path and the loss of virtue and righteousness, they had already lost appreciation of the situation and fallen into a vast emptiness and a void waste In his expositions the worldly scholar neglects nature in order to attain proficiency in the rites of propriety, and forthwith declares that these pertain to nothing further than utensils, rules, measures, and numbers, thereby resolving to follow the lead of circumstances (imitate shadows) and believing that propriety is exhausted in this. Therefore, since all the rules of propriety of former kings were obscured by the smoke, scattered as ashes, and at last burned to ashes in the entire Empire, this cannot all be blamed to the burning of the Ch'in dynasty.[120]

Propriety is to Rites and Ceremonies What Compass and Square are to Circles and Squares

Assuming not to estimate the situation myself, I frequently desire to take what is recorded in the Canon of Rites, that I may exhibit the great invariable relations of mankind and the fundamental virtues of humanity, but discard the rules and regulations, and show that things, truth, source, and end may amount to the same thing But I fear that I am unable to assume the responsibility of that virtue, for at times there are things which I am unable to attain. I have said the following with reference to this matter: "Propriety is to rites and ceremonies as compass and square are to squares and circles. Except for squares and circles there would be no use for compass and square, except for rites and ceremonies there would be no propriety. Although squares and circles are the products of compass and square, one should not think that the squares and circles are the compass and square. If compass and

120 Shih Huang-ti of the Ch'in dynasty burned the books.

square are used to make squares and circles, they can be used indefinitely. If they are not used to make squares and circles, but the squares and circles are used as compass and square, then an end has been put to the use of compass and square. This is because the compass and square are not limited in use to definite squares and circles, while the latter are the result of the definite compass and square." This is the important thing in learning propriety. Men of abundant virtue in action, demeanor, and mutual intercourse, avail themselves of this.

The Rites of Propriety Have Been Carefully Studied and Expounded

Chu Chung-hui of the Sung Dynasty deplored the vague, confused condition of the Li-Ching (Canonical Rites of Propriety) and desired to examine, correct, and revise it, so that the I-Li would be the canon, and the Canon of Rites, the record of traditions and precepts; but he was in the end not able to carry this out.[121] Later when Wu Yu-ch'ing worked at the Tsuan-Yen, he did not discriminate further in that which Chu said, but in the matter of precedence and importance he exhibited and explained much. The point of view held by these two philosophers took its origin from scholars of the Han dynasty, as far as it pertains to the demarcation of rules from the source which says: (96) View this (the Li Chi Tsuan Yen) till you understand it thoroughly, that you may carry out the original canon of propriety.[122] Thus I still deplore the fact that I was born at so late a time that I was not able to hear them. However, insofar as later sages have done anything in this connection, it is not necessary for me to speak; and insofar as they have done nothing, the situation is as the Tsuan-Yen depicts it.[123] Can there be a decrease in the

---

[121] The I-Li is a portion of the Book of Rites devoted to the more general principles of propriety.

[122] Canon of Changes.

[123] That is, he may write a preface.

number of those who continue the calling of devoting themselves to the study of propriety?

My wife's relative, Hu Ju-teng — the prefect of Ning-kuo — a loyal, sincere man who is fond of the rules of propriety, in order to exhibit these and bestow them on the people, had the blocks for the Tsuan-Yen cut, that it could be distributed, and asked me to write a preface. I accept, and adopt Ju-teng's presentation of the truth and carry it forward to its source. For this reason I preface it in this way.

The Rules of Propriety Are True to Nature

Comments — The Doctrine of the Mean extols the greatness of the path of the sage, and uses the rules of ceremony and of demeanor in doing so [124] When the Master (Confucius) spoke to Yen Yüan about virtue, he used the expression, "return to propriety," in his exposition [125] Propriety is the natural expression of disposition, manifested as the rules of all conduct There is nothing that it does not penetrate and include. It should be used daily by all, whether active or at rest. Emulation and debate should not lack the least in this. If benevolence lacks in this, it is not perfect benevolence; if righteousness lacks in this, it is not perfect righteousness; if knowledge lacks in this, it is not perfect knowledge Propriety penetrates and strengthens the four virtues [126] This is in harmony with the saying in the Canon of Changes· "View this till you understand it thoroughly in order that you may carry out the Canon of Propriety." Through the thorough investigation of principles, and the exhausting of one's nature, in order to attain to the ordinances of Heaven, it is possible to get at the very root of propriety

---

[124] *Vide* Doctrine of the Mean, Ch. 27, ¶ 3.

[125] Analects, Book XII, Ch. 1, ¶ 1.

[126] Benevolence, righteousness, knowledge, and propriety.

Instruction to Cheng Te-fu on the Occasion of His Return Home

Given in the tenth year of Emperor Cheng Te

The Record of a Conversation Between Wang Yang-ming and Cheng Te-fu

Cheng Te-fu from Hsian was about to study with Yang-ming when he heard scholars and officials criticise his learning and culture as Buddhistic. Then he gave up the plan. Thus it came that with Chou I-shan from Chiangshan he merely followed the disciples of Yang-ming and critically examined what they said. Finding that the teaching was not Buddhistic, he followed the Teacher and himself heard his exposition. (97) After nineteen days he was perfectly clear that the learning was not like that of the Buddhists. Then he began to offer the respect of student to master. He made inquiry of the Teacher, saying, "What difference exists between Confucianism and Buddhism?"

The Teacher said: "You should not seek for points of difference and agreement in Confucianism and Buddhism. You should seek for, and learn the truth."

Te-fu said: "What distinction is there between truth and error, between right and wrong?"

The Teacher said: "You should not seek for truth and error, right and wrong, in expositions and discussions. Seek to know and attain an understanding of the situation in your mind. If the mind acquiesces, it is true."

Te-fu said: "How can the mind determine what is right and wrong?"

The Teacher said: "He who lacks the capacity of distinguishing between right and wrong is not a man. In tasting sweetness and bitterness, the mouth of any other individual is quite as well able to make distinctions as I Ya's; in judging beauty and ugliness other men's eyes are able to make distinctions quite as well as Li Lou's; and in making distinctions between right and wrong, anyone's mind is like that of the sages.[127] If in matters of interest the relation of the mind to the path of duty is not comparable to the sincerity and earnestness of the mouth to flavor, and of the eyes to beauty and ugliness, selfishness will later obscure it. You should establish its sincerity, and that is all. You should be solicitous lest, in its relation to the path of duty, the mind be not equal in sincerity and earnestness to the mouth in testing flavors, or the eyes in testing color. Why should you fear lest it should not be able to distinguish between sweet and bitter, beauty and ugliness?"

Te-fu said: "In that case would it not be true that what is recorded in the Five Classics and promulgated in the Four Books is all of no use?"

The Teacher said: "Who says that these things are of no use? They are the depository of sweetness, bitterness, beauty, and ugliness. If the individual seeks without sincerity for what they record, nothing but discussions about flavor and color will follow. Who is able to get at the real facts about the bitterness, sweetness, beauty, or ugliness under such circumstances?"

Inasmuch as Te-fu said he wished to return home and asked for a copy of this conversation I forthwith made it.

Comments — That one should learn what is agreeable to and in accord with the mind, it here pointed out and earnestly urged.

Preface to "Instructions Fixed by the Philosopher Chu in Later Life"

Written in the thirteenth year of Emperor Cheng Te

Wang Gives a Statement of His Experience as a Student in Early Life and of the Way in Which He Arrived at His Later Views

The doctrines promulgated and transmitted by Con-

---

127 I Ya was the famous cook of Duke Huan (B C. 684-642). *Vide* Mencius, Book VI, Pt. 1, Ch. 7, ¶ 5.

fucius had lost their influence from the time of Mencius. (98) More than fifteen hundred years after Confucius, Chou Lien-hsi and Ch'eng Ming-tao first again sought for what had been transmitted. Thereafter scholars daily discriminated and distinguished these (doctrines) more carefully and minutely, but at the same time departed so far from them that they were again lost and obscured. I have often earnestly attempted to get at the reason. In general, this is due to the fact that they were reduced to a state of confusion by the great amount of exposition of worldly scholars. Early in life I (Shou-jen) devoted my energies to getting the degree of Chüjen, and sank my purpose into the practice of writing essays. Having gained some knowledge of what is meant by devoting one's self to true learning, I deplored the confusion and lassitude of the expositions of the mass of scholars, as well as their vagueness — a vagueness which made it impossible to understand them. For this reason I sought relief in Taoism and Buddhism. I readily understood these and thought that the learning of the sages amounted to the same thing. However, when I tried to adjust them to the instruction of Confucius, and employed them in daily use, they were constantly deficient. Trusting them and disregarding them, departing from them and returning to them, I both believed and mistrusted them.

Later, as a degraded official I lived in distress among the barbarians. Having been stimulated in mind and hardened in nature, I suddenly realized that this should be carefully investigated and sought out. A year later I substantiated the fact that the sayings of the Six Classics and the four philosophers are as copiously sufficient as a stream bursting its banks and flowing into the sea. After that I lauded the path of the sages as a plain, level, great highway, and deplored the fact that worldly scholars had erroneously opened a narrow road, trodden on thorns, and fallen into a pit. Having examined their expositions, I found that they emanated from a lower level than those of the two religions. Is it not proper that the highly intelligent scholar should despise their expositions and prefer to follow those of the two religions? Should this be considered the fault of the two religions? Occasionally when I use this in speaking to those of common purpose, some cautious and fearful ones criticise me as wrong, as establishing heterodoxy and as being fond of strange things. Nevertheless, whenever I earnestly introspect and profoundly keep my self-possession, while seeking exhaustively my own defects and blemishes, I the more discriminatingly, clearly and truly apprehend that this cannot be doubted.

In Later Life the Philosopher Chu Realized the Mistakes of His Earlier Expositions and Accepted a View in Harmony with Wang's

However, insofar as this contradicted the exposition which the philosopher Chu has given, I was constantly distressed in mind. Privately I doubted, saying, "Can it be that a man of such virtue as the philosopher Chu did not examine into this?" When I was official at Liutu (Nanchang in Kiangsi), I again took up the works of the philosopher Chu and thoroughly investigated them. Thereupon I knew that in later life he fully realized the errors of his old expositions. Repenting to the utmost, he reached the point where he considered himself as having committed the crime of misleading others through his own delusion and deception, and deplored the fact that he could not atone. The transmitted commentaries, and the places where he speaks of some one making inquiry, are all expositions which were fixed by him in middle age. (99) He blamed himself insofar as he held that the original copies were mistaken, and planned to correct his mistakes, but without attaining thereto. As far as his sayings are concerned, his followers have made use of a desire to maintain his superiority in order to annex their own point of view. As compared with the ordinary expositions of the philosopher Chu, their mistakes are great. However, the worldly students who are confined to seeing and hearing do no more than orderly and leisurely discuss and practice these (his earlier expositions). They probably never have heard of the expositions which the philosopher Chu gave after he had come to a state of realization. Why then blame them for not having confidence in what I say? Is it not true that thereby the mind of the philosopher Chu is not made known to later generations?

Since I congratulate myself that my exposition does not depart from that of the philosopher Chu, and since I rejoice that he attained the same position I hold, I also deplore the fact that the ordinary scholars vainly hold to the expositions he gave in middle life, and do not, in addition, realize the necessity of seeking those later expositions which he made after he had come to a state of realization. Violently discussing and clamoring, they confuse true learning. They do not realize that they have entered the realm of heterodoxy. I have hastily selected, recorded, and brought this together, that I may privately exhibit it to those who have a common purpose, so that they may perhaps have no doubt with reference to what I say and that the revelation of this learning and culture may be expected.

Preface to the Ancient Edition of the Great Learning

Written in the thirteenth year of Emperor Cheng Te

A Résumé of the Principles of the Great Learning

The essential principle in the Great Learning is that of making the purpose sincere. The task of making the purpose sincere consists in investigating things. When the task of making the purpose sincere has reached its highest development, it gives what is designated as resting in the highest excellence. The rule which applies to resting in the highest excellence is that of extending knowledge to the utmost. By rectifying the mind, its original nature is reinstated; by cultivating the person, its function can be manifested. Referring to the self, this means manifesting virtue; referring to others, it implies loving the people; referring to the things included in heaven and earth, this is all-complete. For this reason, the highest excellence is really the original and fundamental nature of the mind. When once there has been the stirring of the passions, it is no longer in a state of excellence. But the knowledge of this fundamental nature of the mind is at no time absent. Purpose is the activity of the mind, things are the affairs of the mind. If one is developing the knowledge of the mind considered in its fundamental nature, then, whatever activity there is, is excellent. (100) However, if it is not his own affairs that are investigated, it is not possible for the individual to develop his knowledge. For this reason the development of the intuitive faculty is the root of making the purpose sincere, while the investigation of things is the result of developing the intuitive faculty.

When things have been investigated, knowledge is completed, the purpose sincere, and the original nature of the mind reinstated. This is what is called resting in the highest excellence. The sage fears lest others seek it in external things, and thus reiterates what he says If the old text is divided up, the purpose of the sage is lost. Thus failure to devote one's self to making one's purpose sincere, while one merely investigates things, is spoken of as departing from the path; failure to practice the investigation of things, while one merely makes the purpose sincere, is abstraction; failure to begin with the developing of the intuitive faculty, while one merely investigates things and makes the purpose sincere, is absurd and false. ' Such departure, abstraction, and absurdity are very different from the highest excellence. When brought into relation with the text of the Great Learning, they are checked; but when they are strengthened and patched up by the commentary, the departure from the text is increased. I am afraid that in learning this the students daily depart farther from the highest excellence. If the division into chapters is discarded, and the students, reinstating the old text, rely upon this with its lines and verses in pointing out its meaning, they come very near to seeing the mind of the sage again. Moreover, he who seeks learning has the fundamental principles in the Great Learning. In extending knowledge, it is necessary to cherish the mind. Then the realization of what is meant by extending knowledge to the utmost is complete.

Comments — According to the idea of this preface, the point of departure of the Great Learning consists in the investigation of things. In carrying on the investigation of things, can study, inquiry, reflection, discrimination, and earnest practice be discarded, while the individual vainly engages in abstruse expositions devoted to sudden awakenings and discernments? Scholars do not apprehend the underlying idea, but vainly see that it is somewhat different from the philosopher Chu's saying, that one must investigate the principles of all things with which one comes into contact. Thereupon they say that the Teacher's exposition, regarding the development of the intuitive faculty, obliterates and destroys the investigation of things. Is that a proper way of estimating this?

The Differences in Opinion of Wang and Chu Regarding the Texts of the Great Learning Are Not Important

Since the time that texts and commentaries met with the fire of Ch'in Shih Huang, there are few complete editions. Can it be otherwise than that there are a few mistakes in the ancient transmitted text of the Great Learning? The philosopher Chu adopted the views of the philosopher Ch'eng in his commentary. Is his exposition of necessity in complete accord with the ancient text? The philosophers Chu and Wang are at variance at this point. However, when things have been investigated, knowledge is com-

pleted and the purpose sincere. (101) The rules of the text
are naturally clear. The investigation of things is the real
point of departure for him who is entering the path of
duty   Therefore when things have been investigated,
knowledge is completed. The Teacher cannot really be
different from the philosopher Chu, for Chu cannot be
different from the sacred text. Even if their point of
view and their exposition differs somewhat, they are alike
when they reach the matter of making the purpose sincere,
and regarding the truths of the Great Learning they
are also at one. Students should understand that they
(Chu and Wang) are at one regarding the path of duty
They should not emphasize the differences of exposition.
In the commentary to the ancient text, it is allowable to put
aside all that with reference to which one is in doubt.

INDEX

INDEX

LaVergne, TN USA
02 January 2010
210752LV00004B/44/P